MINTZBERG ON MANAGEMENT

*Inside Our Strange
World of Organizations*

Henry Mintzberg

THE FREE PRESS

NEW YORK LONDON TORONTO SYDNEY SINGAPORE

THE FREE PRESS
A Division of Simon & Schuster Inc.
1230 Avenue of the Americas
New York, NY 10020

THE FREE PRESS and colophon are trademarks
of Simon & Schuster Inc.

Manufactured in the United States of America

10

Library of Congress Cataloging-in-Publication Data

Mintzberg, Henry.
    Mintzberg on management : inside our strange world of
organizations / Henry Mintzberg.
        p.   cm.
    Bibliography: p.
    ISBN 0-02-921371-1
    1. Management   2. Organization   3. Organizational behavior.
I. Title.
HD31.M4568   1989
658—dc 19   89-1241
                                                            CIP

*This book is written for those of us who
spend our public lives dealing with organizations
and our private lives escaping from them.*

*It is dedicated to the memory of Jim Waters,
who spent his career seeking to make those organizations
more humane.*

CONTENTS

Acknowledgment

It is customary here to thank everyone who provided significant help to the book. But since a good part of this book is based on my previous writings, where I already thanked many of those people, I shall not repeat those thank-you's here. They were heartfelt then; they remain so. What I would like to do here, aside from certain special mentions— my colleagues Danny Miller and Frances Westley, who helped my thinking in many ways; Jim Waters, a wonderful friend whose implicit contributions to this book far outweigh the many formally acknowledged in the text and who will be deeply missed; my editor Bob Wallace, who exhibited remarkable tolerance; my support staff Kate Maguire-Devlin and Zinette Khan, who handled my awful scrawl with grace; and my two deans Morty Yalovsky and Wally Crowston, who provided other important kinds of support—is to focus this acknowledgment on one person.

Bill Litwack embodies the word empathy. Not the empathy of the pop psychologist, for he is rude and abrasive, at least to his good friends. But he understands those friends and responds to their needs, not to mention the needs of the books they write.

In 1968, Billy, at the not-so-tender age of twenty, edited my doctoral thesis. It was a harrowing experience. But I learned how to write. In the twenty years since, either I forgot how to write or else his standards went up. I certainly forgot what a harrowing experience it had been. In any event, after our second such experience, I survived, Billy survived, this book survived, and most important, our friendship survived. Billy lived the book for several intense months, getting inside my head and driving me crazy (not so sample comment: "It is hypocrisy to spell 'hypo-cracy' 'hippo-cracy' ") until I turned a portfolio of publications into (what I at least hope is) the book I intended it to be. I thank you for this Bill, but not primarily for this.

The author is supposed to add here, as if anyone doubts it, that despite all the wonderful things everyone else contributed, somehow only he is responsible for what follows. No way. (Billy's not editing this!) I may not have taken his "advice" in some places, may have made some last minute changes he never got to see, but everywhere else Litwack is to blame for any errors or inadequacies that remain in this book. Here's to another twenty years of peace.

Lac Castor
January 1989

OUR WORLD OF ORGANIZATIONS

Ours has become, for better and for worse, a society of organizations. We are born in organizations and are educated in organizations so that we can later work in organizations. At the same time, organizations supply us and entertain us, they govern us and harass us (sometimes concurrently). Finally, we are buried by organizations. Yet aside from a small group of scholars called "organization theorists" who study them, and those managers inclined to look deeply into the subject of their management, few people really understand these strange collective beasts that so influence our daily lives.

If you want to find out about your own psyche, walk into any bookstore and take your pick of dozens of books on how your mind, body, or behavior supposedly works. But if it is your organization you wish to understand, you must instead find a college bookstore and then wade through the dense theory of some academic tome, unless you are willing to settle for a textbook that packages it all very neatly—and probably simplistically.

At least that's what you will find on the management shelves. On those devoted to the older, more traditional disciplines, you will find material that talks around organizations. In economics, the organization takes on the form of a "rational" but otherwise mysterious entity that somehow manages to maximize its profits. I don't know any organizations like that. Psychology teaches us about the behavior of individuals and small groups inside organizations, but not about the behavior of organizations themselves. Political science considers one very important class of organization, government, but more as a legislative or political system than as the network of organizations it significantly is. Sociology and anthropology do consider collective human behavior, but usually in terms of the larger informal society rather than the smaller formal organization.

Organization theory draws on all those disciplines, but it adds something very important, the concept of "organization" itself. Organization to me means collective action in the pursuit of a common mission, a fancy way of saying that a bunch of people have come together under an identifiable label ("General Motors," "Joe's Body Shop") to produce some product or service.

I present this book in the belief that there is a real thirst out there to understand organizations, in society at large no less than among the managers who try to run them (and who often seem as puzzled by their strange behavior as the rest of us). Every time I have discussed organizations with people from diverse backgrounds—including self-employed professionals, homemakers, and others who have *relatively* little contact with them—I have been amazed at the interest in the subject. Someone recounts a bizarre experience in a hospital, another person an incident in an airplane or at an auto dealership. We all need desperately to comprehend these strange beasts that so affect us. The basic conceptual understanding is there; it just has not been readily accessible.

This book presents material on organizations that I have been working on these past twenty years. It contains not just my own ideas, because a certain amount of my work set out to synthesize the work of others, especially that based on systematic research. Over the years, I have considered how managers work; how organizations function, make decisions, develop strategies, and structure themselves; and how power relationships surround and infuse organizations, including how societies try to deal with their organizations.

I present here a series of essays drawing on those parts of my writings that I believe are best suited to a general readership interested in organizations. Some of this material was first published in the more popular business press, while other material received only limited circulation in more obscure academic journals. I have tried to include here, and to render easily readable, that material I believe to be of widest interest. I originally set out to package this material together; I ended up rewriting, or in several cases writing originally, well over half of what appears here. This book is offered, therefore, in the hope of extending the audience for these ideas more deeply inside as well as beyond the management community. Call this "pop org theory" if you like, so long as there is no presumption that I have tried to trivialize the complicated activity of organizations.

I have divided these essays into three sections. The first is on *management,* that process by which the people who are formally in charge of whole organizations or part of them try to direct or at least to guide what they do. The second considers forms of *organizations,* in a way comparable to how biologists consider different species in nature. I believe our greatest mistake in dealing with organizations—one we have made throughout this century and continue to make every day—is in pretending that there is "one best way" to manage every organization. What's good for General Motors is often dead wrong for Joe's Body Shop. We have no more business treating all organizations alike than do doctors in prescribing the same pair of glasses for everyone. The third section looks at *our society of organizations*—how we try to influence them and how they influence us in turn and thereby make our lives happy and miserable.

Read what follows at your leisure; pick and choose, skimming or studying according to your own interests. Whatever you do, think about your own company, your repair shop or supplier of automobiles, the hospital that cured you and the school that made you miserable, the airline you fly, the association that lobbies for the clothing of animals or for the promotion of popcorn. Organizations supply us and exploit us, they nurture us and torment us. We can all escape them occasionally, a few of us can even function relatively free of them. But most of us must resign ourselves to spending a great deal of our public and private lives dealing with them. We all need to understand them better.

Part I
ON MANAGEMENT

In some sense, the twentieth century might be characterized as the age of management. Certainly the more economically developed world has become enamored with the management process over the course of this century. Henri Fayol, the French industrialist, may have done some of the important early thinking on management, but it was really a stream of writers in America, from Frederick Taylor through Peter Drucker and Herbert Simon, among many others, who created and reinforced the love affair America has had with managers and the management process.

That was why the recent Japanese challenge to American industrial supremacy came as such a shock. Here was a people from a very different culture beating America at its own game, the game of management. But it was not the first time. The West Europeans did it first, if not so dramatically. (Volkswagen embarrassed Detroit's Big Three long before Toyota did.) Not so very long ago, in 1968, Jean-Jacques Servan-Schreiber published *The American Challenge,* about how the key to America's economic success lay not in its resources or technologies, but in its attention to the management process itself.[1] Well, America's friends learned that lesson so well that *the European challenge* and later *the Japanese challenge* have been published many times over, if not by those titles.

There has been no such communist challenge. But management has certainly emerged as a critical process in Eastern Europe as well. Indeed, promises of the withering of the state notwithstanding, there is no way to run a communist society without heavy reliance on the management process. In this regard, America and the Soviet Union differ not in their obsession with management but simply in where they tend to locate their most influential managers. Everywhere we look then, where there is economic development there is attention to the management process.

Of course, there is more to organizations than management. Likewise, there is more to economic development than attention to management. Indeed, it can be argued (as I shall in Part III) that the traditional approach to management may now be impeding rather than fostering economic development. But no consideration of organizations is complete without careful attention to the management process. And so we begin our discussion with such attention, at least to management as it really seems to be practiced, not how the traditional literature keeps telling managers how to practice it.

We begin at what I believe should be the beginning: with the nature of managerial work, what those people called "manager" or something equivalent actually do at the office all day long. You may be surprised by what you read—well, not surprised in terms of your own experiences so much as in the light of what decades of literature have made people believe managers are *supposed* to do. This first article will make clear the discrepancy, very common and costly in organizations, between what really does go on and some vague and often misguided ideas of what *should* go on.

Our second article continues in the same vein, but on a different aspect of management. It considers the process of developing strategy. But again, in contrast to the traditional perception of a process of planning, here it is characterized as one of *craft,* which has all kinds of implications for managers and for organizations.

Both articles suggest something else is happening in management, something besides the highly analytical and "rational" processes so long favored. Our third article tries to get at this, drawing on research into the two hemispheres of the human brain to suggest that, in our race to throw the light of analysis on management, we may have lost sight of that darker but no less important process called intuition. The essay that follows, prepared for this book from several sources, probes more deeply into this issue, first considering the fundamental debate between analysis and intuition, then proposing ways in which the two can be coupled to manage complex organizations.

A final essay of this section on management, written especially for this book, takes up a major consequence of this debate, the inclination of our business schools to train MBAs, not managers. I imply here, and argue more fully in the final essay of this book, that this has had serious effects on our organizations, undermining their social as well as their economic effectiveness.

1

THE MANAGER'S JOB
Folklore and Fact

When we think of *organization,* we think of *management.* Of course, there is a great deal more to organizations than managers and the management systems they create. But what distinguishes the formal organization from a random collection of people—a mob, an informal group—is the presence of some system of authority and administration, personified by one manager or several in a hierarchy to knit the whole effort together.

That being the case, and given the love affair the American people in particular have had with the manager for more than a century, from Horatio Alger to Lee Iacocca, it is surprising how little study there has been of what managers actually do. Like thousands of other students at the time, I took an MBA, a degree ostensibly designed to train managers, without questioning the fact that no one ever discussed in a serious way what managers really did. Imagine a program in medicine without ever a comment on the work of the doctor.

There has certainly been no shortage of material on what managers *should* do (for example, follow a whole set of simple prescriptions called "time management" or use computers in the ways recommended by detached technical specialists). Unfortunately, in the absence of any real understanding of managerial work, much of this advice has proved false and wasteful. How can anyone possibly prescribe change in a phenomenon so complex as managerial work without first having a deep comprehension of it?

In the mid-1960s, James Webb, who ran NASA, wanted to be studied. NASA felt the need to justify its existence by spinning off practical applications of its innovations, and Webb counted its management processes among those innovations. Webb raised the idea with a professor of mine at the MIT Sloan School of Management, and since I was the only doctoral student then studying *management* there (as opposed to computer systems or mathematical models or motivating people, etc.), he approached me to study Webb as my doctoral thesis. I declined what seemed to be a crazy idea. This was MIT, after all, the bastion of science. Sitting in a manager's office and writing down what he did all day just didn't seem quite right. (Another professor had told me earlier that what an MIT doctoral thesis had to be above all was "elegant." He was not referring to the results.) In any event, I was going to do a thesis on how to develop a comprehensive strategic planning process for organizations. Luckily, and not for the last time in my life, forces outside of me saved me from myself.

The planning thesis didn't work out, for want of an organization willing to subject itself to such an exercise (or for want of my trying very hard to find one). Then I attended a conference at MIT to which a number of impressive people came to discuss the impact that the computer would have on the manager. They went nowhere; for two days they talked in circles, hardly getting beyond the contention that the managers' use of the computer should have something to do with the fact that their work was "unprogrammed" (whatever that was supposed to mean). It struck me that these people lacked a framework to enable them to understand managerial work. They certainly didn't lack an innate knowledge of the process—they all worked with managers, and a number were managers themselves. What they lacked was a *conceptual* basis to consider the issue.

I learned two things at that conference. The first was that knowing explicitly was different from knowing implicitly, and both had great relevance for running organizations. The second was that there was an urgent need for someone to look carefully at what managers really did, that even at a place like MIT, what mattered in a thesis was not the elegance of the methodology but the relevance of the topic.

And so I did my first research on "the nature of managerial work" (the title of the book that resulted from the thesis). But not with James Webb, who was no longer available. Using a stopwatch (much as Frederick Taylor had done with factory workers years earlier), I observed in the course of one intensive week the activities of five chief executives: of a major consulting firm, a well-known teaching hospital, a school system, a high-technology firm, and a manufacturer of consumer goods. One week was not a long time, but I was more interested in the pace and nature of the work than in the unfolding of issues over the long term. The dissertation was completed in 1968, the book in 1973; two years later, the *Harvard Business Review* published the article that is reprinted here (with minor changes).

In orientation and tone, as well as in some of its central content, this article really set the pattern for my subsequent work. An article that followed in the *New York Times* (on October 29, 1976)[1] labeled this description of managerial work "calculated chaos" and "controlled disorder." It also used a phrase that I have come to prefer for characterizing much of my writing: "celebrating intuition."

If you ask managers what they do, they will most likely tell you that they plan, organize, coordinate, and control. Then watch what they do. Don't be surprised if you can't relate what you see to those four words.

When they are called and told that one of their factories has just burned down, and they advise the caller to see whether temporary arrangements can be made to supply customers through a foreign subsidiary, is that planning, organizing, coordinating, or controlling? How about when they present a gold watch to a retiring employee? Or when they attend a conference to meet people in the trade? Or on returning from that conference, when they tell one of their employees about an interesting product idea they picked up there?

The fact is that those four words, which have dominated management vocabulary since the French industrialist Henri Fayol first introduced them in 1916, tell us little about what managers actually do. At best, they indicate some vague objectives managers have when they work.

My intention here is simple: to break the reader away from Fayol's words and introduce him or her to a more supportable, and what I believe to be a more useful, description of managerial work. This description is based on my own study of the work of five chief executives, supported by a few others on how various managers spent their time.

In some studies, managers were observed intensively ("shadowed" is the term some of them used); in a number of others, they kept detailed diaries of their activities; in a few studies, their records were analyzed. Various kinds of managers were studied—foremen, factory supervisors, staff managers, field sales managers, hospital administrators, presidents of companies and nations, and even street gang leaders. These "managers" worked in the United States, Canada, Sweden, and Great Britain.

A synthesis of these findings paints an interesting picture, one as different from Fayol's classical view as a cubist abstract is from a Renaissance painting. In a sense, this picture will be obvious to anyone who has ever spent a day in a manager's office, either in front of the desk or behind it. Yet at the same time, this picture may turn out to be revolutionary, in that it throws into doubt so much of the folklore that we have accepted about the manager's work.

I first discuss some of this folklore and contrast it with some of the findings of systematic research—the hard facts about how managers spend their time. Then I synthesize those research findings in a description of ten roles that seem to describe the essential content of all managers' jobs. In a concluding section, I discuss a number of implications of this synthesis for those trying to achieve more effective management.

SOME FOLKLORE AND FACTS ABOUT MANAGERIAL WORK

There are four myths about the manager's job that do not bear up under careful scrutiny of the facts.

1. Folklore: The manager is a reflective, systematic planner. The evidence on the issue is overwhelming, but not a shred of it supports this statement.

Fact: Study after study has shown that managers work at an unrelenting pace, that their activities are characterized by brevity, variety, and discontinuity, and that they are strongly oriented to action and dislike reflective activities. Consider this evidence:
- Half the activities engaged in by the five chief executives of my study lasted less than nine minutes, and only 10 percent exceeded one hour.[2] A study of fifty-six U.S. foremen found that they averaged 583 activities per eight-hour shift, one every forty-eight seconds.[3] The work pace for both chief executives and foremen was unrelenting. The chief executives met a steady stream of callers and mail from the moment they arrived in the morning until they left in the evening. Coffee breaks and lunches were inevitably work-related, and ever present subordinates seemed to usurp any free moment.
- A diary study of 160 British middle and top managers found that they worked for a half-hour or more without interruption only about once every two days.[4]
- Of the verbal contacts of the chief executives in my study, 93 percent were arranged on an *ad hoc* basis. Only 1 percent of the executives' time was spent in open-ended observational tours. Only 1 out of 368 verbal contacts was unrelated to a specific issue and could be called general planning.
- No study has found important patterns in the way managers schedule their time. They seem to jump from issue to issue, continually responding to the needs of the moment.

Is this the planner of the classical literature? Hardly. How, then, can we explain this behavior? The manager is simply responding to the pressures of his or her job. I found that my chief executives terminated many of their own activities, often leaving meetings before the end, and interrupted their desk work to call in subordinates. One president not only placed his desk so that he could look down a long hallway but also left his door open when he was alone—an invitation for subordinates to come in and interrupt him.

Clearly, these managers wanted to encourage the flow of current information. But more significantly, they seemed to be conditioned by their own work loads. They appreciated the opportunity cost of their own time, and they were continually aware of their ever present obligations—mail to be answered, callers to attend to, and so on. It seems that no matter what they are doing, managers are plagued by the possibilities of what they might do and what they must do.

When the manager must plan, he or she seems to do so implicitly in the context of daily actions, not in some abstract process reserved for two weeks at the organization's mountain retreat. The plans of the chief executives I studied seemed to exist only in their heads—as flexible, but often specific, intentions. The traditional literature notwithstanding, the job of managing does not breed reflective planners; the manager is a real-time responder to stimuli, an individual who is conditioned by his or her job to prefer live to delayed action.

2. Folklore: The effective manager has no regular duties to perform. Managers are constantly being told to spend more time planning and delegating, and less time seeing customers and engaging in negotiations. Those are not, after all, the true tasks of the manager. To use the popular analogy, the good manager, like the good conductor, carefully orchestrates everything in advance, then sits back to enjoy the fruits of his or her labor, responding occasionally to an unforeseeable exception.

But here again the pleasant abstraction just does not seem to hold up.

Fact: In addition to handling exceptions, managerial work involves performing a number of regular duties, including ritual and ceremony, negotiations, and processing of soft information that links the organization with its environment. Consider some evidence from the research studies:

- A study of the work of the presidents of small companies found that they engaged in routine activities because their companies could not afford staff specialists and were so thin on operating personnel that a single absence often required the president to substitute.[5]

• One study of field sales managers and another of chief executives suggest that it is a natural part of both jobs to see important customers, assuming the managers wish to keep those customers.[6]

• Someone, only half in jest, once described the manager as that person who sees the visitors so that everyone else can get on with his or her work. In my study, I found that certain ceremonial duties— meeting visiting dignitaries, giving out gold watches, presiding at special dinners—were an intrinsic part of the chief executive's job.

• Studies of managers' information flow suggest that managers play a key role in securing "soft" external information (much of it available only to them because of their status) and in passing it along to their subordinates.

3. Folklore: The senior manager needs aggregated information, which a formal management information system best provides. In keeping with the classical view of the manager as that individual perched on the apex of a regulated, hierarchical system, the literature's manager is to receive all important information from a giant, comprehensive MIS. But a look at how managers actually process information reveals a very different picture. Managers have five media at their command—documents, telephone calls, scheduled and unscheduled meetings, and observational tours.

Fact: Managers strongly favor the oral media—namely, telephone calls and meetings. The evidence comes from every single study of managerial work. Consider the following:

• In two British studies, managers spent an average of 66 and 80 percent of their time in oral communication.[7] In my study of five American chief executives, the figure was 78 percent.

• These five chief executives treated mail processing as a burden to be dispensed with. One came in Saturday morning to process 142 pieces of mail in just over three hours, to "get rid of all the stuff." This same manager looked at the first piece of "hard" mail he had received all week, a standard cost report, and put it aside with the comment, "I never look at this."

• These same five chief executives responded immediately to just two of the forty routine reports they received during the five weeks of my study and to four items in the 104 periodicals. They skimmed most of these periodicals in seconds, almost ritualistically. In all, these chief executives of good-size organizations initiated on their own—that is, not in response to something else—a grand total of twenty-five pieces of mail during the twenty-five days I observed them.

An analysis of the mail the executives received reveals an interesting picture: Only 13 percent was of specific and immediate use. So now we have another piece in the puzzle. Not much of the mail provides live, current information—the action of a competitor, the mood of a government legislator, the rating of last night's television show. Yet this is the information that drove the managers, interrupting their meetings and rescheduling their workdays.

Consider another interesting finding. Managers seem to cherish "soft" information, especially gossip, hearsay, and speculation. Why? The reason is its timeliness; today's gossip may be tomorrow's fact. The manager who is not accessible for the telephone call informing him that his biggest customer was seen golfing with his main competitor may read about a dramatic drop in sales in the next quarterly report. But then it's too late.

Consider the words of Richard Neustadt who studied the information-collecting habits of three U.S. Presidents:

> It is not information of a general sort that helps a President see personal stakes; not summaries, not surveys, not the *bland amalgams*. Rather . . . it is the odds and ends of *tangible detail* that pieced together in his mind illuminate the underside of issues put before him. To help himself, he must reach out as widely as he can for every scrap of fact, opinion, gossip, bearing on his interests and relationships as President. He must become his own director of his own central intelligence.[8]

The manager's emphasis on the oral media raises two important points:

First, oral information is stored in the brains of people. Only when people write this information down can it be stored in the files of the organization—whether in metal cabinets or on magnetic tape—and managers apparently do not write down much of what they hear. Thus the strategic data bank of the organization is not in the memory of its computers so much as in the minds of its managers.

Second, the managers' extensive use of oral media helps to explain why they are reluctant to delegate tasks. When we note that most of the managers' important information comes in oral form and is stored in their heads, we can well appreciate their reluctance. It is not as if they can hand a dossier over to someone; they must take the time to "dump memory"—to tell that someone all they know about the subject. But this could take so long that the managers may find it easier to do the task themselves. Thus the manager is damned by his or her own information system to a "dilemma of delegation"—to do too much him or herself or to delegate to subordinates with inadequate briefing.

4. Folklore: Management is, or at least is quickly becoming, a science and a profession. By almost any definitions of *science* and *profession,* this statement is false. Brief observation of any manager will quickly lay to rest the notion that managers practice a science. A science involves the enaction of systematic, analytically determined procedures or programs. If we do not even know what procedures managers use, how can we prescribe them by scientific analysis? And how can we call management a profession if we cannot specify what managers are to learn?

Fact: The managers' programs—to schedule time, process information, make decisions, and so on—remain locked deep inside their brains. Thus, to describe those programs, we rely on words like *judgment* and *intuition,* seldom stopping to realize that they are merely labels for our ignorance.

I was struck during my study by the fact that the executives I observed— all very competent by any standard—were fundamentally indistinguishable from their counterparts of a hundred years ago. The information they needed differed, but they sought it in the same way—by word of mouth. Their decisions concerned modern technology, but the procedures they used to make them were the same as the procedures of the nineteenth-century manager. Even the computer, so important for the specialized work of the organization, had apparently had no influence on the work procedures of general managers. In fact, the manager is in a kind of loop, with increasingly heavy work pressures but no aid forthcoming from management science.

Considering the facts about managerial work, we can see that the manager's job is enormously complicated and difficult. The manager is overburdened with obligations; yet he or she cannot easily delegate his or her tasks. As a result, he or she is driven to overwork and is forced to do many tasks superficially. Brevity, fragmentation, and oral communication characterize the work. Yet these are the very characteristics of managerial work that have impeded scientific attempts to improve it. As a result, management scientists have concentrated their efforts on the specialized functions of the organization, where they could more easily analyze the procedures and quantify the relevant information. Thus the first step in providing the manager with some help is to find out what his or her job really is.

BACK TO A BASIC DESCRIPTION OF MANAGERIAL WORK

Let us try to put some of the pieces of this puzzle together. The manager can be defined as that person in charge of an organization or one of its subunits. Besides chief executive officers, this definition would include vice presidents, bishops, foremen, hockey coaches, and prime ministers. Can all of these people have anything in common? Indeed they can. For an important starting point, all are vested with formal authority over an organizational unit. From formal authority comes status, which leads to various interpersonal relations, and from these comes access to information. Information, in turn, enables the manager to make decisions and strategies for his or her unit.

The manager's job can be described in terms of various "roles," or organized sets of behaviors identified with a position. My description, shown in Figure 1–1, comprises ten roles.

INTERPERSONAL ROLES

Three of the manager's roles arise directly from formal authority and involve basic interpersonal relationships.

1. First is the *figurehead* role. By virtue of his or her position as head of an organizational unit, every manager must perform some duties of a ceremonial nature. The president greets the touring dignitaries, the foreman attends the wedding of a lathe operator, and the sales manager takes an important customer to lunch.

The chief executives of my study spent 12 percent of their contact time on ceremonial duties; 17 percent of their incoming mail dealt with acknowledgments and requests related to their status. For example, a letter to a company president requested free merchandise for a disabled schoolchild; diplomas were put on the desk of the school superintendent for his signature.

Duties that involve interpersonal roles may sometimes be routine, involving little serious communication and no important decision-making.

FIGURE 1–1
The Manager's Roles

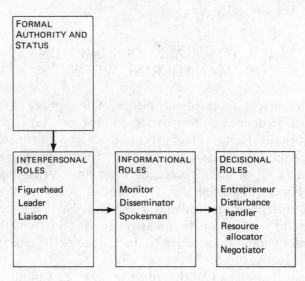

Nevertheless, they are important to the smooth functioning of an organization and cannot be ignored by the manager.

2. Because he or she is in charge of an organizational unit, the manager is responsible for the work of the people of that unit. His or her actions in this regard constitute the *leader* role. Some of those actions involve leadership directly—for example, in most organizations the manager is normally responsible for hiring and training his or her own staff. In addition, there is the indirect exercise of the leader role. Every manager must motivate and encourage his or her employees, somehow reconciling their individual needs with the goals of the organization. In virtually every contact the manager has with those employees, subordinates seeking leadership clues probe his or her actions: "Does he approve?" "How would she like the report to turn out?" "Is he more interested in market share than high profits?"

The influence of the manager is most clearly seen in the leader role. Formal authority vests the manager with great potential power; leadership determines in large part how much of it he or she will in fact use.

3. The literature of management has always recognized the leader role, particularly those aspects of it related to motivation. In comparison,

until recently it has hardly mentioned the *liaison* role, in which the manager makes contacts outside his or her vertical chain of command. This is remarkable in light of the finding of virtually every study of managerial work that managers spend as much time with peers and other people outside their units as they do with their own subordinates, and, surprisingly, very little time with their own superiors (generally on the order of 45, 45, and 10 percent respectively).

The contacts the five CEOs of my study made were with an incredibly wide range of people: subordinates; clients, business associates, and suppliers; managers of similar organizations, government and trade organization officials, fellow directors on outside boards; and so on. Robert Guest's study of foremen shows, likewise, that their contacts were numerous and wideranging, seldom involving fewer than twenty-five individuals, and often more than fifty.

As we shall see shortly, the manager cultivates such contacts largely to find information. In effect, the liaison role is devoted to building up the manager's own external information system—informal, private, oral but nevertheless effective.

INFORMATIONAL ROLES

By virtue of interpersonal contacts, both with subordinates and with the network of contacts, the manager emerges as the nerve center of his or her organizational unit. The manager may not know everything, but he or she typically knows more than any one of his or her subordinates.

Studies have shown this to hold for all managers, from street gang leaders to U.S. Presidents. In *The Human Group,* George C. Homans explains how, because they were at the center of the information flow in their own gangs and were also in close touch with other gang leaders, street gang leaders were better informed than any of their followers.[9] And Richard Neustadt describes the following account from his study of Franklin D. Roosevelt:

> The essence of Roosevelt's technique for information-gathering was competition. "He would call you in," one of his aides once told me, "and he'd ask you to get the story on some complicated business, and you'd come back after a couple of days of hard labor and present the juicy morsel you'd uncovered under a stone somewhere, and *then* you'd find out he knew all about it, along with something else you *didn't* know. Where he got this information from he wouldn't mention, usually, but

after he had done this to you once or twice you got damn careful about *your* information.''[10]

We can see where Roosevelt "got this information" when we consider the relationship between the interpersonal and informational roles. As leader, managers have formal and easy access to each of their subordinates. Hence, as noted earlier, they tend to know more about their own units than anyone else does. In addition, their liaison contacts expose the managers to external information to which their subordinates often lack access. Many of those contacts are with other managers of equal status, who are themselves nerve centers in their own organizations. In this way, managers develops powerful data bases of information.

The processing of information is a key part of the manager's job. In my study, the chief executives spent 40 percent of their contact time on activities devoted exclusively to the transmission of information and 70 percent of their incoming mail was purely informational (as opposed to requests for action). The manager does not leave meetings or hang up the telephone in order to get back to work. In large part, communication *is* his or her work. Three roles describe the informational aspects of managerial work.

4. As *monitor,* the manager perpetually scans his or her environment for information, interrogates liaison contacts and subordinates, and receives unsolicited information, much of it as a result of the network of personal contacts he or she has developed. Remember that a good part of the information the manager collects in the monitor role arrives in oral form, often as gossip, hearsay, and speculation. By virtue of contacts, the manager has a natural advantage in collecting this soft information for his or her organization.

5. Managers must share and distribute much of this information. Information they glean from outside personal contacts may be needed within their organizations. In their *disseminator* role, managers pass some of their privileged information directly to their subordinates, who would otherwise have no access to it. Moreover, when their subordinates lack easy contact with one another, managers will sometimes pass information from one to another.

6. In their *spokesman* role, managers send some of their information to people outside their units—a president makes a speech to lobby for an organizational need, or a foreman suggests a product modification to a supplier. In addition, as part of the role of spokesman, every manager

must inform and satisfy the influential people who control his or her organizational unit. Chief executives especially may spend great amounts of time dealing with hosts of influencers. Directors and shareholders must be advised about financial performance, consumer groups must be assured that the organization is fulfilling its social responsibilities, and so on.

DECISIONAL ROLES

Information is not, of course, an end in itself; it is the basic input to decision-making. One thing is clear in the study of managerial work: The manager plays the major role in his or her unit's decision-making system. As its formal authority, only the manager can commit the unit to important new courses of action; and as its nerve center, only the manager has full and current information to make the set of decisions that determines the unit's strategy. Four roles describe the manager as decision-maker.

7. As *entrepreneur*, the manager seeks to improve his or her unit, to adapt it to changing conditions in the environment. In the monitor role, the president is constantly on the lookout for new ideas; when a good one appears, he or she initiates, in the context of the entrepreneur role, a development project that he or she may supervise or else delegate to an employee (perhaps with the stipulation that the manager must approve the final proposal).

There are two interesting features about development projects at the chief executive level. First, these projects do not involve single decisions or even unified clusters of decisions. Rather, they emerge as a series of small decisions and actions sequenced over time. Apparently, chief executives prolong each project so that they can fit it bit by bit into their busy, disjointed schedule and so that they can gradually come to comprehend the issue, if it is a complex one.

Second, the chief executives I studied supervised as many as fifty of these projects at the same time. Some projects entailed new products or processes; others involved public relations campaigns, resolution of a morale problem in a foreign division, integration of computer operations, various acquisitions, and so on. The chief executives appeared to maintain a kind of inventory of the development projects they themselves supervised—projects at various stages of development, some active and some in limbo. Like a juggler, they seemed to keep a number of projects in the air; periodically, one comes down, is given a new burst of energy and is sent back into orbit. At various intervals, they put new projects onstream and discard old ones.

8. While the entrepreneur role describes the manager as the voluntary initiator of change, the *disturbance handler* role shows the manager involuntarily responding to pressures. Here change is beyond the manager's control: A strike looms, a major customer has gone bankrupt, a supplier reneges on a contract.

It has been fashionable, I noted earlier, to compare the manager to an orchestra conductor, as Peter F. Drucker wrote in *The Practice of Management:*

> The manager has the task of creating a true whole that is larger than the sum of its parts, a productive entity that turns out more than the sum of the resources put into it. One analogy is the conductor of a symphony orchestra, through whose effort, vision and leadership individual instrumental parts that are so much noise by themselves become the living whole of music. But the conductor has the composer's score; he is only interpreter. The manager is both composer and conductor.[11]

Now consider the words of Leonard R. Sayles, who carried out systematic research on the manager's job. The manager

> . . . is like a symphony orchestra conductor, endeavouring to maintain a melodious performance in which the contributions of the various instruments are coordinated and sequenced, patterned and paced, while the orchestra members are having various personal difficulties, stage hands are moving music stands, alternating excessive heat and cold are creating audience and instrument problems, and the sponsor of the concert is insisting on irrational changes in the program.[12]

In effect, every manager must spend a good part of time responding to high-pressure disturbances. No organization can be so well run, so standardized, that it has considered every contingency in advance. Disturbances arise not only because poor managers ignore situations until they reach crisis proportions, but also because good managers cannot possibly anticipate all the consequences of the actions they take.

9. The third decisional role is that of *resource allocator*. To the manager falls the responsibility of deciding who will get what in the organizational unit. Perhaps the most important resource the manager allocates is his or her own time. Access to the manager constitutes exposure to the unit's nerve center and decision-maker. The manager is also charged with designing the unit's structure, that pattern of formal

relationships that determines how work is to be divided and coordinated.

Also, in his or her role as resource allocator the manager authorizes the important decisions of the unit before they are implemented. By retaining this power, the manager can ensure that decisions are interrelated—all must pass through a single brain. To fragment this power is to encourage discontinuous decision-making and a disjointed strategy.

I found that the chief executives of my study faced incredibly complex choices. They had to consider the impact of each decision on other decisions and on the organization's strategy. They had to ensure that the decision would be acceptable to those who influenced the organization, as well as ensure that resources would not be overextended. They had to understand the various costs and benefits as well as the feasibility of the proposal. They also had to consider questions of timing. All this was necessary for the simple approval of someone else's proposal. At the same time, however, delay could lose time, while quick approval could be ill considered and quick rejection could discourage a subordinate who had spent months developing a pet project. One common solution in approving projects seems to have been to pick the person instead of the proposal. That is, managers authorize those projects presented to them by people whose judgment they trust. But they cannot always use this simple dodge.

10. The final decisional role is that of *negotiator*. Studies of managerial work at all levels indicate that managers spend considerable time in negotiations: The president of the football team is called in to work out a contract with the holdout superstar; the corporation president leads his or her company's contingent to negotiate a new strike issue; the foreman argues a grievance problem to its conclusion with the shop steward. As Leonard Sayles puts it, negotiations are a "way of life" for the sophisticated manager.

The negotiations are duties of the manager's job; perhaps routine, they are not to be shirked. They are an integral part of the job, for only the manager has the authority to commit organizational resources in "real time," and only he or she has the nerve center information that important negotiations require.

THE INTEGRATED JOB

It should be clear by now that the ten roles I have been describing are not easily separable. They form a *gestalt,* an integrated whole. No role can be pulled out of the framework and the job be left intact. For example, a manager without liaison contacts lacks external information. As a result, he or she can neither disseminate the information subordinates need nor make decisions that adequately reflect external conditions. (In fact, this is a problem for the new person in a managerial position, since he or she cannot make effective decisions until the network of contacts has been built up.)

Herein lies a clue to the problems of team management. Two or three people cannot share a single managerial position unless they can act as one entity. That means they cannot divide up the ten roles unless they can very carefully reintegrate them. The real difficulty lies with the informational roles. Unless there can be full sharing of managerial information—and, as I pointed out earlier, it is primarily oral—team management breaks down. A single managerial job cannot be arbitrarily split, for example, into internal and external roles, for information from both sources must be brought to bear on the same decisions.

To say that the ten roles form a *gestalt* is not to say that all managers give equal attention to each role. In fact, I found in my review of the various research studies that

- Sales managers seem to spend relatively more of their time in the interpersonal roles, presumably a reflection of the extroverted nature of the marketing activity
- Production managers give relatively more attention to the decisional roles, presumably a reflection of their concern with efficient work flow
- Staff managers spend relatively more time in the informational roles, since they are experts who manage departments that advise other parts of the organization

Nevertheless, in all cases the interpersonal, informational, and decisional roles remain inseparable.

TOWARD MORE EFFECTIVE MANAGEMENT

What are the messages for management in this description? I believe, first and foremost, that this description of managerial work should itself prove more important to managers than any prescription they might derive from it. That is to say, *the managers' effectiveness is significantly influenced by their insight into their own work.* Their performance depends on how well they understand and respond to the pressures and dilemmas of the job.

Let us take a look at three specific areas of concern. For the most part, the managerial logjams—the dilemma of delegation, the data base centralized in one brain, and the problems of working with the management scientist—revolve around the oral nature of the manager's information. There are great dangers in centralizing the organization's data bank in the minds of its managers. When they leave, they take their memory with them. And when subordinates are out of convenient oral reach of the manager, they are at an informational disadvantage.

1. The manager is challenged to find systematic ways to share his or her privileged information. A regular debriefing session with key subordinates, a weekly memory dump on the dictating machine, the maintaining of a diary of important information for limited circulation, or other similar methods may ease the logjam of work considerably. Time spent disseminating this information will be more than regained when decisions must be made. Of course, some will raise the question of confidentiality. But managers would do well to weigh the risks of exposing privileged information against having subordinates who can make effective decisions.

If there is a single theme that runs through this description, it is that the pressures of his job drive the manager to be superficial in his or her actions—to overload him- or herself with work, encourage interruption, respond quickly to every stimulus, seek the tangible and avoid the abstract, make decisions in small increments, and do everything abruptly.

2. Here again, the manager is challenged to deal consciously with the pressures of superficiality by giving serious attention to the issues that require it, by stepping back from tangible bits of information in order to see a broad picture, and by making use of analytical inputs. Although effective managers have to be adept at responding quickly to numerous and varying problems, the danger in managerial work is that they will respond to every issue equally (and that means abruptly) and that they will never work the tangible bits and pieces of informational input into a comprehensive picture of their world.

In dealing with complex issues, the senior manager has much to gain from a close relationship with the management scientists of his or her own organization. They have something important that he lacks—time to probe complex issues. An effective working relationship hinges on the resolution of what a colleague and I have called "the planning dilemma."[13] Managers have the information and the authority; analysts have the time and the technology. A successful working relationship between the two will be effected when the manager learns to share his or her information and the analyst learns to adapt to the manager's needs. For the analyst, adaptation means worrying less about the elegance of the method and more about its speed and flexibility.

3. The manager is challenged to gain control of his or her own time by turning obligations to advantage and by turning those things he or she wishes to do into obligations. The chief executives of my study initiated only 32 percent of their own contacts (and another 5 percent by mutual agreement). And yet to a considerable extent they seemed to control their time. There were two key factors that enabled them to do so.

First, managers have to spend so much time discharging obligations that if they were to view them as just that, they would leave no mark on their organizations. The unsuccessful manager blames failure on the obligations; the effective manager turns obligations to his or her own advantage. A speech is a chance to lobby for a cause; a meeting is a chance to reorganize a weak department; a visit to an important customer is a chance to extract trade information.

Second, managers free some of their time to do those things that they—perhaps no one else—think important by turning them into obligations. Free time is made, not found, in the manager's job; it is forced into the schedule. Hoping to leave some time open for contemplation or general planning is tantamount to hoping that the pressures of the job will go away. The manager who wants to innovate initiates a project and obligates others to report back to him or her; the manager who needs certain external information establishes channels that will automatically keep him or her informed; the manager who has to tour facilities commits him- or herself publicly to doing so.

No job is more vital to our society than that of the manager. It is the manager who determines whether our social institutions serve us well or whether they squander our talents and resources. It is time to strip away the folklore of managerial work so that we can begin the difficult task of making significant improvements in its performance.

2
CRAFTING STRATEGY

One of the more important things managers do is make strategy
for their organizations, or at least oversee the process by which they
and others make strategies. In a narrow sense, strategy-making deals
with the positioning of an organization in market niches, in other
words, deciding on what products will be produced and for whom.
But in a broader sense strategy-making refers to how the collective
system called organization establishes, and when necessary changes,
its basic orientation. Strategy-making also takes up the complex issue
of collective intention—how an organization composed of many people makes up *its* mind, so to speak.

Strategy-making is a fascinating process, involving more than the
simple set of prescriptions called "planning" with which it is usually
associated. This subject has been my central interest throughout
my career. My first article, in 1967, as a doctoral student and entitled
"The Science of Strategy Making," contrasted a Biblical "grand plan"
approach with a Darwinian evolutionary approach. My current writing
involves a two-volume work entitled "Strategy Formation," whose
underlying theme contrasts deliberate and emergent approaches to
the subject.

My ideas on this subject developed through a research project
initiated in 1971. With the aid of a number of doctoral students and
colleagues, especially Jim Waters, the intention was to study how
organizations engage in the process by tracking their strategies across
decades in their histories. Over the next twelve years or so, we carried
out a whole series of studies—on a supermarket chain, a major airline,
a government film agency, a small daily newspaper, our own university, and others. As the project neared its end, I began to search for
a way to bring the conclusions to a general managerial audience.

All the while, my wife was crafting pottery in the basement. One
day she put up a retrospective of her work, and I saw strategy evolving
before my own eyes. An idea struck then, or perhaps it had struck
when she made a presentation to a combined class of pottery and
management students on the source and nature of creativity in craft.
I realized I was hearing from her much the same as I had heard

from creative strategists in business (for example, the serendipitous role of "mistakes" in pottery and of "opportunities" in business, "a feel for the clay" and "a knowledge of the business"). Thus I decided to use crafting as a metaphor and an analogy to capture the difficulties of creating strategy in a dynamic organization. "Crafting Strategy" appeared in the *Harvard Business Review* in 1987.

My ideas may have developed over the years (though you will see shades of Biblical grand plans and Darwinian evolution here too), but you will find here a tone similar to that of the "manager's job" article. What this article presents is a description of how managers who must work in "calculated chaos" deal with the complex and necessarily collective process of making strategy.

Imagine someone *planning* strategy. What most likely springs to mind is an image of orderly thinking: a senior manager, or a group of them, sitting in an office formulating courses of action that everyone else will implement on schedule. The keynote is reason—rational control, the systematic analysis of competitors and markets, of company strengths and weaknesses, the combination of these analyses producing clear, explicit, full-blown strategies.

Now imagine someone *crafting* strategy. An entirely different image most likely results, as different from planning as craft is from mechanization. Craft evokes traditional skill, dedication, perfection through the mastery of detail. What springs to mind is not so much thinking and reason as involvement, a feeling of intimacy and harmony with the materials at hand, developed through long experience and commitment. Formulation and implementation merge into a fluid process of learning, through which creative strategies evolve.

My thesis is simple: The crafting image better captures the process by which effective strategies come to be. The planning image, long popular in the literature, distorts those processes and thereby misguides organizations that embrace it unreservedly.

In developing this thesis, I shall draw on the experiences of a single craftsman, a potter, and compare them with the results of a research project that tracked the strategies of a number of corporations across several decades. Because the two contexts are so obviously different, my metaphor, like my assertion, may seem far-fetched at first. Yet if we think of a craftsman as an organization of one, we can see that he or she must also resolve one of the great challenges the corporate strategist faces: knowing the organization's capabilities well enough to think deeply about its strategic direction. By considering strategy-making from the perspective of one person, free of all the paraphernalia of what has been called the strategy industry, we can learn something about the formation of strategy in the corporation. For much as our potter has to manage her craft, so too managers have to craft their strategy.

At work, the potter sits before a lump of clay on the wheel. Her mind is on the clay, but she is also aware of sitting between her past experiences and her future prospects. She knows exactly what has and has not worked for her in the past. She has an intimate knowledge of her work, her capabilities, and her markets. As a craftsman, she senses rather than analyzes these things; her knowledge is "tacit." All this is working in her mind as her hands are working the clay. The product that emerges on the wheel is likely to be in the tradition of her past work. But she may break away and embark on a new path. Even so, the past is no less present, projecting itself into the future.

In my metaphor, managers are craftsmen and strategy is their clay. Like the potter, they sit between a past of corporate capabilities and a future of market opportunities. And if they are truly craftsmen, they bring to their work an equally intimate knowledge of the materials at hand. That is the essence of crafting strategy.

We will explore this metaphor by looking at how strategies actually get made as opposed to how they are supposed to get made. Throughout, I will be drawing on the two sets of experiences I have mentioned. One is a research project on patterns in strategy formation that went on at McGill University under my direction beginning in 1971. The second is the stream of work of a successful potter, my wife, who began her craft in 1967.

Strategies are both plans for the future and patterns from the past.

Ask almost anyone what strategy is, and they will define it as a plan of some sort, an explicit guide to future behavior. Then ask them what strategy a competitor or a government or even they themselves have actually pursued. Chances are they will describe consistency in *past* behavior—a pattern in action over time. Strategy, it turns out, is one of those words that people define in one way and often use in another, without realizing the difference.

The reason for this is simple. Strategy's formal definition and its Greek military origins notwithstanding, we need the word as much to explain past actions as to describe intended behavior in the future. After all, if strategies can be planned and intended, they can also be pursued and realized (or not realized, as the case may be). And pattern in past action, or what I call *realized* strategy, reflects that pursuit. Moreover, just as a plan need not produce a pattern (some strategies that are intended are simply not realized), so too a pattern need not result from a plan. An organization can develop a pattern (a realized strategy) without knowing it, let alone making it explicit.

Patterns, like beauty, are of course in the mind of the beholder. But anyone reviewing a chronological lineup of our craftsman's work would have little trouble discerning clear patterns, at least in certain periods. Until 1974, for example, she made small, decorative ceramic animals and objects of various kinds. Then this "knickknack strategy" stopped abruptly, and eventually new patterns formed around waferlike sculptures and ceramic bowls, highly textured and unglazed.

Finding equivalent patterns in action for organizations isn't that much more difficult. Indeed, for such large companies as Volkswagenwerk and Air Canada in our research, it proved simpler! (As well it should. A craftsman, after all, can change what she does in a studio a lot more easily than a Volkswagenwerk can retool its assembly lines.) Mapping the product models at Volkswagenwerk from the late 1940s to the late 1970s, for example, uncovers a clear pattern of concentration on the Beetle, followed in the late 1960s by a frantic search for replacements through acquisitions and internally developed new models, until a strategic reorientation developed around more stylish, water-cooled, front-wheel-drive vehicles in the mid-1970s.

But what about *intended* strategies, those formal plans and pronouncements we think of when we use the term *strategy*? Ironically, here we run into all kinds of problems. Even with a single craftsman, how can we know what her intended strategies really were? If we could go back, would we find expressions of intention? And if we did, would we be able to trust them? We often fool ourselves, as well as others, by denying our subconscious motives. And remember that intentions come cheap, at least when compared with realizations.

READING THE ORGANIZATION'S MIND

If you believe all this has more to do with the Freudian recesses of a craftsman's mind than with the practical realities of producing automobiles, then think again. For who knows what the intended strategies of a Volkswagenwerk really mean, let alone what they are? Can we simply assume in this collective context that the company's intended strategies are represented by its formal plans or by other statements emanating from the executive suite? Might these be just vain hopes, or rationalizations, or ploys to fool the competition? And even if such expressed intentions exist, to what extent do other people in the organization share them? How do we read the collective mind? Who is the strategist anyway?

The traditional view of strategic management resolves these problems quite simply, by what organizational theorists call attribution. You see it all the time in the business press. When General Motors acts, it's because its chief executive has made a strategy. Given realization, there must have been intention, and that is automatically attributed to the chief.

In a short magazine article, this assumption is understandable, even if wrong. Journalists don't have a lot of time to uncover the origins of strategy, and GM is a large, complicated organization. But just consider all the complexity and confusion that get swept under this assumption— all the meetings and debates, the many people involved, the dead ends, the folding and unfolding of ideas. Now consider trying to build a formal strategy-making system around that assumption. Is it any wonder that formal strategic planning is often such a resounding failure?

To unravel some of the confusion—and move away from the artificial complexity we have piled around the strategy-making process—we need to get back to some basic concepts. The most basic of all is the intimate connection between thought and action. That is the key to craft, and so also to the crafting of strategy.

Strategies need not be deliberate—they can also emerge, more or less.

Virtually everything that has been written about strategy-making depicts it as a deliberate process. First we think, then we act. We formulate, then we implement. The progression seems so perfectly sensible. Why would anybody wish to proceed differently?

Our potter is in the studio, rolling the clay to make a waferlike sculpture. The clay sticks to the rolling pin, and a round form appears. Why not make a cylindrical vase? One idea leads to another, until a new pattern forms. Action has driven thinking: A strategy has emerged.

Out in the field, a salesman visits a customer. The product isn't quite right, and together they work out some modifications. The salesman returns to the company and puts the changes through; after two or three more rounds, they finally get it right. A new product emerges, which eventually opens up a new market. The company has changed strategic course.

In fact, most salespeople are less fortunate than this one or than our craftsman. In an organization of one, the implementer is the formulator, so innovations can be incorporated into strategy quickly and easily. In a large organization, the innovator may be ten levels removed from the leader who is supposed to dictate strategy, and may also have to sell the idea to dozens of peers doing the same job.

Some salespeople, of course, can proceed on their own, modifying products to suit their customers and convincing skunkworks in the factory to produce them. In effect, they pursue their own strategies. Maybe no one else notices or cares. Sometimes, however, their innovations do get noticed, perhaps years later, when the company's prevalent strategies have broken down and its leaders are groping for something new. Then the salesperson's own strategy may be allowed to pervade the system, to become organizational.

Is this story far-fetched? Certainly not. We have all heard stories like it. But since we tend to see only what we believe, if we believe that strategies have to be planned, we are unlikely to see the real meaning such stories hold.

Consider how the National Film Board of Canada (NFB) came to adopt a feature-film strategy. The NFB is a federal government agency, famous for its creativity and expertise in the production of short documentaries. Some years back, it funded a filmmaker on a project that unexpectedly ran long. To distribute his film, the NFB turned to theaters and so inadvertently gained experience in marketing feature-length films. Other filmmakers caught on to the idea, and eventually the NFB found itself pursuing a feature-film strategy—a pattern of producing such films.

My point is simple, deceptively simple: Strategies can *form* as well as be *formulated*. A realized strategy can emerge in response to an evolving situation, or it can be brought about deliberately, through a process of formulation followed by implementation. But when these planned intentions do not produce the desired actions, organizations are left with unrealized strategies.

Today we hear a great deal about unrealized strategies, almost always in concert with the claim that implementation has failed. Management has been lax, controls have been loose, the implementers haven't been committed. Excuses abound. At times, they may be valid. But often these explanations prove too easy. So some people look beyond implementation, to formulation. The strategists haven't been smart enough.

While it is certainly true that many intended strategies are ill conceived, I believe that the problem often lies one step beyond that, in the distinction we make in the first place between formulation and implementation, the common assumption that thought must be independent of (and precede) action. Sure, people could be smarter—but not only by conceiving smarter strategies. Sometimes they can be smarter by allowing their strategies to develop gradually, through the organization's actions and experiences. Smart strategists appreciate that they cannot always be smart enough to think through everything in advance.

HANDS AND MINDS

No craftsman thinks some days and works others. The craftsman's mind is going constantly, in tandem with her hands. Yet large organizations try to separate the work of minds and hands. In so doing, they often sever the vital feedback link between the two. The salesperson who finds a customer with an unmet need may possess the most strategic bit of information in the entire organization. But that information is useless if he or she cannot create a strategy in response to it, or else convey the information to someone who can—because the channels are blocked or because the formulators have simply finished formulating. The notion that strategy is something that should happen way up there, far removed from the details of running an organization on a daily basis, is one of the great fallacies of conventional management. And it explains a good many of the most dramatic failures in business and public policy today.

We at McGill call strategies that appear without clear intentions—or in spite of them—*emergent* strategies. Actions simply converge into patterns. They may become deliberate, of course, if the pattern is recognized and then legitimized by senior management. But that is after the fact.

All this may sound rather strange, I know. Strategies that emerge? Managers who acknowledge strategies already formed? Over the years, our research group at McGill has met with a good deal of resistance from people upset by what they perceive to be our passive definition of a word so bound up with proactive behavior and free will. After all, strategy means control—the ancient Greeks used it to describe the art of the army general.

STRATEGIC LEARNING

But we have persisted in this usage for one reason: learning. Purely *deliberate* strategy precludes learning once the strategy is formulated; emergent strategy fosters it. People take actions one by one and respond to them, so that patterns eventually form.

Our craftsman tries to make a freestanding sculptural form. It doesn't work, so she rounds it a bit here, flattens it a bit there. The result looks better but still isn't quite right. She makes another and another and another. Eventually, after days or months or years, she finally has what she wants. She is off on a new strategy.

In practice, of course, all strategy-making walks on two feet, one deliberate, the other emergent. For just as purely deliberate strategy-making precludes learning, so purely emergent strategy-making precludes control. Pushed to the limit, neither approach makes much sense. Learning must be coupled with control. That is why the McGill research group uses the word *strategy* for both emergent and deliberate behavior.

Likewise, there is no such thing as a purely deliberate strategy or a purely emergent one. No organization—not even the ones commanded by those ancient Greek generals—knows enough to work everything out in advance, to ignore learning en route. And no one—not even a solitary potter—can be flexible enough to leave everything to happenstance, to give up all mental control. Craft requires control just as it requires responsiveness to the material at hand. Thus deliberate and emergent strategies form the end points of a continuum along which the strategies that are crafted in the real world may be found. Some strategies may approach either end, but many more fall at intermediate points.

Effective strategies develop in all kinds of strange ways.

Effective strategies can show up in the strangest places and develop through the most unexpected means. There is no "one best way" to make strategy.

The form for a cat collapses on the wheel, and our potter sees in the clay a bull taking shape. Clay sticks to a rolling pin, and a line of cylinders results. Waferlike forms come into being because of a shortage of clay and limited kiln space while the potter is working temporarily in a studio in France. Thus errors become opportunities, and limitations stimulate creativity. The natural propensity to experiment, or sometimes just boredom, likewise encourages strategic change.

Organizations that craft their strategies have similar experiences. Recall the National Film Board with its inadvertently long film that brought about a feature-film strategy. Or consider its experiences with experimental films, which made special use of animation and sound. For twenty years, the NFB produced a thin but steady trickle of such films. In fact, every film but one in that trickle was produced by a single person, Norman McLaren, the NFB's most celebrated filmmaker. McLaren pursued a *personal strategy* of experimentation, deliberate for him perhaps (did he intend the whole stream or simply consider one film at a time?) but not for the organization. Then twenty years later, others followed his lead and the trickle widened, his personal strategy becoming more broadly organizational.

Conversely, in 1952, when television came to Canada, a *consensus strategy* emerged at the NFB. Senior management was not keen on producing films for the new medium. But while the arguments raged, one filmmaker quietly went off and made a single series for TV. That precedent being set, one by one his colleagues leapt in, and within months the NFB—and its management—found themselves committed for several years to a new strategy with an intensity unmatched before or since. That consensus strategy arose spontaneously, as a result of many independent decisions made by the filmmakers about the films they wished to make. Can we call the strategy deliberate? For the filmmakers perhaps; for senior management certainly not. But for the organization? It all depends on your perspective, on how you choose to read the organization's mind.

While the NFB may seem like an extreme case, it highlights behavior that can be found, albeit in muted form, in all organizations. Those who doubt this might read Richard Pascale's account of how Honda stumbled into its enormous success in the American motorcycle market. Brilliant as its strategy may have looked after the fact, Honda's managers made almost every conceivable mistake until the market finally hit them over the head with the right formula. The Honda managers on site in

America, driving their products themselves (and thus inadvertently picking up market reaction), did only one thing right: They learned, firsthand.[1]

GRASSROOTS STRATEGY-MAKING

These strategies all reflect, in whole or part, what we like to call a grassroots approach to strategic management. Strategies grow like weeds in a garden. They take root in all kinds of places, wherever people have the capacity to learn (because they are in touch with the situation) and the resources to support that capacity. These strategies become organizational when they become collective, that is, when they proliferate to influence the behavior of the organization at large.

Of course, this view is overstated. But it is no less extreme than the conventional view of strategic management, which might be labeled the hothouse approach. Neither is right. Reality falls between the two. Some of the most effective strategies we uncovered in our research combined deliberation and control with flexibility and organizational learning.

Consider first what we call the *umbrella strategy*. Here senior management sets out broad guidelines (say, to produce only high-margin products at the cutting edge of technology or to produce products using bonding and coating technologies) and leaves the specifics (such as what those products will be) to others lower down in the organization. This strategy is not only deliberate (in its guidelines) and emergent (in its specifics), but it is also deliberately emergent in that the process is consciously managed to allow strategies to develop en route. IBM used the umbrella strategy in the early 1960s with the impending 360 series, when its senior management approved a set of broad criteria for the design of a family of computers later developed in detail throughout the organization.[2]

Deliberately emergent, too, is what we call the *process strategy*. Here management controls the process of strategy formation—concerning itself with the design of the structure, with staffing, development of procedures, and so on—while leaving the actual content to others.

Both process and umbrella strategies seem to be especially prevalent in businesses that require great expertise and creativity—a 3M, a Hewlett-Packard, a National Film Board. Such organizations can be effective only if their implementers are allowed to be formulators, because it is the people way down in the hierarchy who are in touch with the situation at hand and have the requisite technical expertise. In a sense, these are organizations peopled with craftsmen, all of whom must be strategists.

Strategic reorientations happen in brief, quantum leaps.

The conventional view of strategy in the planning literature claims that change must be continuous: The organization should be adapting all the time. Yet this view proves to be ironic, because the very concept of strategy is rooted in stability, not change. As this same literature makes clear, organizations pursue strategies to set direction, to lay out courses of action, and to elicit cooperation from their members around common, established guidelines. By any definition, and especially from the perspective of planning, strategy imposes stability on an organization. No stability means no strategy (no course to the future, no pattern from the past). Indeed, the very fact of having a strategy, and especially of making it explicit (as the conventional literature implores managers to do), creates resistance to strategic change!

What the conventional view fails to come to grips with, then, is how and when to promote change. A fundamental dilemma of strategy-making is the need to reconcile the forces for stability and for change—to focus efforts and gain operating efficiencies on the one hand, yet adapt and maintain currency with a changing external environment on the other.

QUANTUM LEAPS

Our own research and that of colleagues suggest that organizations resolve those opposing forces by attending first to one and then to the other. Distinct periods of stability and of change can usually be identified in organizations; major shifts in strategic orientation occur only rarely.

In our study of Steinberg Inc., a large supermarket chain headquartered in Montreal, we found only two important reorientations in the sixty years from its founding to the mid-1970s: a shift to self-service in 1933 and the introduction of shopping centers and public financing in 1953. At Volkswagenwerk, we saw only one reorientation between the late 1940s and the 1970s, the major shift from the traditional Beetle to the Audi-type design mentioned earlier. And at Air Canada, we found none over the airline's first four decades, following its initial positioning.

Our colleagues at McGill, Danny Miller and Peter Friesen, found this pattern of change so common in their studies of large numbers of companies (especially the high-performance ones) that they built a theory around it which they labeled the *quantum* theory of strategic change.[3] Their basic point is that organizations adopt two distinctly different modes of behavior at different times.

Most of the time organizations pursue a given strategic orientation. Change may seem continuous, but it occurs in the context of that orientation (perfecting a given retailing formula, for example) and usually amounts to doing more of the same, perhaps better as well. Most organizations favor these periods of stability because they achieve success not by changing strategies but by exploiting the ones they have. They, like craftsmen, seek continuous improvement by using their distinctive competencies on established courses.

While this goes on, however, the world continues to change, sometimes slowly, occasionally in dramatic shifts. As a result, whether gradually or suddenly, the organization's strategic orientation moves out of sync with its environment. Then what Miller and Friesen call a strategic revolution must take place. That long period of evolutionary change is suddenly punctuated by a brief bout of revolutionary turmoil in which the organization quickly alters many of its established patterns. In effect, it tries to leap to a new stability quickly to reestablish an integrated posture among a new set of strategies, structure, and culture.

But what about all those emergent strategies, growing like weeds around the organization? What the quantum theory suggests is that the really novel ones are generally held in check in some corner of the organization until a strategic revolution becomes necessary. Then as an alternative to having to develop new strategies from scratch or having to import generic strategies from competitors, the organization can turn to its own emerging patterns to find its new orientation. As the old, established strategy disintegrates, the seeds of the new one begin to spread.

This quantum theory of change seems to apply particularly well to large, established, mass-production organizations. Because they are especially reliant on standardized procedures, their resistance to strategic reorientation tends to be especially fierce. So we find long periods of stability broken by short disruptive periods of revolutionary change.

Volkswagenwerk is a case in point. Long enamored of the Beetle and armed with a tightly integrated set of strategies, the company ignored fundamental changes in its markets throughout the late 1950s and 1960s. The bureaucratic inertia of its mass-production organization combined with the psychological inertia of its leader, the person most responsible for the strategies it had been realizing. When change finally did come, it was tumultuous: The company groped its way through a hodgepodge of models before it settled on a new set of vehicles championed by a new leader. Strategic reorientations really are cultural revolutions.

CYCLES OF CHANGE

In more creative organizations like the National Film Board, we see a somewhat different pattern of change and stability, one that is more balanced. Organizations in the business of producing novel outputs apparently need to fly off in all directions from time to time to sustain their creativity. Yet they also need to settle down after such periods to find some order in the resulting chaos.

The NFB showed a marked tendency to move in and out of focus through remarkably balanced periods of convergence and divergence. Concentrated production of films to aid the war effort in the 1940s gave way to great divergence after the war as the organization sought a new raison d'être. Then the advent of television brought back a very sharp focus in the early 1950s, as noted earlier. But in the late 1950s, this dissipated almost as quickly as it began, giving rise to another period of exploration. Then the social changes in the early 1960s evoked a new period of convergence around experimental films and films on social issues.

We use the label "adhocracy" for organizations, like the National Film Board, that produce individual, or custom-made, products (or designs) in an innovative way, on a project basis.[4] Our craftsman is an adhocracy of sorts too, since each of her ceramic sculptures is unique. And her pattern of strategic change was much like the NFB's, with evident cycles of convergence and divergence: a focus on knickknacks from 1967 to 1972; then a period of exploration to about 1976, which resulted in a refocus on ceramic sculptures; that continued to about 1981, followed by a period of searching for new directions.

Whether through quantum revolutions or cycles of convergence and divergence, however, organizations seem to need to separate in time the basic forces for change and stability, reconciling them by attending to each in turn. Many strategic failures can be attributed either to mixing the two or to an obsession with one of these forces at the expense of the other.

The problems are evident in the work of many craftsmen. On the one hand, there are those who seize on the perfection of a single theme and never change. Eventually the creativity disappears from their work and the world passes them by—much as it did Volkswagenwerk until the company was shocked into its strategic revolution. And then there are those who are always changing, who flit from one idea to another and never settle down. Because no theme or strategy ever emerges in their work, they cannot exploit or even develop any distinctive competence. And because their work lacks definition, identity crises are likely to develop, with neither the craftsmen nor those interested in the craft knowing what to make of it. Miller and Friesen found this behavior in conventional business too; they labeled it "the impulsive firm running blind."[5] How often have we seen it in companies that go on acquisition sprees?

To manage strategy, then, is to craft thought and action, control and learning, stability and change.

The popular view sees the strategist as a planner or as a visionary, someone sitting on a pedestal dictating brilliant strategies for everyone else to implement. While recognizing the importance of thinking ahead and especially of the need for creative vision in a prosaic world, I wish to propose an additional view of the strategist—as a pattern recognizer, a learner if you will, who manages a process in which strategies (and visions) can emerge as well as be deliberately conceived. I also wish to redefine that strategist, to replace that individual with a collective entity, made up of many actors whose interplay expresses an organization's mind. This strategist *finds* strategies no less than creates them, often in patterns that form inadvertently in its own behavior.

What, then, does it mean to craft strategy? Let us return to the words associated with craft: dedication, experience, involvement with the material, the personal touch, mastery of detail, a sense of harmony and integration. Managers who craft strategy do not spend much time in executive suites reading MIS reports or studying industry analyses. They are involved, responsive to their materials, learning about their organizations and industries through personal touch. They are also sensitive to experience, recognizing that while individual vision may be important, other factors must help determine strategy as well.

TO MANAGE STABILITY. To manage strategy is in the first place mostly to manage stability, not change. Indeed, most of the time senior managers should not be formulating strategy at all; they should be getting on with making their organizations as effective as possible in pursuing the strategies they already have. Like distinguished craftsmen, organizations become distinguished because they master the details.

To manage strategy, then, at least in the first instance, is not so much to promote change as to know *when* to do so. Advocates of strategic planning often urge managers to plan for perpetual instability in the environment (for example, by rolling over five-year plans annually). But this obsession with change is dysfunctional. Organizations that reassess their strategies continuously are like individuals who reassess their jobs or their marriages continuously—in both cases, they can drive themselves crazy, or else reduce themselves to inaction. The formal planning process repeats itself so often and so mechanically that it can desensitize organizations to real change, programming them more and more deeply into set patterns, and thereby encouraging them to make only minor adaptations.

So-called strategic planning must be recognized for what it is: a means, not to create strategy, but to program a strategy already created—to work out its implications formally. It is essentially analytic in nature, based on decomposition, while strategy creation is essentially a process of synthesis. That is why trying to create strategies through formal planning most often leads to the extrapolation of existing strategies or to the copying of the strategies of competitors.

This is not to say that planners have no role to play in strategy formation. In addition to programming strategies created by other means, they can feed ad hoc analyses into the strategy-making process at the front end to be sure that the hard data are taken into consideration. They can also stimulate others to think strategically. And of course people called planners can be strategists too, so long as they are creative thinkers who are in touch with what is relevant. But that has nothing to do with the technology of formal planning.

TO DETECT DISCONTINUITY. Environments do not change on any regular or orderly basis. And they seldom undergo continuous dramatic change, claims about our "age of discontinuity" and environmental "turbulence" notwithstanding. (Go tell those claims to people who lived through the Great Depression or survivors of the siege of Leningrad during World War II.) Much of the time, change is minor and even temporary and requires no strategic response. Once in a while there is a truly significant discontinuity or even less often, a *gestalt* shift in the environment, where everything important seems to change at once. But these events, while critical, are also easy to recognize.

The real challenge in crafting strategy lies in detecting the subtle discontinuities that may undermine an organization in the future. And for that, there is no technique, no program, just a sharp mind in touch with the situation. Such discontinuities are unexpected and irregular, essentially unprecedented. They can be dealt with only by minds that are attuned to existing patterns yet able to perceive important breaks in them. Unfortunately, this form of strategic thinking tends to atrophy during the long periods of stability that most organizations experience (just as it did at Volkswagenwerk during the 1950s and 1960s). So the trick is to manage within a given strategic orientation most of the time yet be able to pick out the occasional discontinuity that really matters.

The Steinberg chain was built and run for more than half a century by a man named Sam Steinberg. For twenty years, the company concentrated on perfecting a self-service retailing formula introduced in 1933. Installing fluorescent lighting and figuring out how to package meat in cellophane wrapping were the "strategic" issues of the day. Then in 1952, with the arrival of the first shopping center in Montreal, Steinberg realized he had to redefine his business almost overnight. He knew he needed to control those shopping centers and that control would require public financing and other major changes. So he reoriented his business. The ability to make that kind of switch in thinking is the essence of strategic management. And it has more to do with vision and involvement than it does with analytic technique.

TO KNOW THE BUSINESS. Sam Steinberg was the epitome of the entrepreneur, a man intimately involved with all the details of his business, who spent Saturday mornings visiting his stores. As he told us in discussing his company's competitive advantage:

> Nobody knew the grocery business like we did. Everything has to do with your knowledge. I knew merchandise, I knew cost, I knew selling, I knew customers. I knew everything, and I passed on all my knowledge; I kept teaching my people. That's the advantage we had. Our competitors couldn't touch us.

Note the kind of knowledge involved: not intellectual knowledge, not analytical reports or abstracted facts and figures (though these can certainly help), but personal knowledge, intimate understanding, equivalent to the craftsman's feel for the clay. Facts are available to anyone; this kind of knowledge is not. Wisdom is the word that captures it best. But wisdom is a word that has been lost in the bureaucracies we have built for ourselves, systems designed to distance leaders from operating details. Show me managers who think they can rely on formal planning to create their strategies, and I'll show you managers who lack intimate knowledge of their businesses or the creativity to do something with it.

Craftsmen have to train themselves to see, to pick up things other people miss. The same holds true for managers of strategy. It is those with a kind of peripheral vision who are best able to detect and take advantage of events as they unfold.

TO MANAGE PATTERNS. Whether in an executive suite in Manhattan or a pottery studio in Montreal, a key to managing strategy is the ability to detect emerging patterns and help them take shape. The job of the manager is not just to preconceive specific strategies but also to recognize their emergence elsewhere in the organization and intervene when appropriate.

Like weeds that appear unexpectedly in a garden, some emergent strategies may need to be uprooted immediately. But management cannot be too quick to cut off the unexpected, for tomorrow's vision may grow out of today's aberration. (Europeans, after all, enjoy salads made from the leaves of the dandelion, America's most notorious weed!) Thus some patterns are worth watching until their effects have more clearly manifested themselves. Then those that prove useful can be made deliberate and incorporated into the formal strategy, even if that means shifting the strategic umbrella to cover them.

To manage in this context, then, is to create the climate within which a wide variety of strategies can grow. In more complex organizations, this may mean building flexible structures, hiring creative people, defining broad umbrella strategies, and watching for the patterns that emerge.

TO RECONCILE CHANGE AND CONTINUITY. Finally, managers considering radical departures need to keep the quantum theory of change in mind. As Ecclesiastes reminds us, there is a time to sow and a time to reap. Some new patterns must be held in check until the organization is ready for a strategic revolution, or at least a period of divergence.

Managers who are obsessed with either change or stability are bound eventually to harm their organizations. As pattern recognizer, the manager has to be able to sense when to exploit an established crop of strategies and when to encourage new strains to displace the old.

While strategy is a word that is usually associated with the future, its link to the past is no less central. As Kierkegaard once observed, life is lived forward but understood backward. Managers may have to live strategy in the future, but they must understand it through the past.

Like a potter at the wheel, organizations must make sense of the past if they hope to manage the future. Only by coming to understand the patterns that form in their own behavior do they get to know their capabilities and their potential. Thus crafting strategy, like managing craft, requires a natural synthesis of the future, present, and past.

3

PLANNING ON THE LEFT SIDE, MANAGING ON THE RIGHT

The article reprinted here preceded the last by more than a decade and took me into a somewhat different although perhaps more fundamental issue: the relationship between analysis and intuition, as manifested in the long and sometimes strained relationship between "staff" and "line," with special reference to planners and managers. The first two articles of this book grew out of years of research and contemplation; this third one developed rather spontaneously. In the summer of 1975, on a small farm in the Perigord region of France, I read Robert Ornstein's *The Psychology of Consciousness,* a popular account of the findings on the two hemispheres of the human brain. Although attention to these findings had become faddish at the time, to me they provided a basis for much of what I had been finding in my own research.

There is a lovely irony in the fact that intuition was in some sense brought back to life by the biologists. You see, intuition should really be a psychological concept. But most psychologists, in order to be perceived as good scientists, have long slighted it, when not ignoring it altogether. After all, if intuition is a thought process inaccessible to the *conscious* mind, how could they use *scientific* methods to describe it? Then along came people like Roger Sperry—real scientists, who cut tissue with knives and the like—and they were the ones to rediscover intuition, in a sense hiding all along in the mute right hemisphere of the human brain!

In reading Ornstein's book, I came to realize that I had really been celebrating intuition in my own research, uncovering it in all kinds of odd and clandestine places. This was at odds with the mainline management literature—applied no less than academic—that emphasized, almost to the point of obsession, the role of analysis in organizations, especially under so-called professional management. The title hit me first, then I wrote the article. (Usually it has been the other way around.) My writing almost always goes through many drafts before the editors get their hands on it and propose further changes. "Planning on the Left Side and Managing on the Right" appeared in the *Harvard Business Review* in 1976 almost as I first put it down on that small farm in the Perigord.

In the folklore of the Middle East, the story is told about a man named Nasrudin, who was searching for something on the ground. A friend came by and asked: "What have you lost, Nasrudin?"

"My key," said Nasrudin.

So the friend went down on his knees too, and they both looked for it. After a time, the friend asked: "Where exactly did you drop it?"

"In my house," answered Nasrudin.

"Then why are you looking here, Nasrudin?"

"There is more light here than inside my own house."

This little story has some timeless, mysterious appeal which has much to do with what follows. But let me leave that aside for a moment while I pose some questions—also simple yet mysterious—that have long puzzled me.

• First: Why are some people so smart and so dull at the same time, so capable of mastering certain mental activities yet so incapable of mastering others? Why is it that some of the most creative thinkers cannot comprehend a balance sheet, and that some accountants have no sense of product design? Why do some brilliant management scientists have no ability to handle organizational politics, while some of the most politically adept individuals seem unable to understand the simplest elements of management science?

• Second: Why do people sometimes express such surprise when they read or learn the obvious, something they already must have known? Why is a manager so delighted, for example, when he or she reads a new article on decision-making, every part of which must be patently obvious to him or her even though never before seen in print?

• Third: Why is there such a discrepancy in organizations, at least at the top levels, between formal planning on the one hand and informal managing on the other? Why have none of the techniques of planning and analysis really had much effect on how top managers function?

I intend below to weave answers to those three questions around the theme of the specialization of the hemispheres of the human brain. Later

I shall use my own research to draw out some implications of this for management, returning to our story of Nasrudin.

THE TWO HEMISPHERES OF THE HUMAN BRAIN

Let us first try to answer the three questions by looking at what is known about the hemispheres of the human brain.

QUESTION ONE

Scientists—in particular, neurologists, biologists, and psychologists—have known for a long time that the brain has two distinct hemispheres. They have known, further, that the left hemisphere controls movements on the body's right side while the right hemisphere controls movements on the left. What some have discovered more recently, however, is that the two hemispheres are specialized in more fundamental ways.

In the left hemisphere of most people's brains (lefthanders largely excepted), the mode of operation appears to be largely linear, information being processed sequentially, one bit after another, in an ordered way. Perhaps the most obvious linear faculty is language. In sharp contrast, the right hemisphere appears to be specialized for simultaneous processing; that is, it seems to operate in a more holistic, relational way. Perhaps its most obvious faculty is comprehension of visual images.

Although relatively few specific mental activities have yet been associated with one hemisphere or the other, research has provided some important clues. For example, an article in *The New York Times* cited research which suggests that emotion may be a right-hemispheric function.[1] This notion is based on the finding that victims of right-hemispheric strokes are often comparatively untroubled about their incapacity, while those with strokes of the left hemisphere often suffer profound mental anguish.

What does this specialization of the brain mean for the way people function? Speech, being linear, is a left-hemispheric activity, but other forms of human communication, such as gesturing, are relational and visual rather than sequential and verbal so tend to be associated with the right hemisphere. Imagine what would happen if the two sides of a human brain were detached so that, for example, in reading stimuli, words would be separate from gestures. In other words, in the same person, two separate brains—one specialized for verbal communication, and the other for gestures—would react to the same stimulus.

This, in fact, describes how the main breakthrough in the research on the human brain took place. In trying to treat certain cases of epilepsy, neurosurgeons found that by severing the corpus callosum, which joins the two hemispheres of the brain, they could "split the brain," isolating the epilepsy. A number of experiments run on these "split-brain" patients produced some fascinating results.

In one experiment, doctors showed a woman epileptic's right hemisphere a photograph of a nude woman. (This is done by showing it to the left half of each eye.) The patient said she saw nothing, but almost simultaneously blushed and seemed confused and uncomfortable. Her "conscious" left hemisphere, including her verbal apparatus, was aware only that something had happened to her body, but not what had caused the emotional response. Only her "unconscious" right hemisphere knew. Here neurosurgeons observed a clear split between the two independent consciousnesses that are normally in communication and collaboration.[2]

Scientists have found further that some common human tasks activate one side of the brain while leaving the other largely at rest. For example, learning a mathematical proof might evoke activity in the left hemisphere of the brain, while viewing a piece of sculpture or assessing a political opponent might evoke activity in the right.

So now we seem to have the answer to the first question. An individual may be smart and dull at the same time simply because one side of his or her brain is more developed than the other. Some people—perhaps most lawyers, accountants, planners—may have better developed left-hemispheric thinking processes, while others—perhaps, artists, athletes, politicians—may have better developed right-hemispheric processes. Thus an artist may be incapable of expressing certain feelings in words, while a lawyer may have no facility for painting. Or a politician may not be able to learn mathematics, while a management scientist may be constantly manipulated in political situations.

QUESTION TWO

A number of word opposites have been proposed to distinguish the two hemispheric modes of "consciousness," for example: explicit versus implicit; verbal versus spatial; argument versus experience; intellectual versus intuitive; and analytic versus gestalt.

I should interject at this point that these words, as well as much of the evidence for these conclusions, can be found in the remarkable book entitled *The Psychology of Consciousness* by Robert Ornstein, a research psychologist in California. Ornstein uses the story of Nasrudin to further the points he is making. Specifically, he refers to the linear left hemisphere as synonymous with lightness, with thought processes that we know in an explicit sense. We can *articulate* them. He associates the right hemisphere with darkness, with thought processes that are mysterious to us, at least "us" in the Western world.

Ornstein also points out how the "esoteric psychologies" of the East (Zen, Yoga, Sufism, and so on) have focused on right-hemispheric consciousness (for example, altering pulse rate through meditation). In sharp contrast, Western psychology has been concerned almost exclusively with left-hemispheric consciousness, with logical thought. Ornstein suggests that we might find an important key to human consciousness in the right hemisphere, in what to us in the West has been the darkness.

Now, reflect on this for a moment. (Should I say meditate?) There is a set of thought processes—linear, sequential, analytical—that scientists as well as the rest of us know a good deal about. And there is another set—simultaneous, relational, holistic—that we know little about. More importantly, here we do not "know" what we "know" or more exactly, our left hemispheres do not seem able to articulate explicitly what our right hemispheres know implicitly.

So here, seemingly, is the answer to the second question as well. The feeling of revelation about learning the obvious can be explained with the suggestion that the "obvious" knowledge was implicit, apparently restricted to the right hemisphere. The left hemisphere never "knew." Thus it seems to be a revelation to the left hemisphere when it learns explicitly what the right hemisphere knew all along implicitly.

Now the third question—the discrepancy between planning and managing—remains.

QUESTION THREE

By now, it should be obvious where my discussion is leading (at least, to the reader's right hemisphere and, now that I write it, perhaps to the reader's left hemisphere as well). It may be that management researchers have been looking for the key to management in the lightness of logical analysis whereas perhaps it has always been lost in the darkness of intuition.

Specifically, I propose that there may be a fundamental difference between formal planning and informal managing, a difference akin to that between the two hemispheres of the human brain. The techniques of planning and analysis are sequential and systematic; above all, articulated. Planners and management scientists are expected to proceed in their work through a series of logical, ordered steps, each one involving explicit analysis. (The argument that the successful application of these techniques requires considerable intuition does not really change my point. The occurrence of intuition simply means that the analyst is departing from his or her science.)

Formal planning, then, seems to use processes akin to those identified with the brain's left hemisphere. Furthermore, planners and management scientists seem to revel in a systematic, well-ordered world, and many show little appreciation for the more relational, holistic processes.

What about managing? More exactly, what about the processes used by top managers? (Let me emphasize here that I am focusing this discussion at the senior levels of organizations, where I believe the dichotomy between planning and managing is most pronounced.) Managers plan in some ways, too (that is, they think ahead), and they engage in their share of logical analysis. But I believe there is more than that to the effective managing of an organization. I hypothesize, therefore, that *the important processes of managing an organization rely to a considerable extent on the faculties identified with the brain's right hemisphere.* Effective managers seem to revel in ambiguity, in complex, mysterious systems with relatively little order.

If true, this hypothesis would answer the third question about the discrepancy between planning and managing. It would help to explain why each of the new analytic techniques of planning and analysis has, one after the other, had so little success at the senior levels. PPBS, strategic planning, "management" information systems, and models of the firm—all have been greeted with great enthusiasm, then, in many instances, a few years later quietly ushered out the back door.

MANAGING FROM THE RIGHT HEMISPHERE

Because research has so far told us little about the right hemisphere, I cannot support with evidence my claim that a key to managing lies there. I can only present to the reader a "feel" for the situation, not a reading of concrete data. A number of findings from my own research on senior management processes do, however, suggest that they possess characteristics of right-hemispheric thinking.

One fact recurs repeatedly in all of this research. The key managerial processes are enormously complex and mysterious (to me as a researcher, as well as to the managers who carry them out), drawing on the vaguest of information and using the least articulated of mental processes. These processes seem to be more relational and holistic than ordered and sequential, more intuitive than intellectual; they seem, in other words, to be most characteristic of right-hemispheric activity.

Here are some general findings:

1. The five chief executives I observed strongly favored the oral media of communication, especially meetings, over the written forms, namely reading and writing. Of course oral communication is linear, too, but it is more than that. Managers seem to favor it for two fundamental reasons that suggest a relational mode of operation.

First, oral communication enables the manager to "read" facial expressions, tones of voice, and gestures. As I mentioned earlier, these stimuli seem to be associated with the right hemisphere of the brain. Second, and perhaps more important, oral communication enables the manager to engage in the "real-time" exchange of information. Managers' concentration on the oral media, therefore, suggests that they desire relational, simultaneous methods of acquiring information, rather than the ordered and sequential ones.

2. In addition to noting the media managers use, it is interesting to look at the content of managers' information, and at what they do with it. The evidence here is that a great deal of the managers' inputs are soft and speculative—impressions and feelings about other people, hearsay, gossip, and so on. Furthermore, the very analytical inputs—reports, documents, and hard data in general—seem to be of relatively little interest to many managers.

What can managers do with this soft, speculative information? They "synthesize" rather than "analyze" it, I should think. (How do you analyze the mood of a friend or the grimace someone makes in response to a suggestion?) A great deal of this information helps the manager understand implicitly his or her organization and its environment, to "see the big picture." This very expression, so common in management, implies a relational, holistic use of information.

A number of words managers commonly use suggest this kind of mental process. For example, the word "hunch" seems to refer to the results of using the implicit models that managers develop subconsciously in their brains. "I don't know why, but I have a hunch that if we do x, then they will respond with y.'' Managers also use the word ''intuition'' to refer to thought processes that work but are unknown to them. This seems to be a word that the verbal intellect has given to the mysterious thought processes. Maybe ''a person has good intuition'' simply means that person has good implicit models in his or her right hemisphere.

3. Another consequence of the oral nature of the managers' information is of interest here. Managers tend to be the best-informed members of their organization, but they have difficulty disseminating their information to their subordinates. Therefore, when managers overloaded with work find a new task that needs doing, they face a dilemma: They must either delegate the task without the background information or simply do the task themselves, neither of which is satisfactory.

When I first encountered this ''dilemma of delegation,'' I described it in terms of time and of the nature of the manager's information: Because so much of a manager's information is oral (and stored in his or her head), the dissemination of it consumes much time. But now the split-brain research suggests a second, perhaps more significant, reason for the dilemma of delegation. The manager may simply be incapable of disseminating some relevant information because it is inaccessible to his or her consciousness.

4. Earlier in this article I wrote that managers revel in ambiguity, in complex, mysterious systems without much order. Let us look at evidence of this. What I have discussed so far about the managers' use of information suggests that their work is geared to action, not reflection. We see further evidence for this in the pace of their work (''Breaks are rare. It's one damn thing after another.''); the brevity of their activities (half of the chief executives' activities I observed were completed in less than nine minutes); the variety of their activities (these chief executives had no evident patterns in their workdays); the active preference for interruption in their work (stopping meetings, leaving their doors open); and the lack of routine in their work (few regularly scheduled contacts, and hardly any issues related to general planning).

Clearly, the manager does not operate in a systematic, orderly, and intellectual way, puffing on a pipe in a mountain retreat, as problems are analyzed. Rather, the manager deals with issues in the context of daily activities—one hand on the telephone, the other shaking hands with a departing guest. The manager is involved, plugged in; the mode of operating is relational, simultaneous, experiential, that is, encompassing all the characteristics associated with the right hemisphere.

5. If the most important managerial roles of the ten described in my research were to be isolated, leader, liaison, and disturbance handler would certainly be among them. Yet these are the roles least understood. *Leader* describes how the manager deals with his or her own subordinates. It is ironic that despite an immense amount of research, managers and researchers still know virtually nothing about the essence of leadership, about why some people follow and others lead. Leadership remains a mysterious chemistry; catchall words such as *charisma* proclaim our ignorance.

In the *liaison* role, the manager builds up a network of outside contacts, which serve as his or her personal information system. Again, the activities of this role remain almost completely outside the realm of articulated knowledge. And as a *disturbance handler* the manager handles problems and crises in his or her organization. Here again, despite an extensive literature on analytical decision-making, virtually nothing is written about decision-making under pressure. These activities remain outside the realm of management science, inside only the realm of intuition and experience.

6. Let us turn now to our research on strategic decision-making processes.[3] Two aspects of this—the *diagnosis* of decision situations and the *design* of custom-made solutions—stand out in that almost nothing is known about them. Yet these two stand out for another reason as well: They seem to be the most important aspects. In particular, diagnosis seems to be *the* crucial step in strategic decision-making, for it is here that the whole course of decision-making is set. It is a surprising fact, therefore, that diagnosis goes virtually without mention in the literature of planning or management science, most of which deals with the formal evaluation of given alternatives. The question becomes, *where* and *how* does diagnosis take place? Apparently in the darkness of judgment and intuition.

7. Another point that emerges from studying strategic decision-making processes is the existence and profound influence of a set of dynamic factors. Strategic decision-making processes are stopped by interruptions, delayed and speeded up by timing responses, and forced repeatedly to branch and cycle. Yet it is these dynamic factors that the ordered, sequential techniques of analysis are least able to handle. Thus, despite their importance, the dynamic factors go virtually without mention in the literature of management science.

Let us look at timing, for example. It is evident that timing is crucial in virtually everything the manager does. No manager takes action without considering the effects of moving more or less quickly, of seizing initiatives or of delaying to avoid complications. Yet in one review of the literature of management, the authors found fewer than ten books in 183 that refer directly to the subject of timing.[4] Essentially, managers are left on their own to deal with dynamic factors, which involve simultaneous, relational modes of thinking.

8. When managers do have to make serious choices from among options, how do they in fact make them? Three fundamental modes of selection can be distinguished—analysis, judgment, and bargaining. The first involves the systematic evaluation of options in terms of their consequences on stated organizational goals; the second is a process in the mind of a single decision-maker; and the third involves negotiations between different people.

One of the most surprising facts about how managers made the strategic decisions we studied is that so few reported using explicit analysis. There was considerable bargaining, but in general the selection mode most commonly used was judgment. Typically, the options and all kinds of data associated with them entered the mind of a manager, and somehow a choice later came out. *How* was never explained. *How* is never explained in any of the literature either.

9. Finally, we turn to our research on strategy-making in organizations. This process does not turn out to be the regular, continuous, systematic process depicted in so much of the planning literature. It is most often an irregular, discontinuous process, proceeding in fits and starts. There are periods of stability in strategy development, but also there are periods of flux, of groping, and of global change. To my mind, ''strategy'' represents the mediating force between a dynamic environment and a stable operating system. Strategy is the organization's ''conception'' of how to deal with its environment for a time.

Now, the environment does not change in any set pattern. And even if it did, the human brain would be unlikely to perceive it that way. People tend to underreact to mild stimuli and overreact to strong ones. It stands to reason, therefore, that strategies that mediate between environments and organizations cannot change in regular patterns.

How does strategic planning account for these fits and starts? The fact is that it does not. So again, the burden to cope falls on the manager, specifically on his or her mental processes—intuitional and experiential—that can deal with the irregular inputs from the environment.

10. Where do new strategies come from? This is not the place to probe into that complex question. But research does make one thing

clear. Formal, analytical processes that generally go under the label of planning are not likely to produce innovative strategies so much as "main-line" ones common to organizations in a given industry.[5] Innovative strategies seem to result from informal processes—vague, interactive, and above all oriented to the synthesis of disparate elements. No management process is more demanding of holistic, relational thinking than the creation of an integrated strategy to deal with a complex, intertwined environment. How can analysis, under the label strategic planning, possibly produce such a strategy?

Another famous old story has relevance here. It is the one about the blind men trying to identify an elephant by touch. One grabs the trunk and says the elephant is long and soft; another holds the leg and says it is massive and cylindrical; a third touches the skin and says it is rough and scaly. As Ornstein points out:

> Each person standing at one part of the elephant can make his own limited, analytic assessment of the situation, but we do not obtain an elephant by adding "scaly," "long and soft," "massive and cylindrical" together in any conceivable proportion. Without the development of an overall perspective, we remain lost in our individual investigations. Such a perspective is a province of another mode of knowledge, and cannot be achieved in the same way that individual parts are explored. It does not arise out of a linear sum of independent observations.[6]

What can we conclude from these findings? I must first reemphasize that everything I write about the two hemispheres of the brain falls into the realm of speculation. Researchers have yet to formally relate any management process to the functioning of the human brain.* Nevertheless, these findings do seem to support the hypothesis stated earlier: *The important policy-level processes required to manage an organization rely to a considerable extent on the faculties identified with the brain's right hemisphere.*

This conclusion does not imply that the left hemisphere is unimportant for policy-makers. Every manager engages in considerable explicit calculation when he or she acts, and much intuitive thinking must be translated into the linear order of the left hemisphere if it is to be articulated and

* Almost concurrently with the publication of this article, Robert Doktor was, in fact, reporting on research with senior line managers and staff analysts which uncovered physiological evidence (through EEG measurement of brainwaves) for the lateral specialization implied here. See R. Doktor, "Problem Solving Styles of Executives and Management Scientists," *TIMS Studies in the Management Sciences,* no. 8 (1978), pp. 123–34.

eventually put to use. The great powers that appear to be associated with the right hemisphere are obviously useless without the faculties of the left. The artist can create without verbalizing; the manager cannot.

Truly outstanding managers are no doubt the ones who can couple effective processes of the right (hunch, intuition, synthesis) with effective processes of the left (articulateness, logic, analysis). But there will be little headway in the field of management if managers and researchers continue, like Nasrudin, to search for the key to management in the "lightness" of ordered analysis. Too much will stay unexplained in the "darkness" of intuition.

IMPLICATIONS FOR THE LEFT HEMISPHERE

What does all this mean for those associated with management?

First, I would not like to suggest that planners and management scientists pack up their bags of techniques and leave organizations, or that they take up basket-weaving or meditation in their spare time. (I haven't—at least not yet!) It seems to me that the left hemisphere is alive and well; the analytic community is firmly established, and indispensable, at the operating and middle levels of most organizations. Its real problems occur at the senior levels. Here analysis must coexist with—perhaps even take its lead from—intuition, a fact that many analysts and planners have been slow to accept. To my mind, organizational effectiveness does not lie in that narrow-minded concept called "rationality"; it lies in a blend of clear-headed logic *and* powerful intuition.

For one thing, only under certain circumstances should planners try to plan. When an organization is in a stable environment and has no use for an innovative strategy, then the development of formal, systematic strategic plans (and main-line strategies) may be in order. But when the environment is unstable or the organization needs an innovative strategy, then strategic planning may not be the best approach to strategy making, and planners have no business pushing their organizations to use it. Further, effective decision-making at the senior level requires good analytical input; it is the job of the planner and management scientist to ensure that top management gets it. Managers are very effective at securing soft information. But they tend to underemphasize analytical input that is often important as well. The planners and management scientists can serve their organizations effectively by carrying out ad hoc analyses and feeding the results to top management (need I say orally?), ensuring that the very best of analysis is brought to bear on policy-making.

For teachers of management, if the suggestions in this article turn out to be valid, then educators had better revise drastically some of their notions about management education. Unfortunately, the revolution in that sphere over the last fifteen years—while it has brought so much of value—has virtually consecrated the modern management school to the worship of the left hemisphere.

Should educators be surprised that so many of their graduates end up in staff positions, with no intention of ever managing anything? Some of the best-known management schools have become virtual closed systems in which professors with little interest in the reality of organizational life teach inexperienced students the theories of mathematics, economics, and psychology as ends in themselves. In these management schools, management is accorded little place. There is a need for a new balance in our schools, the balance that the best of human brains can achieve, between the analytic and the intuitive.

As for managers, the first conclusion should be a call for caution. The findings of the human brain should not be taken as license to shroud activities in darkness. Artificially mystifying behavior is a favorite ploy of those seeking to protect a power base; this helps no organization and neither does trying to impose intuition on activities that can be handled effectively by analysis. But a misplaced obsession with analysis is no better, and to my mind represents a far more prevalent problem today.

A major thrust of development in our organizations, ever since Frederick Taylor began experimenting in factories late in the last century, has been to shift activities out of the realm of intuition, toward conscious analysis. That trend will continue. But managers, and those who work with them, need to be careful to distinguish that which is best handled analytically from that which must remain in the realm of intuition. That is where we shall have to continue looking for the lost keys to management.

4
COUPLING ANALYSIS AND INTUITION IN MANAGEMENT

"Planning on the Left Side, Managing on the Right" did not resolve any issue so much as open up a number of difficult and, I believe, fundamental ones. First among these is the question of how our organizations should make use of the processes of analysis and intuition. Excessive use of intuition, perhaps common a century ago, can drive organizations toward idiosyncratic and arbitrary behaviors. But excessive reliance on analysis, which I believe to be the common case now, can make their behavior indifferent and unresponsive. How we couple these two processes has major implications, not only for the effectiveness of our organizations but for the society we are to live in.

I began on the analytic side of management. I was trained in engineering and accepted my first full-time job in the Operational Research Branch of Canadian National Railways. Operational research (called operations research, or OR, in the United States, also known as management science), seeks to apply systematic analysis to the problems of management. Later, when I did my masters degree at the MIT Sloan School of Management, I shifted my attention to the softer side of the field—the policy processes of senior management. But my interest in the role of analysis remained, and one stream of my articles has been directed to that group with which I first identified, the staff analysts of organizations—OR people, planners, information systems designers. Nothing in management has frustrated me more than what has been called the "rule of the tool," the use of technique for its own sake ("Give a little boy a hammer and it just so happens that everything needs pounding!").* These articles sought to help correct that.

* One of the founders of operational research during World War II in Britain, P. M. S. Blackett, defined it as "merely the scientific method applied to the complex data of human society."[1] By the 1970s, a prominent American practioner would define it as "a comprehensive array of tested and proven tools."[2]

I have always considered Herbert Simon the most distinguished organization theorist of our time. Simon was trained in political science but early on joined the Graduate School of Industrial Administration at Carnegie-Mellon University, where he served as a major intellectual force in the development of the contemporary management school.

In the 1950s GSIA, as it is called, literally invented contemporary management education—the notions of basing it in the fundamental disciplines of economics, psychology, and mathematics, and of teaching theory derived from research, which was viewed at GSIA as the main task of the business school academic. Carnegie-Mellon in these respects was at least ten years ahead of other business schools, almost all of which now do (I shall soon argue overdo) these things as their natural way of functioning.

Simon's impact on our understanding of organizations, as well as on our attitudes toward research, has been profound, reflected in a publication list that numbers over five hundred items, including several major books in the field.[3] His contribution was recognized in 1978, when he was awarded the Nobel Prize. This was the prize in Economics, but Simon won it for his work in organization theory. In fact, since the early 1970s Simon has made his home in Carnegie-Mellon's psychology department, where he pursues his interests in decision-making through studies of human cognition.

I sent Simon a copy of "Planning on the Left Side and Managing on the Right" shortly after it was accepted for publication. He responded soon after, suggesting my argument was false. Just then receiving a telegram from the publisher requesting the article immediately, I spent a miserable forty-eight hours. I finally decided to proceed with the publication, which I feel represents a turning point in my career.

To that time, I was a fairly conventional scholar. I toyed with notions of intuition etc., but it was only after I decided to publish the article that I really opened up to them. Herbert Simon knew a great deal more than I about human cognition in decision-making; my problem during those forty-eight hours was to conclude whether he knew enough, in essence whether anyone really understood the full meaning of intuition. By concluding that no one did (I mean formally, not intuitively!), I was also concluding that society has paid a terrible price by rejecting it over the course of almost a century—in organizations, the study of organizations, and, behind that, the field of psychology itself.

I believe it is worth taking the space here to repeat some of the correspondence I had with Herbert Simon about the article, partly because it may be of interest in itself, but primarily because I believe it helps to introduce a critical issue that is addressed in the text that follows.

In earlier correspondence, Simon had mentioned he was revising *The New Science of Management Decision,* a small but important book about the impact of computers on organizations and especially about the need to bring the "modern techniques" of systematic analysis to bear on the "traditional," "nonprogrammed" decision processes of senior management. On March 17, 1976, I wrote him, in part:

I have one question about that revision, which is implied in the enclosed paper. All of my work to date has proceeded on the assumption that we must specify as precisely as possible—"program," if you like—the organizational decision processes. I continue to work in this direction . . . but some reading I have recently done on the brain's two hemispheres (notably the book by Robert Ornstein entitled *The Psychology of Consciousness*) has upset this assumption somewhat. Perhaps the processes we call intuition are fundamentally different from those we can specify or program. Do we really yet understand the meaning of synthesis? This reading as well as gnawing questions which have remained in all of my own research stimulated me to write "Planning on the Left Side, and Managing on the Right," more to raise questions than to answer them. In any event, I am curious whether you will address this issue in the revision, and if so, how. I am beginning to believe that this may be a fundamental issue for us.

His letter of March 24, 1976, read as follows:

I do not discuss the left–right brain evidence in the new revision, but I do discuss ill-structured problem solving. I believe that the left–right distinction is important, but not (a) that Ornstein has described it correctly, or (b) that it has anything to do with the distinction between planning and managing or conscious-unconscious.

What I think it *does* have to do with is the role of perceptual recognition in problem solving. On this, we have done a good deal of work, in the environment of chess. I enclose a couple of reprints, which will give you a general idea of our local views on the matter, and I have incorporated some of these views in the revision. If you want to substitute "right hemisphere" for visual pattern recognition, you will have a first approximation of what I believe to be the case.

The temptations are so great to romanticize about human performance (and even to credit it with ESP for which there is no real evidence)! I will paraphrase one of the French philosophers: "I have no need for that hypothesis." Was that Diderot? Perhaps one of your colleagues at Aix-en-Provence can identify the quotation.

We are now starting some research on managers' versus students' analysis of policy cases, using our perceptual hypothesis as a guide for what kinds of differences to look for. Perhaps in some months, we will have some results. Meanwhile, I would be inclined to go slow with left–right brain explanations of intuition. It is just the latest of a long series of fads—not the phenomenon, but this particular romantic explanation of it.

Simon's comment about ESP was in reference to two sentences in my original paper that both I and the *Harvard Business Review* editor, independently, deleted as too provocative. (In reference to the roles of oral communication and gestures in managerial work, they read in the original version: "I am tempted to raise the issue of extra-sensory perception here. There is clearly too much evidence to dismiss this as a medium of communication, at least for some people, and as Ornstein suggests, it is presumably a right hemisphere activity.") In fact, my decision to publish ultimately turned on that comment of Simon: While the presence of ESP may not have been *proved* in any scientific sense, to dismiss it for "no real evidence" suggested to me more about Simon's thinking than about ESP. The text of my letter to Simon of May 4, 1976, follows:

Your letter about my paper on managing and the two hemispheres of the human brain stimulated me to review it very carefully. When your letter arrived, the paper was already accepted for publication, but I was able to make changes. On balance, while I chose to tone down some of the specific comments linking management process to one hemisphere or the other, and to make clearer what is fact and what is speculation, I feel that it is important to proceed with the general theme. I believe that a number of the points in the paper need to be made, especially to management schools that I find have moved increasingly away from real management process.

As for your disagreement with Ornstein, the issue seems to come down to a question of whether or not there are two fundamentally different thought processes. I am concerned about a number of unexplained phenomena, for example the sudden discovery of a creative insight after a period of intellectual incubation. I'm tempted to side with Ornstein for the moment (that there are fundamentally different thought processes; that they do or not fall into distinct hemispheres interests me less; that is an issue for the physiologists, although the evidence seems tempting), while keeping a watchful eye on how far researchers like yourself can push the frontiers of linear simulation into real-world decision-making. It seems to me that you are uncomfortable with Ornstein's extrapolations from the tangible evidence of the research to date. I am not so uncomfortable, partly because they suggest so much to me and partly, I am sure, because I know so much less than you do about human cognition. But when we get right down to it, how much does anyone really know about creativity, concept formation, and the like? Ornstein's work does have all the trappings of a fad. I am generally opposed to fads; this one is the exception because it seems to explain so much behavior that I have observed informally. (May I say that my right hemisphere "feels" that Ornstein is on to something?) In any event, all of my other papers in one way or another have roots in your work; this one provides a counterpoint. My intention is primarily to provoke, to open some new channels of debate, not to make any definitive claims.

Incidentally, concerning "no real evidence" for ESP, have you by chance seen a book entitled "Psychic Discoveries Behind the Iron Curtain"? No one can invent that many lies. If only one of the hundreds of research studies reported there is valid, then the phenomenon cannot be dismissed as a "residual." The signal may not be identified, but the presence of communication is. Did you know that Turing,* in his paper reprinted in the Feigenbaum and Feldman book, while refuting in an elegant way a number of the arguments about why computers cannot think, hesitates on only one, commenting as follows:

> "I assume that the reader is familiar with the idea of extrasensory perception, and the meaning of the four items of it, viz., telepathy, clairvoyance, precognition and psychokinesis. These disturbing phenomena seem to deny all our usual scientific ideas. How we should like to descredit them! Unfortunately the statistical evidence, at least for telepathy, is overwhelming. It is very difficult to rearrange one's ideas so as to fit these new facts in. . . . This argument is to my mind quite a strong one. One can say in reply that many scientific theories seem to remain workable in practice, in spite of clashing with ESP; that in fact one can get along very nicely if

---

* An eminent British mathematician of the 1930s and 1940s.

one forgets about it. This is rather cold comfort, and one fears that thinking is just the kind of phenomenon where ESP may be especially relevant.'' (p. 29)

A year later, I published a review of Simon's revised *The New Science of Management Decision.* In later publications, in reference to the left and right hemisphere discussion, Simon has made clear his use of the word intuition in management. In the text that follows, I begin with excerpts from my book review, concentrating on my critique of Simon's view of intuition in management. I conclude with the juxtaposition of two single sentence quotations that diametrically oppose each other—one by Herbert Simon, the other by Roger Sperry, who also won a Nobel Prize, in his case in physiology, in 1981 for the split brain research. I then present Simon's more recent views on intuition, quoting from an article in a management journal of 1987. (In my request to him to reprint this correspondence, which also stated my wish to quote his more recent ideas, he suggested this particular article.)

While I continue to disagree with Simon's view of intuition, I agree fully with his final conclusion, that effectiveness in management depends ultimately on the coupling of analytic and intuitive processes. Accordingly, the rest of this chapter presents excerpts from three of my publications that sought to do that, with regard to the practice of strategic decision-making, of management information systems design, and of planning.

REVIEW OF THE NEW SCIENCE OF MANAGEMENT DECISION

A brief word on history: *The New Science of Management Decision* was first published in 1960 as a fifty-page book, based on a series of lectures Herbert Simon gave at New York University on the nature of the executive decision process and the impact of new techniques on organizational decision-making and structure. A second version appeared in 1965 . . . under the title, *The Shape of Automation.* . . . What we have in 1977 is a 175-page revised edition of the 1965 book with the 1960 title. . . . But the changes are not fundamental: ''. . . revising this volume, although the revision is extensive, has been more a matter of updating the evidence and treating a number of topics more fully, than it has been a matter of altering the main findings and conclusions."[4]

The New Science of Management Decision seeks to understand the effects that the computer has had, and by extrapolation will have, on organizations, the people who work in them, and the society in which they are embedded. . . .

If the essence of *The New Science of Management Decision* were to be captured in a single phrase, it would be that the book celebrates the results of technology, particularly of the information processing variety, on decision-making and structure in organizations, on the work of the executives at the top and the workers at the bottom, even on society and its capacity to solve the problems of pollution and overpopulation. . . .

> The processes of nonprogrammed decision making are beginning to undergo as fundamental a revolution as the one that is currently transforming programmed decision making in business organizations. Basic discoveries have been made about the nature of human problem solving, and their first potentialities for business application have already emerged. (p. 63)

My own research as well as my review of others' on the work of senior managers—those people most involved with nonprogrammed decision making—led to a very different conclusion, namely that "there is as yet no science in managerial work" . . . [and] that "even the computer . . . has apparently done little to alter the working methods of the general manager."[5]

[The review then considers the evidence Simon presents for his assumption, including his own research in the psychology laboratory, and ends with:] The sparseness of evidence cited notwithstanding, Simon draws a rather strong conclusion:

> The first thing we have learned—and the evidence for this is by now substantial—is that these human processes (problem solving, thinking, and learning) can be explained *without* postulating mechanisms at subconscious levels that are different from those that are partly conscious and partly verbalized. Much of the iceberg is, indeed, below the surface and inaccessible to verbalization, but its concealed bulk is made of the same kind of ice as the part we can see. The secret of problem solving is that there is no secret. It is accomplished through complex structures of familiar simple elements.[6]

I read [Simon's argument] with a good deal of incredulity. But my biggest surprise came when I discovered that Simon had written essentially the same thing in the 1960 edition of the book.* I had read that version in the mid-60s without surprise; indeed, I positively shared Simon's vision of the coming managerial revolution. What has changed since then? My own research on the work and decision processes of senior managers has certainly opened my eyes to a very different perspective, but that is beside the point in this review. Two fundamental events have taken place in those intervening years which have changed my views. . . . One exposed a fundamental problem with technology and analysis; the other suggests a possible explanation for the problem. . . .

Vietnam represented a critical turning point in the perceptions of many of us toward analysis. It would be trite to say that a reading of Halberstam's *The Best and the Brightest*[7] signaled that the honeymoon with analysis was over. Its relationship with management, which began in the factory with Frederick Taylor, flourished in the office with the introduction of Operations Research, and culminated in Robert McNamara's application of the Hitch and McKean[8] proposals for PPBS and cost-benefit analysis at the policy level, started to come apart in the rice paddies of Vietnam. Halberstam's carefully documented story makes it quite clear that this was no ordinary failure of analysis, not yet another one to be explained away in "implementation." Something was fundamentally wrong with the "formulation," that is, with analysis itself. Here the best and the brightest—not politicians or bureaucrats, but America's finest analytic talent, drawn from the centers of liberal intelligentsia—applied the modern techniques to the White House's nonprogrammed decisions, and the result was a war effort both ill-conceived and fundamentally immoral.

What went wrong? Could it have been the inability of analysis to handle the soft data—the expression on a peasant's face as opposed to a body count, the will of the enemy as opposed to the number of bombs needed to defoliate a jungle? "When [civilian advisers] said the Diem government was losing popularity with the peasants because of the Buddhist crisis, McNamara asked, well, what percentage was dropping off,

---

* The [above] quotation appears almost word-for-word. The only substantive change is the addition in 1977 of the phrase "and inaccessible to verbalization." Most curious is the statement seventeen years after the first edition: "It is only in the past twenty years that we have begun to have a good scientific understanding of the information processes that humans use in problem solving and nonprogrammed decision making." [Much of the research Simon cites is, in fact, discussed in the 1960 edition of the book as well.]

what percentage did the government have and what percentage was it losing? He asked for facts, some statistics, something he could run through the data bank, not just this poetry they were spouting."[9] Could the facts have represented values?* In other words, can values inadvertently creep into the analysis when the number of dead bodies or the acres of defoliated jungle are measurable while the worth of a single human life is not?

Facts become impregnated with value when they consistently line up behind a single set of goals. In Vietnam they supported the military goals; the humanitarian goals, supported only by soft data, were driven out of the analysis. We see the same thing in corporations when the hard data line up behind the economic goals—cost reduction, profit increase, growth in market share—leaving the social goals—product quality, employee satisfaction, protection of the environment—to fend for themselves.[10] And in society itself, when pollution endures pending calculation of its costs, and chemicals continue to be pumped into our bodies until some scientist can "prove" that they are killing us (presumably by more body counts). When these things happen, analysis can no longer be called amoral: It drives even well-intentioned decision makers to make decidedly immoral choices. Shortly after the Bay of Pigs incident, Chester Bowles wrote of the Kennedy administration:

> The question which concerns me most about this new Administration is whether it lacks a genuine sense of conviction about what is right and what is wrong. . . .
>
> Anyone in public life who has strong convictions about the rights and wrongs of public morality, both domestic and international, has a very great advantage in times of strain, since his instincts on what to do are clear and immediate. Lacking such a framework of moral conviction or sense of what is right and what is wrong, he is forced to lean almost entirely upon his mental processes; he adds up the pluses and minuses of any question and comes up with a conclusion. Under normal conditions, when he is not tired or frustrated, this pragmatic approach should successfully bring him out on the right side of the question.
>
> What worries me are the conclusions that such an individual may reach when he is tired, angry, frustrated or emotionally affected. The Cuban fiasco demonstrates how far astray a man as brilliant and well intentioned as Kennedy can go who lacks a basic moral reference point.[11]

---

* In *Administrative Behavior,* Herbert Simon makes what has become a well-known distinction between facts and values in decision-making. See also Chapter 16 of this book.

If Vietnam exposed the problem, then a psychobiologist at the California Institute of Technology may have found the explanation. [The review then presents Roger Sperry's notions of the two hemispheres of the brain, much as discussed in "Planning on the Left Side, Managing on the Right," concluding that the right hemisphere] appears to be the seat of what we call judgment or intuition, the "instincts" Bowles found missing in the Kennedy administration, a likely place to deal with the soft data analysis cannot handle.

[Sperry's] speculation, of course, diametrically opposes that of Simon. To Sperry, the ice is not the same on both sides of the human brain; Simon's [research accesses] only one kind of ice; and sequential programming cannot simulate gestalt thinking.* In fact, Sperry has spoken out on this last point. In sharp contrast to Simon's statement that "We now know a great deal about what goes on in the human head when a person is exercising judgment or having an intuition, to the point where many of these processes can be simulated on a computer," Sperry has written . . . "The right [hemisphere], by contrast [with the left] is spatial, mute and performs with a synthetic spatio-perceptual and mechanical kind of information processing *not yet simulateable in computers*"[13]. . . .

On page 7 of his book, Simon asks: "How does one choose among experts? The easiest and commonest way is to accept an expert who confirms one's present beliefs and prior prejudices." As reviewer, I have not hidden my beliefs or prior prejudices. But then Simon adds, "We choose among experts by forcing the experts to disclose how they reached their conclusions, what reasoning they employed, *what evidence they relied upon*. . . . We do not have to be championship boxers to referee a fight."[14] I suppose that being the reviewer puts me in the ring as referee; I am certainly not here as a championship psychologist. Given the evidence Simon and Sperry rely upon in this match of speculations, I declare Sperry's two modes of thinking, only one that can be simulated in computers, the winner by a technical knockout!

---

* In discussing the simulation of human thought, Simon writes: "In solving problems, human thinking is governed by programs that organize myriads of simple information processes—or symbol manipulating processes if you like—into orderly, complex *sequences* that are responsive to and adaptive to the task environment and the clues that are extracted from that environment as the sequences unfold. Since programs of the same kind can be written for computers, these programs can be used to describe and simulate human thinking."[12]

To conclude, Simon's *The New Science of Management Decision* celebrates the effects of technology, analysis as well as automation. It does so to the point of concluding that all modes of thinking can be represented in sequential form, that what we call judgment or intuition can be simulated in the computer, and that the modern techniques of analysis must be applied to that judgment if society is to solve its problems. But we have also seen that other important [scientists] disagree. And of equal importance, we have seen that the issue has to do with much more than just the physiology of the brain; it may be the key to the management of our organizations and even to the ultimate survival of mankind itself. Many of us are coming to question increasingly the extent to which we can trust analysis untempered by intuition, to question whether truly humanitarian decisions will always have to be made in places inaccessible to Herbert Simon's computer.

SIMON'S CURRENT VIEW OF INTUITION

In an article published in the *Academy of Management Executive* of February 1987, entitled "Making Management Decisions: The Role of Intuition and Emotion," Herbert Simon reviews some evidence from physiological research and then notes that "the more romantic issues of the split-brain doctrine extrapolate this evidence into the two polar forms of thought labelled . . . as analytical and creative." But

> The evidence for this romantic extrapolation does not derive from the physiological research. As I indicated above, that research has provided evidence only for some measure of specialization between the hemispheres. It does not in any way imply that either hemisphere (especially the right hemisphere) is capable of problem solving, decision making, or discovery independent of the other. The real evidence for two different forms of thought is essentially the observation that, in everyday affairs, men and women often make competent judgments or reach reasonable decisions rapidly—without evidence indicating that they have engaged in systematic reasoning, and without their being able to report the thought processes that took them to their conclusion.
>
> There is also some evidence for the very plausible hypothesis that some people, confronted with a particular problem, make more use of intuitive processes in solving it, while other people make relatively more use of analytical processes.[15]

Simon then discusses some research on the "expert's intuition," particularly the ability of chess grandmasters to glance at a chessboard and quickly size up the situation. He argues that the expert recognizes familiar patterns, that "the secret of the grandmaster's intuition or judgment" is "previous learning that has stored the patterns and the information associated with them." Simon's own extrapolation is that "the experienced manager, too, has in his or her memory a large amount of knowledge, gained from training and experience and arranged in terms of recognizable chunks and associated information,"[16] and that the essence of intuition lies in the *organization* of knowledge for quick identification, and not in its rendering for inspired design. He cites, for example, one study in which business people could identify the key features of a case far faster than MBA students.

Simon concludes that "intuition is not a process that operates independently of analysis; rather the two processes are essential complementary components of effective decision-making systems." Therefore:

> It is a fallacy to contrast "analytic" and "intuitive" styles of management. Intuition and judgment—at least good judgment—are simply *analyses frozen into habit* and into the capacity for rapid response through recognition. Every manager needs to be able to analyze problems systematically (and with the aid of the modern arsenal of analytical tools provided by management science and operations research). Every manager needs also to be able to respond to situations rapidly, a skill that requires cultivation of intuition and judgment over many years of experience and training. The effective manager does not have the luxury of choosing between "analytic" and "intuitive" approaches to problems. Behaving like a manager means having command of the whole range of management skills and applying them as they become appropriate.[17]

Simon's view of intuition as "analyses frozen into habit" appears to me to be overly narrow, slighting especially the important phenomenon of creative insight (where did those famous new chess moves come from, anyway?). In none of the evidence he cites do I get a sense of how decision-makers see deeply into a complex problem, how they size up novel situations, how they leap to creative solutions.

Simon is well known for his concept of "bounded rationality," that people are limited in the amount of information they can process at any one time. In one rendition of this by psychologist George Miller, this amounts to about seven "bits" or "chunks" of information in our short and intermediate term memories.[18] The question remains, however, whether other things are going on deeper inside our brains—whether we are in fact restricted to processing discrete units of information (as are computers), as opposed, say, to vague "impressions" or "images," whatever form they may take, and, concomitantly, whether there are complex processes of synthesis taking place there that cannot be studied by the research methods of the cognitive psychologist.

Remember that much of Simon's work has been based on verbal protocols—voice articulations of the person's thoughts as he or she makes a decision. Words are bits; they express the results of thought processes that are available to the conscious mind, and they must be emitted in linear order. Thus, research that accesses the *conscious,* that does so via people's *input/output* devices (notably speech), and that assumes a posture that is essentially reductionist in nature, and therefore basically *analytic* (reflecting conventional "rationality," however "bounded"), has been used to draw inferences about *processes* that appear to be *subconscious* and based in a good part on *synthesis.* Is it any wonder then that intuition gets reduced to "analyses frozen into habit"?

Can attention to the bounded rationality of bits and chunks of information really capture feats of synthesis that take place in human minds—for example, Edwin Land's conception of the instant camera one day in Santa Fe? Can it explain the writing of Simon's own books, full of insights and representing tremendous integration of all kinds of ideas and information? Land himself has commented that during his intense periods of creative insight "atavistic competencies seem to come welling up. You are handling *so many variables* at a barely conscious level that you can't afford to be interrupted"[19] (presumably, even by the researcher's request for protocols!).

As human beings, we may have to articulate the results of our insightful syntheses in the linear order of words. But the processes by which we arrive at them seem to remain mysterious, not irrational so much, perhaps, as *a*rational, locked deep inside our subconscious minds.

But then again, will anyone ever be able to resolve this type of disagreement? If intuition is, by definition, a thought process in the subconscious, then how can we ever know we have probed deeply enough inside anyone's head to be sure we have captured what is going on there? (For example, what if Turing was right about ESP? That would leave not even "cold comfort" for anyone intent on understanding intuitive thought processes through research.) The researcher's tool is essentially analytical, as is the scholar's in debating this issue—words in linear order. How can rational analysis be used to prove or disprove the existence of an arational, nonanalytical thought process?

There is, however, cold comfort in the implication of Herbert Simon's final conclusion: that no matter what intuition really is—anything from the rapid recognition of the expert to the extrasensory perception of the psychic—clearly it must be combined with analysis in managerial decision-making. No organization can afford the luxury of being purely analytic or purely intuitive.

STRENGTHS AND WEAKNESSES OF ANALYSIS AND INTUITION

An expert has been defined as someone who avoids all the many pitfalls on his or her way to the grand fallacy. What makes this quotation of relevance here is that analytical and planning people in the field of management have long been inclined to blame their failures on a set of pitfalls, mostly of "implementation." They have claimed that managers don't understand analysis, that they don't support planning sufficiently, that the politicized climates of organizations impede the use of planning and analysis, and so on. But pitfalls are to organizations what sins are to religions—blemishes to be removed, so that people can get on with the more noble task of serving the almighty. These pitfalls ignore the more deeply rooted causes of the resistance to planning and analysis, which I believe should be labeled the fallacies of formulation—essentially misperceptions of how planning and analysis, as well as managers and organizations, need to work.

Implicit in a good deal of management science, information systems design, and formal planning have long been the assumptions that strategy making is a relatively static, orderly process (it is anything but); that discontinuities can be forecast through systematic procedures (there is no support for this whatsoever); that strategic management can be detached from operating management, with the senior managers informed by "hard" (namely computer-generated) data (managers who believe this are ignorant in two ways); and ultimately that the processes of making decisions and developing strategies can be formalized, or programmed, by systems that rely above all on decomposition. All these fallacies, to my mind, reduce to one grand fallacy: that to decompose is to recombine, in other words, that analysis includes synthesis. In the final analysis (so to speak), synthesis is not analysis, but rather is rooted in the mysteries of intuition.

Analysis and intuition differ not only in how they work but also in their respective strengths and weaknesses. Let us consider several of these.

COST. Ask almost anyone which process is more costly and the quick response will be "analysis." After all, it takes time to study an issue systematically, whereas intuition is right there with an answer. Well, this might be an example of intuition itself leaping to the wrong conclusion, because the question turns out to be more involved than it first seems. The fact is that analysis has a high *operating* cost, but its *investment* cost is relatively low (just hire a few freshly minted MBAs). Intuition, on the other hand (again, so to speak), has almost no operating cost ("Hey, Fred, should we expand into Guadeloupe?"). But its investment cost is high: A person has to know a subject deeply, has to have long and intimate experience with it, to be able to deal with it effectively through intuition. (Simon comments in his article about the need for at least ten years before a chess grandmaster or other "expert" can recognize those chunks quickly.)

ERROR. Also, again on first thought, analysis appears to be systematic, intuition haphazard. But several studies have shown that although analysis, when correct, tends to be precisely correct, when it errs it can produce strange answers. "Analytic thinking involves measurement and calculation and 'resembles the switching of trains at a multiple junction, with each of the possible courses being well organized and of machine-like precision yet leading to drastically different destinations.' "[20] Switch one track incorrectly and you might head in exactly the opposite direction to the one desired; misplace one decimal point, and you might be off by a factor of ten. Intuition, in contrast, while not usually precise, is generally close enough on certain kinds of issues. Figure 4–1 demonstrates this in one experiment, where the intuitive approach had a narrower range of errors while the analytic approach was more often precisely correct.[21] Thus, just as organizations need to confirm the speculations of intuition with systematic analysis, so too do they need to "eyeball" the results of formal analysis with "commonsense" intuition. When they need precision, they must rely on analysis, but when they don't, it is sometimes easier, even safer, to rely on intuition.

EASE. While intuition is subject to the biases of emotion and experience, analysis can sometimes prove terribly cumbersome at tasks that prove simple for intuition. As Polanyi has noted for what here may be an analogy if not an example, any five-year-old can ride a bicycle without conscious thought. But for analysis, "to ride a bicycle . . . it is necessary at any given angle of unbalance for the rider to give a turn to the front

FIGURE 4–1
Distribution of Errors in an Experiment of Intuitive and Analytical Thinking
(*in Peters* et al., *1974:128*)

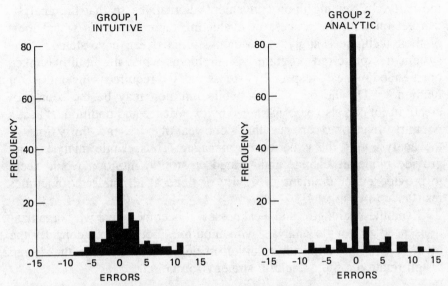

wheel that is by some measure inversely proportional to the square of
the speed at which he is proceeding."[22] Curtis put it well when he
claimed: "The [intuitive] people tend to act before they think, if they
ever think; and the [analytic] people think before they act, if they ever
act."[23] Or more succinctly, being forced to choose only one may amount
to either "extinction by instinct" or "paralysis by analysis."[24]

COMPLEXITY. Jay Forrester has argued in a paper entitled "The
Counter-Intuititve Behavior of Social Systems" that intuitive interventions
in complex social systems (such as urban decay) have often worked to
aggravate rather than correct the problem, because our brains cannot
comprehend complex feedback loops without the aid of formal models.[25]
But someone could also write "the counter-*analytic* behavior of social
systems," because an understanding of some such systems is also dependent on the use of soft data inaccessible to computers, indeed sometimes
even to analysis in any form.

CREATIVITY. Then there is the achievement of creativity. That too requires a form of synthesis beyond just analysis. That is why analytic

techniques—planning included—have tended to produce incremental adaptations more than innovative breakthroughs. "Premature closure" is a major problem in analysis. It tends to impose structure on problems too early, by seizing upon convenient alternatives so that the analysts can get on with the process of evaluating them, which is where most of their techniques apply. As McKinney and Keen have stated, "The systematics preferred program-type problems while the intuitives liked open-ended ones, especially those that required ingenuity or opinion."[26] On the other hand, while intuition may be the source of creativity, it can also be constrained by experience and tradition. "That's not thirty years of experience; that's one year of experience thirty times," the analyst tells the experienced manager. Thus, while analysis may provide moderate change and limited creativity, intuition would seem to provide either dramatic creativity or none at all, indeed sometimes resistance to change.

Given these strengths and weaknesses, it becomes clear why organizations need to couple analysis with intuition. Let us now consider the roles of analysis alongside intuition in decision-making, in the design of information systems, and in strategy formation.

THE ROLE OF ANALYSIS IN STRATEGIC DECISION-MAKING

The first generally recognized operations research study, "a quite elementary analysis of fighter losses over France in May 1940, which helped in the momentous decision not to send any more British fighters over France,"[27] was, according to the group leader, "an impromptu two-hour study."[28]

Operations research seems to have worked best when it involved clever people, comfortable with numbers, who could bring common sense alongside analytical thinking (as opposed to analytical technique) to bear on complex organizational problems. Managers, many of whom are inclined to overlook the hard data, can be helped by analysts who have the time and the inclination to feed such analysis into decision-making. What this amounts to is "soft analysis," in which teams of interdisciplinary analysts couple a certain amount of intuitive sense with their more systematic thinking.

The good systems analyst is a "chochem," a Yiddish word meaning "wise man," with overtones of "wise guy." His forte is creativity. Although he sometimes relates means to ends and fits ends to match means, he ordinarily eschews such pat processes, preferring instead to relate elements imaginatively into new systems that create their own means and ends.[29]

Soft analysis can provide managers not with solutions so much as perspectives they may be inclined to overlook because of the time pressures of their jobs and their orientation toward oral forms of communication. It can suggest new means to consider market or economic forces, or new conceptions of the functioning of their own organizations. Soft analysis can expose errors in intuitive thinking and question long held assumptions. It can be "quick and dirty analysis" on complex, pressing problems, so that a manager who must make a decision in a busy week can benefit from the equivalent of several weeks of the work of a team of analysts.

THE ROLE OF *MIS* IN INFORMATION PROCESSING

Many *management* information systems (MIS) seem not to be for management at all. They are *computer* information systems and proceed on the assumption that managers care that the information has been processed by a machine. In fact, as discussed earlier, what managers seem to care about is that their information is timely and relevant, and much information that comes from the computer is not. As a result, managers have to build their own MIS. The "rule of the tool" strikes again.

What MIS people tend to overlook are the limitations of formal information. In a monograph for the Canadian and American management accounting associations, entitled "Impediments to the Use of Management Information," I reviewed some reasons why managers seem to fail to use information as they apparently should. A number of the reasons lay in the inadequacies of formal information, while others pertained to problems in the functioning of organizations and ones rooted in the human brain.

INADEQUACIES OF FORMAL INFORMATION

1. Formal information is often too limited. Much formal management information is simply not sufficiently rich for the manager (e.g., ignoring information on lost sales or on risk); it precludes much that is nonquantitative (politics, personality, quality, etc.) and noncommunicable (tone of voice, gesture, facial expression, etc.); moreover, it tends to be weak on the external situation.

2. *Formal information, by aggregating data, is often too general for the manager.* It is not the cumulative data on the sales drop that may count so much as the specific reason why a particular Mrs. Consumer didn't buy your toothpaste last month. In other words, one informal discussion can sometimes be far more revealing than reams of statistics.

3. *Much formal information is too late.* It takes time for events to become facts, more time for those facts to be recorded and aggregated, to appear in a periodic report. Thus, while the American leaders in Washington were reading about the dead body counts of Vietnam, live Vietcong were marching down the jungle paths. It is often the necessarily quick response in the short run that dictates performance in the long run, even for the most senior managers of the largest organizations.

4. *Some formal information is unreliable.* Which statistics can anyone be sure of? In those body counts, who was a Vietcong and who an innocent bystander? What about scores on IQ-type tests? In business, what do quality figures really measure; can anyone be sure of market data; does increased profit reflect better performance or forgone investment mistakenly recorded as cut costs?

FUNCTIONING PROBLEMS IN ORGANIZATIONS

Formal information systems do not, of course, contain the only inadequacies. Organizations too have their limitations with regard to the processing of information.

5. *Rigid, dysfunctional objectives can encourage the use of inappropriate information.* Maintenance can, for example, be cut or research forgone as managers react to the pressures of short-term profit measures.

6. *Politics can cause the distortion of information.* People are inclined to send up the hierarchy information that makes them look good. In fact, Robert McNamara, who as U.S. Secretary of Defense probably did more than any other manager to promote analysis in government, is reported to have deliberately distorted the cost estimates sent to Congress on the Vietnam war.[30]

7. *The nature of managerial work introduces a bias in favor of oral channels of information at the expense of documented sources.* This point has already been discussed at length; suffice it here to note that oral channels have their obvious limitations too, in terms of inconsistencies and superficialities.

LIMITATIONS OF THE HUMAN BRAIN

Finally, beyond the inadequacies of information itself and of the arrangements of the organization lie our inadequacies as human beings to process correctly all the information we receive.

8. *Cognitive limitations restrict the amount of information that people consider in a complex decision process.* Herbert Simon has argued this point in much of his work. People can focus on only a few elements at a time; they lose detail in what can be retained in short-term memory and stored in long-term memory. Simon quotes an all too common newspaper story about how the State Department, "drowning in a river" of 15 million words a month, "has turned to the computer for help." Officials claimed that would "eliminate bottlenecks in the system" by "absorbing cable messages electronically at a rate of 1,200 lines a minute." Simon remarks: "A touching faith in more water as an antidote to drowning! Let us hope that Foreign Ministers will not feel themselves obliged to process those 1,200 lines of messages per minute just because they are there."[31]

9. *The brain systematically filters information in line with its established patterns of experience.* In other words, to reverse the old adage, believing is seeing. Marketing people see problems as marketing related, finance people as having to do with the numbers.

10. *Psychological failures and threats further impede the brain's openness to information.* All of our psychological problems get reflected in the information we end up processing and retaining. There is a good deal of evidence on these last two points from psychology.

To summarize, of all the available information, the formal systems capture only a subset; of what is captured, the managers receive only a subset; of what is received, the brain absorbs only a subset; and of what the brain absorbs, only a subset is relevant and accurate in the first place. With all of these impediments, it is a wonder that organizations get anything right!

Of course, they usually do. But there are clear messages for the designer of a true MIS. Above all, it must exist in good part independent of the computer. Systems should feed managers the information they need when and how they need it, based on what they actually use, whether or not that happens to be convenient to the tool called a computer. That tool is a means for handling large quantities of quantitative information, nothing more. Oral channels should be used alongside documentary ones, and information should be stored in convenient places, in paper files and assistants' heads no less than on magnetic disks. The MIS should also filter information for managers on an *intelligent* basis, for example, reducing it not just by aggregating it but also by isolating its key messages. Despite the excitement about so-called expert systems, that will probably continue to require human brains, not electronic ones, in my opinion.

THE ROLE OF PLANNING (AND PLANNERS) IN STRATEGY-MAKING

"Strategic planning" was very popular in the 1960s; by the 1980s, a series of setbacks, not least the energy crisis of the 1970s, to which planning had great difficulty responding, had seriously reduced its role in organizations. But there was no need to throw out the baby with the bathwater—planning as well as planners have important roles to play in organizations.

The grand fallacy expressed itself here in the belief that strategy could be formulated formally, that the analytic procedures of planning could generate the synthesis required in strategy. It was the old machine assumption: Assemble all the parts (steps, checklists, techniques) and you have an operating whole. But machines are first designed somewhere else, whereas the planning machine itself was supposed to produce the blueprint—the strategy. That is why the phrase "strategic planning"—like Progressive Conservative or fresh frozen (or civil engineer?)—has proved to be an oxymoron.

In a forthcoming book on strategic planning, I consider the evidence on this process and its pitfalls and fallacies before considering the roles that planning, plans, and planners might play in various types of organizations.

Part of the problem has been with the definition used for planning itself. To associate planning with future thinking in general, as has often been done, is to render the term so broad as to lose all practical meaning. ("If Planning Is Everything, Maybe It's Nothing," is the title Aaron Wildavsky used for an article.[32]) So too is to associate planning with decision-making, as has also been done. If planning means, as I think it most logically does, formalized procedure to produce articulated results about coordinated systems of decisions, then one thing I think becomes clear: Planning is not a means to create strategy but one to operationalize strategies already created by other means.

Strategic programming would thus seem to be a more appropriate label, entailing the working out of the consequences of strategies in terms of budgets, programs, action plans, and the like. Thus, organizations would logically engage in planning when they already have viable intended strategies and need to formalize them into a future that appears to be stable or at least predictable.

That is not, of course, to deny roles for people called planners, aside from operating the systems of strategic programming. Planners are, in some sense, the analysts of the strategy-making system. They can carry out ad hoc studies to feed managers information they might otherwise overlook: that a market is being undermined by a new technology, that competitor postures seem to be changing, that organizational strengths may be faltering in a certain area. Planners can also scrutinize the viability of strategies managers intend to pursue, and even undertake the search for potentially viable strategies that may be emerging in strange places around the organization itself. These things would, of course, involve a good deal of soft analysis.

Planners can be catalysts too, but not to promote strategic planning as some kind of religion so much as to encourage strategic *thinking* to keep the organization viable. In some sense, the planners are the ones most inclined to think conceptually about the strategy-making process in organizations. They must try to understand its complexities and nuances (including when it is best to avoid formal planning), and feed that understanding to the managers charged with running that process.

Of course, planners can be strategists too—anyone can who happens to be bright, creative, well informed, and adept at synthesis. But that has nothing to do with the fact that they are planners; their techniques give them no advantage in this regard, indeed perhaps a disadvantage.

In a sense, we end up with a planner for each side of the brain. On one hand, we have the highly analytic planner, the strategic programmer who brings order to the managers' strategies for purposes of implementation, and also carries out analyses to feed hard data into the front end of the strategy-making process. On the other hand, we have the soft planner, a more creative, divergent thinker, rather intuitive in addition to being analytical, who seeks to open up the strategy-making process by conducting quick and dirty studies, finding emergent strategies in strange places, and stimulating others to think strategically, perhaps sometimes doing so himself or herself. As we shall see, some organizations need to rely more on the traditional "righthanded planners," others on the less traditional "lefthanded planners." But in the spirit of coupling analysis with intuition, most need some degree of both.

5

TRAINING MANAGERS, NOT MBAs

There remains one last consequence of the analysis–intuition issue, alluded to earlier. In "Planning on the Left Side, Managing on the Right," I commented on how business school education has been virtually consecrated to the worship of the brain's left hemisphere. To my mind, the balance that Simon seeks has been totally lost in most of our business schools.*

In 1980, two Harvard Business School professors, Hayes and Abernathy, published an award-winning article entitled "Managing Our Way to Economic Decline."[1] They argued, among other things, that overly analytical business schools were partly responsible for a misguided obsession with technique and analysis in practice. Few disagreed. Well, since then I have watched business school education become more analytic, not less. I have seen professors of finance continue to search for the respect of economists by teaching increasingly irrelevant mathematical models. I have watched many of the behavioral scientists who have infiltrated business schools strut around like high priests seeking to ensure a degree of "scientific" rigor in research sufficient to detach researchers from the very organizations they are supposed to understand. The field of management information systems, ostensibly concerned with application, continues to try to define itself by what a machine is claimed able to do (but never quite does, although no one dares to find out). Even my own field of strategy, which maintained a balance before 1980, has since tilted in favor of the "number crunchers" more inter-

---

* Though this can be traced to the indiscriminate embracing of the very changes in business school education—an emphasis on rigorous research and theory development rooted in the basic disciplines of economics, psychology, and mathematics—that Simon and his colleagues at Carnegie-Mellon so vigorously promoted in the 1950s. In his book *The Sciences of the Artificial*,[2] Simon does, however, deplore the reluctance of business schools to teach "design" (to train "in the core professional skills") alongside the fundamental disciplines.

ested in the techniques of "competitive analysis" than the nuances of crafting strategies. I do not exaggerate one bit by claiming that if those people in business and government who support today's business schools really knew what was going on inside many of them, including some of the best known, really took the trouble, for example, to interview the professors at random, they would be demanding revolutionary changes in faculty and curriculum instead of passively writing checks.

I don't write such checks, but I do receive them. A few years ago I decided to put my money where my mind was and do the kind of management training I believed in. I proposed a reduction in my teaching and my salary at McGill in order to restrict my academic work to research and doctoral training while focusing my managerial training on experienced practitioners in the field.

My research and writing have always come first in my professional life. Some years ago, in a *Fortune* article entitled "The MBA—the Man, the Myth, and the Method," Zalaznick made the interesting point that the real contribution of the American business school lay not in its graduates from teaching so much as in its insights from research.[3] I still believe this to be true, at least for that portion of research that remains creative and applied to organizations.

I have long had concerns about undergraduate education in management and have not done it for many years (although I do believe in accounting training at that level, since accounting really is a profession). More recently I developed similar concerns about the conventional MBA. Increasingly I have come to believe that it is wrong—socially as well as economically—to train relatively inexperienced people in management. A few years of prior experience does help, but that does not resolve the fundamental problem. We cannot afford to have a society of elitist managers, preselected at a young age on the basis of academic criteria and then promoted on a "fast track" outside of the difficult work of making products and serving customers. Thus, I have come to believe that management training should be directed at people who have substantial organizational experience coupled with proven leadership ability as well as the requisite intelligence.

As a result, three years ago, with the understanding cooperation of the McGill administration, I taught my last MBA class. About a year later I addressed a meeting of the directors of MBA programs in Canada about these issues. What follows is the material of that talk, prepared for publication in this book. It may sound like a diatribe; I stand behind every word of it. Its implications will be pursued further in the final chapter of this book.

I propose to address my concerns about conventional MBA training in terms of how students get into the program in the first place, how they then go through it, and finally how they come out of it—in systems terms, input, throughput, and output.

APPLICANT INPUT

People come into MBA programs largely on the basis of two sets of criteria. First, they select themselves, by virtue of applying to the program in the first place. In other words, the pool of applicants from which the students are chosen is not defined by any leadership ability, real or potential, but simply by their desire for an MBA. This may reflect an interest in management, but all too often it simply reflects an interest in income. Business schools can certainly screen candidates for leadership or managerial potential, but at the age of, say, twenty-four, usually with no more than two or three years of full-time work experience, this is a chancy means of selection at best.

The other set of criteria is the hard numbers of performance. There are no hard numbers of work performance (beyond years of simply doing it), but there certainly are ones of test performance: grades on examinations (the grade point average, or GPA) and the notorious GMAT (Graduate Management Aptitude Test). Don't underestimate business schools' use of these. After all, they provide objective criteria for selection, and anything to do with management (or at least the teaching of management) has to be above all else objective. No matter what the object.

I know of no evidence that relates high GMAT score to success in the practice of management. Certainly a low score (by a native English speaker at least) may signal a problem of intelligence, and good managers must be intelligent. But how intelligent? It has long been known that there is no correlation between intelligence (as measured on IQ tests) and creativity above a certain moderate level. In other words, intelligent people range widely in their creativity. So too, I believe, do they in their managerial ability. In fact, when I see a score of 796 on a GMAT or a GPA of 4.9, I wonder if I am not as likely to be facing an "idiot-savant" as someone who is worldly, a person who can ace tests but can't talk to a customer.

I am a graduate of the MIT Sloan School masters program (yes, a young MBA). In their magazine recently,[4] they published statistics on their 1986 class. "Over 1,500 men and women vied for 185 places." Applicants were put into twelve levels, "based roughly on their numerical addition," which is made up of a variety of factors, including GMAT scores and GPA. "Admission is granted primarily to applicants falling in the top three levels." In fact, no one was rejected or waitlisted in the first two levels (some were deferred), while every single candidate in levels eight to twelve was rejected. The average GMAT scores for Levels I and II were both 680, and the GPAs, 4.6 and 4.5. For Levels VIII to XII, those averages ranged from 590 to 615 and 4.1 to 4.3.* Associate Dean Barks takes issue with my suggestion that MIT makes its decisions on the basis of these two scores. But surely the results suggest considerable attention to them,† unless of course there is a remarkable correlation between these scores and other, softer factors in assessing managerial potential.

A famous article of years ago, entitled "The Myth of the Well-Educated Manager,"[5] by Harvard's Professor Stirling Livingston, in fact suggested contrary evidence for that correlation—the lack of relationship between grades at the Harvard Business School and subsequent success in management jobs. Livingston's implication was that there was a need to assess intuitive skills and street sense, not just academic prowess.

There is a problem with assessing the intuition of MBA applicants, however: Intuition hardly gets a chance to manifest itself at a young age. A person simply cannot be effectively intuitive about things of which he or she has only superficial understanding. So it becomes difficult to know if even the potential for good intuition is present in most MBA applicants.

Moreover, even if the potential for intuition were there, its absence in *developed* form means that it cannot be used in the training process. Thus much of the conventional MBA program reduces to the formally analytical. The students can only appreciate formal knowledge, generally in the form of technique. And that, of course, is what they promote

---

* Which group of applicants would my 1963 GMAT of 602 and GPA of well under 4 have put me in 1986?

† Early in his article, Barks writes: "The aspects of quality that can be measured [for those applying] are indeed impressive, with a median GMAT of 630 and a mean GPA of 4.3 for all applicants" (p. 3). But can management *quality* in fact be measured? In the Zalaznick article in *Fortune,* it can be seen how far back this inclination to rely on numbers goes: He reports that the incoming Stanford class in 1958 was close to the median GMAT of 500; by 1968, it had attained the 96th percentile at 650 (p. 171).

immediately after they graduate—at least if their two years of training in business school is to have had any purpose. No wonder young MBA graduates run around putting down intuition whenever it rears its mysterious head. (In a subsequent talk I gave on these ideas to a class of MBA students, one young student came up with the marvelous comment that "How can you select for intuition when you can't even measure it!")

My criterion for entry to management education is very simple: proven success in managerial work. This would mean two things. First, applicants would need extensive practical experience; most would be in their thirties before even being considered for such education. My preference would be for intensive experience, well within at least one industry, preferably one organization, so that the knowledge base is deep, or "thick," as anthropologists might put it. I would not favor accepting "professional managers," those "birds of passage" who flit from one situation to another. Second, the candidates' leadership and management ability would have to be proven. They would, in other words, be selected not by themselves but by the subordinates who follow them, the peers who respect them, the supervisors who appreciate them. In this way, management training would not be wasted on people who are unlikely to be effective managers—a sizable number of today's MBA students, I should think.

I am, of course, making the assumption here that the MBA means to combine the B with the A. In other words, we are seeking to train for administration as well as for business. It could also be argued that we should decouple the two, train people for certain positions in business—namely the more analytical, such as marketing research or accounting—without pretending that we are training them to be managers. But that would require changing a great many established expectations, including those of the applicants who believe they will attain positions of power quickly because they sat in a classroom for a couple of years, the many recruiting firms that believe they are hiring their future leaders, and the business schools whose budgets are predicated on continuation of the production of about 60,000 MBAs annually (in the United States at least).

I do not mean to suggest that education for management is ineffective, only that it makes little sense when the student lacks the knack for leadership. Some years ago, Herbert Simon suggested in reference to the nature–nurture debate that if you wish to develop a star athlete, you must begin with someone who has the "natural endowment" (not me for instance) and then "by dint of practice, learning and experience develops that . . . into a mature skill."[6] We have good things to teach in management; let's teach them to people who can use them.

Management theory, like any other, is conceptual and abstract. People without experience cannot appreciate it. They are bound to run around like loose cannons believing that linear programming or portfolio models are the answer to all the world's problems. Seasoned managers, in contrast, have the experience on which to hang the concepts. Some of these run around half-cocked too, looking for the quick fix. But at least experience enables one to question the validity of a theory. And philosophers of science like Karl Popper notwithstanding (a secretary of mine once typed his name as Propper), the best test of an applied theory is still whether intelligent practioners find it more helpful than any other to deal with their problems.

CONTENT THROUGHPUT

What to teach those who get into management training? Given a class of the relatively inexperienced, you certainly don't stress the subtleties of intuition. You inundate them with methods and techniques, the more quantitative the better. After all, the teachers are researchers who may well have even less experience and higher GMAT scores than the students. Teach them statistics (for its own sake), mathematics (labeled "finance"), and behaviorial psychology (under "marketing"). Never, absolutely never, utter the word "judgment," let alone "intuition." Under "strategy," teach them to process reams of hard data on markets and competitors, like good economists. I recently had a vigorous exchange with a psychologist teaching in a business school who did not appreciate my assertion that psychologists, mathematicians, and economists who have no interest in adopting an organizational perspective should not be taking up places in the business schools. Business schools may have to *draw* on these disciplines, within limits (which in my opinion have long been surpassed). But that hardly justifies them in trying to *replicate* these disciplines.

My ideal management education would change the priorities. It would contain less analysis and prescription, more soft material and insights into how the world of organizations really does work, as opposed to how it should work. Incidentally, it need not be an MBA program, or even a form of the so-called executive MBA (although that is a fine idea). It might just be a series of ad hoc short courses for busy practioners. (And I have no concern about the B in the MBA. We need to teach *management,* and it really makes little difference whether that be for hospital directors, government administrators, or business people. I believe management schools should call their degree master in administration and then let the students add the B in the middle if they wish to emphasize business.)

First, in my ideal management program I would emphasize *skill training,* "experiential" education if you like, devoting perhaps a third of the effort to it. This would involve much more than the usual interpersonal skills, however. Equally important are skills at collecting information, at conducting negotiations, at making decisions under conditions of ambiguity, and so on. Of course, I refer not only, not even primarily, to skills exercised through systematic technique, but to those that rely on the softer processes of intuition as well.

In fact, a good deal is known about inculcating such skills, but not in the business schools. A few years ago, we started using a simulation called the "Looking Glass" at McGill, developed at the Center for Creative Leadership in Greensboro, North Carolina. It is a kind of elaborate in-basket exercise in which teams of managers compete with each other in a simulated (but not computer) setting. Watching our MBA students run around the building playing manager, it struck me that this was the first time I ever saw anybody practicing management in the management school (unless you put that label on what the dean does!). Finally we were teaching management, even if only for two days a year.*

The fact is that our management schools do not generally hire people capable of teaching true managerial skills. The PhD is the license to teach in a business school. But that degree neither preselects nor trains for skill in pedagogy, certainly not of the experiential kind. The PhD is a research degree, and in good part it attracts introverts, people who want to bury themselves in a library or under a stack of data. (That is why the questionnaire is such a popular research device—not so much because it has any intrinsic advantage as because it allows academics to do research without ever leaving their offices.) There are certainly

---

* I was also struck by the superficiality of the exercise—the "managers" were "managing" something they learned about only a few days earlier. But then it struck me that I had sometimes seen exercises not much less superficial in real-life executive suites! Perhaps it was an all-too-realistic simulation after all!

academics who are great teachers, even some who are great at skill teaching. But that is purely coincidental, and in any event, these are few in my opinion.

Without the innate ability to teach, teacher training (like management training) is of little help. But we don't even try. Some years ago, in the development of our own PhD program in management, we proposed a course in pedagogy. One course. Just 3 percent of the total program devoted to pedagogy, with 97 percent left for research, for a degree, it should be noted, that licenses people to spend about as much time teaching as doing research. Some of my colleagues disagreed—excessive attention to pedagogy, I guess they believed—but we managed to get it accepted. I'll bet there are not many other such courses around.

The ability to train for managerial skills resides largely in the field, with people who teach "in-house" for the big organizations or who work on a consulting basis. These people devote their efforts exclusively to pedagogy, with no need to be skilled at research. Thus, we do have some natural division of labor between scholarship and management training, but we have not pursued it to its logical conclusion. Perhaps the universities have no business trying to train managers, at least not in the sphere of skill development.

Second—and here I believe the universities *do* have the natural advantage—I would devote perhaps another third of my management education to *descriptive insight,* informing managers about how their world works. I refer here to understanding in a formal or conceptual sense, theory based on systematic research—the domain of the scholar.

The trouble with prescription is that it cannot be applied in general. No one approach can solve the problems of managers from many different organizations, all sitting in one classroom. Prescription belongs in context: It has to be done in a specific situation, tailored to the needs of that place at that particular time.

Critical to effective prescription is effective diagnosis, and that depends on the best possible understanding of the situation in question. In management, we simply lack generic categories of problems and their symptoms—quick ways to diagnose issues and prescribe solutions, as perhaps exist in medicine. Each management problem, at least at senior levels, has usually to be studied on its own terms. That is why I believe *description* is the most powerful *pre*scriptive tool we have, in the right hands—those of the *informed* practitioner. (And that is why I see my role as researcher not to create technique but to develop insight, and my role as educator not to prescribe change but to disseminate that insight. Only when I serve as a consultant, in a specific context, do I have any business being prescriptive. Which I guess is what I am doing now—as self-proclaimed consultant to management educators!)

The actual content of this descriptive material could cover two areas. First is the basic functioning of organizations—how they make decisions and form strategies, how they process information, how their managers work, and so on. Second is the basic knowledge about the environments of organizations—the economic, political, social, financial, etc., contexts. But this material must be presented not to preclude intuition, as is so often done now, but to make the very best use of it alongside more formal knowledge.

Theory is a dirty word in some quarters. But we all function on the basis of theories, whether they are formal and explicit or informal and subconscious. Keynes has been paraphrased frequently on this point: The "practical" person is often the prisoner of some defunct theorist. Our job as trainers is to get managers to hold their implicit theories up to scrutiny by challenging them with alternate theories, ones developed more systematically. Managers have to consider when it is beneficial to watch the world through a different lens, for example to think of strategy formation as an informal craft instead of a process of formal planning.

Clearly, there is no shortage of bad theory in our field. You can usually tell it by the ugliness of its labels—the "vertical dyad linkage model" (believe it or not, about leadership) is my favorite example. Abraham Kaplan, in *The Conduct of Inquiry,* talks about the "esthetic qualities of a theory,"[7] and I suspect he is correct that a harmonious theory, one that is nicely constructed and labeled, is more likely to be valid and useful than an ugly one. In any event, intelligent managers with deep-rooted knowledge of their practice can usually sort out the more and less useful theories.

From the outset of my teaching career, I emphasized descriptive theory in the classroom. But soon the questions came: "Hey, listen, Prof, it's fine to hear about how managers do work and how organizations do make strategies, but when are you going to tell us how these things should be done, something we can use the day we graduate." "Wait," I would answer, "it's coming at the end of the course." I stopped saying that a few years later (since I had little to say about it at the end of the course). Instead I began to shoot back: "If you didn't know how the doorknob worked, you would never have been able to get inside this classroom. What makes you think you understand how organizations work? These are immensely complicated systems. What would you do with prescription even if I gave it to you?'' I now say much the same thing to the executives I teach: "Don't expect prescription from me; the best thing I can do for you—in fact, anyone standing up here in front of all your different organizations can do for you—is to provide you with rich description, alternate ways to view your world. If it's good, you'll know what to do with it.''

Why do we in the field of management persist in this premature, all-embracing prescription? It has taken us off course time and time again throughout this century, whether it was participative management (change your leadership style the way you change your clothing), strategic planning (creativity by checklist), or the current obsession with the bottom line (making profits by managing, not products, markets, or customers, but profits themselves). God spare us yet another finance professor arguing that the reason managers are so bored with his teaching is that he is so far ahead of them.

Imagine a student in an engineering class saying, ''Hey, listen, Prof, it's fine to hear about how atoms *do* work, but when are you going to tell us how they *should* work?'' Engineering students learn physics, and medical students physiology, because everyone knows that you cannot practice those jobs without a deep understanding of the phenomena in question. Why do we persist in thinking management is any different in this regard?

Third, I would give some attention to *technique* in my management program. Managers do need to be exposed to certain methods that have proved broadly useful, if only to have a sense of how to deal with the people who promote them. Clearly they need to understand accounting, computers, and certain statistical techniques, among others. But since anyone (with one of those fancy GMAT scores, anyway) can quickly and easily learn many of these things, my ideal management program would give far less time to them than MBA programs now do.

Before we leave throughput, I wish to add a word of caution on the case study method of teaching—not so much on the use of cases as on how cases are used. Cases are a powerful device to bring varieties of reality into the classroom for descriptive purposes. But used in a prescriptive way, I believe they are part of the problem, not the solution.

The game is quite simple. As an eager young MBA student at Harvard, you are handed a neat twenty-page package on General Motors or the Mitsubishi Group, which you read the night before, along with the other cases for the next day. Then you arrive in class all prepared to discuss what it is that the denizens of Detroit or the chiefs of some distant Japanese corporation must do to resolve their problems. Don't claim ignorance, lack of sufficient knowledge: Good managers are decisive, therefore good management students must take a stand. The environment of General Motors must be assessed, its distinctive competencies identified, alternate strategies proposed, these strategies evaluated, and one selected, all before class is dismissed in eighty minutes. All based on that neat twenty-page package. All repeated hundreds of times over the course of the MBA program. Imagine the result.

Of course, the students do not implement the strategy they choose. How can they? But that's okay, because the professor makes a convenient distinction between formulation and implementation. For perhaps no more than "the sake of orderly presentation," as the Harvard authors of a well-known textbook put it,[8] tomorrow's captains of industry are left with the impression that good managers pronounce from on high based on a quick reading of a pithy report, without ever leaving their offices, while everyone else scurries around down below doing the implementing. And we believe the secret to the Japanese success lies in the things *they* do *right*!

When the students are seasoned practitioners, the trainer in fact has an opportunity to use something far better than the case study—the students' own experiences. They need only raise current examples or, better still, work up small "caselettes" of problems they have dealt with in the past, to which the conceptual insights and techniques of the classroom can be applied. This can make for especially powerful pedagogy when all the students come from a single organization, or from just a few whose experiences can be compared.

Let me provide one example from my own experience. When organizations ask me to do in-house programs, I now ask that we do workshops on actual issues that they face. That way they learn better, maybe even help in solving a problem in the process, while I learn too. I lose some work this way, but what I get keeps me stimulated. When I requested this of David Frances, who was working with the Thorn-EMI group in the United Kingdom, the result was a wonderful experience.

The participants were a group of practitioners in organizational development from various divisions of the company. They had been using my book on organizational structuring, so there was a common base of conceptual material. Three division managers from very different contexts—the Computer Software division, the Lighting division, and the Music and Distribution Services division—each drew up a kind of live case, essentially a collection of materials on structural issues they currently faced. The class read this material in advance and then, to begin each of three half-day sessions, the division manager outlined the problem, finishing with a series of questions. The class then split into groups to discuss the questions, after which they presented their conclusions to the division manager and me. The two of us then engaged in a discussion of the issues and the recommendations, the division manager drawing mainly on his understanding of the problem, and I on the concepts that might help to deal with it. What emerged was an intriguing combination of teaching and fishbowl consulting, which helped to drive home the conceptual materials (showing how they might be applied) and perhaps to make a bit of progress on the issues themselves.

MBA OUTPUT

We may accept the wrong people for management training and we may train them in the wrong way, but what *really* bothers me about all this is what happens after they leave. An MBA is a license to bypass the very things that organizations do, to leapfrog over the realities of organizational life into its abstractions, where innate intuition, even if it does exist, hardly gets a chance to develop. This encourages an approach to the practice of management that is "thin" and superficial, to my mind close to the root of certain problems facing American business today.

Organizations generally do only two things of consequence: They make things and they sell things. Not market things, not plan things, not control things, not communicate in retreats or feed masses of data into computers. Just physically make something, or provide some service, and then get someone to buy or use it. It can be said, then, without great overstatement, that our MBA programs take people who have hardly ever made anything or sold anything and then make damn sure they never will. How many MBA graduates go into sales or production? How many even manage these things, let alone do them? I recently polled two MBA classes. One student expressed an interest in production, none in sales.

Just consider the most popular jobs of the graduates: finance, where the abstractions of money, so compatible with the whole thrust of quantitative MBA training, shield them from the messiness of people and products; consulting, where the case study lives on in the quick fix of the detached expert; planning, where specialists dream about the abstract futures of organizations they seldom get a chance to know; and marketing, where manipulating concepts and numbers in the aggregate replaces selling one-on-one.

In his article, Livingston condemns the second-handedness of management education; here we have it perpetuated in the world of work. By the time these whiz kids reach the executive suite, having won the race down the "fast track," they may never have had their hands on anything more than sheets of numbers and abstractions, may never have dirtied themselves with anything beyond a malfunctioning photocopying machine, may never have met a customer who was not a statistic in a computer. And then they pretend to practice what they like to call "hands-on" management, while ceding their markets to those clever Japanese.

My ideal management education would take proven leaders well steeped in the making and the buying of one industry and then superimpose on their tacit knowledge and innate intuition the best of skill development, conceptual knowledge, and practical technique, so that they can take a fresh perspective on the very things they know well. Sure any intelligent person can learn good things in the classroom. But let's not promote widespread superficiality in the name of so-called professional management. Our organizations are simply too important for that.

Part II
ON
ORGANIZATIONS

As noted earlier, we can no more talk of *the* organization than we can talk of *the* mammal, no more prescribe one best way to run all organizations than prescribe one pair of glasses for all people. There are species in the world of organizations much as there are species in the world of biology. Too much effort has been wasted in trying to treat all organizations alike—governments that require the same procedures of all their ministries, conglomerates that do the same with their many divisions, consulting firms that seek to impose the latest technique on all their clients, whether they be post offices or hospitals, stable mass producers or fast-moving firms in high technology.

Much of my work has focused on trying to classify organizations, first from the perspective of structure and later from the perspective of power. We like to think of categorizing schemes as fixed by some law of nature. After all, dogs are different from elephants. But any classification scheme is also somewhat arbitrary, especially in the number of categories presented. In other words, every such scheme is to some degree the invention of the classifier and exists as much for convenience of understanding as to represent some scientific truth. Biologists define species by their mating capacity, but we have no such simple rule to classify organizations. (Besides, horses can mate with donkeys, even though the offspring mules are sterile.)

In a famous article entitled "The Magic Number Seven Plus or Minus Two: Some Limits on Our Capacity for Processing Information," the psychologist George Miller suggested that our inclination as human beings to classify things into sevens (the seven wonders of the world, the seven days of the week, and so on) reflects the number of "chunks" of information we are able to retain in our short-term memories.[1] Three wonders of the world would fall a little flat, so to speak, while eighteen would be daunting.

In my book *The Structuring of Organizations,* I proposed five types of organizations. I added two more—more or less—in my book *Power In and Around Organizations.* So I too happened to end up with seven, another of one of those "pernicious Pythagorean coincidences" Miller referred to. In this section, I present these seven—labeled entrepreneurial, machine, diversified, professional, innovative, missionary, and political—as a way to help identify and sort out the variety of things that happen in organizations.

I begin with a derivation of the seven in terms of a number of basic attributes, or building blocks, of organizations that can be used to understand how they function. These attributes include the component parts of organizations, the mechanisms they use to coordinate their work, and elements of their structures, power systems, and contexts. My basic point is that these attributes tend to *configure* in various ways, hence I refer to the different types of organizations as *configurations.* The seven chapters that follow discuss each of the configurations identified, adding other attributes (strategy-making processes, the nature of their managerial work, strengths and weaknesses, social issues, and so forth), while a final chapter of this section looks "beyond configuration" at the broader issues of forces and forms in organizations—really presenting a theory of organizational effectiveness.

6
DERIVING CONFIGURATIONS
Combining the Basic Attributes of Organizations

A few years ago, Danny Miller (my first doctoral student) and I published a paper entitled "The Case for Configuration." To introduce this chapter, which derives the seven basic configurations discussed in this section of the book, I would like to present the argument we developed in that paper.

That argument in fact originated in the earlier work of another colleague at McGill, Pradip Khandwalla, who found in his doctoral thesis at Carnegie-Mellon that the success of different businesses could be explained not by their use of any single organizational attribute (such as a particular type of planning system or form of decentralization), but by how they interrelated various attributes.[1] In other words, there were alternate paths to success, based on an organization's ability to configure the attributes it used. "Getting it all together" proved more important than any "one best way." Configuration subsequently became an important theme in my work.

In making the case for configuration, Danny and I argued that academic research on organizations has tended to limit its insight by favoring analysis over synthesis. In particular, it has tended to focus on how individual variables arrange themselves along linear scales rather than on how sets of attributes configure into types, referred to as configurations, archetypes, or gestalts. On one hand, an organization might be described as more or less decentralized, with the research seeking to correlate that variable with a second (say, the amount of planning). On the other hand, a type of decentralization (say, to grant autonomy to division managers) might be combined with other attributes (say, the use of performance controls and giving each manager responsibility over a distinct set of products) to suggest a type of organization (the divisionalized form).

Configurations are, in essence, systems, in which it makes more sense to talk of networks of interrelationships than of any one variable driving another.

Danny and I presented a number of reasons for the existence of configurations, some to do with the needs of organizations themselves, others with the needs of people trying to understand organizations. Of the former, one is that Darwinian-type forces may encourage only a few basic forms of organizations to survive in a given setting. In other words, like species, perhaps organizations survive only if they evolve in ways suitable to particular niches in the environment. Given that the types of environments are limited, then so too must be the types of organizations.

Our second argument was that organizations may be drawn toward configuration in order to achieve consistency in their internal characteristics, to create synergy in their working processes, and to establish a fit with their external contexts. Configuration in essence means harmony. Instead of trying to do everything well, the effective organization may be able to adapt *itself* (unlike the member of a Darwinian species, it should be noted) by concentrating on a specific theme around which it can configure its attributes.

Third, based on some of the findings of Danny's own research, we argued that it makes more sense for organizations to change, not by adapting continuously and gradually, in piecemeal fashion, but rather by engaging in quantum leaps from one integrated configuration to another. (This is akin to the current notions in ecology of "punctuated equilibrium," except that in our case, individual organizations rather than generations of them can adapt). In effect, it may be more efficient to hold on to a form that is going out of synchronization with its environment until a major transition can be made to a new, more suitable one. That way, internal configuration can be maintained, even if at the expense of external fit, and the costliness and disruption of organizational change can be concentrated into brief periods of "strategic revolution."

But configuration exists also in the mind of the beholder. As we argued in the paper, visitors to an art museum first consider a painting holistically, roaming over the entire canvas with their eyes to take in the gestalt of the work, its image, mood, and theme. Only afterward might attention be focused on a particular attribute—say, the coarseness of brushstrokes, the intensity of hues, the flow of lines. In other words, we appreciate a complex system first through synthesis, perhaps only later through analysis (even though it might have been created in the opposite order). Only a world controlled by a malevolent deity would force us to perceive systems in the reverse order, for example, having to study a painting a square inch at a time before putting it all together ourselves. In such a world, either paintings would be very small or museums would be very empty.

In our opinion, the main reason the museums of organizational theory have been so empty (even though its archives are rather busy) is that most of the writings ask the reader to do just that—survey the attributes of organizations one at a time without ever exposing the whole. The readers need organizational theory for the same reason some viewers need paintings: to gain insight into their world. And the observer of organizations perceives much as does the appreciator of art. Thus we need configuration also to help us understand our world—to allow us to observe whole canvases, if you like. Unlike the famous blind men, each of whom touched a different part of the elephant and then argued about its nature, describing organizations as configurations can open the eyes of the beholder to the nature of whole beasts. Each can be seen as a logical combination of its own particular attributes, similar to other members of its own species (configurations) but fundamentally different from other ones.

Hence, we proceed from the perspective of configuration. But first we must understand the attributes that make them up. This chapter presents those attributes and shows how they were combined into seven distinct forms of configuration. We begin with the people and parts of organizations, then consider the basic mechanisms by which they coordinate their work, look next at various elements of structure and how they are influenced by context (the latter in the spirit of the traditional, analytical research), and conclude by deriving the configurations.

I shall introduce a diagram here that, since first developed for my book on structuring, has become my personal "logo" in a sense, the symbol of my work. Organizations are not linear, but words to describe them in a book must be. So it helps to rely on diagrams as much as possible. I shall use this one in various ways in the discussion that follows.

I have had great fun with this diagram. The young woman artist I first engaged to draw it properly immediately saw but one thing there and claimed everyone else would. Well, I hadn't, and in China recently, someone saw an upside-down mushroom; others have seen lungs, the female uterus, a fly's head, a kidney bean; one person even told me he believed AT&T was using my book in executive programs because it looked like a telephone! In any event, while this may be a kind of Rorschach, I see only an organization. Feel free to experiment with this diagram; just let me know if you find anything interesting!

THE PARTS AND PEOPLE OF AN ORGANIZATION

At the base of any organization can be found its operators, those people who perform the basic work of producing the products and rendering the services. They form the *operating core*. All but the simplest organizations also require at least one full-time manager who occupies what we shall call the *strategic apex*, where the whole system is overseen. And as the organization grows, more managers are needed—not only managers of operators but also managers of managers. A *middle line* is created, a hierarchy of authority between the operating core and the strategic apex.

As the organization becomes still more complex, it generally requires another group of people, whom we shall call the analysts. They, too, perform administrative duties—to plan and control formally the work of others—but of a different nature, often labeled "staff." These analysts form what we shall call the *technostructure,* outside the hierarchy of line authority. Most organizations also add staff units of a different kind, to provide various internal services, from a cafeteria or mailroom to a legal counsel or public relations office. We call these units and the part of the organization they form the *support staff*.

Finally, every active organization has a sixth part, which we call its *ideology* (an alternate popular term recently has been "culture"). Ideology encompasses the traditions and beliefs of an organization that distinguish it from other organizations and infuse a certain life into the skeleton of its structure.

This gives us six basic parts of an organization. As shown in Figure 6–1, our logo, we have a small strategic apex connected by a flaring middle line to a large, flat operating core at the base. These three parts of the organization are drawn in one uninterrupted sequence to indicate that they are typically connected through a single chain of formal authority. The technostructure and the support staff are shown off to either side to indicate that they are separate from this main line of authority, influencing the operating core only indirectly. The ideology is shown as a kind of halo that surrounds the entire system.

These people, all of whom work inside the organization to make its decisions and take its actions—full-time employees or, in some cases, committed volunteers—may be thought of as *influencers* who form a kind of *internal coalition*. By this term, we mean a system within which people vie among themselves to determine the distribution of power.

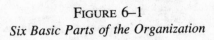

FIGURE 6–1
Six Basic Parts of the Organization

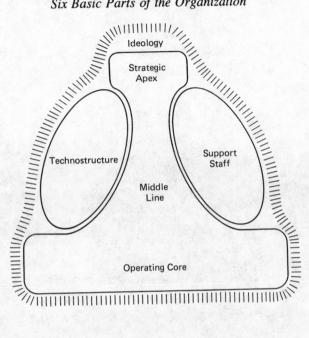

In addition, as shown in Figure 6–2, various outside people also try to exert influence on the organization, seeking to affect the decisions and actions taken inside. These external influencers, shown in Figure 6–2 as creating a field of forces around the organization, can include owners, unions and other employee associations, suppliers, clients, partners, competitors, and all kinds of publics, in the form of governments, special interest groups, and so forth. Together they can all be thought to form an *external coalition.*

Sometimes the external coalition is relatively *passive* (as in the typical behavior of the shareholders of a widely held corporation or the members of a large union). Other times it is *dominated* by one active influencer or some group of them acting in concert (such as an outside owner of a business firm or a community intent on imposing a certain philosophy on its school system). And in still other cases, the external coalition may be *divided,* as different groups seek to impose contradictory pressures on the organization (as in a prison buffeted between two community groups, one favoring custody, the other rehabilitation).

FIGURE 6–2
Internal and External Influencers of an Organization

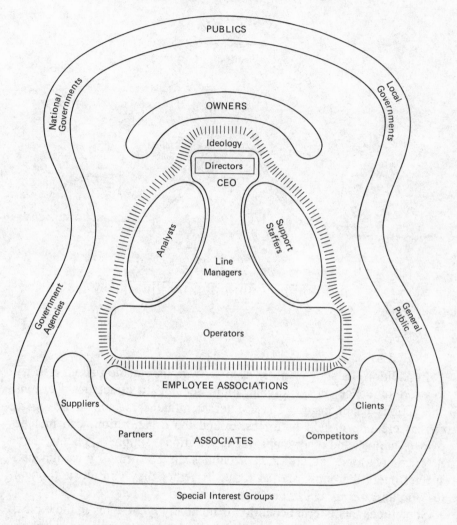

THE ESSENCE OF ORGANIZATIONAL STRUCTURE

Every organized human activity—from the making of pottery to the placing of a man on the moon—gives rise to two fundamental and opposing requirements: the *division of labor* into various tasks to be performed and the *coordination* of those tasks to accomplish the activity. The structure of an organization can be defined simply as the total of the ways in which its labor is divided into distinct tasks and then its coordination achieved among those tasks.

COORDINATING MECHANISMS

A number of coordinating mechanisms seem to describe the fundamental ways in which organizations can coordinate their work, shown in Figure 6–3 and listed below.

1. *Mutual adjustment,* which achieves coordination by the simple process of informal communication (as between two operating employees)

2. *Direct supervision,* in which coordination is achieved by having one person issue orders or instructions to several others whose work interrelates (as when a boss tells others what is to be done, one step at a time)

3. *Standardization of work processes,* which achieves coordination by specifying the work processes of people carrying out interrelated tasks (those standards usually being developed in the technostructure to be carried out in the operating core, as in the case of the work instructions that come out of time-and-motion studies)

4. *Standardization of outputs,* which achieves coordination by specifying the results of different work (again usually developed in the technostructure, as in a financial plan that specifies subunit performance targets or specifications that outline the dimensions of a product to be produced)

5. *Standardization of skills (*as well as *knowledge),* in which different work is coordinated by virtue of the related training the workers have received (as in medical specialists—say a surgeon and an anesthetist in an operating room—responding almost automatically to each other's standardized procedures)

6. *Standardization of norms,* in which it is the norms infusing the work that are controlled, usually for the entire organization, so that everyone functions according to the same set of beliefs (as in a religious order)

These coordinating mechanisms can be considered the most basic elements of structure, the glue that holds organizations together. They seem to fall into a rough order: As organizational work becomes more complicated, the favored means of coordination seems to shift from mutual adjustment (the simplest mechanism) to direct supervision, then

FIGURE 6–3
The Coordinating Mechanisms

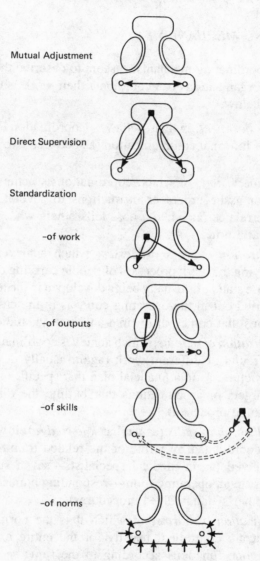

Mutual Adjustment

Direct Supervision

Standardization

–of work

–of outputs

–of skills

–of norms

to standardization, preferably of work processes or norms, otherwise of outputs or of skills, finally reverting back to mutual adjustment (paradoxically also the mechanism best able to deal with the most complex forms of work).

No organization, of course, can rely on a single one of those mechanisms. The mechanisms may be somewhat substitutable for each other, but all will typically be found in every reasonably developed organization. In particular, mutual adjustment and direct supervision are almost always important, no matter what use is made of the various forms of standardization. Contemporary organizations simply cannot exist without leadership and informal communication, even if only to override the rigidities of standardization.

But the important point for us here is that many organizations do favor one mechanism over the others, at least at certain stages of their lives. In fact, organizations that favor none seem most prone to becoming politicized, simply because of the conflicts that naturally arise when people have to vie for influence in a relative vacuum of power (bearing in mind, for example, that little use of direct supervision means a weak system of authority, little use of standardization of norms means a weak ideology, and so on).

DESIGN PARAMETERS

The essence of organizational design is the manipulation of a series of parameters that determine the division of labor and the achievement of coordination. Some of these concern the design of individual positions, others the design of the superstructure (the overall network of subunits, reflected in the organizational chart), some the design of lateral linkages to flesh out that superstructure, and a final group concerns the design of the decision-making system of the organization. Listed below are the main parameters of structural design, with links to the coordinating mechanisms.

- *Job specialization* refers to the number of tasks in a given job and the worker's control over these tasks. A job is *horizontally* specialized to the extent that it encompasses a few narrowly defined tasks, *vertically* specialized to the extent that the worker lacks control of the tasks performed. *Unskilled* jobs are typically highly specialized in both dimensions; skilled or *professional* jobs are typically specialized horizontally but not vertically. "Job enrichment" refers to the enlargement of jobs in both the vertical and horizontal dimensions.
- *Behavior formalization* refers to the standardization of work processes by the imposition of operating instructions, job descriptions,

rules, regulations, and the like. Structures that rely on any form of standardization for coordination may be defined as *bureaucratic*, those that do not as *organic*.

- *Training* refers to the use of formal instructional programs to establish and standardize in people the requisite skills and knowledge to do particular jobs in organizations. Training is a key design parameter in all work we call professional. Training and formalization are basically substitutes for achieving the standardization (in effect, the bureaucratization) of behavior. In one, the standards are learned as skills, in the other they are imposed on the job as rules.

- *Indoctrination* refers to programs and techniques by which the norms of the members of an organization are standardized, so that they become responsive to its ideological needs and can thereby be trusted to make its decisions and take its actions. Indoctrination too is a substitute for formalization, as well as for skill training, in this case the standards being internalized as deeply rooted beliefs.

- *Unit grouping* refers to the choice of the bases by which positions are grouped together into units, and those units into higher-order units. Grouping encourages coordination by putting different jobs under common supervision, by requiring them to share common resources and achieve common measures of performance, and by facilitating mutual adjustment among them. The various bases for grouping—by work process, product, client, area, and so on—can be reduced to two fundamental ones—the *function* performed and the *market* served. The former refers to a single link in the chain of processes by which products or services are produced, the latter to the whole chain for specific end products.

- *Unit size* refers to the number of positions (or units) contained in a single unit. The equivalent term, *span of control*, is not used here, because sometimes units are kept small despite an absence of close supervisory control. For example, when experts coordinate extensively by mutual adjustment, as in an engineering team in a space agency, they will form into small teams. In this case, unit size is small and span of control is low despite a relative absence of direct supervision. In contrast, when work is highly standardized (because of either formalization or training), unit size can be very large, because there is little need for direct supervision. One foreman can supervise dozens of assemblers, because they work according to very tight instructions.

- *Planning and control systems* are used to standardize outputs. They may be divided into two types: *action planning* systems, which specify the results of specific actions before they are taken (for example, that holes should be drilled with diameters of 3 centimeters); and *performance control* systems, which specify the desired results of whole ranges of actions after the fact (for example, that sales of a division should grow by 10 percent in a given year).
- *Liaison devices* refer to a whole series of mechanisms used to encourage mutual adjustment within and between units. They range from *liaison positions* (such as the purchasing engineer who stands between purchasing and engineering), through *task forces* and *integrating managers* (such as brand managers), finally to fully developed *matrix structures*.
- *Decentralization* refers to the diffusion of decision-making power. When all the power rests at a single point in an organization, we call its structure centralized; to the extent that the power is dispersed among many individuals, we call it relatively decentralized. We can distinguish *vertical decentralization*—the delegation of formal power down the hierarchy to line managers—from *horizontal decentralization*—the extent to which formal or informal power is dispersed out of the line hierarchy to nonmanagers (operators, analysts, and support staffers). We can also distinguish *selective* decentralization—the dispersal of power over different decisions to different places in the organization—from *parallel* decentralization—where the power over various kinds of decisions is delegated to the same place. Six forms of decentralization may thus be described: (1) vertical and horizontal centralization, where all the power rests at the strategic apex; (2) limited horizontal decentralization (selective), where the strategic apex shares some power with the technostructure that standardized everybody else's work; (3) limited vertical decentralization (parallel), where managers of market-based units are delegated the power to control most of the decisions concerning their line units; (4) vertical and horizontal decentralization, where most of the power rests in the operating core, at the bottom of the structure; (5) selective vertical and horizontal decentralization, where the power over different decisions is dispersed to various places in the organization, among managers, staff experts, and operators who work in teams at various levels in the hierarchy; and (6) pure decentralization, where power is shared more or less equally by all members of the organization.

STRUCTURE IN CONTEXT

A number of "contingency" or "situational" factors influence the choice of these design parameters, and vice versa. They include the age and size of the organization; its technical system of production; various characteristics of its environment, such as stability and complexity; and its power system, for example, whether or not it is tightly controlled by outside influencers. Some of the effects of these factors, as found in an extensive body of research literature, are summarized below as hypotheses.

AGE AND SIZE

• *The older an organization, the more formalized its behavior.* What we have here is the "we've-seen-it-all-before" syndrome. As organizations age, they tend to repeat their behaviors: as a result, these become more predictable and so more amenable to formalization.

• *The larger an organization, the more formalized its behavior.* Just as the older organization formalizes what it has seen before, so the larger organization formalizes what it sees often. ("Listen mister, I've heard that story at least five times today. Just fill in the form like it says.")

• *The larger an organization, the more elaborate its structure; that is, the more specialized its jobs and units and the more developed its administrative components.* As organizations grow in size, they are able to specialize their jobs more finely. (The big barbershop can afford a specialist to cut children's hair; the small one cannot.) As a result, they can also specialize—or "differentiate"—the work of their units more extensively. This requires more effort at coordination. And so the larger organization tends also to enlarge its hierarchy to effect direct supervision and to make greater use of its technostructure to achieve coordination by standardization, or else to encourage more coordination by mutual adjustment.

• *Structure reflects the age of the industry from its founding.* This is a curious finding, but one that we shall see holds up remarkably well. An organization's structure seems to reflect the age of the industry in which it operates, no matter what its own age. Industries that predate the industrial revolution seem to favor one kind of structure, those of the age of the early railroads another, and so on. We should obviously expect different structures in different periods; the surprising thing is that these structures seem to carry through to new periods, old industries remaining relatively true to earlier structures.

TECHNICAL SYSTEM

Technical system refers to the instruments used in the operating core to produce the outputs. (This should be distinguished from "technology," which refers to the knowledge base of an organization.)

• *The more regulating the technical system—that is, the more it controls the work of the operators—the more formalized the operating work and the more bureaucratic the structure of the operating core.* Technical systems that regulate the work of the operators—for example, mass production assembly lines—render that work highly routine and predictable, and so encourage its specialization and formalization, which in turn create the conditions for bureaucracy in the operating core.

• *The more complex the technical system, the more elaborate and professional the support staff.* Essentially, if an organization is to use complex machinery, it must hire staff experts who can understand that machinery—who have the capability to design, select, and modify it. And then it must give them considerable power to make decisions concerning that machinery, and encourage them to use the liaison devices to ensure mutual adjustment among them.

• *The automation of the operating core transforms a bureaucratic administrative structure into an organic one.* When unskilled work is coordinated by the standardization of work processes, we tend to get bureaucratic structure throughout the organization, because a control mentality pervades the whole system. But when the work of the operating core becomes automated, social relationships tend to change. Now it is machines, not people, that are regulated. So the obsession with control tends to disappear—machines do not need to be watched over—and with it go many of the managers and analysts who were needed to control the operators. In their place come the support specialists to look after the machinery, coordinating their own work by mutual adjustment. Thus, automation reduces line authority in favor of staff expertise and reduces the tendency to rely on standardization for coordination.

ENVIRONMENT

Environment refers to various characteristics of the organization's outside context, related to markets, political climate, economic conditions, and so on.

• *The more dynamic an organization's environment, the more organic its structure.* It stands to reason that in a stable environment—when nothing changes—an organization can predict its future conditions and so, all other things being equal, can easily rely on standardization for coordination. But when conditions become dynamic—when the need for product change is frequent, labor turnover is high, and political conditions are unstable—the organization cannot standardize but must instead remain flexible through the use of direct supervision or mutual adjustment for coordination, and so it must use a more organic structure. Thus, for example, armies, which tend to be highly bureaucratic institutions in peacetime, can become rather organic when engaged in highly dynamic, guerilla-type warfare.

• *The more complex an organization's environment, the more decentralized its structure.* The prime reason to decentralize a structure is that all the information needed to make decisions cannot be comprehended in one head. Thus, when the operations of an organization are based on a complex body of knowledge, there is usually a need to decentralize decision-making power. Note that a simple environment can be stable or dynamic (the manufacturer of dresses faces a simple environment yet cannot predict style from one season to another), as can a complex one (the specialist in perfected open heart surgery faces a complex task, yet knows what to expect).

• *The more diversified an organization's markets, the greater the propensity to split it into market-based units, or divisions, given favorable economies of scale.* When an organization can identify distinct markets—geographical regions, clients, but especially products and services—it will be predisposed to split itself into high-level units on that basis, and to give each a good deal of control over its own operations (that is, to use what we called "limited vertical decentralization"). In simple terms, diversification breeds divisionalization. Each unit can be given all the functions associated with its own markets. But this assumes favorable economies of scale: If the operating core cannot be divided, as in the case of an aluminum smelter, also if some critical function must be centrally coordinated, as in purchasing in a retail chain, then full divisionalization may not be possible.

• *Extreme hostility in its environment drives any organization to centralize its structure temporarily.* When threatened by extreme hostility in its environment, the tendency for an organization is to centralize power, in other words, to fall back on its tightest coordinating mechanism, direct supervision. Here a single leader can ensure fast and tightly coordinated response to the threat (at least temporarily).

POWER

• *The greater the external control of an organization, the more centralized and formalized its structure.* This important hypothesis claims that to the extent that an organization is controlled externally, for example by a parent firm or a government that dominates its external coalition—it tends to centralize power at the strategic apex and to formalize its behavior. The reason is that the two most effective ways to control an organization from the outside are to hold its chief executive officer responsible for its actions and to impose clearly defined standards on it. Moreover, external control forces the organization to be especially careful about its actions.

• *A divided external coalition will tend to give rise to a politicized internal coalition, and vice versa.* In effect, conflict in one of the coalitions tends to spill over to the other, as one set of influencers seeks to enlist the support of the others.

• *Fashion favors the structure of the day (and of the culture), sometimes even when inappropriate.* Ideally, the design parameters are chosen according to the dictates of age, size, technical system, and environment. In fact, however, fashion seems to play a role too, encouraging many organizations to adopt currently popular design parameters that are inappropriate for themselves. Paris has its salons of haute couture; likewise New York has its offices of "haute structure," the consulting firms that sometimes tend to oversell the latest in structural fashion.

BASIC TYPES OF ORGANIZATIONS

We have now introduced various attributes of organizations—parts, coordinating mechanisms, design parameters, situational factors. How do they all combine?

For years, the literature of management promoted the "one best way"; it largely still does. A good structure was one with a rigid hierarchy of authority, spans of control no greater than six, heavy use of strategic planning, and so on. In the 1960s, organizational theory developed the contingency approach—"it all depends"—characterized by the situational hypotheses we have just presented. Organizations were to pick their attributes independently, but according to context, much as diners pick their food at a buffet table. As discussed earlier, we have come to favor a third approach, which we characterize as "getting it all to-gether"—the configuration approach. The elements of structure, even those of situation, should be selected to achieve consistency.

Our basic premise here is that a limited number of configurations can help explain much of what can be observed in organizations. We have introduced in our discussion six basic parts of the organization, six basic mechanisms of coordination, as well as six basic types of decentralization. In fact, there seems to be a fundamental correspondence between all of these sixes, which can be explained by a set of pulls exerted on the organization by each of its six parts, as shown in Figure 6–4. When conditions favor one of these pulls, the organization is drawn to design itself as a particular configuration. We list below and then introduce briefly the six resulting configurations, together with a seventh that tends to appear when no one pull or part dominates.

Configuration	Prime Coordinating Mechanism	Key Part of Organization	Type of Decentralization
Entrepreneurial organization	Direct supervision	Strategic apex	Vertical and horizontal centralization
Machine organization	Standardization of work processes	Technostructure	Limited horizontal decentralization
Professional organization	Standardization of skills	Operating core	Horizontal decentralization
Diversified organization	Standardization of outputs	Middle line	Limited vertical decentralization
Innovative organization	Mutual adjustment	Support staff	Selected decentralization
Missionary organization	Standardization of norms	Ideology	Decentralization
Political organization	None	None	Varies

FIGURE 6–4

Basic Pulls on the Organization

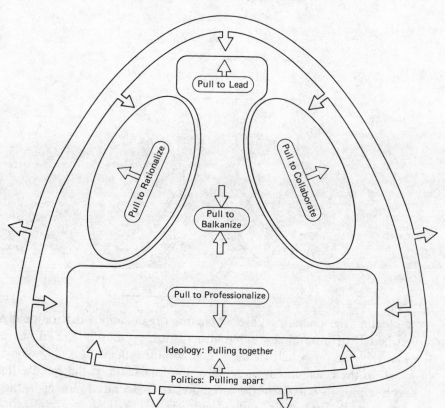

• The strategic apex exerts a pull to *lead*, by which it retains control over decision-making, with coordination achieved by direct supervision. When the organization cedes to this pull, often due to an overriding need for strategic vision, the centralized configuration called *entrepreneurial* results. As shown in Figure 6–5, the strategic apex sits over the operating core directly, with little else in the way of line managers or staff specialists.

• The technostructure exerts its pull to *rationalize*, ideally through the standardization of work processes, encouraging only limited horizontal decentralization (which empowers itself). Organizations that cede to this pull, usually due to an overriding need for routine efficiency, take on the *machine* configuration, shown in Figure 6–6 with a fully elaborated line and staff structure concentrated on controlling and

FIGURE 6–5
The Entrepreneurial Organization

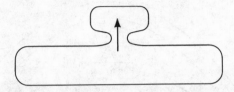

FIGURE 6–6
The Machine Organization

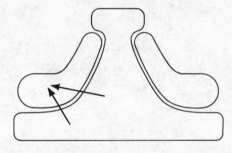

protecting the operating core. (Machine organizations that rationalize on behalf of a dominant external constituency may be called *instruments;* those on behalf of their own administrators, *closed systems.*)

• In their search for autonomy, the managers of the middle line exert a pull to *balkanize* the structure, to concentrate power in their own units through only limited (and parallel) vertical decentralization to themselves. When the organization cedes to this pull, generally by dividing itself into distinct units in order to serve different markets effectively, restricting itself to controlling the performance of those units largely through the standardization of outputs, the *diversified* configuration results. As indicated in Figure 6–7, a small strategic apex at "headquarters" supported by small staff units oversees a set of divisions usually structured as machine configurations (for reasons to be explained later).

• The members of the operating core exert a pull to *professionalize,* in order to minimize the influence that others, colleagues as well as line and technocratic administrators, have over their work. When the organization cedes to this pull, generally due to an overriding need to perfect expert programs, the *professional* configuration results, with full horizontal and vertical decentralization of power to the operating

FIGURE 6–7
The Diversified Organization

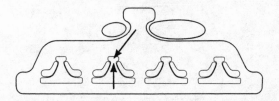

core, with coordinating achieved largely through the standardization of knowledge and skills. As shown in Figure 6–8, the organization has only a small technostructure and middle line, since there is little need for administrative control. But it has a large support staff to back up its high-priced professionals.

• The support staff exerts a pull to *collaborate* in order to involve itself in the central activity of the organization. The organization that has need for sophisticated innovation must usually cede to this pull, welding staff and line, and sometimes operating personnel as well, into multidisciplinary teams of experts that achieve coordination within and between themselves through mutual adjustment. The organization takes on the *innovative* configuration, shown in Figure 6–9, with many of the distinctions of conventional organizations falling away, as its various parts meld into a single system of vertical and horizontal decentralization on a selective basis.

• Ideology exists primarily as a force in organizations of other types, encouraging their members to *pull together,* as shown in Figure 6–10. But sometimes it too can dominate, as the standardization of norms becomes the prime coordinating mechanism. Then the organization takes on the *missionary* configuration, achieving the purest form of decentralization, as each member is trusted to decide and act for the overall good of the organization.

FIGURE 6–8
The Professional Organization

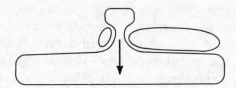

FIGURE 6–9
The Innovative Organization

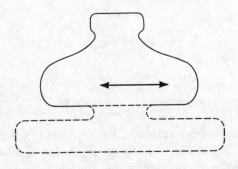

FIGURE 6–10
The Missionary Organization

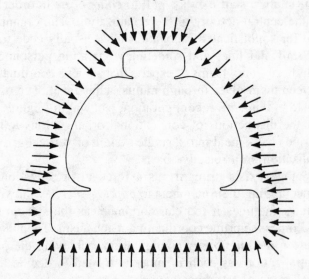

• Finally, politics also exists in organizations of other types, the force of conflict that causes people to *pull apart*, as shown in Figure 6–11. But it too can sometimes dominate, especially when no one part of the organization and no one mechanism of coordination is dominant. Then the organization takes on the *political* configuration, with no stable form of centralization or decentralization.

Together these configurations, as well as the pulls and needs represented by each, seem to encompass and integrate a good deal of what we

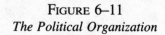

FIGURE 6–11
The Political Organization

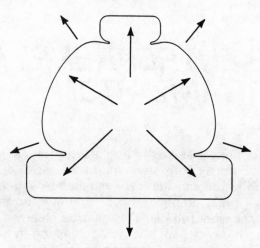

know about organizations. It should be emphasized that, as presented, each configuration is idealized—a simplification, really a caricature of reality. No real organization is ever exactly like any one of them. But some do come remarkably close, while others seem to reflect combinations of them, sometimes in transition from one to another.

Individually then, these configurations reflect leading tendencies in organizations, while collectively they seem to define the boundaries of a space within which real organizations may be considered to lie. In order to map a space, however, the boundaries must first be identified. Thus we begin by describing, in the seven chapters that follow, each of the configurations. Then, in a final chapter we can consider the whole space, by using the framework of the seven to describe the many and varied forms that real-world organizations seem to take.

7

THE ENTREPRENEURIAL ORGANIZATION

Simple organizations that are run firmly and personally by their leaders (even if not strictly entrepreneurs, in the sense of being owner-managers), are fun to consider: They make for wonderful stories of the building of great empires and of dramatic turnarounds. They are also the place where strategic vision most clearly manifests itself, a hot topic these days, though largely remaining in the darkness of human intuition. But, like every other configuration, the entrepreneurial one has its problems too. Indeed, it is not coincidental that this form of organization declined in popularity during much of this century, although it has experienced a resurgence recently as the big bureaucracies have faltered.

Here I set out to describe the entrepreneurial organization: how it organizes itself (or at least resists doing so); how it functions, and especially makes its strategy; the conditions that are likely to foster its development; the problems it encounters; and finally, what can be said about its strategic vision, based on studies we have done at McGill of visionary leaders.

The Entrepreneurial Organization

Structure: • simple, informal, flexible, with little staff or middle-line hierarchy
  • activities revolving around the chief executive, who controls personally, through direct supervision
Context: • simple and dynamic environment
  • strong leadership, sometimes charismatic, autocratic
  • startup, crisis, and turnaround
  • small organizations, "local producers"
Strategy: • often visionary process, broadly deliberate but emergent and flexible in details
  • leader positions malleable organization in protected niches
Issues: • responsive, sense of mission
      but
  • vulnerable, restrictive
  • danger of imbalance toward strategy or operations

Consider an automobile dealership with a flamboyant owner, a brand-new government department, a corporation or even a nation run by an autocratic leader, or a school system in a state of crisis. In many respects, those are vastly different organizations. But the evidence suggests that they share a number of basic characteristics. They form a configuration we shall call the *entrepreneurial organization*.

THE BASIC STRUCTURE

The structure of the entrepreneurial organization is simple, characterized above all by what it is not: elaborated. As shown in the opening figure, typically it has little or no staff, a loose division of labor, and a small managerial hierarchy. Little of its activity is formalized, and it makes minimal use of planning procedures or training routines. In a sense, it is nonstructure; in my "structuring" book, I called it *simple structure*.

Power focuses on the chief executive, who exercises it personally. Formal controls are discouraged as a threat to that person's authority, as are strong pockets of expertise and even aspects of ideology that are not in accord with his or her vision. Under the leader's watchful eye, politics cannot arise. Should outsiders, such as particular customers or suppliers, seek to exert influence, the leader is as likely as not to take the organization to a less exposed niche in the marketplace.

Thus, it is not uncommon in small entrepreneurial organizations for everyone to report to the chief. Even in ones not so small, communication flows informally, much of it between the chief executive and others. As one group of McGill MBA students commented in their study of a small manufacturer of pumps: "It is not unusual to see the president of the company engaged in casual conversation with a machine shop mechanic. [That way he is] informed of a machine breakdown even before the shop superintendent is advised."

Decision-making is likewise flexible, with a highly centralized power system allowing for rapid response. The creation of strategy is, of course, the responsibility of the chief executive, the process tending to be highly intuitive, often oriented to the aggressive search for opportunities. It is not surprising, therefore, that the resulting strategy tends to reflect the chief executive's implicit vision of the world, often an extrapolation of his or her own personality.

Handling disturbances and innovating in an entrepreneurial way are perhaps the most important aspects of the chief executive's work. In contrast, the more formal aspects of managerial work—figurehead duties, for example—receive less attention, as does the need to disseminate information and allocate resources internally, since knowledge and power remain at the top.

CONDITIONS OF THE ENTREPRENEURIAL ORGANIZATION

The entrepreneurial configuration is fostered by an external context that is both simple and dynamic. It must be relatively simple (say retailing food as opposed to designing jet aircraft) in order for one person at the top to retain so much influence, and it is the dynamic context that requires the flexible structure, which in turn enables this organization to outmaneuver the bureaucracies. Entrepreneurial leaders are naturally attracted to such conditions.

The classic case of this is, of course, the entrepreneurial firm, where the leader is the owner. Entrepreneurs often found their own firms to escape the procedures and control of the bureaucracies where they previously worked. At the helm of their own enterprises, they continue to loathe the ways of bureaucracy, and the staff analysts that accompany them, and so they keep their organizations lean and flexible. Figure 7–1 shows the organigram for Steinberg's, a supermarket chain we shall be discussing shortly, during its most classically entrepreneurial years. Notice the identification of people above positions, the simplicity of the structure (the firm's sales by this time were on the order of $27 million), and the focus on the chief executive (not to mention the obvious family connections).

Entrepreneurial firms are often young and aggressive, continually searching for the risky markets that scare off the bigger bureaucracies. But they are also careful to avoid the complex markets, preferring to remain in niches that their leaders can comprehend. Their small size and focused strategies allow their structures to remain simple, so that the leaders can retain tight control and maneuver flexibly. Moreover, business entrepreneurs are often visionary, sometimes charismatic or autocratic as well (sometimes both, in sequence!). Of course, not all "entrepreneurs" are so aggressive or visionary; many settle down to pursue common strategies in small geographic niches. Labeled the *local producers*, these can include the corner restaurant, the town bakery, the regional supermarket chain.

But an organization need not be owned by an entrepreneur, indeed need not even operate in the profit sector, to adopt the configuration

FIGURE 7–1

Organization of Steinberg's, an Entrepreneurial Firm (circa 1948)

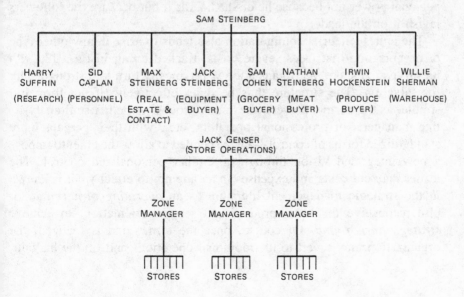

we call entrepreneurial. In fact, most new organizations seem to adopt this configuration, whatever their sector, because they generally have to rely on personalized leadership to get themselves going—to establish their basic direction, or *strategic vision,* to hire their first people and set up their initial procedures. Of course, strong leaders are likewise attracted to new organizations, where they can put their own stamp on things. Thus, we can conclude that most organizations in business, government, and not-for-profit areas pass through the entrepreneurial configuration in their formative years, during *startup.*

Moreover, while new organizations that quickly grow large or that require specialized forms of expertise may make a relatively quick transition to another configuration, many others seem to remain in the entrepreneurial form, more or less, as long as their founding leaders remain in office. This reflects the fact that the structure has often been built around the personal needs and orientation of the leader and has been staffed with people loyal to him or her.

This last comment suggests that the personal power needs of a leader can also, by themselves, give rise to this configuration in an existing organization. When a chief executive hoards power and avoids or destroys the formalization of activity as an infringement on his or her right to rule by fiat, then an autocratic form of the entrepreneurial organization will tend to appear. This can been seen in the cult of personality of the leader, in business (the last days of Henry Ford) no less than in government (the leadership of Stalin in the Soviet Union). Charisma can have a similar effect, though different consequences, when the leader gains personal power not because he or she hoards it but because the followers lavish it on the leader.

The entrepreneurial configuration also tends to arise in any other type of organization that faces severe crisis. Backed up against a wall, with its survival at stake, an organization will typically turn to a strong leader for salvation. The structure thus becomes effectively (if not formally) simple, as the normal powers of existing groups—whether staff analysts, line managers, or professional operators, etc., with their perhaps more standardized forms of control—are suspended to allow the chief to impose a new integrated vision through his or her personalized control. The leader may cut costs and expenses in an attempt to effect what is known in the strategic management literature as an *operating turnaround,* or else reconceive the basic product and service orientation, to achieve *strategic turnaround.* Of course, once the turnaround is realized, the organization may revert to its traditional operations and, in the bargain, spew out its entrepreneurial leader, now viewed as an impediment to its smooth functioning.

STRATEGY FORMATION IN THE ENTREPRENEURIAL ORGANIZATION

How does strategy develop in the entrepreneurial organization? And what role does that mysterious concept known as "strategic vision" play? We know something of the entrepreneurial mode of strategy-making, but less of strategic vision itself, since it is locked in the head of the individual. But some studies we have done at McGill do shed some light on both these questions. Let us consider strategic vision first.

VISIONARY LEADERSHIP

In a paper she co-authored with me, my McGill colleague Frances Westley contrasted two views of visionary leadership. One she likened to a hypodermic needle, in which the active ingredient (vision) is loaded into a syringe (words) which is injected into the employees to stimulate all kinds of energy. There is surely some truth to this, but Frances prefers another image, that of drama. Drawing from a book on theater by Peter Brook,[1] the legendary director of the Royal Shakespeare Company, she conceives strategic vision, like drama, as becoming magical in that moment when fiction and life blend together. In drama, this moment is the result of endless "rehearsal," the "performance" itself, and the "attendance" of the audience. But Brook prefers the more dynamic equivalent words in French, all of which have English meanings—"repetition," "representation," and "assistance." Frances likewise applies these words to strategic vision.

"Repetition" suggests that success comes from deep knowledge of the subject at hand. Just as Sir Laurence Olivier would repeat his lines again and again until he had trained his tongue muscles to say them effortlessly,[2] so too Lee Iacocca "grew up" in the automobile business, going to Chrysler after Ford because cars were "in his blood."[3] The visionary's inspiration stems not from luck, although chance encounters can play a role, but from endless experience in a particular context.

"Representation" means not just to perform but to make the past live again, giving it immediacy, vitality. To the strategist, that is vision articulated, in words and actions. What distinguishes visionary leaders is their profound ability with language, often in symbolic form, as metaphor. It is not just that they "see" things from a new perspective but that they get others to so see them.

Edwin Land, who built a great company around the Polaroid camera he invented, has written of the duty of "the inventor to build a new gestalt for the old one in the framework of society."[4] He himself described photography as helping "to focus some aspect of [your] life"; as you look through the viewfinder, "it's not merely the camera you are focusing: you are focusing yourself . . . when you touch the button, what is inside of you comes out. It's the most basic form of creativity. Part of you is now permanent."[5] Lofty words for fifty tourists filing out of a bus to record some pat scene, but powerful imagery for someone trying to build an organization to promote a novel camera. Steve Jobs, visionary (for a time) in his promotion, if not invention, of the personal computer, placed a grand piano and a BMW in Apple's central foyer, with the claim that "I believe people get great ideas from seeing great products."[6]

"Assistance" means that the audience for drama, whether in the theater or in the organization, empowers the actor no less than the actor empowers the audience. Leaders become visionary because they appeal powerfully to specific constituencies at specific periods of time. That is why leaders once perceived as visionary can fall so dramatically from grace—a Steve Jobs, a Winston Churchill. Or to take a more dramatic example, here is how Albert Speer, arriving skeptical, reacted to the first lecture he heard by his future leader: "Hitler no longer seemed to be speaking to convince; rather, he seemed to feel that he was experiencing what the audience, by now transformed into a single mass, expected of him."[7]

Of course, management is not theater; the leader who becomes a stage actor, playing a part he or she does not live, is destined to fall from grace. It is integrity—a genuine feeling behind what the leader says and does—that makes leadership truly visionary, and that is what makes impossible the transition of such leadership into any formula.

This visionary leadership is style and strategy, coupled together. It is drama, but not play-acting. The strategic visionary is born and made, the product of a historical moment. Brook closes his book with the following quotation:

> In everyday life, "if" is a fiction, in the theatre "if" is an experiment.
> In everyday life, "if" is an evasion, in the theatre "if" is the truth.
> When we are persuaded to believe in this truth, then the theatre and life are one.

This is a high aim. It sounds like hard work.
To play needs much work. But when we experience the work as play,
then it is not work any more.
A play is play.[8]

In the entrepreneurial organization, at best "theater," namely strategic vision, becomes one with "life," namely organization. That way leadership creates drama; it turns work into play.

Let us now consider the entrepreneurial approach to strategy formation in terms of two specific studies we have done, one of a supermarket chain, the other of a manufacturer of women's undergarments.

THE ENTREPRENEURIAL MODE OF STRATEGY FORMATION IN A SUPERMARKET CHAIN

Steinberg's is a Canadian retail chain that began with a tiny food store in Montreal in 1917 and grew to sales in the billion-dollar range during the almost sixty-year reign of its leader. Most of that growth came from supermarket operations. In many ways, Steinberg's fits the entrepreneurial model rather well. Sam Steinberg, who joined his mother in the first store at the age of eleven and personally made a quick decision to expand it two years later, maintained complete formal control of the firm (including every single voting share) to the day of his death in 1978. He also exercised close managerial control over all its major decisions, at least until the firm began to diversify after 1960, primarily into other forms of retailing.

It has been popular to describe the "bold stroke" of the entrepreneur.[9] In Steinberg's we saw only two major reorientations of strategy in the sixty years, moves into self-service in the 1930s and into the shopping center business in the 1950s. But the stroke was not bold so much as tested. The story of the move into self-service is indicative. In 1933 one of the company's eight stores "struck it bad," in the chief executive's words, incurring "unacceptable" losses ($125 a week). Sam Steinberg closed the store one Friday evening, converted it to self-service, changed its name from "Steinberg's Service Stores" to "Wholesale Groceteria," slashed its prices by 15–20 percent, printed handbills, stuffed them into neighborhood mailboxes, and reopened on Monday morning. That's strategic change! But only once these changes proved successful did he convert the other stores. Then, in his words, "We grew like Topsy."

This anecdote tells us something about the bold stroke of the entrepreneur—"controlled boldness" is a better expression. The ideas were bold, the execution careful. Sam Steinberg could have simply closed the one unprofitable store. Instead he used it to create a new vision, but he tested that vision, however ambitiously, before leaping into it. Notice the interplay here of problems and opportunities. Steinberg took what most businessmen would probably have perceived as a *problem* (how to cut the losses in one store) and by treating it as a *crisis* (what is wrong with our *general* operation that produces these losses) turned it into an *opportunity* (we can grow more effectively with a new concept of retailing). That was how he got energy behind actions and kept ahead of his competitors. He "oversolved" his problem and thereby remade his company, a characteristic of some of the most effective forms of entrepreneurship.

But absolutely central to this form of entrepreneurship is intimate, detailed knowledge of the business or of analogous business situations, the "repetition" discussed earlier. The leader as conventional strategic "planner"—the so-called architect of strategy—sits on a pedestal and is fed aggregate data that he or she uses to "formulate" strategies that are "implemented" by others. But the history of Steinberg's belies that image. It suggests that clear, imaginative, integrated strategic vision depends on an involvement with detail, an intimate knowledge of specifics. And by closely controlling "implementation" personally, the leader is able to reformulate en route, to adapt the evolving vision through his or her own process of learning. That is why Steinberg tried his new ideas in one store first. And that is why, in discussing his firm's competitive advantage, he told us: "Nobody knew the grocery business like we did. Everything has to do with your knowledge." He added: "I knew merchandise, I knew cost, I knew selling, I knew customers, I knew everything . . . and I passed on all my knowledge; I kept teaching my people. That's the advantage we had. They couldn't touch us."

Such knowledge can be incredibly effective when concentrated in one individual who is fully in charge (having no need to convince others, not subordinates below, not superiors at some distant headquarters, nor market analysts looking for superficial pronouncements) and who retains a strong, long-term commitment to the organization. So long as the business is simple and focused enough to be comprehended in one brain, the entrepreneurial approach is powerful, indeed unexcelled. Nothing else can provide so clear and complete a vision, yet also allow the flexibility to elaborate and rework that vision when necessary. The conception of a new strategy is an exercise in synthesis, which is typically best carried out in a single, informed brain. That is why the entrepreneurial approach is at the center of the most glorious corporate successes.

But in its strength lies entrepreneurship's weakness. Bear in mind that strategy for the entrepreneurial leader is not a formal, detailed plan on paper. It is a personal vision, a concept of the business, locked in a single brain. It may need to get "represented," in words and metaphors, but that must remain general if the leader is to maintain the richness and flexibility of his or her concept. But success breeds a large organization, public financing, and the need for formal planning. The vision must be articulated to drive others and gain their support, and that threatens the personal nature of the vision. At the limit, as we shall see in the case of Steinberg's in the next chapter, the leader can get captured by his or her very success.

In Steinberg's, moreover, when success in the traditional business encouraged diversification into new ones (new regions, new forms of retailing, new industries), the organization moved beyond the realm of its leader's personal comprehension, and the entrepreneurial mode of strategy formation lost its viability. Strategy-making became more decentralized, more analytic, in some ways more careful, but at the same time less visionary, less integrated, less flexible, and ironically, less deliberate.

CONCEIVING A NEW VISION IN A GARMENT FIRM

The genius of an entrepreneur like Sam Steinberg was his ability to pursue one vision (self-service and everything that entailed) faithfully for decades and then, based on a weak signal in the environment (the building of the first small shopping center in Montreal), to realize the need to shift that vision. The planning literature makes a big issue of forecasting such discontinuities, but as far as I know there are no formal techniques to do so effectively (claims about "scenario analysis" notwithstanding). The ability to perceive a sudden shift in an established pattern and then to conceive a new vision to deal with it appears to remain largely in the realm of informed intuition, generally the purview of the wise, experienced, and energetic leader. Again, the literature is largely silent on this. But another of our studies, also concerning entrepreneurship, did reveal some aspects of this process.

Canadelle produces women's undergarments, primarily brassieres. It too was a highly successful organization, although not on the same scale as Steinberg's. Things were going well for the company in the late 1960s, under the personal leadership of Larry Nadler, the son of its founder, when suddenly everything changed. A sexual revolution of sorts was accompanying broader social manifestations, with bra-burning a symbol of its resistance. For a manufacturer of brassieres the threat was obvious. For many other women the miniskirt had come to dominate the fashion scene, obsoleting the girdle and giving rise to pantyhose. As the executives of Canadelle put it, "the bottom fell out of the girdle business." The whole environment—long so receptive to the company's strategies—seemed to turn on it all at once.

At the time, a French company had entered the Quebec market with a light, sexy, molded garment called "Huit," using the theme, "just like not wearing a bra." Their target market was 15–20-year-olds. Though the product was expensive when it landed in Quebec and did not fit well in Nadler's opinion, it sold well. Nadler flew to France in an attempt to license the product for manufacture in Canada. The French firm refused, but, in Nadler's words, what he learned in "that one hour in their offices made the trip worthwhile." He realized that what women wanted was a more natural look, not no bra but less bra. Another trip shortly afterward, to a sister American firm, convinced him of the importance of market segmentation by age and life-style. That led him to the realization that the firm had two markets, one for the more mature customer, for whom the brassiere was a cosmetic to look and feel more attractive, and another for the younger customer who wanted to look and feel more natural.

Those two events led to a major shift in strategic vision. The CEO described it as sudden, the confluence of different ideas to create a new mental set. In his words, "all of a sudden the idea forms." Canadelle reconfirmed its commitment to the brassiere business, seeking greater market share while its competitors were cutting back. It introduced a new line of more natural brassieres for the younger customers, for which the firm had to work out the molding technology as well as a new approach to promotion.

We can draw on Kurt Lewin's three-stage model of unfreezing, changing, and refreezing to explain such a gestalt shift in vision.[10] The process of *unfreezing* is essentially one of overcoming the natural defense mechanisms, the established "mental set" of how an industry is supposed to operate, to realize that things have changed fundamentally. The old assumptions no longer hold. Effective managers, especially effective strategic managers, are supposed to scan their environments continually, looking for such changes. But doing so continuously, or worse, trying to use technique to do so, may have exactly the opposite effect. So much attention may be given to strategic monitoring when nothing important is happening that when something really does, it may not even be noticed. The trick, of course, is to pick out the discontinuities that matter, and as noted earlier that seems to have more to do with informed intuition than anything else.

A second step in unfreezing is the willingness to step into the void, so to speak, for the leader to shed his or her conventional notions of how a business is supposed to function. The leader must above all avoid premature closure—seizing on a new thrust before it has become clear what its signals really mean. That takes a special kind of management, one able to live with a good deal of uncertainty and discomfort. "There is a period of confusion," Nadler told us, "you sleep on it . . . start looking for patterns . . . become an information hound, searching for [explanations] everywhere."

Strategic *change* of this magnitude seems to require a shift in mindset before a new strategy can be conceived. And the thinking is fundamentally conceptual and inductive, probably stimulated (as in this case) by just one or two key insights. Continuous bombardment of facts, opinions, problems, and so on may prepare the mind for the shift, but it is the sudden *insight* that is likely to drive the synthesis—to bring all the disparate elements together in one "eureka"-type flash.

Once the strategist's mind is set, assuming he or she has read the new situation correctly and has not closed prematurely, then the *refreezing* process begins. Here the object is not to read the situation, at least not in a global sense, but in effect to block it out. It is a time to work out the consequences of the new strategic vision.

It has been claimed that obsession is an ingredient in effective organizations.[11] Only for the period of refreezing would we agree, when the organization must focus on the pursuit of the new orientation—the new mindset—with full vigor. A management that was open and divergent in its thinking must now become closed and convergent. But that means that the uncomfortable period of uncertainty has passed, and people can now get down to the exciting task of accomplishing something new. Now the organization knows where it is going; the object of the exercise is to get there using all the skills at its command, many of them formal and analytic. Of course, not everyone accepts the new vision. For those steeped in old strategies, *this* is the period of discomfort, and they can put up considerable resistance, forcing the leader to make greater use of his or her formal powers and political skills. Thus, refreezing of the leader's mindset often involves the unfreezing, changing, and refreezing of the organization itself! But when the structure is simple, as it is in the entrepreneurial organization, that problem is relatively minor.

LEADERSHIP TAKING PRECEDENCE IN THE ENTREPRENEURIAL CONFIGURATION

To conclude, entrepreneurship is very much tied up with the creation of strategic vision, often with the attainment of a new concept. Strategies can be characterized as largely deliberate, since they reside in the intentions of a single leader. But being largely personal as well, the details of those strategies can emerge as they develop. In fact, the vision can change too. The leader can adapt en route, can learn, which means new visions can emerge too, sometimes, as we have seen, rather quickly.

In the entrepreneurial organization, as shown in Figure 7–2, the focus of attention is on the leader. The organization is malleable and responsive to that person's initiatives, while the environment remains benign for the most part, the result of the leader's selecting (or "enacting") the correct niche for his or her organization. The environment can, of course, flare up occasionally to challenge the organization, and then the leader must adapt, perhaps seeking out a new and more appropriate niche in which to operate.

FIGURE 7–2

Leadership Taking Precedence in the Entrepreneurial Organization

SOME ISSUES ASSOCIATED WITH THE ENTREPRENEURIAL ORGANIZATION

We conclude briefly with some broad issues associated with the entrepreneurial organization. In this configuration, decisions concerning both strategy and operations tend to be centralized in the office of the chief executive. This centralization has the important advantage of rooting strategic response in deep knowledge of the operations. It also allows for flexibility and adaptability: Only one person need act. But this same executive can get so enmeshed in operating problems that he or she loses sight of strategy; alternatively, he or she may become so enthusiastic about strategic opportunities that the more routine operations can wither for lack of attention and eventually pull down the whole organization. Both are frequent occurrences in entrepreneurial organizations.

This is also the riskiest of organizations, hinging on the activities of one individual. One heart attack can literally wipe out the organization's prime means of coordination. Even a leader in place can be risky. When change becomes necessary, everything hinges on the chief's response to it. If he or she resists, as is not uncommon where that person developed the existing strategy in the first place, then the organization may have no means to adapt. Then the great strength of the entrepreneurial organization—the vision of its leader plus its capacity to respond quickly—becomes its chief liability.

Another great advantage of the entrepreneurial organization is its sense of mission. Many people enjoy working in a small, intimate organization where the leader—often charismatic—knows where he or she is taking it. As a result, the organization tends to grow rapidly, with great enthusiasm. Employees can develop a solid identification with such an organization.

But other people perceive this configuration as highly restrictive. Because one person calls all the shots, they feel not like the participants on an exciting journey, but like cattle being led to market for someone else's benefit. In fact, the broadening of democratic norms into the sphere of organizations has rendered the entrepreneurial organization unfashionable in some quarters of contemporary society. It has been described as paternalistic and sometimes autocratic, and accused of concentrating too much power at the top. Certainly, without countervailing powers in the organization the chief executive can easily abuse his or her authority.

Perhaps the entrepreneurial organization is an anachronism in societies that call themselves democratic. Yet there have always been such organizations, and there always will be. This was probably the only structure known to those who first discovered the benefits of coordinating their activities in some formal way. And it probably reached its heyday in the era of the great American trusts of the late nineteenth century, when powerful entrepreneurs personally controlled huge empires. Since then, at least in Western society, the entrepreneurial organization has been on the decline. Nonetheless, it remains a prevalent and important configuration, and will continue to be so as long as society faces the conditions that require it: the prizing of entrepreneurial initiative and the resultant encouragement of new organizations, the need for small and informal organizations in some spheres and of strong personalized leadership despite larger size in others, and the need periodically to turn around ailing organizations of all types.

8
THE MACHINE ORGANIZATION

These are supposedly the big bad guys of the organization world, the homes of red tape and the sources of curious tales. Yet if we think of McDonald's or the Swiss railroad, a different impression develops, of organizations—when they get it right—that can be enormously efficient and can provide an unmatchable reliability of service (can you think any other way to deliver millions of pieces of mail every day?). Thus, like every other configuration, the machine one cuts both ways too: It can serve us or drive us crazy (or the two concurrently). I am not terribly partial to these personally—you won't find me working in one, except to flit in and out on a consulting basis—but I do not hesitate to fly them to conferences, have them print my books or deliver my mail, even provide me and the kids with the occasional hamburger. Like many other people, I can't live without them even though I choose not to live within them.

In my structuring book, I called these *machine bureaucracies.* To most people, bureaucracy is a pejorative term—the locus of excessive controls, of managers lording authority over workers and workers lording control over the clients. Just as it is always the other guy who causes pollution, so too do we never think of ourselves as the bureaucrats. Well, I hope in this chapter I can dispel these two myths: first, as noted above, by showing that there is a constructive side to machine bureaucracy (though no lack of that destructive side too, as we shall see), and second, by showing that we can all be bureaucrats. Like the tango, it can take only two to make a bureaucracy—two who set up procedures, two obsessed with control to avoid the unexpected, two intent on sticking to the plans. The spirit of bureaucracy is to set course and to stay on it, to ensure that everything comes out as intended. Bureaucracy means no surprises. It is epitomized by the comment of a General Motors chairman some years ago that "In the automotive business, uncertainty is the biggest enemy."[1]

I begin with a description of the machine bureaucracy structure, then consider the well-defined conditions of machine organizations, raising a distinction between this configuration as an externally controlled "instrument" and as an internally controlled "closed system." I then consider some social issues associated with the machine organization—critical ones in a society inundated with these types. Finally, I close by drawing again on our McGill research to describe how these configurations make strategy or, more commonly in this case, use formal planning to resist making strategy, so that they can get on with being the bureaucratic machines that they are designed to be.

The Machine Organization

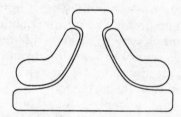

Structure:
- centralized bureaucracy
- formal procedures, specialized work, sharp divisions of labor, usually functional groupings, extensive hierarchy
- key is technostructure, charged with standardizing the work, but clearly separated from middle line (itself highly developed)
- also extensive support staff to reduce uncertainty

Context:
- simple and stable environment
- usually larger, more mature organization
- rationalized work, rationalizing (but not automated) technical system
- external control→*instrument* form
- otherwise can be *closed system* form
- common in mass production mass service, government, organizations in business of control and safety

Strategy:
- ostensibly planning process, but that is really strategic programming
- resistance to strategic change, necessary to overlay innovative configuration for revitalization or else revert to entrepreneurial configuration for turnaround
- hence quantum pattern of change: long periods of stability interrupted by occasional bursts of strategic revolution

Issues:
- efficient, reliable, precise, consistent
    but
- obsession with control leads to
- human problems in operating core, leads to
- coordination problems in administrative center, leads to
- adaptation problems at strategic apex

A national post office, a custodial prison, an airline, a giant automobile company, even a small security agency—all these organizations appear to have a number of characteristics in common. Above all, their operating work is routine, the greatest part of it rather simple and repetitive; as a result, their work processes are highly standardized. These characteristics give rise to the machine organizations of our society, structures fine-tuned to run as integrated, regulated, highly bureaucratic machines.

THE BASIC STRUCTURE

A clear configuration of the attributes has appeared consistently in the research: highly specialized, routine operating tasks; very formalized communication throughout the organization; large-size operating units; reliance on the functional basis for grouping tasks; relatively centralized power for decision making; and an elaborate administrative structure with a sharp distinction between line and staff.

THE OPERATING CORE AND ADMINISTRATION

The obvious starting point is the operating core, with its highly rationalized work flow. This means that the operating tasks are made simple and repetitive, generally requiring a minimum of skill and training, the latter often taking only hours, seldom more than a few weeks, and usually in-house. This in turn results in narrowly defined jobs and an emphasis on the standardization of work processes for coordination, with activities highly formalized. The workers are left with little discretion, as are their supervisors, who can therefore handle very large spans of control.

To achieve such high regulation of the operating work, the organization has need for an elaborate administrative structure—a fully developed middle-line hierarchy and technostructure—but the two clearly distinguished.

The managers of the middle line have three prime tasks. One is to handle the disturbances that arise in the operating core. The work is so standardized that when things fall through the cracks, conflict flares, because the problems cannot be worked out informally. So it falls to managers to resolve them by direct supervision. Indeed, many problems get bumped up successive steps in the hierarchy until they reach a level of common supervision where they can be resolved by authority (as with a dispute in a company between manufacturing and marketing that may have to be resolved by the chief executive). A second task of the middle-line managers is to work with the staff analysts to incorporate their standards down into the operating units. And a third task is to support the vertical flows in the organization—the elaboration of action plans flowing down the hierarchy and the communication of feedback information back up.

The technostructure must also be highly elaborated. In fact this structure was first identified with the rise of technocratic personnel in early-nineteenth-century industries such as textiles and banking.[1a] Because the machine organization depends primarily on the standardization of its operating work for coordination, the technostructure—which houses the staff analysts who do the standardizing—emerges as the key part of the structure. To the line managers may be delegated the formal authority for the operating units, but without the standardizers—the cadre of work-study analysts, schedulers, quality control engineers, planners, budgeters, accountants, operations researchers, and many more—these structures simply could not function. Hence, despite their lack of formal authority, considerable informal power rests with these staff analysts, who standardize everyone else's work. Rules and regulations permeate the entire system: The emphasis on standardization extends well beyond the operating core of the machine organization, and with it follows the analysts' influence.

A further reflection of this formalization of behavior are the sharp divisions of labor all over the machine organization. Job specialization in the operating core and the pronounced formal distinction between line and staff have already been mentioned. In addition, the administrative structure is clearly distinguished from the operating core; unlike the entrepreneurial organization, here managers seldom work alongside operators. And they themselves tend to be organized along functional lines, meaning that each runs a unit that performs a single function in the chain that produces the final outputs. Figure 8–1 shows this, for example, in the organigram of a large steel company, traditionally machinelike in structure.

All this suggests that the machine organization is a structure with an obsession—namely, control. A control mentality pervades it from top to bottom. At the bottom, consider how a Ford Assembly Division general foreman described his work:

> I refer to my watch all the time. I check different items. About every hour I tour my line. About six thirty, I'll tour labor relations to find out

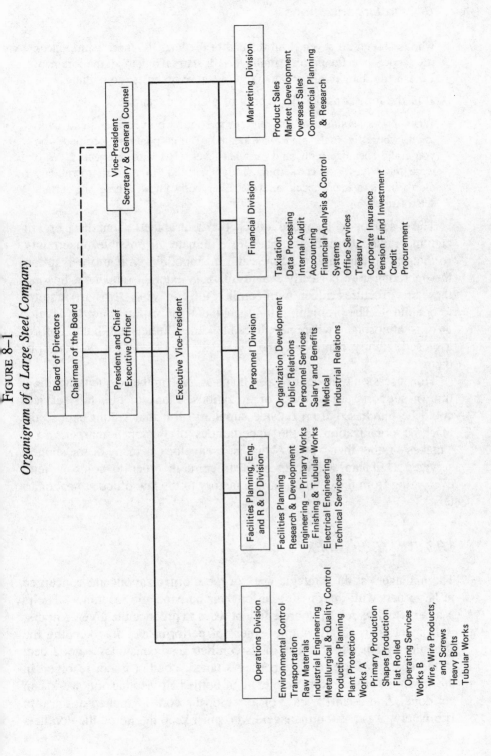

FIGURE 8–1

Organigram of a Large Steel Company

who is absent. At seven, I hit the end of the line. I'll check paint, check my scratches and damage. Around ten I'll start talking to all the foremen. I make sure they're all awake. We can't have no holes, no nothing.

And at the top, consider the words of a chief executive:

When I was president of this big corporation, we lived in a small Ohio town, where the main plant was located. The corporation specified who you could socialize with, and on what level. (His wife interjects: "Who were the wives you could play bridge with."). In a small town they didn't have to keep check on you. Everybody knew. There are certain sets of rules.[2]

The obsession with control reflects two central facts about these organizations. First, attempts are made to eliminate all possible uncertainty, so that the bureaucratic machine can run smoothly, without interruption, the operating core perfectly sealed off from external influence. Second, these are structures ridden with conflict; the control systems are required to contain it. The problem in the machine organization is not to develop an open atmosphere where people can talk the conflicts out, but to enforce a closed, tightly controlled one where the work can get done despite them.

The obsession with control also helps to explain the frequent proliferation of support staff in these organizations. Many of the staff services could be purchased from outside suppliers. But that would expose the machine organization to the uncertainties of the open market. So it "makes" rather than "buys," that is, it envelops as many of the support services as it can within its own structure in order to control them, everything from the cafeteria in the factory to the law office at headquarters.

THE STRATEGIC APEX

The managers at the strategic apex of these organizations are concerned in large part with the fine-tuning of their bureaucratic machines. Theirs is a perpetual search for more efficient ways to produce the given outputs.

But not all is strictly improvement of performance. Just keeping the structure together in the face of its conflicts also consumes a good deal of the energy of top management. As noted, conflict is not resolved in the machine organization; rather it is bottled up so that the work can get done. And as in the case of a bottle, the cork is applied at the top: Ultimately, it is the top managers who must keep the lid on the conflicts through their role of handling disturbances. Moreover, the managers of the strategic apex must intervene frequently in the activities of the middle line to ensure that coordination is achieved there. The top managers are the only generalists in the structure, the only managers with a perspective broad enough to see all the functions.

All this leads us to the conclusion that considerable power in the machine organization rests with the managers of the strategic apex. These are, in other words, rather centralized structures: The formal power clearly rests at the top; hierarchy and chain of authority are paramount concepts. But so also does much of the informal power, since that resides in knowledge, and only at the top of the hierarchy does the formally segmented knowledge of the organization come together.

Thus, our introductory figure shows the machine organization with a fully elaborated administrative and support structure—both parts of the staff component being focused on the operating core—together with large units in the operating core but narrower ones in the middle line to reflect the tall hierarchy of authority.

CONDITIONS OF THE MACHINE ORGANIZATION

Work of a machine bureaucratic nature is found, above all, in environments that are simple and stable. The work associated with complex environments cannot be rationalized into simple tasks, and that associated with dynamic environments cannot be predicted, made repetitive, and so standardized.

In addition, the machine configuration is typically found in mature organizations, large enough to have the volume of operating work needed for repetition and standardization, and old enough to have been able to settle on the standards they wish to use. These are the organizations that have seen it all before and have established standard procedures to deal with it. Likewise, machine organizations tend to be identified with technical systems that regulate the operating work, so that it can easily be programmed. Such technical systems cannot be very sophisticated or automated (for reasons that will be discussed later).

Mass production firms are perhaps the best-known machine organizations. Their operating work flows through an integrated chain, open at one end to accept raw materials, and after that functioning as a sealed system that processes them through sequences of standardized operations. Thus, the environment may be stable because the organization has acted aggressively to stabilize it. Giant firms in such industries as transportation, tobacco, and metals are well known for their attempts to influence the forces of supply and demand by the use of advertising, the development of long-term supply contacts, sometimes the establishment of cartels. They also tend to adopt strategies of "vertical integration," that is, extend their production chains at both ends, becoming both their own suppliers and their own customers. In that way they can bring some of the forces of supply and demand within their own planning processes.

Of course, the machine organization is not restricted to large, or manufacturing, or even private enterprise organizations. Small manufacturers—for example producers of discount furniture or paper products—may sometimes prefer this structure because their operating work is simple and repetitive. Many service firms use it for the same reason, such as banks or insurance companies in their retailing activities. Another condition often found with machine organizations is external control. Many government departments, such as post offices and tax collection agencies, are machine bureaucratic not only because their operating work is routine but also because they must be accountable to the public for their actions. Everything they do—treating clients, hiring employees, etc.—must be seen to be fair, and so they proliferate regulations.

Since control is the forte of the machine bureaucracy, it stands to reason that organizations in the business of control—regulatory agencies, custodial prisons, police forces—are drawn to this configuration, sometimes in spite of contradictory conditions. The same is true for the special need for safety. Organizations that fly airplanes or put out fires must minimize the risks they take. Hence they formalize their procedures extensively to ensure that they are carried out to the letter: A fire crew cannot arrive at a burning house and then turn to the chief for orders or discuss informally who will connect the hose and who will go up the ladder.

MACHINE ORGANIZATIONS AS INSTRUMENTS AND CLOSED SYSTEMS

Control raises another issue about machine organizations. Being so pervasively regulated, they themselves can easily be controlled externally, as the *instruments* of outside influencers. In contrast, however, their obsession with control runs not only up the hierarchy but beyond, to control of their own environments, so that they can become *closed systems* immune to external influence. From the perspective of power, the instrument and the closed system constitute two main types of machine organizations.

In our terms, the instrument form of machine organization is dominated by one external influencer or by a group of them acting in concert. In the "closely held" corporation, the dominant influencer is the outside owner; in some prisons, it is a community concerned with the custody rather than the rehabilitation of prisoners.

Outside influencers render an organization their instrument by appointing the chief executive, charging that person with the pursuit of clear goals (ideally quantifiable, such as return-on-investment or prisoner escape measures), and then holding the chief responsible for performance. That way outsiders can control an organization without actually having to manage it. And such control, by virtue of the power put in the hands of the chief executive and the numerical nature of the goals, acts to centralize and bureaucratize the internal structure, in other words, to drive it to the machine form. (Recall the proposition in Chapter 6 about the centralizing and formalizing effects of the external control of an organization.)

In contrast to this, Charles Perrow, the colorful and outspoken organizational sociologist, does not quite see the machine organization as anyone's instrument:

> Society is adaptive to organizations, to the large, powerful organizations controlled by a few, often overlapping, leaders. To see these organizations as adaptive to a "turbulent," dynamic, very changing environment is to indulge in fantasy. The environment of most powerful organizations is well controlled by them, quite stable, and made up of other organizations with similar interests, or ones they control.[3]

Perrow is, of course, describing the closed system form of machine organization, the one that uses its bureaucratic procedures to seal itself off from external control and control others instead. It controls not only its own people but its environment as well: perhaps its suppliers, customers, competitors, even government and owners too.

Of course, autonomy can be achieved not only by controlling others (for example, buying up customers and suppliers in so-called vertical integration) but simply by avoiding the control of others. Thus, for example, closed system organizations sometimes form cartels with ostensible competitors or, less blatantly, diversify markets to avoid dependence on particular customers, finance internally to avoid dependence on particular financial groups, and even buy back their own shares to weaken the influence of their own owners. Key to being a closed system is to ensure wide dispersal, and therefore pacification, of all groups of potential external influence.

What goals does the closed system organization pursue? Remember that to sustain centralized bureaucracy the goals should be operational, ideally quantifiable. What operational goals enable an organization to serve itself, as a system closed to external influence? The most obvious answer is growth. Survival may be an indispensable goal and efficiency a necessary one, but beyond those what really matters here is making the system larger. Growth serves the system by providing greater rewards for its insiders—bigger empires for managers to run or fancier private jets to fly, greater programs for analysts to design, even more power for unions to wield by virtue of having more members. (The unions may be external influencers, but the management can keep them passive by allowing them more of the spoils of the closed system.) Thus the classic closed system machine organization, the large, widely held industrial corporation, has long been described as oriented far more to growth than to the maximization of profit per se.[4]

Of course, the closed system form of machine organization can exist outside the private sector too, for example in the fundraising agency that, relatively free to external control, becomes increasingly charitable to itself (as indicated by the plushness of its managers' offices), the agricultural or retail cooperative that ignores those who collectively own it, even government that becomes more intent on serving itself than the citizens for which it supposedly exists.

The communist state seems to fit all the characteristics of the closed system bureaucracy. It has no dominant external influencer (at least in the case of the Soviet Union, if not the other East European states, its "instruments"). And the population to which it is ostensibly responsible must respond to its own plethora of rules and regulations. Its election procedures, traditionally offering a choice of one, are similar to those for the directors of the "widely held" Western corporation. The government's own structure is heavily bureaucratic, with a single hierarchy of authority and a very elaborate technostructure, ranging from state planners to KGB agents. (As James Worthy noted, Frederick Taylor's "Scientific Management had its fullest flowering not in America but in Soviet Russia."[5]) All significant resources are the property of the state—the collective system—not the individual. And, as in other closed systems, the administrators tend to take the lion's share of the benefits, as one writer noted some time ago:

> . . . far from increased productivity benefiting the majority, increases in productive capacity primarily benefit the bureaucracy itself. In the case of the Soviet Union, the standard of living of the bureaucracy has risen far more than that of any other group, and its tendency is to go higher still.[6]*

SOME ISSUES ASSOCIATED WITH THE MACHINE ORGANIZATION

No structure has evoked more heated debate than the machine organization. As Michel Crozier, one of its most eminent students, has noted:

> On the one hand, most authors consider the bureaucratic organization to be the embodiment of rationality in the modern world, and, as such, to be intrinsically superior to all other possible forms of organizations. On the other hand, many authors—often the same ones—consider it a sort of Leviathan, preparing the enslavement of the human race.[7]

Max Weber, who first wrote about this form of organization, emphasized its rationality; in fact, the word *machine* comes directly from his writings.[8] A machine is certainly precise; it is also reliable and easy to control; and it is efficient—at least when restricted to the job it has been designed to do. Those are the reasons many organizations are structured as machine bureaucracies. When an integrated set of simple, repetitive tasks must be performed precisely and consistently by human beings, this is the most efficient structure—indeed, the only conceivable one.

But in these same advantages of machinelike efficiency lie all the disadvantages of this configuration. Machines consist of mechanical parts; organizational structures also include human beings—and that is where the analogy breaks down.

---

*On the day that Alexei Kosygin, Chairmain of the USSR Council of Ministers, died, a Canadian diplomat who knew him was interviewed on the CBC radio network. Kosygin reminded him of an American businessman more than the head of a totalitarian state, he said, seemingly surprised at the point. He should not have been. The Soviet Union is organized much like a large Western business, with its divisions, planning procedures, and performance control measures, and, conversely, in many fundamental respects the large Western business is managed internally much like a centralized state.

HUMAN PROBLEMS IN THE OPERATING CORE

James Worthy, when he was an executive of Sears, wrote a penetrating and scathing criticism of the machine organization in his book *Big Business and Free Men*. Worthy traces the root of the human problems in these structures to the "scientific management" movement led by Frederick Taylor that swept America early in this century. Worthy acknowledges Taylor's contribution to efficiency, narrowly defined. Worker initiative did not, however, enter into his efficiency equation. Taylor's pleas to remove "all possible brain work" from the shop floor also removed all possible initiative from the people who worked there: The "machine has no will of its own. Its parts have no urge to independent action. Thinking, direction—even purpose—must be provided from outside or above." This had the "consequence of destroying the meaning of work itself," which has been "fantastically wasteful for industry and society," resulting in excessive absenteeism, high worker turnover, sloppy workmanship, costly strikes, even outright sabotage.[9] Of course, there are people who like to work in highly structured situations. But increasing numbers do not, at least not *that* highly structured.

Taylor was fond of saying, "In the past the man has been first; in the future the system must be first."[10] Prophetic words, indeed. Modern man seems to exist for his systems; many of the organizations he created to serve him have come to enslave him. The result is that several of what Victor Thompson has called "bureaupathologies"—dysfunctional behaviors of these structures—reinforce each other to form a vicious circle in the machine organization.[11] The concentration on means at the expense of ends, the mistreatment of clients, the various manifestations of worker alienation—all lead to the tightening of controls on behavior. The implicit motto of the machine organization seems to be, "When in doubt, control." All problems have to be solved by the turning of the technocratic screws. But since that is what caused the bureaupathologies in the first place, increasing the controls serves only to magnify the problems, leading to the imposition of further controls, and so on.

COORDINATION PROBLEMS IN THE ADMINISTRATIVE CENTER

Since the operating core of the machine organization is not designed to handle conflict, many of the human problems that arise there spill up and over, into the administrative structure.

It is one of the ironies of the machine configuration that to achieve the control it requires, it must mirror the narrow specialization of its operating core in its administrative structure (for example, differentiating marketing managers from manufacturing managers, much as salesmen are differentiated from factory workers). This, in turn, means problems of communication and coordination. The fact is that the administrative structure of the machine organization is also ill suited to the resolution of problems through mutual adjustment. All the communication barriers in these structures—horizontal, vertical, status, line/staff—impede informal communication among managers and with staff people. "Each unit becomes jealous of its own prerogatives and finds ways to protect itself against the pressure or encroachments of others."[12] Thus narrow functionalism not only impedes coordination; it also encourages the building of private empires, which tends to produce topheavy organizations that can be more concerned with the political games to be won than with the clients to be served.

ADAPTATION PROBLEMS IN THE STRATEGIC APEX

But if mutual adjustment does not work in the administrative center— generating more political heat than cooperative light—how does the machine organization resolve its coordination problems? Instinctively, it tries standardization, for example, by tightening job descriptions or proliferating rules. But standardization is not suited to handling the nonroutine problems of the administrative center. Indeed, it only aggravates them, undermining the influence of the line managers and increasing the conflict. So to reconcile these coordination problems, the machine organization is left with only one coordinating mechanism, direct supervision from above. Specifically, nonroutine coordination problems between units are "bumped" up the line hierarchy until they reach a common level of supervision, often at the top of the structure. The result can be excessive centralization of power, which in turn produces a host of other problems. In effect, just as the human problems in the operating core become coordination problems in the administrative center, so too do the coordination problems in the administrative center become adaptation problems at the strategic apex. Let us take a closer look at these by concluding with a discussion of strategic change in the machine configuration.

STRATEGY FORMATION IN THE
MACHINE ORGANIZATION

Strategy in the machine organization is supposed to emanate from the top of the hierarchy, where the perspective is broadest and the power most focused. All the relevant information is to be sent up the hierarchy, in aggregated, MIS-type form, there to be formulated into integrated strategy (with the aid of the technostructure). Implementation then follows, with the intended strategies sent down the hierarchy to be turned into successively more elaborated programs and action plans. Notice the clear division of labor assumed between the formulators at the top and the implementors down below, based on the assumption of perfectly deliberate strategy produced through a process of planning.

That is the theory. The practice has been shown to be another matter. Drawing on our strategy research at McGill, we shall consider first what planning really proved to be in one machinelike organization, how it may in fact have impeded strategic thinking in a second, and how a third really did change its strategy. From there we shall consider the problems of strategic change in machine organizations and their possible resolution.

PLANNING AS PROGRAMMING IN A
SUPERMARKET CHAIN

What really is the role of formal planning? Does it produce original strategies? Let us return to the case of Steinberg's in the later years of its founder, as large size drove the organization toward the machine form, and as is common in that form, toward a planning mode of management at the expense of entrepreneurship.

One event in particular encouraged the start of planning at Steinberg's: the company's entry into capital markets in 1953. Months before it floated its first bond issue (stock, always nonvoting, came later), Sam Steinberg boasted to a newspaper reporter that "not a cent of any money outside the family is invested in the company." And asked about future plans, he replied: "Who knows? We will try to go everywhere there seems to be a need for us." A few months later he announced a $5 million debt issue and with it a $15 million five-year expansion program, one new store every two months for a total of thirty, the doubling of sales, new stores to average double the size of existing ones.

What happened in those ensuing months was Sam Steinberg's realization, after the opening of Montreal's first shopping center, that he needed to enter the shopping center business himself to protect his supermarket chain and that he could not do so with the company's traditional methods of short-term and internal financing. And, of course, no company is allowed to go to capital markets without a plan. You can't just say: "I'm Sam Steinberg and I'm good," though that was really the issue. In a "rational" society, you have to plan (or at least appear to do so).

But what exactly was that planning? One thing for certain: It did not formulate a strategy. Sam Steinberg already had that. What planning did was justify, elaborate, and articulate the strategy that already existed in Sam Steinberg's mind. Planning operationalized his strategic vision, programmed it. It gave order to that vision, imposing form on it to comply with the needs of the organization and its environment. Thus, planning followed the strategy-making process, which had been essentially entrepreneurial.

But its effect on that process was not incidental. By specifying and articulating the vision, planning constrained it and rendered it less flexible. Sam Steinberg retained formal control of the company to the day of his death. But his control over strategy did not remain so absolute. The entrepreneur, by keeping his vision personal, is able to adapt it at will to a changing environment. But by being forced to program it, the leader loses that flexibility. The danger, ultimately, is that the planning mode forces out the entrepreneurial one; procedure replaces vision. As its structure became more machinelike, Steinberg's required planning in the form of strategic programming. But that planning also accelerated the firm's transition toward the machine form of organization.

Is there, then, such a thing as "strategic planning"? I suspect not. To be more explicit, I do not find that major new strategies are formulated through any formal procedure. Organizations that rely on planning procedures to formulate strategies seem to extrapolate existing strategies, perhaps with marginal changes in them, or else copy the strategies of other organizations. This came out most clearly in another of our McGill studies.

PLANNING AS AN IMPEDIMENT TO STRATEGIC THINKING IN AN AIRLINE

From about the mid-1950s, Air Canada engaged heavily in planning. Once the airline was established, particularly once it developed its basic route structure, a number of factors drove it strongly to the planning mode. Above all was the need for coordination, both of flight schedules with aircraft, crews, and maintenance, and of the purchase of expensive aircraft with the structure of the route system. (Imagine someone calling out in the hangar: "Hey, Fred, this guy says he has two 747s for us; do you know who ordered them?") Safety was another factor: The intense need for safety in the air breeds a mentality of being very careful about what the organization does on the ground, too. That is the airlines' obsession with control. Other factors included the lead times inherent in key decisions, such as ordering new airplanes or introducing new routes, the sheer cost of the capital equipment, and the size of the organization. You don't run an intricate system like an airline, necessarily very machinelike, without a great deal of formal planning.

But what we found to be the consequence of planning at Air Canada was the absence of a major reorientation of strategy during our study period (up to the mid-1970s). Aircraft certainly changed—they became larger and faster—but the basic route system did not, nor did markets. Air Canada gave only marginal attention, for example, to cargo, charter, and shuttle operations. Formal planning, in our view, impeded strategic thinking.

The problem is that planning, too, proceeds from the machine perspective, much as an assembly line or a conventional machine produces a product. It all depends on the decomposition of analysis: You split the process into a series of steps or component parts, specify each, and then by following the specifications in sequence you get the desired product. There is a fallacy in this, however, noted back in Chapter 4. Assembly lines and conventional machines produce standardized products, while planning is supposed to produce a novel strategy. It is as if the machine is supposed to design the machine; the planning machine is expected to create the original blueprint—the strategy. To repeat another point made there, planning is analysis oriented to decomposition, while strategy-making depends on synthesis oriented to integration. That is why the term "strategic planning" has proved to be an oxymoron.

STRATEGIC CHANGE IN AN AUTOMOBILE FIRM

How then does the planning-oriented machine bureaucracy change its strategy when it has to? Volkswagenwerk was an organization that had to. We interpreted its history from 1934 to 1974 as one long life cycle of a single strategic perspective. The original "people's car," the famous "Beetle," was conceived by Ferdinand Porsche; the factory to produce it was built just before the war but did not go into civilian automobile production until after. In 1948, a man named Heinrich Nordhoff was given control of the devastated plant and began the rebuilding of it, as well as of the organization and the strategy itself, rounding out Porsche's original conception. The firm's success was dramatic.

By the late 1950s, however, problems began to appear. Demand in Germany was moving away from the Beetle. The typically machine-bureaucratic response was not to rethink the basic strategy—"it's okay" was the reaction—but rather to graft another piece onto it. A new automobile model was added, larger than the Beetle but with a similar no-nonsense approach to motoring, again air-cooled with the engine in the back. Volkswagenwerk added position but did not change perspective.

But that did not solve the basic problem, and by the mid-1960s the company was in crisis. Nordhoff, who had resisted strategic change, died in office and was replaced by a lawyer from outside the business. The company then underwent a frantic search for new models, designing, developing, or acquiring a whole host of them with engines in the front, middle, and rear; air- and water-cooled; front- and rear-wheel drive. To paraphrase the humorist Stephen Leacock, Volkswagenwerk leaped onto its strategic horse and rode off in all directions. Only when another leader came in, a man steeped in the company and the automobile business, did the firm consolidate itself around a new strategic perspective, based on the stylish front-wheel-drive, water-cooled designs of one of its acquired firms, and thereby turn its fortunes around.

What this story suggests, first of all, is the great force of bureaucratic momentum in the machine organization. Even leaving planning aside, the immense effort of producing and marketing a new line of automobiles locks a company into a certain posture. But here the momentum was psychological, too. Nordhoff, who had been the driving force behind the great success of the organization, became a major liability when the environment demanded change. Over the years, he too had been captured by bureaucratic momentum. Moreover, the uniqueness and tight integration of Volkswagenwerk's strategy—we labeled it *gestalt*—impeded strategic change. Change an element of a tightly integrated gestalt and it *dis*integrates. Thus does success eventually breed failure.

BOTTLENECK AT THE TOP

Why the great difficulty in changing strategy in the machine organization? Here we take up that question and show how changes generally have to be achieved in a different configuration, if at all.

As discussed earlier, unanticipated problems in the machine organization tend to get bumped up the hierarchy. When these are few, which means conditions are relatively stable, things work smoothly enough. But in times of rapid change, just when new strategies are called for, the number of such problems magnifies, resulting in a bottleneck at the top, where senior managers get overloaded. And that tends either to impede strategic change or else to render it ill-considered.

A major part of the problem is information. Senior managers face an organization decomposed into parts, like a machine itself. Marketing information comes up one channel, manufacturing information up another, and so on. Somehow it is the senior managers themselves who must integrate all that information. But the very machine bureaucratic premise of separating the administration of work from the doing of it means that the top managers often lack the intimate, detailed knowledge of issues necessary to effect such an integration. In essence, the necessary power is at the top of the structure, but the necessary knowledge is often at the bottom.

Of course, there is a machinelike solution to that problem too—not surprisingly in the form of a system. It is called a management information system, or MIS, and what it does is combine all the necessary information and package it neatly so that top managers can be informed about what is going on—the perfect solution for the overloaded executive. At least in theory.

Unfortunately, a number of real-world problems arise in the MIS. For one thing, in the tall administrative hierarchy of the machine organization, information must pass through many levels before it reaches the top. Losses take place at each one. Good news gets highlighted while bad news gets blocked on the way up. And "soft" information, so necessary for strategy formation, cannot easily pass through, while much of the hard MIS-type information arrives only slowly. In a stable environment, the manager may be able to wait; in a rapidly changing one, he or she cannot. The president wants to be told right away that the firm's most important customer was seen playing golf yesterday with a main competitor, not to find out six months later in the form of a drop in a sales report. Gossip, hearsay, speculation—the softest kinds of information—warn the manager of impending problems; the MIS all too often records for posterity ones that have already been felt. The manager who depends on an MIS in a changing environment generally finds himself or herself out of touch.

The obvious solution for top managers is to bypass the MIS and set up their own informal information systems, networks of contacts that bring them the rich, tangible, instant information they need. But that violates the machine organization's presuppositions of formality and respect for the chain of authority. Also, that takes the managers' time, the lack of which caused the bottleneck in the first place. So a fundamental dilemma faces the top managers of the machine organization as a result of its very own design: In times of change, when they most need the time to inform themselves, the system overburdens them with other pressures. They are thus reduced to acting superficially, with inadequate, abstract information.

THE FORMULATION / IMPLEMENTATION DICHOTOMY

The essential problem lies in one of the chief tenets of the machine organization, that strategy formation must be sharply separated from strategy implementation. One is thought out at the top, the other then acted out lower down. For this to work assume two conditions: first, that the formulator has full and sufficient information, and second, that the world will hold still, or at least change in predictable ways, during the implementation, so that there is no need for *re*formulation.

Now consider why the organization needs a new strategy in the first place. It is because its world has changed in an unpredictable way, indeed may continue to do so. We have just seen how the machine bureaucratic structure tends to violate the first condition—it misinforms the senior manager during such times of change. And when change continues in an unpredictable way (or at least the world unfolds in a way not yet predicted by an ill-informed management), then the second condition is violated too—it hardly makes sense to lock in by implementation a strategy that does not reflect changes in the world around it.

What all this amounts to is a need to collapse the formulation/implementation dichotomy precisely when the strategy of machine bureaucracy must be changed. This can be done in one of two ways.

In one case, the formulator implements. In other words, power is concentrated at the top, not only for creating the strategy but also for implementing it, step by step, in a personalized way. The strategist is put in close personal touch with the situation at hand (more commonly a strategist is appointed who has or can develop that touch) so that he or she can, on one hand, be properly informed and, on the other, control the implementation en route in order to reformulate when necessary. This, of course, describes the entrepreneurial configuration, at least at the strategic apex.

In the other case, the implementers formulate. In other words, power is concentrated lower down, where the necessary information resides. As people who are naturally in touch with the specific situations at hand take individual actions—approach new customers, develop new products, etc.—patterns form, in other words, strategies emerge. And this, as we shall see, describes the innovative configuration, where strategic initiatives often originate in the grass roots of the organization, and then are championed by managers at middle levels who integrate them with one another or with existing strategies in order to gain their acceptance by senior management.

We conclude, therefore, that the machine configuration is ill-suited to change its fundamental strategy, that the organization must in effect change configuration temporarily in order to change strategy. Either it reverts to the entrepreneurial form, to allow a single leader to develop vision (or proceed with one developed earlier), or else it overlays an innovative form on its conventional structure (for example, creates an informed network of lateral teams and task forces) so that the necessary strategies can emerge. The former can obviously function faster than the latter; that is why it tends to be used for drastic *turnaround,* while the latter tends to proceed by the slower process of *revitalization.* (Of course, quick turnaround may be necessary because there has been no slow revitalization.) In any event, both are characterized by a capacity to *learn*—that is the essence of the entrepreneurial and innovative configurations, in one case learning centralized for the simpler context, in the other, decentralized for the more complex one. The machine configuration is not so characterized.

This, however, should come as no surprise. After all, machines are specialized instruments, designed for productivity, not for adaptation. In Hunt's words, machine bureaucracies are performance systems, not problem-solving ones.[13] Efficiency is their forte, not innovation. An organization cannot put blinders on its personnel and then expect peripheral vision. Managers here are rewarded for cutting costs and improving standards, not for taking risks and ignoring procedures. Change makes a mess of the operating systems: Change one link in a carefully coupled system, and the whole chain must be reconceived. Why, then, should we be surprised when our bureaucratic machines fail to adapt?

Of course, it is fair to ask why we spend so much time trying to make them adapt. After all, when an ordinary machine becomes redundant, we simply scrap it, happy that it served us for as long and as well as it did. Converting it to another use generally proves more expensive than simply starting over. I suspect the same is often true for bureaucratic machines. But here, of course, the context is social and political. Mechanical parts don't protest, nor do displaced raw materials. Workers, suppliers, and customers do, however, protest the scrapping of organizations, for obvious reasons. But that the cost of this is awfully high in a society of giant machine organizations will be the subject of the final chapter of this book.

STRATEGIC REVOLUTIONS IN MACHINE ORGANIZATIONS

Machine organizations do sometimes change, however, at times effectively but more often it would seem at great cost and pain. The lucky ones are able to overlay an innovative structure for periodic revitalization (in ways I shall suggest in the closing chapter of this section), while many of the other survivors somehow manage to get turned around in entrepreneurial fashion.

Overall, the machine organizations seem to follow what my colleagues Danny Miller and Peter Friesen call a "quantum theory" of organization change.[14] They pursue their set strategies through long periods of stability (naturally occurring or created by themselves as closed systems), using planning and other procedures to do so efficiently. Periodically these are interrupted by short bursts of change, which Miller and Friesen characterize as "strategic revolutions" (although another colleague, Mihaela Firsirotu, perhaps better labels it "strategic turnaround as cultural revolution"[15]).

ORGANIZATION TAKING PRECEDENCE IN THE MACHINE ORGANIZATION

To conclude, as shown in Figure 8–2, it is organization—with its systems and procedures, its planning and its bureaucratic momentum—that takes

FIGURE 8–2
Organization Takes Precedence

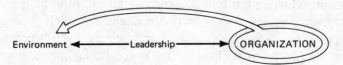

precedence over leadership and environment in the machine configuration. Environment fits organization, either because the organization has slotted itself into a context that matches its procedures, or else because it has forced the environment to do so. And leadership generally falls into place too, supporting the organization, indeed often becoming part of its bureaucratic momentum.

This generally works effectively, though hardly nonproblematically, at least in times of stability. But in times of change, efficiency becomes ineffective and the organization will falter unless it can find a different way to organize for adaptation.

All of this is another way of saying that the machine organization is a configuration, a species, like the others, suited to its own context but ill-suited to others. But unlike the others, it is the dominant configuration in our specialized societies. As long as we demand inexpensive and so necessarily standardized goods and services, and as long as people continue to be more efficient than real machines at providing them, and remain willing to do so, then the machine organization will remain with us—and so will all its problems.

9

THE DIVERSIFIED ORGANIZATION

The waves of mergers that have taken place in American business over the last century, first to combine businesses into larger entities, sometimes enormous trusts, then to add activities at either end of the production chain under the label "vertical integration" (though always, for some curious reason, displayed horizontally), and finally, especially, to move the firms into new businesses, have led to the formation of giant corporations and to the so-called divisionalized forms of structure. The "conglomerate" is, of course, the ultimate example of this, where a corporation doesn't much care about any relationship among its different businesses other than financial.

American business probably reached its peak of conglomerate diversification sometime in the 1970s, after the great merger movement of the 1960s, when so-called professional management—the assumption that a good manager could manage anything—was itself at its peak. But then conglomeration waned. Perhaps there was a realization that it sometimes helps to know a business deeply, more deeply than can executives at a distant headquarters who have to deal with chinaware in the morning and steam shovels in the afternoon. Or maybe it was simply the market forces taking over, the failure of conglomeration allowing outside financial types, even more removed from products and services than the professional managers inside, to strip and restructure excessively diversified corporations.

In any event, the strategy of diversification and the associated structure of divisionalization have hardly disappeared. A chief concern of almost all large corporations remains how to expand while exercising some control over the range of business they are in, and then how to knit these various businesses together to exploit what is now popularly called "synergy" (the 2 + 2 = 5 effect).

In fact, enormous amounts of energy have gone into trying to figure out what to do with overgrown and overextended businesses. It's been great for the consulting professional and the financial houses, but I'm not sure anyone else has benefited very much. The large corporation may have achieved its initial success by being smarter in its core business, but I am not sure that many have been very smart in their programs of conglomerate diversification. A few have persevered and achieved new and viable definition (that is, strategy), but many have been forced into expensive bouts of divestment.

"Put him down as undecided," a friend of mine would say. Well, my biases stem from a belief that power has been allowed to take precedence over performance, rooted in a most superficial view of what it means to manage a business. The relevant distinction for me is between what I prefer to call "thick" and "thin" management. Thin management involves moving pieces around a chessboard, throwing money at people to motivate them and money at facilities to improve them; in the diversified corporation it has meant "portfolio management" and "restructuring" and "shareholder value." Thick management means getting deeply inside a business, coming to know its needs and its processes and its people well enough to weld them all together into a smoothly functioning entity that serves its markets with care and understanding. Conglomerate diversification has given us more than enough of the former, in my opinion.

Severe as those problems have been on the economic side, I believe the greatest ones have been social. Organizations that become too large, too diversified, and too superficial have deadening effects on the people who work for them, and they pose grave threats to the social order, including democracy itself. This applies not only to business but to other spheres as well, governments run as giant conglomerates, multiversities likewise managed, massive divisionalized school systems, and so on through almost every social service. All have caused a great deal of misery.

After discussing the divisionalized form of structure, the conditions that foster it, and the stages that lead up to its fully developed (conglomerate) form, this chapter will delve at some length into what I believe are the threatening social issues that accompany it. I hope you will bear with me as I display my biases rather openly in this latter discussion.

The Diversified Organization

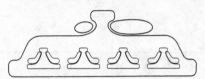

Structure: • market based "divisions" loosely coupled together under central administrative headquarters
 • divisions run businesses autonomously (implying no more than limited decentralization to division managers), subjected to performance control system that standardizes their outputs
 • tendency to drive structures of divisions toward machine configuration, as instruments of headquarters (though tendency of overall organization to be closed system type)

Context: • market diversity, especially of products and services (as opposed to clients or regions); by-product and related-product diversification encourages intermediate forms, conglomerate diversification being purest form
 • typically found in largest and most mature organizations, especially business corporations but also, increasingly, government and other public spheres (e.g. multiversities)

Strategy: • headquarters manages "corporate" strategy as portfolio of businesses, divisions manage individual business strategies

Issues: • resolves some problems of integrated functional (machine) structures (spreading risk, moving capital, adding and deleting businesses, etc.)

 but

 • conglomerate diversification sometimes costly and discouraging of innovation; improvements in functioning of capital markets and boards may make independent businesses more effective than divisions
 • performance control system risks driving organization toward socially unresponsive or irresponsible behavior
 • despite tendency to use in public sphere, dangers there even greater due to non-measurable nature of many goals

THE BASIC DIVISIONALIZED STRUCTURE

The diversified organization is not so much an integrated entity as a set of semi-autonomous units coupled together by a central administrative structure. The units are generally called *divisions,* and the central administration, the *headquarters.* This is a widely used configuration in the private sector of the industrialized economy; the vast majority of the Fortune 500, America's largest corporations, use this structure or a variant of it. But, as we shall see, it is also found in other sectors as well.

In what is commonly called the "divisionalized" form of structure, units, called "divisions," are created to serve distinct markets and are given control over the operating functions necessary to do so, as shown

FIGURE 9–1

Typical Organigram for a Divisionalized Manufacturing Firm

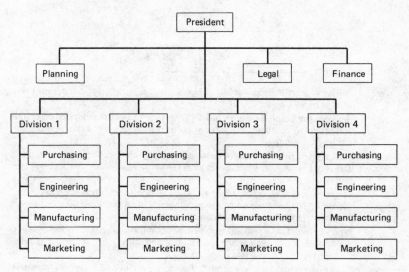

in Figure 9–1. Each is therefore relatively free of direct control by headquarters or even of the need to coordinate activities with other divisions. Each, in other words, appears to be a self-standing business. Of course, none is. There *is* a headquarters, and it has a series of roles that distinguish this overall configuration from a collection of independent businesses providing the same set of products and services.

ROLES OF THE HEADQUARTERS

Above all, the headquarters exercises performance control. It sets standards of achievement, generally in quantitative terms (such as return on investment or growth in sales), and then monitors the results. Coordination between headquarters and the divisions thus reduces largely to the standardization of outputs. Of course, there is some direct supervision—headquarters' managers have to have personal contact with and knowledge of the divisions. But that is largely circumscribed by the key assumption in this configuration that if the division managers are to be responsible for the performance of their divisions, they must have considerable autonomy to manage them as they see fit. Hence there is extensive delegation of authority from headquarters to the level of division manager.

Certain important tasks do, however, remain for the headquarters. One is to develop the overall *corporate* strategy, meaning to establish the portfolio of businesses in which the organization will operate. The headquarters establishes, acquires, divests, and closes down divisions in order to change its portfolio. Popular in the 1970s in this regard was the Boston Consulting Group's "growth share matrix," where corporate managers were supposed to allocate funds to divisions on the basis of their falling into the categories of dogs, cash cows, wildcats, and stars. But enthusiasm for that technique waned, perhaps mindful of Pope's warning that a little learning can be a dangerous thing.

Second, the headquarters manages the movement of funds between the divisions, taking the excess profits of some to support the greater growth potential of others. Third, of course, the headquarters, through its own technostructure, designs and operates the performance control system. Fourth, it appoints and therefore retains the right to replace the division managers. For a headquarters that does not directly manage any division, its most tangible power when the performance of a division lags—short of riding out an industry downturn or divesting the division— is to replace its leader. Finally, the headquarters provides certain support services that are common to all the divisions—a corporate public relations office or legal counsel, for example.

STRUCTURE OF THE DIVISIONS

It has been common to label divisionalized organizations "decentralized." That is a reflection of how *certain* of them came to be, most notably DuPont early in this century. When organizations that were structured functionally (for example, in departments of marketing, manufacturing, and engineering, etc.) diversified, they found that coordination of their different product lines across the functions became increasingly complicated. The central managers had to spend great amounts of time intervening to resolve disputes. But once these corporations switched to a divisionalized form of structure, where all the functions for a given business could be contained in a single unit dedicated to that business, management became much simpler. In effect, their structures became *more* decentralized, power over distinct businesses being delegated to the division managers.

But more decentralized does not mean *decentralized*. That word, as was noted in Chapter 6, refers to the dispersal of decision-making power in an organization, and in many of the diversified corporations much of the power tended to remain with the few managers who ran the businesses. Indeed, the most famous case of divisionalization was one of relative *centralization:* Alfred P. Sloan introduced the divisionalized structure to General Motors in the 1920s to *reduce* the power of its autonomous business units, to impose systems of financial controls on what had been a largely unmanaged agglomeration of different automobile businesses.

In fact, I would argue that it is the *centralization* of power within the divisions that is most compatible with the divisionalized form of structure. In other words, the effect of having a headquarters over the divisions is to drive them toward the machine configuration, namely a structure of centralized bureaucracy. That is the structure most compatible with headquarters control, in my opinion. If true, this would seem to be an important point, because it means that the proliferation of the diversified configuration in many spheres—business, government, and the rest—has the effect of driving many suborganizations toward machine bureaucracy, even where that configuration may be inappropriate (school systems, for example, or government departments charged with innovative project work).

The explanation for this lies in the standardization of outputs, the key to the functioning of the divisionalized structure. Bear in mind the headquarters' dilemma: to respect divisional autonomy while exercising control over performance. This it seeks to resolve by after-the-fact monitoring of divisional results, based on clearly defined performance standards. But two main assumptions underlie such standards.

First, each division must be treated as a single integrated system with a single, consistent set of goals. In other words, although the divisions may be loosely coupled with each other, the assumption is that each is tightly coupled internally.*

Second, these goals must be operational ones, in other words, lend themselves to quantitative measurement. But in the less formal configurations—entrepreneurial and innovative—which are less stable, such performance standards are difficult to establish, while in the professional configuration, the complexity of the work makes it difficult to establish such standards. Moreover, while the entrepreneurial configuration may

---

* Unless, of course, there is a second layer of divisionalization, which simply takes this conclusion down another level in the hierarchy.

lend itself to being integrated around a single set of goals, the innovative and professional configurations do not. Thus, only the machine configuration of the major types fits comfortably into the conventional divisionalized structure, by virture of its integration and its operational goals.

In fact, when organizations with another configuration are drawn under the umbrella of a divisionalized structure, they tend to be forced toward the machine bureaucratic form, to make them conform with *its* needs. How often have we heard stories of entrepreneurial firms recently acquired by conglomerates being descended upon by hordes of headquarters technocrats bemoaning the loose controls, the absence of organigrams, the informality of the systems? In many cases, of course, the very purpose of the acquisition was to do just this, tighten up the organization so that its strategies can be pursued more pervasively and systematically. But other times, the effect is to destroy the organization's basic strengths, sometimes including its flexibility and responsiveness. Similarly, how many times have we heard tell of government administrators complaining about being unable to control public hospitals or universities through conventional (meaning machine bureaucratic) planning systems?

This conclusion is, in fact, a prime manifestation of one of the hypotheses presented in Chapter 6: that concentrated external control of an organization (through what was called a dominated external coalition) has the effect of formalizing and centralizing its structure, in other words, of driving it toward the machine configuration. Headquarters' control of divisions is, of course, concentrated; indeed, when the diversified organization is itself a *closed system,* as I shall argue later many tend to be, then it is a most concentrated form of control. And, the effect of that control is to render the divisions its *instruments*.

There is, in fact, an interesting irony in this, in that the less society controls the overall diversified organization, the more the organization itself controls its individual units. The result is increased autonomy for the largest organizations coupled with decreased autonomy for their many activities. In other words, the systems are free, the people are not!

To conclude this discussion of the basic structure, the diversified configuration is represented in the opening figure, symbolically in terms of our logo, as follows. Headquarters has three parts: a small strategic apex of top managers, a small technostructure to the left concerned with the design and operation of the performance control system, and a slightly larger staff support group to the right to provide support services common to all the divisions. Each of the divisions is shown below the headquarters as a machine configuration.

CONDITIONS OF THE DIVERSIFIED ORGANIZATION

While the diversified configuration may arise from the federation of different organizations, which come together under a common headquarters umbrella, more often it appears to be the structural response to a machine organization that has diversified its range of product or service offerings. In either case, it is the diversity of markets above all that drives an organization to use this configuration. An organization faced with a single integrated market simply cannot split itself into autonomous divisions; the one with distinct markets, however, has an incentive to create a unit to deal with each.

There are three main kinds of market diversity—product and service, client, and region. In theory, all three can lead to divisionalization. But when diversification is based on variations in clients or regions as opposed to products or services, divisionalization often turns out to be incomplete. With identifical products or services in each region or for each group of clients, the headquarters is encouraged to maintain central control of certain critical functions, to ensure common operationg standards for all the divisions. And that seriously reduces divisional autonomy, and so leads to a less than complete form of divisionalization.

Thus, one study found that insurance companies concentrate at headquarters the critical function of investment, and retailers concentrate that of purchasing, also controlling product range, pricing, and volume.[1] One need only look at the individual outlets of a typical retail chain to recognize the absence of divisional autonomy: Usually they all look alike. The same conclusion tends to hold for other businesses organized by regions, such as bakeries, breweries, cement producers, and soft drink bottlers: Their "divisions," distinguished only by geographical location, lack the autonomy normally associated with ones that produce distinct products or services.

What about the conditions of size? Although large size itself does not bring on divisionalization, surely it is not coincidental that most of America's largest corporations use some variant of this configuration. The fact is that as organizations grow large, they become inclined to diversify and then to divisionalize. One reason is protection: Large organizations tend to be risk-averse—they have too much to lose—and diversification spreads the risk. Another is that as firms grow large, they come to dominate their traditional market, and so must often find growth opportunities elsewhere, through diversification. Moreoever, diversification feeds on itself. It creates a cadre of aggressive general managers, each running his or her own division, who push for further diversification and further growth. Thus, most of the giant corporations—with the exception of the "heavies," those with enormously high fixed-cost operating systems, such as the oil or aluminum producers—not only were able to reach their status by diversifying but also feel great pressures to continue to do so.

Age is another factor associated with this configuration, much like size. In larger organizations, the management runs out of places to expand in its traditional markets; in older ones, the managers sometimes get bored with the traditional markets and find diversion through diversification. Also, time brings new competitors into old markets, forcing the management to look elsewhere for growth opportunities.

As governments grow large, they too tend to adopt a kind of divisionalized structure. The central administrators, unable to control all the agencies and departments directly, settle for granting their managers considerable autonomy and then trying to control their results through planning and performance controls. Indeed, the "accountability" buzzword so often heard in governments these days reflects just this trend—to move closer to a divisionalized structure.

One can, in fact, view the entire government as a giant diversified configuration (admittedly an oversimplification, since all kinds of links exist among the departments), with its three main coordinating agencies corresponding to the three main forms of control used by the headquarters of the large corporation. The budgetary agency, technocratic in nature, concerns itself with performance control of the departments; the public service commission, also partly technocratic, concerns itself with the recruiting and training of government managers; and the executive office, top management in nature, reviews the principal proposals and initiatives of the departments.

In the preceding chapter, the communist state was described as a closed system machine bureaucracy. But it may also be characterized as the ultimate closed system diversified configuration, with the various state enterprises and agencies its instruments, machine bureaucracies tightly regulated by the planning and control systems of the central government.

STAGES IN THE TRANSITION TO THE DIVERSIFIED ORGANIZATION

There has been a good deal of research on the transition of the corporation from the functional to the diversified form. Figure 9–2 and the discussion that follows borrow from this research to describe four stages in that transition.

At the top of Figure 9–2 is the pure *functional* structure, used by the corporation whose operating activities form one integrated, unbroken chain from purchasing through production to marketing and sales. Only

FIGURE 9–2
Stages in the Transition to the Pure Diversified Form

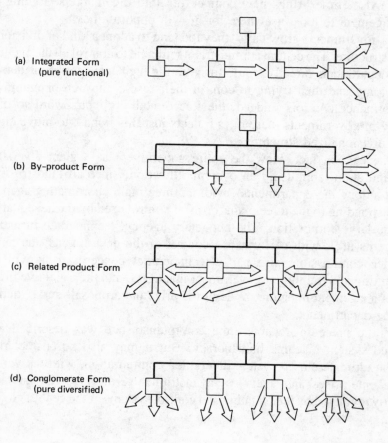

(a) Integrated Form
   (pure functional)

(b) By-product Form

(c) Related Product Form

(d) Conglomerate Form
   (pure diversified)

the final output is sold to the customers.* Autonomy cannot, therefore, be granted to the units, so the organization tends to take on the form of one overall machine configuration.

As an integrated firm seeks wider markets, it may introduce a variety of new end products and so shift all the way to the pure diversified form. A less risky alternative, however, is to start by marketing its intermediate products on the open market. This introduces small breaks in its processing chain, which in turn calls for a measure of divisionalization in its structure, giving rise to the *by-product* form. But because the processing chain remains more or less intact, central coordination must largely remain. Organizations that fall into this category tend to be vertically integrated, basing their operations on a single raw material, such as wood, oil, or aluminum, which they process to a variety of consumable end products. The example of Alcoa is shown in Figure 9–3.

Some corporations further diversify their by-product markets, breaking down their processing chain until what the divisions sell on the open market becomes more important than what they supply to each other. The organization then moves to the *related-product* form. For example, a firm manufacturing washing machines may set up a division to produce the motors. When the motor division sells more motors to outside customers than to its own sister division, a more serious form of divisionalization is called for. What typically holds the divisions of these firms together is some common thread among their products, perhaps a core skill or technology, perhaps a central market theme, as in a corporation such as 3M that likes to describe itself as being in the coating and bonding business. A good deal of the control over the specific product-market strategies can now revert to the divisions, but the central strategic theme means that headquarters may retain certain functions common to the divisions, such as research and development.

As a related-product firm expands into new markets or acquires other firms with less regard to a central strategic theme, the organization moves

---

* It should be noted that this is in fact the definition of a functional structure: Each activity contributes just one step in a chain toward the creation of the final product. Thus, for example, engineering is a functionally organized unit in the firm that produces and markets its own designs, while it would be a market organized unit in a consulting firm that sells its design services, among others, directly to clients.

FIGURE 9–3
By-Product and End-Product Sales of Alcoa[2]

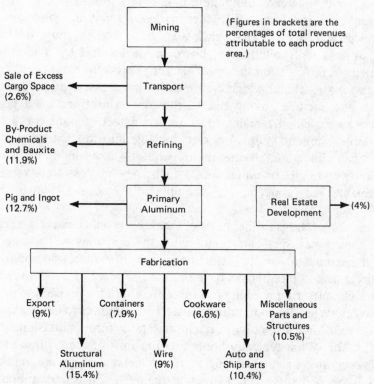

Note: Percentages for 1969 prepared by Richard Rumelt from data in company's annual reports.

See Notes section, page 379, for source.

to the *conglomerate* form and so adopts a pure diversified configuration, the one described at the beginning of this chapter. Each division serves its own markets, producing products unrelated to those of the other divisions—chinaware in one, steam shovels in a second, and so on.* The result is that the headquarters planning and control system becomes simply a vehicle for regulating performance, and the headquarters staff can diminish to almost nothing—a few general and group managers supported by a few financial analysts with a minimum of support services.

---

* I wrote this example here and in the introduction to this chapter somewhat whimsically before I encountered a firm in Finland with divisions that actually produce, among other things, the world's largest icebreaker ships and fine pottery!

SOME ISSUES ASSOCIATED WITH THE DIVERSIFIED ORGANIZATION

THE ECONOMIC ADVANTAGES OF DIVERSIFICATION?

It has been argued that the diversified configuration offers four basic advantages over the functional structure with integrated operations, namely an overall machine configuration. First, it encourages the efficient allocation of capital. Headquarters can choose where to put its money and so can concentrate on its strongest markets, milking the surpluses of some divisions to help others grow. Second, by opening up opportunities to run individual businesses, the diversified configuration helps to train general managers. Third, this configuration spreads its risk across different markets, whereas the focused machine bureaucracy has all its strategic eggs in one market basket, so to speak. Fourth, and perhaps most important, the diversified configuration is strategically responsive. The divisions can fine-tune their bureaucratic machines while the headquarters can concentrate on the strategic portfolio. It can acquire new businesses and divest itself of old, unproductive ones.

But is the single machine organization the correct basis of comparison? Is not the real alternative, at least from society's perspective, the taking of a further step along the same path, to the point of eliminating the headquarters altogether and allowing the divisions to function as independent organizations? Beatrice Foods, described in a 1976 *Fortune* magazine article, had 397 different divisions.[3] The issue is whether this arrangement was more efficient than 397 separate corporations.* In this regard, let us reconsider the four advantages discussed above.

In the diversified corporation, headquarters allocates the capital resources among the divisions. In the case of 397 independent corporations, the capital markets do that job instead. Which does it better? Studies suggest that the answer is not simple.

Some people, such as the economist Oliver Williamson, have argued that the diversified organization may do a better job of allocating money

---

* The example of Beatrice was first written as presented here in the 1970s, when the company was the subject of a good deal of attention and praise in the business press. At the time of this writing, in 1988, the company is being disassembled. It seemed appropriate to leave the example as first presented, among other reasons to question the tendency to favor fashion over investigation in the business press.

because the capital markets are inefficient.[4] Managers at headquarters who know their divisions can move the money around faster and more effectively. But others find that arrangement more costly and, in some ways, less flexible. Moyer, for example, argued early on that conglomerates pay a premium above stock market prices to acquire businesses, whereas the independent investor need pay only small brokerage fees to diversify his or her own portfolio, and can do so easier and more flexibly.[5] Moreover, that provides the investor with full information on all the businesses owned, whereas the diversified corporation provides only limited information to stockholders on the details inside its portfolio.

On the issue of management development, the question becomes whether the division managers receive better training and experience than they would as company presidents. The diversified organization is able to put on training courses and to rotate its managers to vary their experience; the independent firm is limited in those respects. But if, as the proponents of diversification claim, autonomy is the key to management development, then presumably the more autonomy the better. The division managers have a headquarters to lean on—and to be leaned on by. Company presidents, in contrast, are on their own to make their own mistakes and to learn from them.

On the third issue, risk, the argument from the diversified perspective is that the independent organization is vulnerable during periods of internal crisis or economic slump; conglomeration offers support to see individual businesses through such periods. The counter-argument, however, is that diversification may conceal bankruptcies, that ailing divisions are sometimes supported longer than necessary, whereas the market bankrupts the independent firm and is done with it. Moreover, just as diversification spreads the risk, so too does it spread the consequences of that risk. A single division cannot go bankrupt; the whole organization is legally responsible for its debts. So a massive enough problem in one division can pull down the whole organization. Loose coupling may turn out to be riskier than no coupling!

Finally, there is the issue of strategic responsiveness. Loosely coupled divisions may be more responsive than tightly coupled functions. But how responsive do they really prove to be? The answer appears to be negative: This configuration appears to inhibit, not encourage, the taking of strategic initiatives. The problem seems to lie, again, in its control system. It is designed to keep the carrot just the right distance in front of the divisional managers, encouraging them to strive for better and better financial performance. At the same time, however, it seems to dampen their inclination to innovate. It is that famous "bottom line" that creates the problem, encouraging short-term thinking and shortsightedness; attention is focused on the carrot just in front instead of the fields of vegetables beyond. As Bower has noted:

> [T]he risk to the division manager of a major innovation can be considerable if he is measured on short-run, year-to-year, earnings performance. The result is a tendency to avoid big risk bets, and the concomitant phenomenon that major new developments are, with few exceptions, made outside the major firms in the industry. Those exceptions tend to be single-product companies whose top managements are committed to true product leadership. . . . Instead, the diversified companies give us a steady diet of small incremental change.[6]

Innovation requires entrepreneurship, or intrapreneurship, and these, as we have already argued, do not thrive under the diversified configuration. The entrepreneur takes his or her own risks to earn his or her own rewards; the intrapreneur (as we shall see) functions best in the loose structure of the innovative adhocracy. Indeed, many diversified corporations depend on those configurations for their strategic responsiveness, since they diversify not by innovating themselves but by acquiring the innovative results of independent firms. Of course, that may be their role—to exploit rather than create those innovations—but we should not, as a result, justify diversification on the basis of its innovative capacity.

THE CONTRIBUTION OF HEADQUARTERS

To assess the effectiveness of conglomeration, it is necessary to assess what actual contribution the headquarters makes to the divisions. Since what the headquarters does in a diversified organization is otherwise performed by the various boards of directors of a set of independent firms, the question then becomes, what does a headquarters offer to the divisions that the independent board of directors of the autonomous organization does not?

One thing that neither can offer is the management of the individual business. Both are involved with it only on a part-time basis. The management is, therefore, logically left to the full-time managers, who have the required time and information. Among the functions a headquarters *does* perform, as noted earlier, are the establishment of objectives for the divisions, the monitoring of their performance in terms of these objectives, and the maintenance of limited personal contacts with division managers, for example to approve large capital expenditures. Interestingly, those are also the responsibilities of the directors of the individual firm, at least in theory.

In practice, however, many boards of directors—notably those of widely held corporations—do those things rather ineffectively, leaving business managements carte blanche to do what they like. Here, then, we seem to have a major advantage of the diversified configuration. It exists as an administrative mechanism to overcome another prominent weakness of the free-market system, the ineffective board.

There is a catch in this argument, however, for diversification by enhancing an organization's size and expanding its number of markets, renders the corporation more difficult to understand and so to control by its board of part-time directors. Moreover, as Moyer has noted, one common effect of conglomerate acquisition is to increase the number of shareholders, and so to make the corporation more widely held, and therefore less amenable to director control. Thus, the diversified configuration in some sense resolves a problem of its own making—it offers the control that its own existence has rendered difficult. Had the corporation remained in one business, it might have been more narrowly held and easier to understand, and so its directors might have been able to perform their functions more effectively. Diversification thus helped to create the problem that divisionalization is said to solve. Indeed, it is ironic that many a diversified corporation that does such a vigorous job of monitoring the performance of its own divisions is itself so poorly monitored by its own board of directors!

All of this suggests that large diversified organizations tend to be classic closed systems, powerful enough to seal themselves off from much external influence while able to exercise a good deal of control over not only their own divisions, as instruments, but also their external environments. For example, one study of all 5,995 directors of the Fortune 500 found that only 1.6 percent of them represented major shareholder interests,[7] while another survey of 855 corporations found that 84 percent of them did not even formally require their directors to hold any stock at all![8]

What does happen when problems arise in a division? What can a headquarters do that various boards of directors cannot? The chairman of one major conglomerate told a meeting of the New York Society of Security Analysts, in reference to the headquarters vice presidents who oversee the divisions, that "it is not too difficult to coordinate five companies that are well run."[9] True enough. But what about five that are badly run? What could the small staff of administrators at a corporation's headquarters really do to correct problems in that firm's thirty operating divisions or in Beatrice's 397? The natural tendency to tighten the control screws does not usually help once the problem has manifested itself, nor does exercising close surveillance. As noted earlier, the headquarters managers cannot manage the divisions. Essentially, that leaves them with two choices. They can either replace the division manager, or they can divest the corporation of the division. Of course, a board of directors can also replace the management. Indeed, that seems to be its only real prerogative; the management does everything else.

On balance, then, the economic case for one headquarters versus a set of separate boards of directors appears to be mixed. It should, therefore, come as no surprise that one important study found that corporations with "controlled diversity" had better profits than those with conglomerate diversity.[10] Overall, the pure diversified configuration (the conglomerate) may offer some advantages over a weak system of separate boards of directors and inefficient capital markets, but most of those advantages would probably disappear if certain problems in capital markets and boards of directors were rectified. And there is reason to argue, from a social no less than an economic standpoint, that society would be better off trying to correct fundamental inefficiencies in its economic system rather than encourage private administrative arrangements to circumvent them, as we shall now see.

THE SOCIAL PERFORMANCE OF THE PERFORMANCE CONTROL SYSTEM

This configuration requires that headquarters control the divisions primarily by quantitative performance criteria, and that typically means financial ones—profit, sales growth, return on investment, and the like. The problem is that these performance measures often become virtual obsessions in the diversified organization, driving out goals that cannot be measured—product quality, pride in work, customers well served. In effect, the economic goals drive out the social ones. As the chief of a famous conglomerate once remarked, "We, in Textron, worship the god of New Worth."[11]

That would pose no problem if the social and economic consequences of decisions could easily be separated. Governments would look after

the former, corporations the latter. But the fact is that the two are intertwined; every strategic decision of every large corporation involves both,
largely inseparable. As a result, its control systems, by focusing on
economic measures, drive the diversified organization to act in ways
that are, at best, socially unresponsive, at worst, socially irresponsible.
Forced to concentrate on the economic consequences of decisions, the
division manager is driven to ignore their social consequences.* Thus,
Bower found that "the best records in the race relations area are those
of single-product companies whose strong top managements are deeply
involved in the business."[12]

Robert Ackerman, in a study carried out at the Harvard Business
School, investigated this point. He found that social benefits such as
"a rosier public image . . . pride among managers . . . an attractive
posture for recruiting on campus" could not easily be measured and so
could not be plugged into the performance control system. The result
was that

> . . . the financial reporting system may actually inhibit social responsive-
> ness. By focusing on economic performance, even with appropriate safe-
> guards to protect against sacrificing long-term benefits, such a system
> directs energy and resources to achieving results measured in financial
> terms. It is the only game in town, so to speak, at least the only one
> with an official scoreboard.[13]

Headquarters managers who are concerned about legal liabilities or
the public relations effects of decisions, or even ones personally interested
in broader social issues, may be tempted to intervene directly in the
divisions' decision-making process to ensure proper attention to social
matters. But they are discouraged from doing so by this configuration's
strict division of labor: Divisional autonomy requires no meddling by
the headquarters in specific business decisions.

As long as the screws of the performance control system are not
turned too tight, the division managers may retain enough discretion to
consider the social consequences of their actions, if they so choose.
But when those screws are turned tight, as they often are in the diversified
corporation with a bottom-line orientation, then the division managers
wishing to keep their jobs may have no choice but to act socially unrespon-
sively, if not actually irresponsibly. As Bower has noted of the General
Electric price-fixing scandal of the 1960s, "a very severely managed
system of reward and punishment that demanded yearly improvements

---

* Indeed, that manager is also driven to ignore the intangible economic consequences
too, such as product quality or research effort, another manifestation of the problem of
the short-term, bottom-line thinking mentioned earlier.

in earnings, return and market share, applied indiscriminately to all divisions, yielded a situation which was—at the very least—conducive to collusion in the oligopolistic and mature electric equipment markets.''[14]

THE DIVERSIFIED ORGANIZATION IN THE PUBLIC SPHERE

Ironically, for a government intent on dealing with these social problems, solutions are indicated in the very arguments used to support the diversified configuration. Or so it would appear.

For example, if the administrative arrangements are efficient while the capital markets are not, then why should a government hesitate to interfere with the capital markets? And why shouldn't it use those same administrative arrangements to deal with the problems? If Beatrice Foods really can control those 397 divisions, then what is to stop Washington from believing it can control 397 Beatrices? After all, the capital markets don't much matter. In his book on ''countervailing power,'' John Kenneth Galbraith argued that bigness in one sector, such as business, promotes bigness in other sectors, such as unions and government.[15] That has already happened. How long before government pursues the logical next step and exercises direct controls?

While such steps may prove irresistible to some governments, the fact is that they will not resolve the problems of power concentration and social irresponsibility but rather will aggravate them, but not just in the ways usually assumed in Western economics. All the existing problems would simply be bumped up to another level, and there increase. By making use of the diversified configuration, government would magnify the problems of size. Moreover, government, like the corporation, would be driven to favor measurable economic goals over intangible social ones, and that would add to the problems of social irresponsibility—a phenomenon of which we have already seen a good deal in the public sector.

In fact, these problems would be worse in government, because its sphere is social, and so its goals are largely ill-suited to performance control systems. In other words, many of the goals most important for the public sector—and this applies to not-for-profit organizations in spheres such as health and education as well—simply do not lend themselves to measurement, no matter how long and how hard public officials continue to try. And without measurement, the conventional diversified configuration cannot work.

There are, of course, other problems with the application of this form of organization in the public sphere. For example, government cannot divest itself of subunits quite so easily as can corporations. And public service regulations on appointments and the like, as well as a host of other rules, preclude the degree of division manager autonomy available in the private sector. (It is, in fact, these central rules and regulations that make governments resemble integrated machine configurations as much as loosely coupled diversified ones, and that undermine their efforts at "accountability.")

Thus, we conclude that, appearances and even trends notwithstanding, the diversified configuration is generally not suited to the public and not-for-profit sectors of society. Governments and other public-type institutions that wish to divisionalize to avoid centralized machine bureaucracy may often find the imposition of performance standards an artificial exercise. They may thus be better off trying to exercise control of their units in a different way. For example, they can select unit managers who reflect their desired values, or indoctrinate them in those values, and then let them manage freely, the control in effect being normative rather than quantative (and their structure therefore a hybrid between the diversified and the missionary configurations). But as we shall see in Chapter 12, managing ideology, even creating it in the first place, is no simple matter, especially in a highly diversified organization.

IN CONCLUSION: A STRUCTURE ON THE EDGE OF A CLIFF

Our discussion has led to a "damned if you do, damned if you don't" conclusion. The pure (conglomerate) diversified configuration emerges as an organization perched symbolically on the edge of the cliff, at the end of a long path. Ahead, it is one step away from disintegration— breaking up into separate organizations on the rocks below. Behind it is the way back to a more stable integration, in the form of the machine configuration at the start of that path. And ever hovering above is the eagle, representing the broader social control of the state, attracted by the organization's position on the edge of the cliff and waiting for the chance to pull it up to a higher cliff, perhaps more dangerous still. The edge of the cliff is an uncomfortable place to be, perhaps even a temporary one that must inevitably lead to disintegration on the rocks below, a trip to that cliff above, or a return to a safer resting place somewhere on that path behind.

10
THE PROFESSIONAL ORGANIZATION

I work in a professional organization, and probably chose to do so initially because it is the one place in the world where you can act as if you were self-employed yet regularly receive a paycheck. These seemingly upside-down organizations, where the workers sometimes appear to manage the bosses, are fascinating in the way they work. As the nursery rhyme goes, when they're good, they're very, very good, but when they're bad, they're horrid. It all hinges on that fine line between collegiality (working for the common good) and politics (working for self-interest). We need professional organizations to carry out highly skilled yet highly stable tasks in society, such as replacing someone's heart or auditing a company's books. But as a society we have yet to learn how to control their excesses: professionals who mistreat their clients, professional organizations that mistreat their supporters.

The place to start, as always for me, is in understanding how they work. MIT just doesn't function like McDonald's; everyone knows that, but I suspect few people fully appreciate the differences. I begin, once again, by describing the unique structure, internal processes, and context of this configuration. Then, drawing from an article I co-authored with Cynthia Hardy, Ann Langley, and Janet Rose, I explain the very unusual ways in which the professional organization makes and changes its strategy, probing into the issue of collegiality versus politics. The chapter closes with a discussion of some of the social issues surrounding the professional organization, including a comment on the threat that I believe unionization poses for the practice of professional work.

The Professional Organization

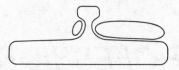

Structure: • bureaucratic yet decentralized, dependent on training to standardize the skills of its many operating professionals

• key to functioning is creation of system of pigeonholes within which individual professionals work autonomously, subject to controls of the profession

• minimal technostructure and middle-line hierarchy, meaning wide spans of control over professional work, and large support staff, more machinelike, to support the professionals

Context: • complex yet stable

• simple technical system

• often, but not necessarily, service sector

Strategy: • many strategies, largely fragmented, but forces for cohesion too

• most made by professional judgment and collective choice (collegially and politically), some by administrative fiat

• overall strategy very stable but in detail continually changing

Issues: • advantages of democracy and autonomy

but

• problems of coordination between the pigeonholes, of misuse of professional discretion, of reluctance to innovate

• public responses to these problems often dysfunctional (machinelike)

• unionization exacerbates these problems

THE BASIC STRUCTURE

An organization can be bureaucratic without being centralized. This happens when its work is complex, requiring that it be carried out and controlled by professionals, yet at the same time remains stable, so that the skills of those professionals can be perfected through standardized operating programs. The structure takes on the form of *professional* bureaucracy, which is common in universities, general hospitals, public accounting firms, social work agencies, and firms doing fairly routine engineering or craft work. All rely on the skills and knowledge of their operating professionals to function; all produce standardized products or services.

THE WORK OF THE PROFESSIONAL OPERATORS

Here again we have a tightly knit configuration of the attributes of structure. Most important, the professional organization relies for coordination on the standardization of skills, which is achieved primarily through formal training. It hires duly trained specialists—professionals—for the operating core, then gives them considerable control over their own work.

Control over their work means that professionals work relatively independently of their colleagues but closely with the clients they serve—doctors treating their own patients and accountants who maintain personal contact with the companies whose books they audit. Most of the necessary coordination among the operating professionals is then handled automatically by their set skills and knowledge—in effect, by what they have learned to expect from each other. During an operation as long and as complex as open-heart surgery, "very little needs to be said [between the anesthesiologist and the surgeon] preceding chest opening and during the procedure on the heart itself . . . [most of the operation is] performed in absolute silence."[1] The point is perhaps best made in reverse by the cartoon that shows six surgeons standing around a patient on an operating table with one saying, "Who opens?"

Just how standardized the complex work of professionals can be is illustrated in a paper read by Spencer before a meeting of the International Cardiovascular Society. Spencer notes that an important feature of surgical training is "repetitive practice" to evoke "an automatic reflex." So automatic, in fact, that this doctor keeps a series of surgical "cookbooks" in which he lists, even for "complex" operations, the essential steps as chains of thirty to forty symbols on a single sheet, to "be reviewed mentally in sixty to 120 seconds at some time during the day preceding the operation."[2]

But no matter how standardized the knowledge and skills, their complexity ensures that considerable discretion remains in their application. No two professionals—no two surgeons or engineers or social workers—ever apply them in exactly the same way. Many judgments are required.

Training, reinforced by indoctrination, is a complicated affair in the professional organization. The initial training typically takes place over a period of years in a university or special institution, during which the skills and knowledge of the profession are formally programmed into the students. There typically follows a long period of on-the-job training, such as internship in medicine or articling in accounting, where the formal knowledge is applied and the practice of skills perfected. On-the-job training also completes the process of indoctrination, which began during the formal education. As new knowledge is generated and new skills develop, of course (so it is hoped) the professional upgrades his or her expertise.

All that training is geared to one goal, the internalization of the set procedures, which is what makes the structure technically bureaucratic (structure defined earlier as relying on standardization for coordination). But the professional bureaucracy differs markedly from the machine bureaucracy. Whereas the latter generates its own standards—through its technostructure, enforced by its line managers—many of the standards of the professional bureaucracy originate outside its own structure, in the self-governing associations its professionals belong to with their colleagues from other institutions. These associations set universal standards, which they ensure are taught by the universities and are used by all the organizations practicing the profession. So whereas the machine bureaucracy relies on authority of a hierarchical nature—the power of office— the professional bureaucracy emphasizes authority of a professional nature—the power of expertise.

Other forms of standardization are, in fact, difficult to rely on in the professional organization. The work processes themselves are too complex to be standardized directly by analysts. One need only try to imagine a work-study analyst following a cardiologist on rounds or timing the activities of a teacher in a classroom. Similarly, the outputs of professional work cannot easily be measured and so do not lend themselves to standardization. Imagine a planner trying to define a cure in psychiatry, the amount of learning that takes place in a classroom, or the quality of an accountant's audit. Likewise, direct supervision and mutual adjustment cannot be relied upon for coordination, for both impede professional autonomy.

THE PIGEONHOLING PROCESS

To understand how the professional organization functions at the operating level, it is helpful to think of it as a set of standard programs—in effect, the repertoire of skills the professionals stand ready to use—that are applied to known situations, called contingencies, also standardized. As Weick notes of one case in point, "schools are in the business of building and maintaining categories."[3] The process is sometimes known as *pigeonholing*. In this regard, the professional has two basic tasks: (1) to categorize, or "diagnose," the client's need in terms of one of the contingencies, which indicates which standard program to apply, and (2) to apply, or execute, that program. For example, the management consultant carries a bag of standard acronymic tricks: MBO, MIS, LRP, OD. The client with information needs gets MIS; the one with managerial conflicts, OD. Such pigeonholing, of course, simplifies matters enormously; it is also what enables each professional to work in a relatively autonomous manner.

It is in the pigeonholing process that the fundamental differences among the machine organization, the professional organization, and the innovative organization (to be discussed next) can best be seen. The machine organization is a single-purpose structure. Presented with a stimulus, it executes its one standard sequence of programs, just as we kick when tapped on the knee. No diagnosis is involved. In the professional organization, diagnosis is a fundamental task, but one highly circumscribed. The organization seeks to match a predetermined contingency to a standardized program. Fully open-ended diagnosis—that which seeks a creative solution to a unique problem—requires the innovative form of organization. No standard contingencies or programs can be relied upon there.

THE ADMINISTRATIVE STRUCTURE

Everything we have discussed so far suggests that the operating core is the key part of the professional organization. The only other part that is fully elaborated is the support staff, but that is focused very much on serving the activities of the operating core. Given the high cost of the professionals, it makes sense to back them up with as much support as possible. Thus, universities have printing facilities, faculty clubs, alma mater funds, publishing houses, archives, libraries, computer facilities, and many, many other support units.

The technostructure and middle-line management are not highly elaborated in the professional organization. They can do little to coordinate the professional work. Moreover, with so little need for direct supervision of, or mutual adjustment among, the professionals, the operating units can be very large. For example, the McGill Faculty of Management functions effectively with fifty professors under a single manager, its dean, and the rest of the university's academic hierarchy is likewise thin.

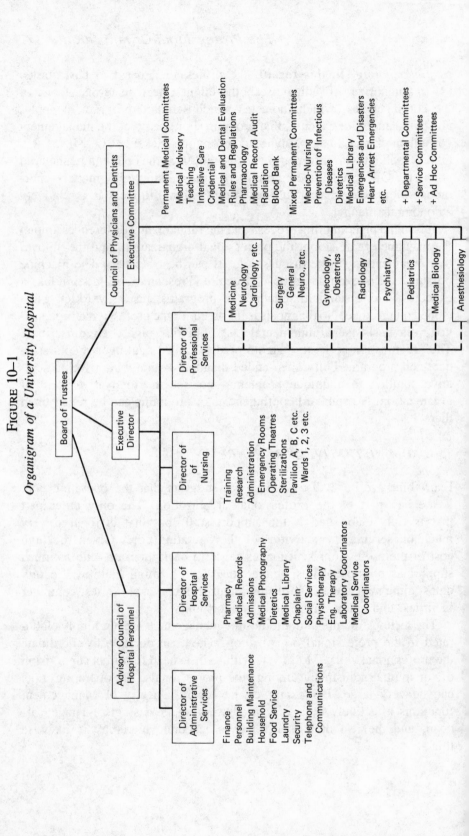

FIGURE 10–1
Organigram of a University Hospital

Thus, the diagram at the beginning of this chapter shows the professional organization, in terms of our logo, as a flat structure with a thin middle line, a tiny technostructure, but a fully elaborated support staff. All these characteristics are reflected in the organigram of a university hospital, shown in Figure 10–1.

Coordination within the administrative structure is another matter, however. Because these configurations are so decentralized, the professionals not only control their own work but they also gain much collective control over the administrative decisions that affect them—decisions, for example, to hire colleagues, to promote them, and to distribute resources. This they do partly by doing some of the administrative work themselves (most university professors, for example, sit on various administrative committees) and partly by ensuring that important administrative posts are staffed by professionals or at least sympathetic people appointed with the professionals' blessing. What emerges, therefore, is a rather democratic administrative structure. But because the administrative work requires mutual adjustment for coordination among the various people involved, task forces and especially standing committees abound at this level, as is in fact suggested in Figure 10–1.

Because of the power of their professional operators, these organizations are sometimes described as inverse pyramids, with the professional operators on top and the administrators down below to serve them—to ensure that the surgical facilities are kept clean and the classrooms well supplied with chalk. Such a description slights the power of the administrators of professional work, however, although it may be an accurate description of those who manage the support units. For the support staff—often more numerous than the professional staff, but generally less skilled—there is no democracy in the professional organization, only the oligarchy of the professionals. Such support units as housekeeping in the hospital or printing in the university are likely to be managed tightly from the top, in effect as machinelike enclaves within the professional configuration. Thus, what frequently emerges in the professional organization are parallel and separate administrative hierarchies, one democratic and bottom-up for the professionals, a second machinelike and top-down for the support staff.

THE ROLES OF THE ADMINISTRATORS
OF PROFESSIONAL WORK

Where does all this leave the administrators of the professional hierarchy, the executive directors and chiefs of the hospitals and the presidents and deans of the universities? Are they powerless? Compared with their counterparts in the entrepreneurial and machine organizations, they certainly lack a good deal of power. But that is far from the whole story. The administrator of professional work may not be able to control the professionals directly, but he or she does perform a series of roles that can provide considerable indirect power.

First, this administrator spends much time handling disturbances in the structure. The pigeonholing process is an imperfect one at best, leading to all kinds of jurisdictional disputes between the professionals. Who should perform mastectomies in the hospitals, surgeons who look after cutting or gynecologists who look after women? Seldom, however, can one administrator impose a solution on the professionals involved in a dispute. Rather, various administrators must often sit down together and negotiate a solution on behalf of their constituencies.

Second, the administrators of professional work—especially those at higher levels—serve in key roles at the boundary of the organization, between the professionals inside and the influencers outside: governments, client associations, benefactors, and so on. On the one hand, the administrators are expected to protect the professionals' autonomy, to ''buffer'' them from external pressures. On the other hand, they are expected to woo those outsiders to support the organization, both morally and financially. And that often leads the outsiders to expect these administrators, in turn, to control the professionals, in machine bureaucratic ways. Thus, the external roles of the manager—maintaining liaison contacts, acting as figurehead and spokesman in a public relations capacity, negotiating with outside agencies—emerge as primary ones in the administration of professional work.

Some view the roles these administrators are called upon to perform as signs of weakness. They see these people as the errand boys of the professionals, or else as pawns caught in various tugs of war—between one professional and another, between support staffer and professional, between outsider and professional. In fact, however, these roles are the very sources of administrators' power. Power is, after all, gained at the locus of uncertainty, and that is exactly where the administrators of professionals sit. The administrator who succeeds in raising extra funds for his or her organization gains a say in how they are distributed; the one who can reconcile conflicts in favor of his or her unit or who can effectively buffer the professionals from external influence becomes a valued, and therefore powerful, member of the organization.

We can conclude that power in these structures does flow to those professionals who care to devote effort to doing administrative instead of professional work, so long as they do it well. But that, it should be stressed, is not laissez-faire power; the professional administrator maintains power only as long as the professionals perceive him or her to be serving their interests effectively.

CONDITIONS OF THE PROFESSIONAL ORGANIZATION

The professional form of organization appears wherever the operating work of an organization is dominated by skilled workers who use procedures that are difficult to learn yet are well defined. This means a situation that is both complex and stable—complex enough to require procedures that can be learned only through extensive training yet stable enough so that their use can become standardized.

Note that an elaborate technical system can work against this configuration. If highly regulating or automated, the professionals' skills might be amenable to rationalization, in other words, to be divided into simple, highly programmed steps that would destroy the basis for professional autonomy and thereby drive the structure to the machine form. And if highly complicated, the technical system would reduce the professionals' autonomy by forcing them to work in multidisciplinary teams, thereby driving the organization toward the innovative form. Thus the surgeon uses a scalpel, and the accountant a pencil. Both must be sharp, but both are otherwise simple and commonplace instruments. Yet both allow their users to perform independently what can be exceedingly complex functions.

The prime example of the professional configuration is the personal-service organization, at least the one with complex, stable work not reliant on a fancy technical system. Schools and universities, consulting firms, law and accounting offices, and social work agencies all rely on this form of organization, more or less, so long as they concentrate not on innovating in the solution of new problems but on applying standard programs to well-defined ones. The same seems to be true of hospitals, at least to the extent that their technical systems are simple. (In those areas that call for more sophisticated equipment—apparently a growing number, especially in teaching institutions—the hospital is driven toward a hybrid structure, with characteristics of the innovative form. But this tendency is mitigated by the hospital's overriding concern with safety.

Only the tried and true can be relied upon, which produces a natural aversion to the looser innovative configuration.)

So far, our examples have come from the service sector. But the professional form can be found in manufacturing too, where the above conditions hold up. Such is the case of the craft enterprise, for example the factory using skilled workers to produce ceramic products. The very term *craftsman* implies a kind of professional who learns traditional skills through long apprentice training and then is allowed to practice them free of direct supervision. Craft enterprises seem typically to have few administrators, who tend to work, in any event, alongside the operating personnel. The same would seem to be true for engineering work oriented not to creative design so much as to modification of existing dominant designs.

STRATEGY FORMATION IN THE PROFESSIONAL ORGANIZATION

It is commonly assumed that strategies are formulated before they are implemented, that planning is the central process of formulation, and that structures must be designed to implement these strategies. At least this is what one reads in the conventional literature of strategic management. In the professional organization, these imperatives stand almost totally at odds with what really happens, leading to the conclusion either that such organizations are confused about how to make strategy, or else that the strategy writers are confused about how professional organizations must function. I subscribe to the latter explanation.

Using the definition of strategy as pattern in action, strategy formation in the professional organization takes on a new meaning. Rather than simply throwing up our hands at its resistance to formal strategic planning or, at the other extreme, dismissing professional organizations as "organized anarchies" with strategy-making processes as mere "garbage cans,"[4] we can focus on how decisions and actions in such organizations order themselves into patterns over time.

Taking strategy as pattern in action, the obvious question becomes, which actions? The key area of strategy-making in most organizations concerns the elaboration of the basic mission (the products or services offered to the public); in professional organizations, we shall argue, this is significantly controlled by individual professionals. Other important areas of strategy here include the inputs to the system (notably the choice of professional staff, the determination of clients, and the raising of external funds), the means to perform the mission (the construction of buildings and facilities, the purchase of research equipment, and so on), the structure and forms of governance (design of the committee system, the hierarchies, and so on), and the various means to support the mission.

Were professional organizations to formulate strategies in the conventional ways, central administrators would develop detailed and integrated plans about these issues. This sometimes happens, but in a very limited number of cases. Many strategic issues come under the direct control of individual professionals, while others can be decided neither by individual professionals nor by central administrators, but instead require the participation of a variety of people in a complex collective process. As illustrated in Figure 10–2, we examine in turn the decisions controlled

FIGURE 10–2
Three Levels of Decision-Making in the Professional Organization

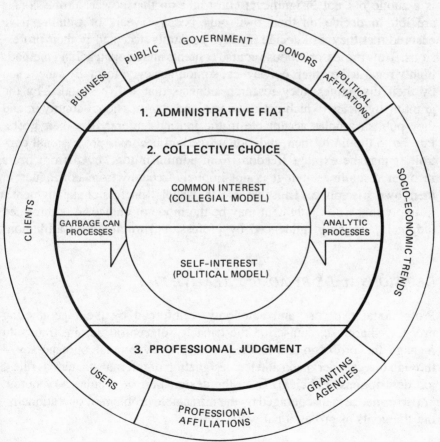

by individual professionals, by central administrators, and by the collectivity.

DECISIONS MADE BY PROFESSIONAL JUDGMENT

Professional organizations are distinguished by the fact that the determination of the basic mission—the specific services to be offered and to whom—is in good part left to the judgment of professionals as individuals. In the university, for example, each professor has a good deal of control over what is taught and how, as well as what is researched and how. Thus the overall product-market strategy of McGill University must be seen as the composite of the individual teaching and research postures of its 1,200 professors.

That, however, does not quite constitute full autonomy, because there is a subtle but not insignificant constraint on that power. Professionals are left to decide on their own only because years of training have ensured that they will decide in ways generally accepted in their professions. Thus professors choose course contents and adopt teaching methods highly regarded by their colleagues, sometimes even formally sanctioned by their disciplines; they research subjects that will be funded by the granting agencies (which usually come under professional controls); and they publish articles acceptable to the journals refereed by their peers. Pushed to the limit, then, individual freedom becomes professional control. It may be explicit freedom from administrators, even from peers in other disciplines, but it is not implicit freedom from colleagues in their own discipline. Thus we use the label "professional judgment" to imply that while judgment may be the mode of choice, it is informed judgment, mightily influenced by professional training and affiliation.

DECISIONS MADE BY ADMINISTRATIVE FIAT

Professional expertise and autonomy, reinforced by the pigeonholing process, sharply circumscribe the capacity of central administrators to manage the professionals in the ways of conventional bureaucracy— through direct supervision and the designation of internal standards (rules, job descriptions, policies). Even the designation of standards of output or performance is discouraged by the intractable problem of operationalizing the goals of professional work.

Certain types of decisions, less related to the professional work per se, do however fall into the realm of what can be called administrative fiat, in other words, become the exclusive prerogative of the administrators. They include some financial decisions, for example, to buy and sell property and embark on fundraising campaigns. Because many of the support services are organized in a conventional top-down hierarchy, they too tend to fall under the control of the central administration. Support services more critical to professional matters, however, such as libraries or computers in the universities, tend to fall into the realm of collective decision-making, where the central administrators join the professionals in the making of choices.

Central administrators may also play a prominent role in determining the procedures by which the collective process functions: what committees exist, who gets nominated to them, and so on. It is the administrators, after all, who have the time to devote to administration. This role can give skillful administrators considerable influence, however indirect, over the decisions made by others. In addition, in times of crisis administrators may acquire more extensive powers, as the professionals become more inclined to defer to leadership to resolve the issues.

DECISIONS MADE BY COLLECTIVE CHOICE

Many decisions are, however, determined neither by administrators nor by individual professionals. Instead they are handled in interactive processes that combine professionals with administrators from a variety of levels and units. Among the most important of these decisions seem to be ones related to the definition, creation, design, and discontinuation of the pigeonholes, that is, the programs and departments of various kinds. Other important decisions here include the hiring and promotion of professionals and, in some cases, budgeting and the establishment and design of the interactive procedures themselves (if they do not fall under administrative fiat).

Decision-making may be considered to involve the three phases of *identification* of the need for a decision, *development* of solutions, and *selection* of one of them. Identification seems to depend largely on individual initiative. Given the complexities of professional work and the rigidities of pigeonholing, change in this configuration is difficult to imagine without an initiating "sponsor" or "champion." Development may involve the same individual but often requires the efforts of collective task forces as well. And selection tends to be a fully interactive process, involving several layers of standing committees composed of professionals and administrators, and sometimes outsiders as well (such as government representatives). It is in this last phase that we find the full impact and complexity of mutual adjustment in the administration of professional organizations.

MODELS OF COLLECTIVE CHOICE

How do these interactive processes in fact work? Some writers have traditionally associated professional organizations with a *collegial* model, where decisions are made by a "community of individuals and groups, all of whom may have different roles and specialties, but who share common goals and objectives for the organization."[5] *Common interest* is the guiding force, and decision-making is therefore by consensus. Other writers instead propose a *political* model, in which the differences of interest groups are irreconcilable. Participants thus seek to serve their *self-interest,* and political factors become instrumental in determining outcomes.

Clearly, neither common interest nor self-interest will dominate decision processes all the time; some combination is naturally to be expected. Professionals may agree on goals yet conflict over how they should be achieved; alternatively, consensus can sometimes be achieved even where goals differ—Democrats do, after all, sometimes vote with Republicans in the U.S. Congress. In fact, we need to consider motivation, not just behavior, in order to distinguish collegiality from politics. Political success sometimes requires a collegial posture—one must cloak self-interest in the mantle of the common good. Likewise, collegial ends sometimes require political means. Thus, we should take as collegial any behavior that is *motivated* by a genuine concern for the good of the institution, and politics as any behavior driven fundamentally by self-interest (of the individual or his or her unit).

A third model that has been used to explain decision-making in universities is the *garbage can.* Here decision-making is characterized by "collections of choices looking for problems, issues and feelings looking for decision situations in which they may be aired, solutions looking for issues to which they might be an answer, and decision makers looking for work."[6] Behavior is, in other words, nonpurposeful and often random, because goals are unclear and the means to achieve them problematic.

Furthermore, participation is fluid because of the cost of time and energy. Thus, in place of the common interest of the collegial model and the self-interest of the political model, the garbage can model suggests a kind of *disinterest*.

The important question is not whether garbage can processes exist—we have all experienced them—but whether they matter. Do they apply to key issues or only to incidental ones? Of course, decisions that are not significant to anyone may well end up in the garbage can, so to speak. There is always someone with free time willing to challenge a proposal for the sake of so doing. But I have difficulty accepting that individuals to whom decisions are important do not invest the effort necessary to influence them. Thus, like common interest and self-interest, I conclude that disinterest neither dominates decision processes nor is absent from them.

Finally, *analysis* may be considered a fourth model of decision-making. Here calculation is used, if not to select the best alternative, then at least to assess the acceptability of different ones. Such an approach seems consistent with the machine configuration, where a technostructure stands ready to calculate the costs and benefits of every proposal. But, in fact, analysis figures prominently in the professional configuration too, but here carried out mostly by professional operators themselves. Rational analysis structures arguments for communication and debate and enables champions and their opponents to support their respective positions. In fact, as each side seeks to pick holes in the position of the other, the real issues are more likely to emerge.

Thus, as indicated in Figure 10–2, the important collective decisions of the professional organization seem to be most influenced by collegial and political processes, with garbage can pressures encouraging a kind of haphazardness on one side (especially for less important decisions) and analytical interventions on the other side encouraging a certain rationality (serving as an invisible hand to keep the lid on the garbage can, so to speak!).

STRATEGIES IN THE PROFESSIONAL ORGANIZATION

Thus, we find here a very different process of strategy-making, and very different resulting strategies, compared with conventional (especially machine) organizations. While it may seem difficult to create strategies in these organizations, due to the fragmentation of activity, the politics, and the garbage can phenomenon, in fact the professional organization is inundated with strategies (meaning patterning in its actions). The standardization of skills encourages patterning, as do the pigeonholing process and the professional affiliations. Collegiality promotes consistency of behavior; even politics works to resist changing existing patterns. As for the garbage can model, perhaps it just represents the unexplained variance in the system; that is, whatever is not understood looks to the outside observer like organized anarchy.

Many different people get involved in the strategy-making process here, including administrators and the various professionals, individually and collectively, so that the resulting strategies can be very fragmented (at the limit, each professional pursues his or her own product-market strategy). There are, of course, forces that encourage some overall cohesion in strategy too: the common forces of administrative fiat, the broad negotiations that take place in the collective process (for example, on new tenure regulations in a university), even the forces of habit and tradition, at the limit ideology, that can pervade a professional organization (such as hiring certain kinds of people or favoring certain styles of teaching or of surgery).

Overall, the strategies of the professional organization tend to exhibit a remarkable degree of stability. Major reorientations in strategy—''strategic revolutions''—are discouraged by the fragmentation of activity and the influence of the individual professionals and their outside associations. But at a narrower level, change is ubiquitous. Inside tiny pigeonholes, services are continually being altered, procedure redesigned, and clientele shifted, while in the collective process, pigeonholes are constantly being added and rearranged. Thus, the professional organization is, paradoxically, extremely stable at the broadest level and in a state of perpetual change at the narrowest one.

SOME ISSUES ASSOCIATED WITH THE PROFESSIONAL ORGANIZATION

The professional organization is unique among the different configurations in answering two of the paramount needs of contemporary men and women. It is democratic, disseminating its power directly to its workers (at least those lucky enough to be professional). And it provides them with extensive autonomy, freeing them even from the need to coordinate closely with their colleagues. Thus, the professional has the best of both worlds. He or she is attached to an organization yet is free to serve clients in his or her own way, constrained only by the established standards of the profession.

The result is that professionals tend to emerge as highly motivated individuals, dedicated to their work and to the clients they serve. Unlike the machine organization, which places barriers between the operator and the client, this configuration removes them, allowing a personal relationship to develop. Moreover, autonomy enables the professionals to perfect their skills free of interference, as they repeat the same complex programs time after time.

But in these same characteristics, democracy and autonomy, lie the chief problems of the professional organization. For there is no evident way to control the work, outside of that exercised by the profession itself, no way to correct deficiencies that the professionals choose to overlook. What they tend to overlook are the problems of coordination, of discretion, and of innovation that arise in these configurations.

PROBLEMS OF COORDINATION

The professional organization can coordinate effectively in its operating core only by relying on the standardization of skills. But that is a loose coordinating mechanism at best; it fails to cope with many of the needs that arise in these organizations. One need is to coordinate the work of professionals with that of support staffers. The professionals want to give the orders. But that can catch the support staffers between the vertical power of line authority and the horizontal power of professional expertise. Another need is to achieve overriding coordination among the professionals themselves. Professional organizations, at the limit, may be viewed as collections of independent individuals who come together only to draw on common resources and support services. Though the pigeonholing process facilitates this, some things inevitably fall through the cracks between the pigeonholes. But because the professional organization lacks any obvious coordinating mechanism to deal with these, they inevitably provoke a great deal of conflict. Much political blood is spilled in the continual reassessment of contingencies and programs that are either imperfectly conceived or artificially distinguished.

PROBLEMS OF DISCRETION

Pigeonholing raises another serious problem. It focuses most of the discretion in the hands of single professionals, whose complex skills, no matter how standardized, require the exercise of considerable judgment. Such discretion works fine when professionals are competent and conscientious. But it plays havoc when they are not. Inevitably, some professionals are simply lazy or incompetent. Others confuse the needs of their clients with the skills of their trade. They thus concentrate on a favored program to the exclusion of all others (like the psychiatrist who thinks that all patients, indeed all people, need psychoanalysis). Clients incorrectly sent their way get mistreated (in both senses of that word).

Various factors confound efforts to deal with this inversion of means and ends. One is that professionals are notoriously reluctant to act against their own, for example, to censure irresponsible behavior through their professional associations. Another (which perhaps helps to explain the first) is the intrinsic difficulty of measuring the outputs of professional work. When psychiatrists cannot even define the words *cure* or *healthy,* how are they to prove that psychoanalysis is better for schizophrenics than chemical therapy?

Discretion allows professionals to ignore not only the needs of their clients but also those of the organization itself. Many professionals focus their loyalty on their profession, not on the place where they happen to practice it. But professional organizations have needs for loyalty too—to support their overall strategies, to staff their administrative committees, to see them through conflicts with the professional associations. Cooperation is crucial to the functioning of the administrative structure, yet many professionals resist it furiously.

PROBLEMS OF INNOVATION

In the professional organizaton, major innovation also depends on cooperation. Existing programs may be perfected by the single professional, but new ones usually cut across the established specialties—in essence, they require a rearrangement of the pigeonholes—and so call for collective action. As a result, the reluctance of the professionals to cooperate with each other and the complexity of the collective processes can produce resistance to innovation. These are, after all, professional *bureaucracies,* in essence, performance structures designed to perfect given programs in stable environments, not problem-solving structures to create new programs for unanticipated needs.

The problems of innovation in the professional organization find their roots in convergent thinking, in the deductive reasoning of the professional who sees the specific situation in terms of the general concept. That means new problems are forced into old pigeonholes, as is excellently illustrated in Spencer's comments: "All patients developing significant complications or death among our three hospitals . . . are reported to a central office with a narrative description of the sequence of events, with reports varying in length from a third to an entire page." And six to eight of these cases are discussed in the one-hour weekly "mortality-morbidity" conferences, including presentation of it by the surgeon and "questions and comments" by the audience.[7] An "entire" page and ten minutes of discussion for a case with "significant complications"! Maybe that is enough to list the symptoms and slot them into pigeonholes. But it is hardly enough even to begin to think about creative solutions. As Lucy once told Charlie Brown, great art cannot be done in half an hour; it takes at least forty-five minutes!

The fact is that great art and innovative problem-solving require *inductive* reasoning—that is, the inference of the new general solution from the particular experience. And that kind of thinking is *divergent;* it breaks away from old routines or standards rather than perfecting existing ones. And that flies in the face of everything the professional organization is designed to do.

PUBLIC RESPONSES TO THESE PROBLEMS

What responses do the problems of coordination, discretion, and innovation evoke? Most commonly, those outside the profession see the problems as resulting from a lack of external control of the professional and the profession. So they do the obvious: try to control the work through other, more traditional means. One is direct supervision, which typically means imposing an intermediate level of supervision to watch over the professionals. But we already discussed why this cannot work for jobs that are complex. Another is to try to standardize the work or its outputs. But we also discussed why complex work cannot be formalized by rules, regulations, or measures of performance. All these types of controls really do, by transferring the responsibility for the service from the professional to the administrative structure, is destroy the effectiveness of the work. It is not the government that educates the student, not even the school system or the school itself; it is not the hospital that delivers the baby. These things are done by the individual professional. If that professional is incompetent, no plan or rule fashioned in the technostructure, no order from any administrator or government official, can ever make him or her competent. But such plans, rules, and orders can impede the competent professional from providing his or her service effectively.

Are there then no solutions for a society concerned about the performance of its professional organizations? Financial control of them and legislation against irresponsible professional behavior are obviously in order. But beyond that, solutions must grow from a recognition of professional work for what it is. Change in the professional organization does not *sweep* in from new administrators taking office to announce wide reforms, or from government officials intent on bringing the professionals under technocratic control. Rather, change *seeps* in through the slow process of changing the professionals—changing who enters the profession in the first place, what they learn in its professional schools (norms as well as skills and knowledge), and thereafter how they upgrade their skills. Where desired changes are resisted, society may be best off to call on its professionals' sense of public responsibility or, failing that, to bring pressure on the professional associations rather than on the professional bureaucracies.

A NOTE ON THE UNIONIZATION OF PROFESSIONALS

Professionals subjected to dysfunctional administrative pressures have sometimes been driven to unionization. But that, in my opinion, aggravates the problem, diminishing the quality of the professional service even further.

Much like unskilled workers, it is when professionals feel powerless that they are most inclined to unionize. Governments are often at the root of such pressures, with efforts to impose machine bureaucratic controls. That is presumably why the vast majority of faculty unions in the United States are found in the public universities. Of course, internal university administrators with the same intentions can have the same effect. Also, weak professionals may favor unionization to protect themselves from their clients and even from their more capable colleagues. In effect, they may try to use collective power to conceal the illegitimacy of their individual power. Thus, even in states with laws supporting the unionization of university faculty, the few institutions that have not been organized "include most of the largest and most prestigious schools."[8]

Probably no group of specialists has been more subjected to technocratic controls, nor has any been more prone to unionize, than that of public school systems. The controls reflect a number of factors—the high cost of education, the absence of a technical mystique in this field, the zeal of certain politicians, the callousness of certain teachers, the sensitivity of certain parents, and so on. So rules are piled on rules. Yet true education remains, as someone so aptly put it, a teacher and a pupil on a log. In other words, the process, when it works well, simply brings a competent educator face to face with a receptive student.* The role of the institution is to facilitate the exchange between these two, not to interfere with it. All manners of standards cannot make an incompetent teacher competent or a callous one responsible. They can, however, discourage the competent, responsible teacher and turn him or her to unionization.

Thus, we have a vicious circle of dysfunction. Bottom-up professional organizations are progressively transformed through increasing technocratic controls and administrative centralization into top-down machine ones; the response of the professionals is to seek unionization, which, instead of arresting the process, only accelerates it.

The key to the effective functioning of the professional organization is *individual* responsibility: the dedication of the professional to his or her client. Individual responsibility is often based on a personal working relationship between the professional and the client—the professor with the students, the physician with the patient. A subtle but crucial point must be stressed here. Professional bureaucracy may be a highly decentralized structure in which the professionals hold a good deal of the power. But they do so, first individually and then in small specialist units, but

---

* I say competent educator rather than *professional* because this example is unfortunate in one respect. In general, the professional is someone who "knows better" than his or her client. The client must therefore remain rather passive in the exchange, as does a patient operated on by a surgeon. But education is not like that, and teachers who take their professional status to mean that they must largely control the learning process—for example, through detailed curriculum design and the like—in my opinion diminish the commitment of the learner and so damage the learning process. It is for this reason that I have mixed feelings about the "professionalization" of education as well (although not about teacher autonomy).

not in one homogeneous collectivity. Professional organizations typically house all kinds of professionals, each with his or her own needs and interests.

Unionization, by blurring professional and subunit differences and by undermining *individual* control of the operating work, can seriously damage professional responsibility. It provides collective action instead, but that can never replace individual responsibility in the professional organization. Unionization can also damage another characteristic critical to the effective functioning of these organizations, a close coordination of operating and administrative efforts through the involvement of the same professionals in both. Unionization assumes a conflict of interest between these two levels. It takes a we–they attitude, which views administrators as authority figures or ''bosses'' instead of colleagues. The result is that unionization either drives a wedge between the operating core and the administrative structure or else drives an existing wedge in deeper.

More significantly, unionization diminishes the influence of professionals in the administrative structure. Unionized professionals act collectively through their representatives, who bargain with senior administrators directly, as if they were outside suppliers. The effect, ironically, is to cede control of the organization's administrative apparatus to the senior administrators, thereby centralizing power in the organization. Middle-level administrators and professionals on administrative committees are bypassed in the play of power between union representative and senior administrator. And once these wedges are driven in and held fast by collective bargaining, the likelihood of removing them becomes remote. ''Thus far, [academic] institutions once unionized have maintained their status.''[9]

Through collective bargaining, the union seeks to impose specific demands on the organization on behalf of its membership at large. But what needs do the various groups of professionals of one organization have in common? On many issues, they in fact disagree. But having to present a united front in its negotiations with the administration, the union must deny these differences and focus instead on the uniformities. And so it tends to be left with the one need the professionals have in common: remuneration in its various forms. Unionization may thus benefit the professionals on this one parochial dimension, but at a great price on some others of great importance to most of them as well, including the quality of their work and their control over it. Thus, clients may have suffered as a result of unionization, but no less than the professionals themselves, especially the most competent and responsible of these.

Note that many union demands amount to standards, in the form of rules and regulations, imposed on the entire organization—not professional standards, but machinelike ones. In other words, though ostensibly imposed on behalf of the professionals, these demands serve to formalize the structure and strengthen the senior administration, which, ironically, implements the standards negotiated by the union. Thus, the direct effect of unionization is to drive whatever is left of professional bureaucracy toward machine bureaucracy, which may be precisely opposite of the reasons professionals unionized in the first place. Everyone loses in the bargain, save a few union officials and some weak members who should never have been allowed into the profession in the first place. The other professionals would have been better off to fight through the administrative system for the reinstatement of collegiality instead.

11

THE INNOVATIVE ORGANIZATION

There is this wonderful passage in A. A. Milne's Introduction to *Win-nie-the-Pooh:*

> There are some people who begin the Zoo at the beginning, called WAYIN, and walk as quickly as they can past every cage until they get to the one called WAYOUT, but the nicest people go straight to the animal they love the most, and stay there.

Well, without claiming to be a nice person, I will admit that this is the organizational beast I love the most. Not to live there, mind you, but at least to observe it from a safe distance (the professional organization being just that, since it is the more subdued alternative for expert-type work).*

The label I use here for this configuration is the *innovative organization,* although I shall also make use of the one in my structuring book, *adhocracy.* Some people refer to this type as "high technology," and to its basic orientation as "intrapreneurship," an indication that whereas the entrepreneurial configuration innovates from a central individual at the top, this one depends on a variety of people for its strategic initiatives.

These initiatives tend to be many, because what adhocracy provides is sophisticated innovation. That comes at the price of a good deal of disruption, if not chaos, and wasted resources. As I note in the text, this type achieves its effectiveness by being *in*efficient. Perhaps that explains why it confuses many people: The innovative organization may be necessary, but it is not conventional, at least not by the standards of the traditional literature of management.

A personal anecdote might explain this best. Some time ago, I submitted an article on the different configurations to the *Harvard Business Review.* They accepted it, but the question came back,

---

* Incidentally, you might get an interesting surprise if you go back to the quotation and trace back the reference to the word "one."

"What's adhocracy?" I didn't quite understand; the description seemed clear enough. But I fixed it up a bit and sent the article back. A call came a little while later: "We're ready to go, just one last question: What's adhocracy?" "Wait a minute," I pleaded, "we've been through this already." The editor with whom I was working, Liza Collins, read through her colleagues' comments. When she came to "Is this the lack of structure?" I suddenly understood. The problem lay not with adhocracy, but with the machine organization.

To many people—especially conventional consultants and government people, as well as at least one *Harvard Business Review* editor—machine bureaucracy is not just one possible form of structure, it *is* structure. It is not the "one best way," it is the *only* way. Structure to those people means hierarchy of authority, top-down control, unity of command, detailed planning, formalization of procedure, and all the rest. Like water to the fish, these are the concepts they have swum around in for the better part of a century. Adhocracy, which violates every one of those notions, therefore looks to them like chaos, like the absence of structure.

But it is nothing of the kind. Make no mistake about it, adhocracy is structure too, in its proper context as logical and as reasonable as any other. That context is, above all, one of complexity and unpredictability. "It's all so simple, Anjin-san," was a comment in the novel *Shogun,* "just change your concept of the world." And many conventional management thinkers will have to, because a fascinating thing I found in my book on structure is that almost every major industry established since World War II relies on the innovative configuration. (One of the few important exceptions is the airline industry, which seems to be a classic machine type.) Adhocracy is the structure of *our* age.

The first part of our discussion considers structure, process, context, and then issues. The second part considers the strange ways in which these organizations form their strategies (strange, at least, to those who think the chief executive has to be the architect of strategy, and all the others "implementors"). So on to my favorite beast. But beware!

The Innovative Organization

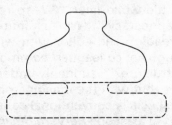

Structure: • fluid, organic, selectively decentralized, "adhocracy"
• functional experts deployed in multidisciplinary teams of staff, operators, and managers to carry out innovative projects
• coordination by mutual adjustment, encouraged by liaison personnel, integrating managers, and matrix structure

Context: • complex and dynamic environment, including high technology, frequent product change (due to severe competition), temporary and mammoth projects
• typically young due to bureaucratic pressure with aging
• common in young industries
• two basic types: operating adhocracy for contract project work, administrative adhocracy for own project work, the latter often when operating core truncated or automated

Strategy: • primarily learning, or "grassroots" process
• largely emergent, evolving through a variety of bottom-up processes, shaped rather than directed by management
• characteristic cycles of convergence and divergence in strategic focus

Issues: • combines more democracy with less bureaucracy, and so fashionable structure
• effective at innovation (an *extra*ordinary configuration)
     but
• effectiveness achieved at the price of inefficiency
• also human problems of ambiguity and dangers of inappropriate transition to another configuration

---

None of the configurations so far discussed is capable of sophisticated innovation, the kind required of a high-technology research organization, an avant-garde film company, or a factory manufacturing complex prototypes. The entrepreneurial organization can certainly innovate, but only in relatively simple ways. The machine and professional organizations are performance, not problem-solving types, designed to perfect standardized programs, not to invent new ones. And although the diversified organization resolves some problem of strategic inflexibility found in the machine organization, as noted earlier it too is not a true innovator. A focus on control by standardizing outputs does not encourage innovation.

Sophisticated innovation requires a very different configuration, one that is able to fuse experts drawn from different disciplines into smoothly functioning ad hoc project teams. To borrow the word coined by Bennis and Slater in 1964 and later popularized in Alvin Toffler's *Future Shock,* these are the *adhocracies* of our society.[1]

THE BASIC STRUCTURE

Here again we have a distinct configuration of the attributes of design: highly organic structure, with little formalization of behavior; specialized jobs based on expert training; a tendency to group the specialists in functional units for housekeeping purposes but to deploy them in small project teams to do their work; a reliance on teams, on task forces, and on integrating managers of various sorts in order to encourage mutual adjustment, the key mechanism of coordination, within and between these teams; and considerable decentralization to and within these teams, which are located at various places in the organization and involve various mixtures of line managers and staff and operating experts.

To innovate means to break away from established patterns. Thus the innovative organization cannot rely on any form of standardization for coordination. In other words, it must avoid all the trappings of bureaucratic structure, notably sharp divisions of labor, extensive unit differentiation, highly formalized behaviors, and an emphasis on planning and control systems. Above all, it must remain flexible. A search for organigrams to illustrate this description elicited the following response from one corporation thought to have an adhocracy structure: "[W]e would prefer not to supply an organization chart, since it would change too quickly to serve any useful purpose." Of all the configurations, this one shows the least reverence for the classical principles of management, especially unity of command. Information and decision processes flow flexibly and informally, wherever they must, to promote innovation. And that means overriding the chain of authority if need be.

The entrepreneurial configuration also retains a flexible, organic structure, and so is likewise able to innovate. But that innovation is restricted to simple situations, ones easily comprehended by a single leader. Innovation of the sophisticated variety requires another kind of flexible structure, one that can draw together different forms of expertise. Thus the adhocracy must hire and give power to experts, people whose knowledge and skills have been highly developed in training programs. But unlike the professional organization, the adhocracy cannot rely on the standardized skills of its experts to achieve coordination, because that would discourage innovation. Rather, it must treat existing knowledge and skills as bases on which to combine and build new ones. Thus the adhocracy must break through the boundaries of conventional specialization and differentiation, which it does by assigning problems not to individual experts in preestablished pigeonholes but to multidisciplinary teams that merge their efforts. Each team forms around one specific project.

Despite organizing around market-based projects, the organization must still support and encourage particular types of specialized expertise. And so the adhocracy tends to use a matrix structure: Its experts are grouped in functional units for specialized housekeeping purposes—hiring, training, professional communication, and the like—but are then deployed in the project teams to carry out the basic work of innovation.

As for coordination in and between these project teams, as noted earlier standardization is precluded as a significant coordinating mechanism. The efforts must be innovative, not routine. So, too, is direct supervision precluded because of the complexity of the work: Coordination must be accomplished by those with the knowledge, namely the experts themselves, not those with just authority. That leaves just one of our coordinating mechanisms, mutual adjustment, which we consider foremost in adhocracy. And, to encourage this, the organization makes use of a whole set of liaison devices, liaison personnel and integrating managers of all kinds, in addition to the various teams and task forces.

The result is that managers abound in the adhocracy: functional managers, integrating managers, project managers. The last-named are particularly numerous, since the project teams must be small to encourage mutual adjustment among their members, and each, of course, needs a designated manager. The consequence is that "spans of control" found in adhocracy tend to be small. But the implication of this is misleading, because the term is suited to the machine, not the innovative configuration: The managers of adhocracy seldom "manage" in the usual sense of giving orders; instead, they spend a good deal of time acting in a liaison capacity, to coordinate the work laterally among the various teams and units.

With its reliance on highly trained experts, the adhocracy emerges as highly decentralized, in the "selective" sense. That means power over its decisions and actions is distributed to various places and at various levels according to the needs of the particular issue. In effect, power flows to wherever the relevent expertise happens to reside—among managers or specialists (or teams of those) in the line structure, the staff units, and the operating core.

To proceed with our discussion and to elaborate on how the innovative organization makes decisions and forms strategies, we need to distinguish two basic forms that it takes.

THE OPERATING ADHOCRACY

The *operating adhocracy* innovates and solves problems directly on behalf of its clients. Its multidisciplinary teams of experts often work under contract, as in the think-tank consulting firm, creative advertising agency, or manufacturer of engineering prototypes.

In fact, for every operating adhocracy, there is a corresponding professional bureaucracy, one that does similar work but with a narrower orientation. Faced with a client problem, the operating adhocracy engages in creative efforts to find a novel solution; the professional bureaucracy pigeonholes it into a known contingency to which it can apply a standard program. One engages in divergent thinking aimed at innovation, the other in convergent thinking aimed at perfection. Thus, one theater company might seek out new avant-garde plays to perform, while another might perfect its performance of Shakespeare year after year.

A key feature of the operating adhocracy is that its administrative and operating work tend to blend into a single effort. That is, in ad hoc project work it is difficult to separate the planning and design of the work from its execution. Both require the same specialized skills, on a project-by-project basis. Thus it can be difficult to distinguish the middle levels of the organization from its operating core, since line managers and staff specialists may take their place alongside operating specialists on the project teams.

Figure 11–1 shows the organigram of the National Film Board of Canada, a classic operating adhocracy (even though it does produce a chart—one that changes frequently, it might be added). The Board is an agency of the Canadian federal government and produces mostly short films, many of them documentaries. At the time of this organigram, the characteristics of adhocracy were particularly in evidence: It shows a large number of support units as well as liaison positions (for example,

FIGURE 11–1
The National Film Board of Canada: An Operating Adhocracy
(circa 1975; used with permission)

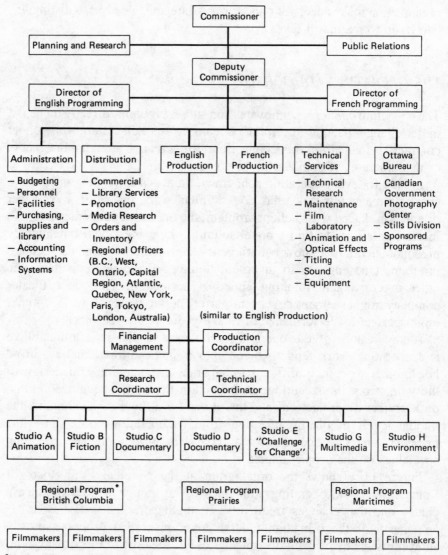

*No lines shown on original organigram connecting Regional Programs to Studios or Filmmakers.

research, technical, and production coordinators), with the operating core containing loose concurrent functional and market groupings, the latter by region as well as by type of film produced and, as can be seen, some not even connected to the line hierarchy!

THE ADMINISTRATIVE ADHOCRACY

The second type of adhocracy also functions with project teams, but toward a different end. Whereas the operating adhocracy undertakes projects to serve its clients, the *administrative adhocracy* undertakes projects to serve itself, to bring new facilities or activities on line, as in the administrative structure of a highly automated company. And in sharp contrast to the operating adhocracy, the administrative adhocracy makes a clear distinction between its administrative component and its operating core. That core is *truncated*—cut right off from the rest of the organization—so that the administrative component that remains can be structured as an adhocracy.

This truncation may take place in a number of ways. First, when the operations have to be machinelike and so could impede innovation in the administration (because of the associated need for control), it may be established as an independent organization. Second, the operating core may be done away with altogether—in effect, contracted out to other organizations. That leaves the organization free to concentrate on the development work, as did NASA during the Apollo project. A third form of truncation arises when the operating core becomes automated. This enables it to run itself, largely independent of the need for direct controls from the administrative component, leaving the latter free to structure itself as an adhocracy to bring new facilities on line or to modify old ones.

Oil companies, because of the high degree of automation of their production process, are in part at least drawn toward administrative adhocracy. Figure 11–2 shows the organigram for one oil company, reproduced exactly as presented by the company (except for modifications to mask its identity, done at the company's request). Note the domination of "Administration and Services," shown at the bottom of the chart; the operating functions, particularly "Production," are lost by comparison. Note also the description of the strategic apex in terms of standing committees instead of individual executives.

FIGURE 11–2

Organigram of an Oil Company: An Administrative Adhocracy

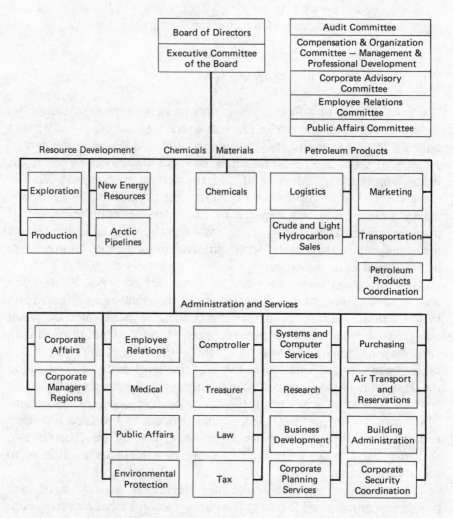

THE ADMINISTRATIVE COMPONENT OF THE ADHOCRACIES

The important conclusion to be drawn from this discussion is that in both types of adhocracy the relation between the operating core and the administrative component is unlike that in any other configuration. In the administrative adhocracy, the operating core is truncated and becomes a relatively unimportant part of the organization; in the operating adhocracy, the two merge into a single entity. Either way, the need for traditional direct supervision is diminished, so managers derive their influence more from their expertise and interpersonal skills than from formal position. And that means the distinction between line and staff blurs. It no longer makes sense to distinguish those who have the formal power to decide from those who have only the informal right to advise. Power over decision-making in the adhocracy flows to anyone with the required expertise, regardless of position.

In fact, the support staff plays a key role in adhocracy, because that is where many of the experts reside (especially in administrative adhocracy). As suggested above, however, that staff is not sharply differentiated from the other parts of the organization, not off to one side, to speak only when spoken to, as in the bureaucratic configurations. The other type of staff, however, the technostructure, is less important here, because the adhocracy does not rely for coordination on standards that it develops. Technostructure analysts may, of course, be used for some action planning and other forms of analysis—marketing research and economic forecasting, for example—but these analysts are as likely to take their place alongside the other specialists on the project teams as to stand back and design systems to control them.

To summarize, the administrative component of the adhocracy emerges as an organic mass of line managers and staff experts, combined with operators in the operating adhocracy, working together in ever shifting relationships on ad hoc projects. Our logo figure at the start of this chapter shows adhocracy with its parts mingled together in one amorphous mass in the middle. In the operating adhocracy, that mass includes the middle line, support staff, technostructure, and operating core. Of these, the administrative adhocracy excludes just the operating core, which is truncated, as shown by the dotted section below the central mass. The reader will also note that the strategic apex of the figure is shown partly merged into the central mass as well, for reasons we shall present in our discussion of strategy formation.

THE ROLES OF THE STRATEGIC APEX

The top managers of the strategic apex of this configuration do not spend much time formulating explicit strategies (as we shall see). But they must spend a good deal of their time in the battles that ensue over strategic choices and in handling the many other disturbances that arise all over these fluid structures. The innovative configuration combines fluid working arrangements with power based on expertise, not authority. Together those breed aggressiveness and conflict. But the job of the managers here, at all levels, is not to bottle up that aggression and conflict so much as to channel them to productive ends. Thus, the managers of adhocracy must be masters of human relations, able to use persuasion, negotiation, coalition, reputation, and rapport to fuse the individualistic experts into smoothly functioning teams.

Top managers must also devote a good deal of time to monitoring the projects. Innovative project work is notoriously difficult to control. No MIS can be relied upon to provide complete, unambiguous results. So there must be careful personal monitoring of projects to ensure that they are completed according to specifications, on schedule and within budget (or, more likely, not excessively late and not too far in excess of cost estimates).

Perhaps the most important single role of the top management of this configuration (especially the operating adhocracy form) is liaison with the external environment. The other configurations tend to focus their attention on clearly defined markets and so are more or less assured of a steady flow of work. No so the operating adhocracy, which lives from project to project and disappears when it can find no more. Since each project is different, the organization can never be sure where the next one will come from. So the top managers must devote a great deal of their time to ensuring a steady and balanced stream of incoming projects. That means developing liaison contacts with potential customers and negotiating contracts with them. Nowhere is this more clearly illustrated than in the consulting business, particularly where the approach is innovative. When a consultant becomes a partner in one of these firms, he or she normally hangs up the calculator and becomes virtually a full-time salesperson. It is a distinguishing characteristic of many an operating adhocracy that the selling function literally takes place at the strategic apex.

Project work poses related problems in the administrative adhocracy. Reeser asked a group of managers in three aerospace companies, "What are some of the human problems of project management?" Among the common answers: "[M]embers of the organization who are displaced because of the phasing out of [their] work . . . may have to wait a long time before they get another assignment at as high a level of responsibility" and "the temporary nature of the organization often necessitates 'make work' assignments for [these] displaced members."[2] Thus senior managers must again concern themselves with a steady flow of projects, although in this case, internally generated.

CONDITIONS OF THE INNOVATIVE ORGANIZATION

This configuration is found in environments that are both dynamic and complex. A dynamic environment, being unpredictable, calls for organic structure; a complex one calls for decentralized structure. This configuration is the only type that provides both. Thus we tend to find the innovative organization wherever these conditions prevail, ranging from guerrilla warfare to space agencies. There appears to be no other way to fight a war in the jungle or to put the first man on the moon.

As we have noted for all the configurations, organizations that prefer particular structures also try to "choose" environments appropriate to them. This is especially clear in the case of the operating adhocracy. Advertising agencies and consulting firms that prefer to structure themselves as professional bureaucracies seek out stable environments; those that prefer the innovative form find environments that are dynamic, where the client needs are difficult and unpredictable.*

A number of organizations are drawn toward this configuration because of the dynamic conditions that result from very frequent product change. The extreme case is the unit producer, the manufacturing firm that custom-makes each of its products to order, as in the engineering company that produces prototypes or the fabricator of extremely expensive machinery. Because each customer order constitutes a new project, the organization is encouraged to structure itself as an operating adhocracy.

Some manufacturers of consumer goods operate in markets so competitive that they must be constantly changing their product offerings, even though each product may itself be mass-produced. A company that records rock music would be a prime example, as would some cosmetic and

---

* I like to tell a story of the hospital patient with an appendix about to burst who presents himself to a hospital organized as an adhocracy: "Who wants to do another appendectomy? We're into livers now," as they go about exploring new procedures. But the patient returning from a trip to the jungle with a rare tropical disease had better beware of the hospital organized as a professional bureaucracy. A student came up to me after I once said this and explained how hospital doctors puzzled by her bloated stomach and not knowing what to do took out her appendix. Luckily, her problem resolved itself, some time later.

pharmaceutical companies. Here again, dynamic conditions, when coupled with some complexity, drive the organization toward the innovative configuration, with the mass production operations truncated to allow for adhocracy in product development.

Youth is another condition often associated with this type of organization. That is because it is difficult to sustain any structure in a state of adhocracy for a long period—to keep behaviors from formalizing and thereby discouraging innovation. All kinds of forces drive the innovative configuration to bureaucratize itself as it ages. On the other hand, young organizations prefer naturally organic structures, since they must find their own ways and tend to be eager to innovate. Unless they are entrepreneurial, they tend to become intrapreneurial.

The operating adhocracy is particularly prone to a short life, since it faces a risky market which can quickly destroy it. The loss of one major contract can literally close it down overnight. But if some operating adhocracies have short lives because they fail, others have short lives because they succeed. Success over time encourages metamorphosis, driving the organization toward a more stable environment and a more bureaucratic structure. As it ages, the successful organization develops a reputation for what it does best. That encourages it to repeat certain activities, which may suit the employees who, themselves aging, may welcome more stability in their work. So operating adhocracy is driven over time toward professional bureaucracy to perfect the activities it does best, perhaps even toward the machine bureaucracy to exploit a single invention. The organization survives, but the configuration dies.

Administrative adhocracies typically live longer. They, too, feel the pressures to bureaucratize as they age, which can lead them to stop innovating or else to innovate in stereotyped ways and thereby to adopt bureaucratic structure. But this will not work if the organization functions in an industry that requires sophisticated innovation from all its participants. Since many of the industries where administrative adhocracies are found do, organizations that survive in them tend to retain this configuration for long periods.

In recognition of the tendency for organizations to bureaucratize as they age, a variant of the innovative configuration has emerged—"the organizational equivalent of paper dresses or throw-away tissues"[3]— which might be called the "temporary adhocracy." It draws together specialists from various organizations to carry out a project, and then it disbands. Temporary adhocracies are becoming increasingly common in modern society: the production group that performs a single play, the election campaign committee that promotes a single candidate, the guerrilla group that overthrows a single government, the Olympic committee that plans a single games. Related is what can be called the "mammoth project adhocracy," a giant temporary adhocracy that draws on thousands of experts for a number of years to carry out a single major task, the Manhattan Project of World War II being one famous example.

Sophisticated and automated technical systems also tend to drive organizations toward the administrative adhocracy. When an organization's technical system is sophisticated, it requires an elaborate, highly trained support staff, working in teams, to design or purchase, modify, and maintain the equipment. In other words, complex machinery requires specialists who have the knowledge, power, and flexible working arrangements to cope with it, which generally requires the organization to structure itself as an adhocracy.

Automation of a technical system can evoke even stronger forces in the same direction. That is why a machine organization that succeeds in automating its operating core tends to undergo a dramatic metamorphosis. The problem of motivating bored workers disappears, and with it goes the control mentality that permeates the structure; the distinction between line and staff blurs (machines being indifferent to who turns their knobs), which leads to another important reduction in conflict; the technostructure loses its influence, since control is built into the machinery by its own designers rather than having to be imposed on workers by the standards of the analysts. Overall, then, the administrative structure becomes more decentralized and organic, emerging as an adhocracy. Of course, for automated organizations with simple technical systems (as in the production of hand creams), the entrepreneurial configuration may suffice instead of the innovative one.

Fashion is most decidedly another condition of the innovative configuration. Every one of its characteristics is very much in vogue today: emphasis on expertise, organic structure, project teams, task forces, decentralization of power, matrix structure, sophisticated technical systems, automation, and young organizations. Thus, if the entrepreneurial and machine forms were earlier configurations, and the professional and the diversified forms yesterday's, then the innovative is clearly today's.

This is the configuration for a population growing ever better educated and more specialized, yet under constant encouragement to adopt the "systems" approach—to view the world as an integrated whole instead of a collection of loosely coupled parts. It is the configuration for environments that are becoming more complex and more insistent on innovation, and for technical systems that are growing more sophisticated and more highly automated. It is the only configuration among our types appropriate for those who believe organizations must become at the same time more democratic and less bureaucratic.

Yet despite our current infatuation with it, adhocracy is not the structure for all organizations. Like all the others, it too has its place. And that place, as our examples make clear, seems to be in the new industries of our age—aerospace, electronics, think-tank consulting, research, advertising, filmmaking, petrochemicals—virtually all of which experienced their greatest development since World War II. The innovative adhocracy appears to be the configuration for the industries of the last half of the twentieth century.

STRATEGY FORMATION IN THE INNOVATIVE ORGANIZATION

The structure of the innovative organization may seem unconventional, but its strategy-making is even more so, upsetting virtually everything we have been taught to believe about that process.

Because the innovative organization must respond continuously to a complex, unpredictable environment, it cannot rely on deliberate strategy. In other words, it cannot predetermine precise patterns in its activities and then impose them on its work through some kind of formal planning process. Rather, many of its actions must be decided upon individually, according to the needs of the moment. It proceeds incrementally; to use Charles Lindblom's words, it prefers "continual nibbling" to a "good bite."[4]

Here, then, the process is best thought of as strategy *formation,* because strategy is not formulated consciously in one place so much as formed implicitly by the specific actions taken in many places. That is why action planning cannot be extensively relied upon in these organizations: Any process that separates thinking from action—planning from execution, formalization from implementation—would impede the flexibility of the organization to respond creatively to its dynamic environment.

STRATEGY FORMATION IN THE OPERATING ADHOCRACY

In the operating adhocracy, a project organization never quite sure what it will do next, the strategy never really stabilizes totally but is responsive to new projects, which themselves involve the activities of a whole host of people. Take the example of the National Film Board. Among its most important strategies are those related to the content of the hundred or so mostly short, documentary-type films that it makes each year. Were the Board structured as a machine bureaucracy, the word on what films to make would come down from on high. Instead, when we studied it some years ago, proposals for new films were submitted to a standing committee, which included elected filmmakers, marketing people, and the heads of production and programming—in other words, operators, line managers, and staff specialists. The chief executive had to approve the committee's choices, and usually did, but the vast majority of the proposals were initiated by the filmmakers and the executive producers lower down. Strategies formed as themes developed among these individual proposals. The operating adhocracy's strategy thus evolves continuously as all kinds of such decisions are made, each leaving its imprint on the strategy by creating a precedent or reinforcing an existing one.

STRATEGY FORMATION IN THE ADMINISTRATIVE ADHOCRACY

Similar things can be said about the administrative adhocracy, although the strategy-making process is slightly neater there. That is because the organization tends to concentrate its attention on fewer projects, which involve more people. NASA's Apollo project, for example, involved most of its personnel for almost ten years.

Administrative adhocracies also need to give more attention to action planning, but of a loose kind—to specify perhaps the ends to be reached while leaving flexibility to work out the means en route. Again, therefore, it is only through the making of specific decisions—namely, those that determine which projects are undertaken and how these projects unfold—that strategies can evolve.

STRATEGIES NONETHELESS

With their activities so disjointed, one might wonder whether adhocracies (of either type) can form strategies (that is, patterns) at all. In fact, they do, at least at certain times.

At the Film Board, despite the little direction from the management, the content of films did converge on certain clear themes periodically and then diverge, in remarkably regular cycles. In the early 1940s, there was a focus on films related to the war effort. After the war, having lost that raison d'être as well as its founding leader, the Board's films went off in all directions. They converged again in the mid-1950s around series of films for television, but by the late 1950s were again diverging widely. And in the mid-1960s and again in the early 1970s (with a brief period of divergence in between), the Board again showed a certain degree of convergence, this time on the themes of social commentary and experimentation.

This habit of cycling in and out of focus is quite unlike what takes place in the other configurations. In the machine organization especially, and somewhat in the entrepreneurial one, convergence proves much stronger and much longer (recall Volkswagenwerk's concentration on the Beetle for twenty years), while divergence tends to be very brief. The machine organization, in particular, cannot tolerate the ambiguity of change and so tries to leap from one strategic orientation to another. The innovative organization, in contrast, seems not only able to function at times without strategic focus, but positively to thrive on it. Perhaps that is the way it keeps itself innovative—by periodically cleansing itself of some of its existing strategic baggage.

THE VARIED STRATEGIES OF ADHOCRACY

Where do the strategies of adhocracy come from? While some may be imposed deliberately by the central management (as in staff cuts at the Film Board), most seem to emerge in a variety of other ways (mentioned back in Chapter 2).

In some cases, a single ad hoc decision sets a precedent which evokes a pattern. That is how the National Film Board got into making series of films for television. While a debate raged over the issue, with management hesitant, one filmmaker slipped out and made one such series, and when many of his colleagues quickly followed suit, the organization suddenly found itself deeply, if unintentionally, committed to a major new strategy. It was, in effect, a strategy of spontaneous but implicit consensus on the part of its operating employees. In another case, even the initial precedent-setting decision wasn't deliberate. One film inadvertently ran longer than expected, it had to be distributed as a feature, the first for the organization, and as some other filmmakers took advantage of the precedent, a feature film strategy emerged.

Sometimes a strategy will be pursued in a pocket of an organization (perhaps in a clandestine manner, in a so-called "skunkworks"), which then later becomes more broadly organizational when the organization, in need of change and casting about for new strategies, siezes upon it. Some salesman has been pursuing a new market, or some engineer has developed a new product, and is ignored until the organization has need for some fresh strategic thinking. Then it finds it, not in the vision of its leaders or the procedures of its planners, not elsewhere in its industry, but hidden in the bowels of its own operations, developed through the learning of its workers.

What then becomes the role of the leadership of the innovative configuration in making strategy? If it cannot impose deliberate strategies, what does it do? The answer is that it manages patterns, seeking partial control over strategies but otherwise attempting to influence what happens to those strategies that do emerge lower down.

These are the organizations in which, as noted earlier in this book, trying to manage strategy is a little like trying to drive an automobile without having your hands on the steering wheel. You can accelerate and brake but cannot determine direction. But there do remain important forms of control. First the leaders can manage the *process* of strategy-making if not the content of strategy. In other words, they can set up the structures to encourage certain kinds of activities and hire the people who themselves will carry out these activities. Second, they can provide general guidelines for strategy—what we have called *umbrella* strategies—seeking to define certain boundaries outside of which the specific patterns developed below should not stray. Then they can watch the patterns that do emerge and use the umbrella to decide which to encourage and which to discourage, remembering, however, that the umbrella can be shifted too.

A GRASSROOTS MODEL OF STRATEGY FORMATION

We can summarize this discussion in terms of a "grassroots" model of strategy formation, comprising six points.

1. Strategies grow initially like weeds in a garden, they are not cultivated like tomatoes in a hothouse. In other words, the process of strategy formation can be overmanaged; sometimes it is more important to let patterns emerge than to force an artificial consistency upon an organization prematurely. The hothouse, if needed, can come later.

2. These strategies can take root in all kinds of places, virtually anywhere people have the capacity to learn and the resources to support that capacity. Sometimes an individual or unit in touch with a particular opportunity creates his, her, or its own pattern. This may happen inadvertently, when an initial action sets a precedent. Even senior managers can fall into strategies by experimenting with ideas until they converge on something that works (though the final result may appear to the observer to have been deliberately designed). At other times, a variety of actions converge on a strategic theme through the mutual adjustment of various people, whether gradually or spontaneously. And then the external environment can impose a pattern on an unsuspecting organization. The point is that organizations cannot always plan where their strategies will emerge, let alone plan the strategies themselves.

3. Such strategies become organizational when they become collective, that is, when the patterns proliferate to pervade the behavior of the organization at large. Weeds can proliferate and encompass a whole garden; then the conventional plants may look out of place. Likewise, emergent strategies can sometimes displace the existing deliberate ones. But, of course, what is a weed but a plant that wasn't expected? With a change of perspective, the emergent strategy, like the weed, can become what is valued (just as Europeans enjoy salads of the leaves of America's most notorious weed, the dandelion!).

4. The processes of proliferation may be conscious but need not be; likewise they may be managed but need not be. The processes by which the initial patterns work their way through the organization need not be consciously intended, by formal leaders or even informal ones. Patterns may simply spread by collective action, much as plants proliferate themselves. Of course, once strategies are recognized as valuable, the processes by which they proliferate can be managed, just as plants can be selectively propagated.

5. *New strategies, which may be emerging continuously, tend to pervade the organization during periods of change, which punctuate periods of more integrated continuity.* Put more simply, organizations, like gardens, may accept the biblical maxim of a time to sow and a time to reap (even though they can sometimes reap what they did not mean to sow). Periods of convergence, during which the organization exploits its prevalent, established strategies, tend to be interrupted periodically by periods of divergence, during which the organization experiments with and subsequently accepts new strategic themes. The blurring of the separation between these two types of periods may have the same effect on an organization that the blurring of the separation between sowing and reaping has on a garden—the destruction of the system's productive capacity.

6. *To manage this process is not to preconceive strategies but to recognize their emergence and intervene when appropriate.* A destructive weed, once noticed, is best uprooted immediately. But one that seems capable of bearing fruit is worth watching, indeed sometimes even worth building a hothouse around. To manage in this context is to create the climate within which a wide variety of strategies can grow (to establish flexible structures, develop appropriate processes, encourage supporting ideologies, and define guiding "umbrella" strategies) and then to watch what does in fact come up. The strategic initiatives that do come "up" may in fact originate anywhere, although often low down in the organization, where the detailed knowledge of products and markets resides. (In fact, to be successful in some organizations, these initiatives must be recognized by middle-level managers and "championed" by combining them with each other or with existing strategies before promoting them to the senior management.) In effect, the management encourages those initiatives that appear to have potential, otherwise it discourages them. But it must not be too quick to cut off the unexpected: Sometimes it is better to pretend not to notice an emerging pattern to allow it more time to unfold. Likewise, there are times when it makes sense to shift or enlarge an umbrella to encompass a new pattern—in other words, to let the organization adapt to the initiative rather than vice versa. Moreover, a management must know when to resist change for the sake of internal efficiency and when to promote it for the sake of external adaptation. In other words, it must sense when to exploit an established

crop of strategies and when to encourage new strains to displace them. It is the excesses of either—failure to focus (running blind) or failure to change (bureaucratic momentum)—that most harms organizations.

I call this a "grassroots" model because the strategies grow up from the base of the organization, rooted in the solid earth of its operations rather than the ethereal abstractions of its administration. (Even the strategic initiatives of the senior management itself are in this model rooted in its tangible involvement with the operations.)

Of course, the model is overstated. But no more so than the more widely accepted deliberate one, which we might call the "hothouse" model of strategy formulation. Management theory must encompass both, perhaps more broadly labeled the *learning* model and the *planning* model, as well as a third, the *visionary* model.

I have discussed the learning model under the innovative configuration, the planning model under the machine configuration, and the visionary model under the entrepreneurial configuration. But in truth, all organizations need to mix these approaches in various ways at different times in their development. For example, our discussion of strategic change in the machine organization concluded, in effect, that they had to revert to the learning model for revitalization and the visionary model for turnaround. Of course, the visionary leader must learn, as must the learning organization evolve a kind of strategic vision, and both sometimes need planning to program the strategies they develop. And overall, no organization can function with strategies that are always and purely emergent; that would amount to a complete abdication of will and leadership, not to mention conscious thought. But none can function either with strategies that are always and purely deliberate; that would amount to an unwillingness to learn, a blindness to whatever is unexpected.

ENVIRONMENT TAKING PRECEDENCE IN THE INNOVATIVE ORGANIZATION

To conclude our discussion of strategy formation, as shown in Figure 11–3, in the innovative configuration it is the environment that takes precedence. It drives the organization, which responds continuously and eclectically, but does nevertheless achieve convergence during certain periods.* The formal leadership seeks somehow to influence both sides

---

* We might take this convergence as the expression of an "organization's mind"—the focusing on a strategic theme as a result of the mutual adjustments among its many actors.

FIGURE 11–3
Environment Taking the Lead in Adhocracy

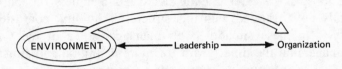

in this relationship, negotiating with the environment for support and attempting to impose some broad general (umbrella) guidelines on the organization.

If the strategist of the entrepreneurial organization is largely a concept attainer and that of the machine organization largely a planner, then the strategist of the innovative organization is largely a *pattern recognizer*, seeking to detect emerging patterns within and outside the strategic umbrella. Then strategies deemed unsuitable can be discouraged while those that seem appropriate can be encouraged, even if that means moving the umbrella. Here, then, we may find the curious situation of leadership changing its intentions to fit the realized behavior of its organization. But that is curious only in the perspective of traditional management theory.

SOME ISSUES ASSOCIATED WITH THE INNOVATIVE ORGANIZATION

Three issues associated with the innovative configuration merit attention here: its ambituities and the reactions of people who must live with them, its inefficiencies, and its propensity to make inappropriate transitions to other configurations.

HUMAN REACTIONS TO AMBIGUITY

Many people, especially creative ones, dislike both structural rigidity and the concentration of power. That leaves them only one configuration, the innovative, which is both organic and decentralized. Thus they find it a great place to work. In essence, adhocracy is the only structure for people who believe in more democracy with less bureaucracy.

But not everyone shares those values (not even everyone who professes to). Many people need order, and so prefer the machine or professional type of organization. They see adhocracy as a nice place to visit but no place to spend a career. Even dedicated members of adhocracies periodically get frustrated with this structure's fluidity, confusion, and ambiguity. "In these situations, all managers some of the time and many managers all the time, yearn for more definition and structure."[5] The managers of innovative organizations report anxiety related to the eventual phase-out of projects; confusion as to who their boss is, whom to impress to get promoted; a lack of clarity in job definitions, authority relationships, and lines of communication; and intense competition for resources, recognition, and rewards.[6] This last point suggests another serious problem of ambiguity here, the politicization of these configurations. Combining its ambiguities with its interdependencies, the innovative form can emerge as a rather politicized and ruthless organization— supportive of the fit, as long as they remain fit, but destructive of the weak.

PROBLEMS OF EFFICIENCY

No configuration is better suited to solving complex, ill-structured problems than this one. None can match it for sophisticated innovation. Or, unfortunately, for the costs of that innovation. This is simply not an efficient way to function. Although it is ideally suited for the one-of-a-kind project, the innovative configuration is not competent at doing *ordinary* things. It is designed for the *extra*ordinary. The bureaucracies are all mass producers; they gain efficiency through standardization. The adhocracy is a custom producer, unable to standardize and so be efficient. It gains its effectiveness (innovation) at the price of efficiency.

One source of inefficiency lies in the unbalanced workload, mentioned earlier. It is almost impossible to keep the personnel of a project structure—high-priced specialists, it should be noted—busy on a steady basis. In January they may be working overtime with no hope of completing the new project on time; by May they may be playing cards for want of work.

But the real root of inefficiency is the high cost of communication. People talk a lot in these organizations; that is how they combine their knowledge to develop new ideas. But that takes time, a great deal of time. Faced with the need to make a decision in the machine organization, someone up above gives an order and that is that. Not so in the innovative one, where everyone must get into the act—managers of all kinds (functional, project, liaison), as well as all the specialists who believe their point of view should be represented. A meeting is called, probably to schedule another meeting, eventually to decide who should participate in the decision. The problem then gets defined and redefined, ideas for its solution get generated and debated, alliances build and fall around different solutions, until eventually everyone settles down to the hard bargaining over which one to adopt. Finally a decision emerges—that in itself is an accomplishment—although it is typically late and will probably be modified later.

THE DANGERS OF INAPPROPRIATE TRANSITION

Of course, one solution to the problems of ambiguity and inefficiency is to change the configuration. Employees no longer able to tolerate the ambiguity and customers fed up with the inefficiency may try to drive the organization to a more stable, bureaucratic form.

That is relatively easily done in the operating adhocracy, as noted earlier. The organization simply selects the set of standard programs it does best, reverting to the professional configuration, or else innovates one last time to find a lucrative market niche in which to mass produce, and then becomes a machine configuration. But those transitions, however easily effected, are not always appropriate. The organization came into being to solve problems imaginatively, not to apply standards indiscriminately. In many spheres, society has more mass producers than it needs; what it lacks are true problem-solvers—the consulting firm that can handle a unique problem instead of applying a pat solution, the advertising agency that can come up with a novel campaign instead of the common imitation, the research laboratory that can make the really serious breakthrough instead of just modifying an existing design. The television networks seem to be classic examples of bureaucracies that provide largely standardized fare when the creativity of adhocracy is called for (except, perhaps, for the newsrooms and the specials, where an ad hoc orientation encourages more creativity).

The administrative adhocracy can run into more serious difficulties when it succumbs to the pressures to bureaucratize. It exists to innovate for itself, in its own industry. Unlike the operating adhocracy, it often cannot change orientation while remaining in the same industry. And so its conversion to the machine configuration (the natural transition for an administrative adhocracy tired of perpetual change), by destroying the organization's ability to innovate, can eventually destroy the organization itself.

To reiterate a central theme of our discussion throughout this section: In general, there is no one best structure; in particular, there may be at a cost of something forgone, so long as the different attributes combine to form a coherent configuration that is consistent with the situation.

12
IDEOLOGY AND THE MISSIONARY ORGANIZATION

In my book on structure, I discussed five configurations. There were no more than hints of a sixth in that literature at the time (the mid-1970s), and since the book was designed to be "a synthesis of the literature" (its subtitle), I mentioned it only as a brief afterthought in the book's final pages, mostly to suggest that we needn't limit our perspective to five types.

Well, our Japanese friends have changed all that. I subsequently found a sixth configuration in the literature of organizational sociology while doing my book on power. But ever since the Japanese showed us how to manage organizations through the use of ideology—norms and beliefs in place of standards and procedures—these concepts came out of the classrooms of sociology and moved into the boardrooms of management. Now you can hardly avoid them, or at least the homilies that accompany them—the four easy steps to the building of a better culture promoted by some management consultants.

Well, homilies are to culture what rules are to wisdom—superficial distillations that distort the phenomenon. You can't change an organization's culture the way those consultants change their clients. So we had better understand the roots of this important concept.

I shall use the word *ideology* in this chapter, rather than *culture.* Every organization has a culture, which describes its own way of doing things. Our concern here is a very special culture—a richly developed and deeply rooted system of values and beliefs that distinguishes a particular organization from all others. I prefer to call this an ideology, which I mean in the organizational, not the political sense. (An organization that reflects a common political ideology—say, bottom-line economic or participative liberal—cannot be described as having its own unique set of beliefs, in other words, its own particular ideology.)

Sometimes an organization's ideology becomes so strong that its whole structure is built around it. Then a sixth configuration appears, which I labeled the *missionary* in my power book. But more commonly, it seems to me, organizational ideologies "overlay" on more conventional structures—a McDonald's, classic machine structure that uses its own vigorous culture to fire up its employees, a Hewlett-Packard that seems to blend its own particular ideology with, perhaps, an innovative, adhocracy-type structure. Accordingly, in this chapter (like the next on politics), I shall depart from the format of the previous five and focus on *force* as much as *form.* In other words, the discussion will be concerned with ideology as a force in organization as much as with the missionary as a distinct form of organization.

Organizations with established ideologies of their own are fascinating ones, once again for better and for worse. They represent some of the most exciting moments in organizational history as well as some of the worst violations of human rights. (Try the Chinese Cultural Revolution for both.) While we adore the way a Toyota motivates its workers for production, we abhor the way a Jonestown drives its members to destruction, perhaps without stopping to realize the similarities in their methods of control. Ideologies can serve us and can enslave us, sometimes indistinguishably.

This chapter begins with a brief discussion of the development of organizational ideology through three stages. It then considers the structure of the missionary configuration, where ideology predominates, and finally concludes with a brief discussion of ideology as an overlay on more conventional types of organizations.

Ideology

- rich system of values and beliefs that distinguishes an organization
- rooted in sense of mission associated with charismatic leadership, developed through traditions and sagas and then reinforced through identifications
- can be overlaid on conventional configuration, most commonly entrepreneurial, followed by innovative, professional, and then machine
- sometimes so strong that evokes own configuration:

The Missionary Organization

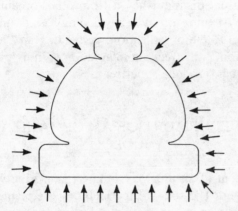

- clear, focused, inspiring, distinctive mission
- coordination through the standardization of norms ("pulling together"), reinforced by selection, socialization, and indoctrination of members
- small units ("enclaves"), loosely organized and highly decentralized but with powerful normative controls
- reformer, converter, and cloister forms
- threats of isolation on one side, assimilation on the other

---

We all know that $2 + 2 = 4$. But general systems theory, through the concept of synergy, suggests that it can also equal 5, that the parts of a system may produce more working together than they can apart. A flashlight and a battery add up to just so many pieces of hardware; together they form a working system. Likewise an organization is a working system that can entice from its members more than they would produce apart—more effort, more creativity, more output (or, of course, less). This may be "strategic"—deriving from the way components have been combined in the organization. Or it may be motivational: The group is said to develop a "mood," an "atmosphere," to have some kind of "chemistry." In organizations, we talk of a "style," a "culture," a "character." One senses something unique when one walks into the offices of IBM; the chemistry of Hewlett-Packard just doesn't feel the same as that of Texas Instruments, even though the two have operated in some similar businesses.

All these words are used to describe something—intangible yet very real, over and above the concrete components of an organization—that we refer to as its *ideology*. Specifically, an ideology is taken here to mean a rich system of values and beliefs about an organization, shared by its members, that distinguishes it from other organizations. For our purposes, the key feature of such an ideology is its unifying power: It ties the individual to the organization, generating an "esprit de corps," a "sense of mission," in effect, an integration of individual and organizational goals that can produce synergy.

THE DEVELOPMENT OF AN ORGANIZATIONAL IDEOLOGY

The development of an ideology in an organization will be discussed here in three stages. The roots of the ideology are planted when a group of individuals band together around a leader and, through a sense of mission, found a vigorous organization, or invigorate an existing one. The ideology then develops over time through the establishment of traditions. Finally, the existing ideology is reinforced when new members enter the organization and identify with its system of beliefs.

STAGE 1: THE ROOTING OF IDEOLOGY IN A SENSE OF MISSION

Typically, an organization is founded when a single prime mover identifies a mission—some product to be produced, service to be rendered—and collects a group around him or her to accomplish it. Some organizations are, of course, founded by other means, as when a new agency is created by a government or a subsidiary by a corporation. But a prime mover often can still be identified behind the founding of the organization.

The individuals who come together don't do so at random, but coalesce because they share some values associated with the fledgling organization. At the very least they see something in it for themselves. But in some cases, in addition to the mission per se there is a "sense of mission," that is, a feeling that the group has banded together to create something unusual and exciting. This is common in new organizations for a number of reasons.

First, unconstrained by procedure and tradition, new organizations offer wide latitude for maneuver. Second, they tend to be small, enabling the members to establish personal relationships. Third, the founding members frequently share a set of strong basic beliefs, sometimes including a sense that they wish to work together. Fourth, the founders of new organizations are often "charismatic" individuals, and so energize the followers and knit them together. Charisma, as Weber used the term, means a sense of "personal devotion" to the leader for the sake of his or her personal qualities rather than formal position.[1] People join and remain with the organization because of dedication to the leader and his or her mission. Thus the roots of strong ideologies tend to be planted in the founding of organizations.

Of course, such ideologies can also develop in existing organizations. But a review of our above points suggests why this should be much more difficult to accomplish. Existing organizations *are* constrained by procedures and traditions, many are *already* large and impersonal, and their *existing* beliefs tend to impede the establishment of new ones. Nonetheless, with the introduction of strong charismatic leadership reinforced by a strong new sense of mission, an existing organization can sometimes be invigorated by the creation of a new ideology.

To my mind, key to the development of an organizational ideology, in a new or existing organization, is a leadership with a genuine belief in mission and an honest dedication to the people who must carry it out. Mouthing the right words might create the veneer of an organizational ideology, but it is only an authentic feeling on the part of the leadership—which followers somehow sense—that sets the roots of the ideology deep enough to sustain it when other forces, such as impersonal administration (bureaucracy) or politics, challenge it.

STAGE 2: THE DEVELOPMENT OF IDEOLOGY THROUGH TRADITIONS AND SAGAS

As a new organization establishes itself or an existing one establishes a new set of beliefs, it makes decisions and takes actions that serve as commitments and establish precedents. Behaviors reinforce themselves over time, and actions become infused with value. When those forces are strong, ideology begins to emerge in its own right. That ideology is strengthened by stories—sometimes called "myths"—that develop around important events in the organization's past. Gradually the organization establishes its own unique sense of history. All of this—the precedents, habits, myths, history—form a common base of tradition, which the members of the organization share, thus solidifying the ideology. Gradually, in Selznick's terms, the organization is converted from an expendable "instrument" for the accomplishment of externally imposed goals into an "institution," a system with a life of its own. It "acquires a self, a distinctive identity."[2]

Thus Clark described the "distinctive college," with reference particularly to Reed, Antioch, and Swarthmore. Such institutions develop, in his words, an "organizational saga," "a collective understanding of a unique accomplishment based on historical exploits," which links the organization's present with its past and "turns a formal place into a beloved institution."[3] The saga captures allegience, committing people to the institution.[4]

STAGE 3: THE REINFORCEMENT OF IDEOLOGY THROUGH IDENTIFICATIONS

Our description to this point makes it clear that an individual entering an organization does not join a random collection of individuals, but rather a living system with its own culture. He or she may come with a certain set of values and beliefs, but there is little doubt that the culture of the organization can weigh heavily on the behavior he or she will exhibit once inside it. This is especially true when the culture is rich—when the organization has an emerging or fully developed ideology. Then the individual's *identification* with and *loyalty* to the organization can be especially strong. Such identification can develop in a number of ways:

- Most simply, identification occurs *naturally* because the new member is attracted to the organization's system of beliefs.
- Identification may also be *selected*. New members are chosen to "fit in" with the existing beliefs, and positions of authority are likewise filled from among the members exhibiting the strongest loyalty to those beliefs.
- Identification may also be *evoked*. When the need for loyalty is especially great, the organization may use informal processes of

socialization and formal programs of *indoctrination* to reinforce natural or selected commitment to its system of beliefs.

- Finally, and most weakly, identification can be *calculated*. In effect, individuals conform to the beliefs not because they identify naturally with them nor because they even necessarily fit in with them, not because they have been socialized or indoctrinated into them, but simply because it pays them to identify with the beliefs. They may enjoy the work or the social group, may like the remuneration, may work to get ahead through promotion and the like. Of course, such identification is fragile. It disappears as soon as an opportunity calculated to be better appears.

Clearly, the higher up this list an organization's member identifications tend to be, the more likely it is to sustain a strong ideology, or even to have such an ideology in the first place. Thus, strong organizational belief systems can be recognized above all by the presence of much natural identification. Attention to selected identification indicates the presence of an ideology, since it reflects an organization's efforts to sustain its ideology, as do efforts at socialization and indoctrination. Some organizations require a good deal of the latter two, because of the need to instill in their new members a complex system of beliefs. When the informal processes of socialization tend to function naturally, perhaps reinforced by more formal programs of indoctrination, then the ideology would seem to be strong. But when an organization is forced to rely almost exclusively on indoctrination, or worse to fall back on forms of calculated identification, then its ideology would appear to be weakening, if not absent to begin with.

THE MISSIONARY ORGANIZATION

Organizations whose identifications are so strong and natural (whether at the outset or after selection, socialization, and indoctrination) that they can be used to effect much of the necessary coordination—in place of the more conventional mechanisms such as direct supervision or the standardization of work, output, or skills—tend to adopt a configuration we label the *missionary*. Here rich traditions and a unique history combine to form an especially strong ideology. What counts above all in such organizations is the mission, some endeavor that is typically (1) clear and focused, so that its members are easily able to identify with it, (2) inspiring, so that the members do, in fact, develop such identifications, and (3) distinctive, so that the organization and its members are deposited into a unique niche where the ideology can flourish.

That is not, however, to conclude that all organizations with such missions end up taking the missionary form. When private interests and needs—for example, those of the administrators or of the members at large—are allowed to take precedent, then even the most noble of missions can be overwhelmed. After all, bingo sometimes ends up being more important in some churches than service to the Almighty. Likewise, there is the story in the literature of sociology of certain rehabilitation agencies that kept their "desirable blind" clients in a state of dependence in order to use them to help raise funds, while ignoring the greater needs of older, less attractive blind people.[5] In these organizations, the mission serves the administrators rather than vice versa, and so the configuration, in our terms, ends up being a closed system machine.

The missionary form is another distinct configuration of the attributes of structure, internally highly integrated yet different from the other configurations we have discussed. What holds this organization together—that is, provides for its coordination—is the standardization of its norms, in other words, the sharing of values and beliefs among its members. As was noted, that can happen informally, either through natural selection or else the informal process of socialization. But from the perspective of structural design—meaning systematic intervention to determine behavior—the key attribute is indoctrination, meaning formalized programs to develop or reinforce identification with the ideology. And once the new member has been selected, socialized, and indoctrinated, he or she is accepted into the system as an equal partner, able to participate in decision-making alongside everyone else. Thus, at the limit, the missionary organization can achieve the purest form of decentralization: All who are accepted into the system share its power.

But that does not mean an absence of control. Quite the contrary. No matter how subtle, control tends to be very powerful in this configuration. For here, the organization controls not just people's behavior but their very souls. The machine organization buys the "workers' " attention through imposed rules; the missionary organization captures the "members' " hearts through shared values. As Jay noted in his book *Management and Machiavelli,* teaching new Jesuit recruits to "love God and do what you like" is not to do what they like at all but to act in strict conformance with the order's beliefs.[6] In this way, of course, the missionary organization minimizes political conflict. The only acceptable debates concern interpretation of the established ideology.

But in another important respect, the missionary organization is not unlike the machine one: Because it too relies on a form of standardization for coordination, it is also fundamentally a bureaucracy. Its form of bureaucracy may seem loose, for, after all, standardized norms allow for more fluid structure than do standardized work processes. But don't be misled by this. The standards of the missionary can be so deeply internalized (not just accepted from nine to five in return for a paycheck) that this can turn out to be the most bureaucratic structure of all, at least in the sense of being the most rigid. Bear in mind that ideological standards tend to be immutable: The missionary organization is more inclined to change the world than to change itself. In other words, it is usually too busy interpreting ''the word'' to call that word into question.

Because the standardization of norms is so powerful in these organizations, other forms of coordination need hardly be relied upon, neither standards of work or output nor direct supervision, nor even much mutual adjustment. Everyone simply acts in accordance with the pervasive beliefs and so can do the operating work relatively independently. This means there tends to be few *formal* rules and regulations in the missionary organization, not much planning or formal control, not even much managerial control, and so hardly any technostructure or hierarchy of authority. (In the Chinese Cultural Revolution, for example, the managers had to work in the factories for a certain number of days each year.) Leadership then becomes not the imposition of direction so much as the protection and enhancement of the common ideology; the leader is expected to inspire others to pursue the mission, perhaps also to interpret the mission, but never to change the mission.

Even professional skills may be discouraged in the missionary organization as incompatible with the ideology. A dependence on particular bodies of expertise might force the organization to surrender some ''normative'' control to the professional institutions that train and license its members and also introduce status differences between members that true missionary organizations try to minimize. For example, the Foundation for Infantile Paralysis, a missionary organization that ran the famous March of Dimes campaign, forbade medical doctors to hold office in its local chapters to avoid the establishment of a specialized elite.[7]

Thus, as shown in the logo, the missionary organization tends to end up as an amorphous mass of members all pulling together within the common ideology, with minimum specialization as to job, differentiation as to part, division as to status. At the limit, managers, staffers, and operators, once selected, socialized, and indoctrinated, all seem rather alike and may, in fact, rotate into each other's positions.

Important for the missionary organization, however, is that its units remain small, because strong ideology depends on personal contact. Thus, when the missionary organization grows past a certain size, beyond which its members can no longer interact with one another on a personal basis, it tends to divide itself, like an amoeba, forming what may best be thought of as enclaves, self-contained replicas of the initial unit, based on the same ideology.

The traditional Israeli kibbutz is a classic example of the missionary configuration. In certain seasons, everyone pitches in and picks fruit in the fields by day and then attends the meetings to decide administrative issues by night. Managerial positions exist but are generally filled on a rotating basis so that no one emerges with the status of office for long. Likewise, staff support positions exist, but they too tend to be filled on a rotating basis from the same pool of members, as are the operating positions in the fields. (Kitchen duty is, for example, considered drudgery that everyone must do periodically.)

As mentioned, this describes the traditional kibbutz. Internal growth was found to threaten the kibbutz's traditional ideology, with the result that efforts were made to keep them small (six hundred adults being considered the upper limit), or to encourage the spinning off of new ones—the creation of what amount to new "enclaves"—from those that became large. A more serious threat to the traditional ideology was the conversion from agriculture to industry, which became necessary as the kibbutzim sought to enhance their influence and wealth. As suggested, it was relatively easy to sustain the egalitarian ideology when the work was agricultural. Industry, in contrast, generally called for greater levels of technology, specialization, and expertise, with a resulting increase in the need for administrative hierarchy and functional differentiation, all of these, as already noted, threatening to the missionary orientation. The kibbutzim continue to struggle with this problem.

A number of our points about the traditional kibbutz are summarized in a table developed by Rosner, which contrasts the "principles of kibbutz organization"—classic missionary—with those of "bureaucratic organization," in our terms, the classic machine.

Principles of Bureaucratic Organization	Principles of Kibbutz Organization
1. Permanency of office	Impermanency of office
2. The office carries with it impersonal, fixed privileges and duties.	The definition of office is flexible—privileges and duties are not formally fixed and often depend on the personality of the official.
3. A hierarchy of functional authorities expressed in the authority of the officials	A basic assumption of the equal value of all functions without a formal hierarchy of authority
4. Nomination of officials is based on formal objective qualifications.	Officials are elected, not nominated. Objective qualifications are not decisive, personal qualities are more important in election.
5. The office is a full-time occupation.	The office is usually supplementary to the full-time occupation of the official.[8]

FORMS OF THE MISSIONARY ORGANIZATION

We can distinguish three different forms of the pure missionary configuration. Some missionary organizations are *reformers*. They set out to change the world directly—anything from overthrowing a government to ensuring that all domestic animals are "decently" clothed. Of course, the label "missionary" comes from the religious orders that are basically reformers. A secular example is the Foundation for Infantile Paralysis, already mentioned, whose mission was to help eradicate that dreaded disease.

Other missionaries can be called *converters*. Their mission is to change the world indirectly, by attracting members and changing them. The difference between the first two types of missionaries is the difference between the Women's Christian Temperance Union and Alcoholics Anonymous. Their ends were similar, but their means differed, seeking to reduce alcoholism in one case by promoting a general ban on liquor sales, in the other by discouraging certain individuals, namely joined members, from drinking. Converters often take the form of what Erving Goffman labeled "total institutions," meaning organizations that house all aspects of their members' private and working lives so that they can control them totally.[9]

Finally there are the *cloister* missionaries, total institutions too, but ones that seek not to change things so much as to allow their members to pursue a unique style of life. The monasteries that close themselves off from the outside world are good examples, as are groups that go off to found new isolated colonies. These are "closed system," but not in the sense that term was used earlier, of an organization that deflects external influence in order to control its environment. The cloisters are not interested in controlling anything but their members' own behavior: They try to close themselves off in every respect.

Of course, no organization can completely seal itself off from the world. All missionary organizations, in fact, face the twin opposing pressures of isolation and assimilation. Together these make them vulnerable, as configurations if not as organizations. On one side is the threat of *isolation,* of growing ever inward in order to protect the unique ideology from the pressures of the ordinary world until the organization eventually dies for lack of renewal. The cloister missionary especially faces the problem of not replenishing its membership (how can it find new people when it is so detached). On the other side is the threat of *assimilation,* of reaching out so far to promote the ideology that it eventually gets compromised. The reformer missionary especially runs this risk, since it must develop intimate contacts with the very world of "contaminated" reality that it wishes to change. When this happens, the organization may survive but the ideology dies, and so the configuration changes (typically to the machine form).

IDEOLOGY AS AN OVERLAY ON CONVENTIONAL ORGANIZATIONS

So far we have discussed what amounts to the extreme form of ideological organization, the missionary. But more organizations have strong ideologies that can afford to structure themselves in this way. In Max Weber's terms, the missionary is an "ideal type," something to be approached but perhaps seldom attained. It may work for an Israeli kibbutz in a remote corner of the Negev desert, but this is hardly a way to run a Hewlett-Packard or a McDonald's, let alone a dynamic university or perhaps even a kibbutz closer to the worldly pressures of Tel Aviv.

What such organizations, with strong ideologies but also important needs for centralized authority or sophisticated expertise, tend to do is

overlay ideological characteristics on a more conventional structure—
perhaps machinelike in the case of McDonald's and that second kibbutz,
professional in the case of Clark's distinctive colleges, innovative in
the case of Hewlett-Packard. The mission may sometimes seem ordinary—
serving hamburgers, teaching students, developing instruments—but it
is carried out with a good dose of ideological fervor by employees firmly
committed to it.

Best known for this are, of course, certain of the Japanese corporations,
Toyota being a prime example. Ouchi and Jaeger contrast in the table
reproduced below the typical large American corporation (Type A) with
its Japanese counterpart (Type J):

Type A (for American)	*Type J (for Japanese)*
Short-term employment	Lifetime employment
Individual decision-making	Consensual decision-making
Individual responsibility	Collective responsibility
Rapid evaluation and promotion	Slow evaluation and promotion
Explicit, formalized control	Implicit, informal control
Specialized career path	Nonspecialized career path
Segmented concern	Holistic concern[10]

Every characteristic of what these authors call the Type J firm is
consistent with our description of the effects of an ideology on an organization: the personal relationship between the individual and the organization,
the collective nature of responsibility and choice, the holistic concern
in place of specialization, the discouragement of formal controls in favor
of implicit (normative) ones. All point to loyalty and ideology as the
central elements in the system. Ouchi and Jaeger in fact make their
point best with an example in which a classic Japanese ideological orientation confronts a conventional American bureaucratic one:

> [D]uring one of the author's visits to a Japanese bank in California, both
> the Japanese president and the American vice-presidents of the bank accused
> the other of being unable to formulate objectives. The Americans meant
> that the Japanese president could not or would not give them explicit,
> quantified targets to attain over the next three or six months, while the
> Japanese meant that the Americans could not see that once they understood
> the company's philosophy, they would be able to deduce for themselves
> the proper objective for any conceivable situation.[11]

In another study, however, Ouchi together with Johnson discusses a
native American corporation that does resemble the Type J firm (labeled

"Type Z"; Ouchi later published a best-seller about such organizations[12]). In it, they found greater loyalty, a strong collective orientation, less specialization, and a greater reliance on informal controls. For example, "a new manager will be useless for at least four or five years. It takes that long for most people to decide whether the new person really fits in, whether they can really trust him." That was in sharp contrast to the "auction market" atmosphere of a typical American firm: It "is almost as if you could open up the doors each day with 100 executives and engineers who had been randomly selected from the country, and the organization would work just as well as it does now."[13]

We have suggested above that ideology can overlay on any of the conventional configurations and have provided several different examples of this. But it is perhaps better to conclude that ideology is more likely to be found overlaid on some configurations than others. Some tentative conclusions in this regard are summarized below:

• Ideologies are perhaps to be most commonly expected overlaid on the *entrepreneurial* configuration. That is because it is the one that can most easily develop a sense of mission, and is most likely to be led by a charismatic individual. Indeed, it is here that we are most likely to find the first stage in the development of an ideology, as described at the beginning of this chapter. But it should be noted that the missionary configuration is fundamentally different from the entrepreneurial one, in that power is centralized in one, widely shared in the other. Thus, we might expect to find the beginnings of ideology in this configuration more commonly than a fully developed one (although the latter may follow after the leader departs and his or her beliefs get institutionalized).

• Ideologies can be overlaid on a *machine* configuration too, as suggested in the examples of McDonald's and Toyota. But because formalization is anathema to ideology—turning informal beliefs into formal rules imposed down a centralized hierarchy of authority—we would also expect to find strong forces for the destruction of fledgling ideologies in this configuration. Thus, while this overlay may not be a rarity, it is not likely to be common.

• A similar conclusion might be reached for the *diversified* configuration, only more so. The debilitating effects of formality and of detached calculation, especially as manifested in "bottom line" thinking, are there, and so too is a diversity of missions that makes it difficult to engender enthusiasm for any one. Thus, while we may be able to find diversified configurations overlaid with ideological energy, we should expect these to be relatively rare.

- Expertise acts, as noted, to introduce status differences that work against the egalitarian nature of organizational ideologies. This discourages ideological overlays on the *professional* and *innovative* configurations, where expertise is pervasive. Moreover, the professional configuration promotes fragmentation of effort, while the innovative one gives rise to considerable political activity, both of which are incompatible with the cooperative needs of ideology. On the other hand, these organizations often have missions that are either intrinsically noble or exciting (such as curing the ill or developing high-technology products). Therefore, ideological overlays may in fact occur with some frequency, as in the earlier examples of Clark's distinctive colleges or Hewlett-Packard. This may be especially true for the operating adhocracy, which tends to combine youth, energy, and informality with the excitement of an ever changing stream of products and services.

The trends in American businesses over several decades—"professional" management, emphasis on technique and rationalization, "bottom-line" mentality—have certainly worked against the development of organizational ideologies. Certainly the missionary configuration has hardly been fashionable in the West, especially the United States. But ideology may have an important role to play there, given the enormous success many Japanese firms have had in head-on competition with American corporations organized in machine and diversified ways, with barren cultures. At the very least, we might expect more ideological overlays on the conventional forms of organizations in the West. But this, as we hope our discussion has made clear, may be both for better and for worse.

13

POLITICS AND THE POLITICAL ORGANIZATION

So far this discussion of the different configurations has revolved around the various mechanisms by which organizations achieve coordination. Politics is obviously something very different. In fact, if coordination is the means by which organizations find order and integration, then politics acts to the detriment of coordination, by *dis*ordering and *dis*integrating what currently exists. Politics has to do with power, not structure, and so it was in my book on that subject that I developed my ideas on politics and on the political organization, which I there called the "political arena." I was also reminded there how much politics can influence all of the processes normally considered alongside structure—managerial work, decision-making, strategy formation, and so on. Thus, no description of the basic forces and forms of organizations can be complete without the consideration of politics.

I am no fan of politics in organizations. But neither am I a fan of illness. Yet I know we have to understand one like the other. In fact, politics can be viewed as a form of organizational illness, working both against and for the system. On one hand, politics can undermine healthy processes, infiltrating them to destroy them. But on the other, it can also work to strengthen a system, acting like fever to alert a system to a graver danger, even evoking the system's own protective and adaptive mechanisms.

Political activity can be found in every organization, indeed every human system, more or less. So it is necessary to discuss politics as a general force in organizations, much as we so discussed ideology in the preceding chapter. Accordingly, we begin this chapter with a discussion of the role of politics in organizations and then consider a variety of political games that tend to be played there. Thirteen are discussed in all, a rough but fascinating little group that most of us have encountered in one form or another.

But again, like ideology, politics can also capture an organization, dominating its processes. Thus, we turn next to a discussion of the political organization, how it arises and evolves, based on the different forms it can take. We have "confrontation," the "shaky alliance," the "politicized organization," and the "complete political arena," each a nasty little viper in its own way, but all capable of doing constructive good in certain circumstances (as, of course, do real vipers). Thus, the chapter concludes with a discussion of how politics can serve a functional role in organizations.

Politics

- means of power technically illegitimate, often in self-interest, resulting in conflict that pulls individuals or units apart
- expresses itself in political games, some coexistent with, some antagonistic to, some that substitute for legitimate systems of power
- usually overlaid on conventional organization, but sometimes strong enough to create own configuration:

The Political Organization

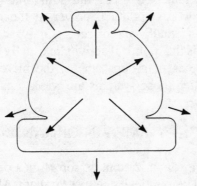

- conventional notions of concentrated coordination and influence absent, replaced by the play of informal power
- dimensions of conflict—moderate/intense, confined/pervasive, as well as enduring/brief—combine into four forms: confrontation, shaky alliance, politicized organization, complete political arena
- can trace development of forms through life cycle of impetus, development, resolution of the conflict
- politics and political organizations serve a series of functional roles in organizations, especially to help bring about necessary change blocked by legitimate systems of influence

---

How does conflict arise in an organization, why, and with what consequences? Years ago, the literature of organization theory avoided such questions. But in the last decade or so, conflict and the politics that go along with it have become not just acceptable topics but fashionable ones. Yet these topics, like most others in the field, have generally been discussed in fragments. Here we seek to consider them somewhat more comprehensively, first by themselves and then in the context of what will be called the political organization—the organization that comes to be dominated by politics and conflict.

POLITICS IN ORGANIZATIONS

What do we mean by "politics" in organizations? An organization may be described as functioning on the basis of a number of systems of influence: authority, ideology, expertise, politics. The first three can be considered legitimate in some sense: Authority is based on legally sanctioned power, ideology on widely accepted beliefs, expertise on power that is officially certified. The system of politics, in contrast, reflects power that is technically illegitimate (or, perhaps more accurately, *a*legitimate), in the means it uses, and sometimes also in the ends it promotes. In other words, political power in the organization (unlike government) is not formally authorized, widely accepted, or officially certified. The result is that political activity is usually divisive and conflictive, pitting individuals or groups against the more legitimate systems of influence and, when those systems are weak, against each other.

POLITICAL GAMES IN ORGANIZATIONS

Political activity in organizations is sometimes described in terms of various "games." The political scientist Graham Allison, for example, has described political games in organizations and government as "intricate and subtle, simultaneous, overlapping," but nevertheless guided by rules: "some rules are explicit, others implicit, some rules are quite clear, others fuzzy. Some are very stable; others are ever changing. But the collection of rules, in effect, defines the game."[1] I have identified thirteen political games in particular, listed here together with their main players, the main reasons they seem to be played, and how they relate to the other systems of influence.

- *Insurgency game:* usually played to resist authority, although can be played to resist expertise or established ideology or even to effect change in the organization; ranges "from protest to rebellion,"[2] and is usually played by "lower participants,"[3] those who feel the greatest weight of formal authority

- *Counterinsurgency game:* played by those with legitimate power who fight back with political means, perhaps with legitimate means as well (e.g., excommunication in the church)
- *Sponsorship game:* played to build power base, in this case by using superiors; individual attaches self to someone with more status, professing loyalty in return for power
- *Alliance-building game:* played among peers—often line managers, sometimes experts—who negotiate implicit contracts of support for each other in order to build power base to advance selves in the organization
- *Empire-building game:* played by line managers, in particular, to build power bases, not cooperatively with peers but individually with subordinates
- *Budgeting game:* played overtly and with rather clearly defined rules to build power base;[4] similar to last game, but less divisive, since prize is resources, not positions or units per se, at least not those of rivals
- *Expertise game:* nonsanctioned use of expertise to build power base, either by flaunting it or by feigning it; true experts play by exploiting technical skills and knowledge, emphasizing the uniqueness, criticality, and irreplaceability of the expertise,[5] also by seeking to keep skills from being programmed, by keeping knowledge to selves; nonexperts play by attempting to have their work viewed as expert, ideally to have it declared professional so they alone can control it
- *Lording game:* played to build power base by "lording" legitimate power over those without it or with less of it (i.e., using legitimate power in illegitimate ways); manager can lord formal authority over subordinate or civil servant over a citizen; members of missionary configuration can lord its ideology over outsiders; experts can lord technical skills over the unskilled
- *Line versus staff game:* a game of sibling-type rivalry, played not just to enhance personal power but to defeat a rival; pits line managers with formal decision-making authority against staff advisers with specialized expertise; each side tends to exploit legitimate power in illegitimate ways
- *Rival camps game:* again played to defeat a rival; typically occurs when alliance or empire-building games result in two major power

blocs, giving rise to two-person, zero-sum game in place of
n-person game; can be most divisive game of all; conflict can be
between units (e.g., between marketing and production in manufacturing firm), between rival personalities, or between two competing
missions (as in prisons split between custody and rehabilitation
orientations)

- *Strategic candidates game:* played to effect change in an organization; individuals or groups seek to promote through political means
  their own favored changes of a strategic nature; many play—analysts, operating personnel, lower-level managers, even senior
  managers and chief executives (especially in the professional configurations), who must promote own candidates politically before
  they can do so formally; often combines elements of other games—
  empire-building (as purpose of game), alliance-building (to win
  game), rival camps, line versus staff, expertise, and lording (evoked
  during game), insurgency (following game), and so on
- *Whistle-blowing game:* a typically brief and simple game, also
  played to effect organizational change; privileged information is
  used by an insider, usually a lower participant, to "blow the whistle" to an influential outsider on questionable or illegal behavior
  by the organization
- *Young Turks game:* played for highest stakes of all, not to effect
  simple change or to resist legitimate power per se, but to throw
  the latter into question, perhaps even to overthrow it, and institute
  major shift; small group of "young Turks," close to but not at
  center of power, seeks to reorient organization's basic strategy,
  displace a major body of its expertise, replace its ideology, or rid
  it of its leadership; Zald and Berger discuss a form of this game
  they call "organizational coup d'état," where the object is "to
  effect an unexpected succession"—to replace *holders* of authority
  while maintaining *system* of authority intact[6]

Some of these games, such as sponsorship and lording, while themselves technically illegitimate, can nevertheless *coexist with* strong legitimate systems of influence, as found for example in the machine and
missionary configurations; indeed, they could not exist without these
systems of influence. Other political games, such as insurgency and
young Turks—usually highly divisive games—arise in the presence of
legitimate power but are *antagonistic to it,* designed to destroy or at
least weaken it. They work against configurations such as the machine.

And still others, such as rival camps, often arise when legitimate power is weak and *substitute for* it, for example in the professional and innovative configurations.

The implication of this is that politics and conflict may exist at two levels in an organization. They may be present but not dominant, existing as an overlay on a more conventional organization, perhaps a kind of fifth column acting on behalf of some challenging power. Or else politics may be the dominant system of influence, and conflict strong, having weakened the legitimate systems of influence or having arisen in their weakness. It is this second level that gives rise to the configuration we shall call the *political organization*.

FORMS OF POLITICAL ORGANIZATIONS

What characterizes the organization dominated by politics is a lack of any of the forms of order found in conventional organizations. In other words, the organization is best described in terms of power, not structure, and that power is exercised in ways not legitimate in conventional organizations. Thus, there is no preferred method of coordination, no single dominant part of the organization, no clear type of decentralization. Everything depends on the fluidity of informal power, marshaled to win individual issues.

How does such an organization come to be? There is little published research on the question. But some ideas can be advanced tentatively. First, conflict would seem to arise in a circumscribed way in an organization, say between two units (such as marketing and production) or between an influential outside group and a powerful insider (such as between a part owner and the CEO). That conflict may develop gradually or it may flare up suddenly. It may eventually be resolved, but when it becomes intense, it may tend to spread, as other influencers get drawn in on one side or the other. But since few organizations can sustain intense political activity for long, that kind of conflict must eventually moderate itself (unless it kills off the organization first). In moderated form, however, the conflict may endure, even when it pervades the whole system, so long as the organization can make up for its losses, perhaps by being in a privileged position (as in the case of a conflict-ridden regulatory agency that is sustained by a government budget, or a politicized corporation that operates in a secure cartel).

What we end up with are two dimensions of conflict, first moderate or intense and second confined or pervasive. A third dimension—enduring or brief—really combines with the first (intense conflict having to be typically brief, moderate conflict possibly enduring). Combining these dimensions, we end up with four forms of the political organization:

- *Confrontation,* characterized by conflict that is *intense, confined,* and *brief* (unstable)
- *Shaky alliance,* characterized by conflict that is *moderate, confined,* and possibly *enduring* (relatively stable)
- *Politicized organization,* characterized by conflict that is *moderate, pervasive,* and possibly *enduring* (relatively stable, so long as it is sustained by privileged position)
- *Complete political arena,* characterized by conflict that is *intense, pervasive,* and *brief* (unstable)*

One of these forms is called *complete* because its conflict is both intense and pervasive. In this form, the external influencers disagree among themselves; they try to form alliances with some insiders, while clashing with others. The internal activities are likewise conflictive, permeated by divisive political games. Authority, ideology, and expertise are all subordinated to the play of political power. An organization so politicized can pursue no goal with any consistency. At best, it attends to a number of goals inconsistently over time, at worst it consumes all its energy in disputes and never accomplishes anything. In essense, the complete political arena is less a coherent organization than a free-for-all of individuals. As such, it is probably the form of political organization least commonly found in practice, or, at least, the most unstable when it does appear.

In contrast, the other three forms of political organization manage to remain partial, one by moderating its conflict, a second by containing it, and the third by doing both. As a result, these forms are more stable than the complete form and so are probably more common, with two of them in particular appearing to be far more viable.

In the *confrontational* form, conflict may be intense, but it is also contained, focusing on two parties. Typical of this is the takeover situation, where, for example, an outside stockholder tries to seize control of a closed system corporation from its management. Another example is the situation, mentioned earlier, of two rival camps in and around a

---

* I do not consider conflict that is moderate, confined, and brief to merit inclusion under the label of political organization.

prison, one promoting the mission of custody, the other that of rehabilitation.

The *shaky alliance* commonly emerges when two or more major systems of influence or centers of power must coexist in roughly equal balance. The symphony orchestra, for example, must typically combine the strong personal authority of the conductor (entrepreneurial orientation) with the extensive expertise of the musicians (professional orientation). As Fellini demonstrated so well in his film *Orchestra Rehearsal,* this alliance, however uncomfortable (experts never being happy in the face of strong authority), is nevertheless a necessary one. Common today is the professional organization operating in the public sector, which must somehow sustain an alliance of experts and government officials, one group pushing upward for professional autonomy, the other downward for technocratic control.

Our final form, the *politicized organization,* is characterized by moderate conflict that pervades the entire system of power. This would appear to describe a number of today's largest organizations, especially ones in the public sector whose mandates are visible and controversial—many regulatory agencies, for example, and some public utilities. Here it is government protection, or monopoly power, that sustains organizations captured by conflict. This form seems to be increasingly common in the private sector too, among some of the largest corporations that are able to sustain the inefficiencies of conflict through their market power and sometimes by their ability to gain government support as well.

LIFE CYCLES OF POLITICAL ORGANIZATIONS

How do these forms of political organizations develop over time and relate with one another? To describe this, we can postulate a life cycle model of political organizations, presented in three stages—impetus, development, and resolution.

IMPETUS

A necessary, and sometimes also a sufficient, condition for the appearance of a political organization is substantial pressure on the part of some influencer, or influencing group, to realign the basic system of power. For example, an outside owner group may seek to consolidate power over an entrepreneurial firm it has just bought, or a group of inside experts, hitherto not influential, may seek to exploit a new and necessary technology to enhance its own power, for example by demanding seats on key administrative committees.

Such pressures may arise by themselves—certain influencers simply demand a new deal—or else they may be provoked by other changes. As in the examples presented—change of ownership, advent of a new technology—some fundamental condition of the organization may have shifted, leading to new demands for influence. Or else the established order of power may have weakened of its own accord, creating a power vacuum that other influencers seek to fill, as when the autocratic chief of an entrepreneurial configuration falls gravely ill.

DEVELOPMENT

Such pressures challenge the existing order of power, if there is one; if not, they produce challenges among different groups vying for new influence in a power vacuum. Of course, since it is the challenge that leads to the conflict, quick resolution of it can avoid politicization, as when a shift of power at the top of a hierarchy is so long overdue and therefore so widely supported that it takes place as a kind of instant coup d'état.

But many important power challenges are not resolved quite so easily. They instead incite resistance, and so it falls to politics to lubricate their movement. As noted earlier, such conflicts tend to be confined at first, for example between "young Turks" promoting change and an "old guard" resisting it. But they can spread.

When the conflict erupts with suddenness and intensity—taking the confrontation form of political organization—unless soon checked it can spread to become a complete political arena. But that form, being intense and pervasive, must be resolved before it kills the entire organization. When the conflict develops gradually, however, it may lead to the more stable form we called the politicized organization, and so can endure (hence we shall discuss it under "resolution"). Of course, the moderate conflict of the politicized form can itself flare up at any time, leading to the confrontation form and then perhaps the complete form of political arena.

RESOLUTION

Three results of such political conflicts are likely. In the simplest case, someone wins—challenger or those challenged—and the organization settles down again to a quiet, relatively nonconflictive existence. That is what we would usually expect from a confrontation. If, however, the side that wins reflects sheer power as opposed to organizational need, then subsequent confrontations may be expected, at least if the organization is to remain effective.

The second possible result is that the conflict kills the organization. When this happens, it is likely to take place via the form of complete political arena. On one hand, this form may arise of its own accord (for example, through a major confrontation that endures and so pervades the organization) and thereby kill the organization. On the other hand, the complete political arena may arise in the death throes of an organization already doomed for other reasons (say, because its technology is hopelessly outmoded or its markets have disappeared). Here, the intense and pervasive conflict of the complete political arena represents a kind of free-for-all in which individuals try to extract whatever resources are left for their own benefit, and so quickly destroy the organization.

The third possible result is that the conflict continues, but in moderated form so that the organization can survive. The shaky alliance and politicized organization are the two moderate forms of political configuration.

When the result of a confrontation is a standoff, we might expect to see the rise of a shaky alliance. Neither side can win, neither wishes to give up, yet both know they must moderate their conflict if the organization is to survive. So they reach some kind of implicit accord, agreeing to tolerate each other. Of course, there are also organizations that must exist in perpetuity as shaky alliances, as in our example of the symphony orchestra or of the professionals who must coexist with government technocrats. In these cases, confrontation does not lead to the shaky alliance so much as the opposite: The alliance, being shaky, flares up into confrontation periodically.

The politicized organization form tends to arise when conflict builds up slowly and spreads throughout an organization, also perhaps when the pervasive conflict of the complete political arena abates, as influencers back off to allow the organization to survive. But as noted earlier, an organization cannot generally survive even with the politicized organizational form unless it is able to exploit a privileged position, such as an established hold on a market or artificial support from a granting agency.

Of course, there is really no such thing as true and final resolution of conflict. Any organization, even the most stable, can flare up into conflict at any time. Even the most formalized bureaucracy, the most secure entrepreneur, the most established ideology can be challenged, either arbitrarily by some group in search of power or because changed conditions have undermined its basis of power. Likewise, the shaky alliance is just that: shaky. The potential for intense conflict—hot war in place of cold—is never far from the surface. Any small perturbation can upset the delicate balance, driving it to outright confrontation. Thus, its power system may best be described as one of homeostasis—a dynamic balance. In the same way, the politicized organization can easily flare up into the intense conflict of the complete political arena. Most of the time, however, most organizations seem to be relatively free of major conflict, which allows them to get on with performing their missions. But politics is never far away. Thus, the only true and permanent stability, for organizations as for all other living systems, is death!

POLITICS IN THE CONVENTIONAL CONFIGURATIONS

Clearly the level of politics will vary in the conventional configurations, some being more prone to this kind of activity (or even to easy transition to a political configuration) than others. Let us consider each in turn.

• The *entrepreneurial* configuration should experience a minimum of politics, since one powerful individual closely supervises all activity. Political games are clearly not encouraged, especially those that cannot coexist with the personalized rule of the chief executive. Sponsorship may take place, but given that the chief does most of the sponsoring, that is hardly political. Likewise, strategic candidates may sometimes be promoted by the chief, but that too is hardly political. Confrontations or shaky alliances may arise between the chief executive and important outside influencers, or a group of young Turks may challenge a faltering chief, but these games are so incompatible with the entrepreneurial organization that they will generally drive it to a new configuration, the political one, for the duration of the conflict in order, perhaps, to make a transition to another stable type.

• The *machine* configuration and the *diversified* one have strong systems of formal authority, which should discourage political activity. But the rigidities of those systems in fact give rise to the milder forms of conflict, as things fall through the bureaucratic cracks. Thus, the political games that can coexist with legitimate authority tend to be prevalent here—empire building, budgeting, sponsorship, strategic candidates, line versus staff, and lording. In effect, machinelike and diversified structures, by introducing sharp divisions of labor, focus attention on the individual unit and so encourage parochialism and efforts to enhance narrow bases of power. That is what all these games do, each in its own way (through accumulating subordinates, enlarging budgets, adding programs, and so on). Games that challenge formal authority—insurgency (responded to by counter-insurgency), young Turks, and whistle-blowing—may also arise periodically to correct deficiencies in the system of formal authority, especially in the closed system form of these configurations where the authority is not constrained by external influence. Given the number of games played here, and the relatively moderate nature of most of them, these configurations can easily tilt over to the politicized organization form. While this tendency tends to be muted in the instrument form, where the presence of external control can discourage excessive political activity, it tends to be exaggerated in the closed system form, where insiders are drawn to share in the distribution of surpluses, and the administrators, on shaky grounds of external legitimacy to begin with, may simply defer to them (e.g., give in to strong union demands so as to avoid the embarrassment of a strike). Moreover, in the closed system form, external influencers may eventually be drawn to challenge the legitimacy of the administration's authority and so further politicize the organization.

• The *professional* and *innovative* configurations have relatively weak systems of authority, though strong ones of expertise. This means that their power tends to be rather diffused, distributed in a fluid way among many individuals. As a result, there is considerable room for political games in these configurations, especially ones that pit groups of insiders against each other—rival camps, alliance building, and young Turks. There is, in addition, a propensity to play the games that build narrow power bases, such as sponsorship, empire building, budgeting, and strategic candidates. Also, of course, the games associated with highly skilled operating work, namely expertise games and those of lording, are commonly played. The professional configuration may have a relatively stable operating core, where activities are highly standardized, but its administrative structure, where all kinds of professionals and managers interact to make choices, is hardly stable and, in fact, very supportive of games such as strategic candidates, empire building, and rival camps. The innovative configuration is far less stable, generally having a highly fluid structure throughout that literally promotes games such as alliance building, rival camps, and strategic candidates. Given the number of games played and the intensity of some of them in these two configurations, transition to a form of the political organization, at least temporarily, would seem to be a natural occurrence, particularly that of confrontation (say, between conflicting groups of experts, each professing to represent pure truth) or the politicized organization, where political activity spreads across the entire system. Transition can also occur to the shaky alliance form, for example when the experts are confronted by an influential group of outside influencers (such as government technocrats), or even to the complete form of political arena for a time, when the experts engage in outright wars with each other.

• The *missionary* is probably the configuration least tolerant of political activity, since the belief system and the encouragement to cooperate are so strong. People in these organizations are not supposed to build private alliances or empires, not hoard budgets, not blow the whistle on their colleagues, not challenge the existing ideology. In fact, the occurrence of these games would suggest the demise of the ideology as well as the configuration, if not the organization itself. Of course, strategic candidates may sometimes be promoted, and lording is one game that might be commonly found, as members flaunt their ideology over outsiders. Conflicts can arise over the interpretation of the "word"—indeed, these can sometimes become quite heated, as each side professes to be the purer. But these must be decidedly internal, the missionary organization always being very careful to present a united front to the outside world. It might be added in closing that ideology as an overlay on another configuration should have a similar, although muted, effect in reducing political activity, for example by discouraging some of the more divisive political games in a machine configuration or encouraging cooperation over conflict in a professional one.

THE FUNCTIONAL ROLE OF POLITICS IN ORGANIZATIONS

Little space need be devoted to the dysfunctional influence of politics in organizations. Politics is divisive and costly; it burns up energies that could instead go into the operations. It can also lead to all kinds of aberrations. Politics is often used to sustain outmoded systems of power, and sometimes to introduce new ones that are not justified. Politics can also paralyze an organization to the point where its effective functioning comes to a halt and nobody benefits. The purpose of an organization, after all, is to produce goods and services, not to provide an arena in which people can fight with one another.

What does deserve space, however, because they are less widely appreciated, are those conditions in which politics and the political organization serve a functional role. Let us first consider in this regard the force of politics, and then the form of political organization.

In general, the system of politics is necessary in an organization to correct certain deficiencies in its other, legitimate systems of influence— above all to provide for certain forms of flexibility discouraged by those other systems. The other systems of influence were labeled legitimate because their *means*—authority, ideology, or expertise—have some basis of legitimacy. But sometimes those means are used to pursue *ends* that are illegitimate (as in the example of the lording game, where legitimate power is flaunted unreasonably). In contrast, the system of politics, whose *means* are (by definition) illegitimate, can sometimes be used to pursue *ends* that are in fact legitimate (as in certain of the whistle-blowing and young Turks games, where political pressures are used against formal authority to correct irresponsible or ineffective behaviors). We can elaborate on this in terms of four specific points.

First, politics as a system of influence can act in a Darwinian way to ensure that the strongest members of an organization are brought into positions of leadership. Authority favors a single chain of command; weak leaders can suppress strong subordinates. Politics, on the other hand, can provide alternate channels of information and promotion, as when the sponsorship game enables someone to leap over a weak superior. Moreover, since effective leaders have been shown to exhibit a need for power,[7] the political games can serve as tests to demonstrate the potential for leadership. The second-string players may suffice for the scrimmages, but only the stars can be allowed to meet the competition. Political games not only suggest who those players are but also help to remove their weak rivals from contention.

Second, politics can also ensure that all sides of an issue are fully debated, whereas the other systems of influence may promote only one. The system of authority, by aggregating information up a central hierarchy, tends to advance only a single point of view, often the one already known to be favored above. So, too, does the system of ideology, since every issue is interpreted in terms of "the word," the prevailing set of beliefs. As for the system of expertise, people tend to defer to the expert on any particular issue. But experts are often closed to new ideas, ones that developed after they received their training. Politics, however, by obliging "responsible men . . . to fight for what they are convinced is right,''[8] encourages a variety of voices to be heard on any issue. And, because of attacks by its opponents, each voice is forced to justify its conclusions in terms of the broader good. That means it must marshal arguments and support proposals that can at least be justified in terms of the interests of the organization at large rather than the parochial needs of a particular group. As Burns has noted in an amusing footnote:

> It is impossible to avoid some reference from the observations made here to F. M. Cornford's well known ''Guide for the Young Academic Politician.'' Jobs ''fall into two classes, My Jobs and Your Jobs. My Jobs are public-spirited proposals, which happen (much to my regret) to involve the advancement of a personal friend, or (still more to my regret) of myself. Your Jobs are insidious intrigues for the advancement of yourself and your friends, spuriously disguised as public-spirited proposals.''[9]

Third, the system of politics is often required to stimulate necessary change that is blocked by the legitimate systems of influence. Internal change is generally threatening to the ''vested interest'' of an organization. Even when the change must be from one form of legitimate power to another, say from the personalized leadership of an entrepreneur to the more formalized leadership of administrators, it is often illegitimate power—namely political power—that must bring it about. The system of authority concentrates power up the hierarchy, often in the hands of those who were responsible for initiating the existing strategies in the first place. It also contains the established controls, which are designed to sustain the status quo. Similarly, the system of expertise concentrates power in the hands of senior and established experts, not junior ones who may possess newer, more necessary skills. Likewise, the system of ideology, because it is rooted in the past, in tradition, acts as a deterrent to change. In the face of these resistances, it is politics that is able to work as a kind of ''invisible hand''—''invisible underhand'' would be a better term—to promote necessary change, through such games as strategic candidates, whistle-blowing, and young Turks.

Fourth and finally, the system of politics can ease the path for the execution of decisions. Senior managers, for example, often use politics to gain acceptance for their decisions, playing the strategic candidates game early in promoting proposals to avoid having to play the more divisive and risky counterinsurgency game later in the face of resistance to them. They persuade, negotiate, and build alliances to smooth the path for the decisions they wish to make.

If the system of politics can sometimes be functional, then so too, presumably, can the organization in which it dominates, the one captured by conflict. Specifically, the political configuration would appear to be functional when:

1. It encourages a realignment in the organization's power necessitated by change in one of its fundamental conditions or breakdown in its established focus of power
2. It corrects an earlier change in power that was itself dysfunctional
3. It exists as a shaky alliance that reflects natural, balanced, and irreconcilable forces in the organization
4. It speeds up the death of a spent organization

The first point argues that when the established order of power has outlived its usefulness, then a confrontation form of political organization that flares up to change it can itself be useful. In effect, extensive politics can sometimes be the only way to displace legitimate power that itself has become counterproductive—outmoded expertise, inappropriate controls, a spent ideology, detached leadership. Then the political organization must be viewed as productive. No matter how illegitimate and disruptive its own power may be, it serves as the functional bridge from one legitimate system of power to another. In effect, the organization reverts to the political configuration for a time to achieve a necessary change. For example, a detached leadership is confronted and the organization becomes politicized until a new, more in-touch leadership is installed. We can conclude that the political configuration serves as a prime means by which society corrects deficiencies in its organizations.

Obviously, political confrontation does not always correct a bad situation. Sometimes it aggravates it; the solution proves worse than the problem. Likewise, politics can be used by those at the center of power to block change that the organization requires. But, as argued earlier, such situations are unlikely to remain stable for long. Our second point argues that renewed confrontation is to be expected, with political pressures building up until they burst their confines to effect the necessary change. Just as anarchists, who lurk in all societies, are able to foment revolution only when large segments of the population feel the need for change, so too does politics, which lurks in all organizations, tend to become dominant only when change widely regarded as necessary has been repeatedly thwarted.

Some political challenges are, of course, arbitrary or neutral. An influencer simply wants a new deal. In those cases, we cannot label the resolution of the conflict functional or dysfunctional. We can, however, call the period during which the conflict endures dysfunctional, since it wastes resources that could have been doing other things. Thus a shaky alliance—an enduring political organization—that reflects no natural set of forces on the organization may be considered dysfunctional because of the resources it uses up. But a third point argues that a shaky alliance that does reflect opposing forces that are natural, roughly equal in importance, and irreconcilable—say, between research people promoting innovation and manufacturing people promoting efficiency in a firm that needs the two in balance—must be considered functional. This is because the organization could not function if it did not accommodate each of these forces. It has no choice but to take the form of a shaky alliance. Some conflict is the inevitable consequence of getting its work done.*

Our final point considers the organization that is about to succumb anyway, perhaps because it can no longer perform its mission effectively or because that mission is no longer required. Little hope exists for improving the organization's effectiveness or for converting to another mission (or, more to the point, it may be more efficient to allow new organizations to arise in its place). In any event, when demise is inevitable, from society's perspective the sooner it comes the better. That way a minimum of resources is wasted during the organization's death throes. Thus, the complete political arena that tends to arise as an organization dies, by speeding up its demise, can be considered functional. Much as the scavengers that swarm over a carcass serve a positive function in nature, so too can the political conflicts that engulf a dying organization serve a positive function in society. Both help to speed up the recycling of useful resources.

To be sure, this assumes that the final conflict is allowed to take its natural course. When, however, artificial forces sustain an organization in a state of pervasive conflict—as governments will sometimes do with giant, essentially bankrupt corporations for fear of the political ramifications of their demise—then the political organization must be considered significantly dysfunctional.

To conclude our discussion, while I am not personally enthusiastic about organizational politics and have no desire to live in a political organization, even the forms I have described as functional, I do accept, and hope I have persuaded the reader to accept, that this configuration, like the others, does have useful roles to play in a society of organizations. Organizational politics may irritate us, but it can also serve us.

---

* I do not draw the same conclusion for the politicized organization, because the pervasiveness of its conflict usually means that too much energy is wasted in political activity.

14

BEYOND CONFIGURATION
Forces and Forms in Effective Organizations

I originally saw this chapter as a kind of mopping-up operation, to tie together some loose ends and encourage the reader to look beyond the configurations per se. But in an intense period of two or three weeks just before this book went into production (and, to the chagrin of some very tolerant people at The Free Press, again after) things began to develop. As discussed in the text, a student some years earlier had upset my thinking with his question about playing "jigsaw puzzle" or LEGO. That and a number of comments on an earlier draft of this chapter, as well as some consulting experiences just when I was revising it, all suddenly converged to lead me to what has emerged as a statement on organizational effectiveness—the first time I have written directly on this issue. I found myself going not just beyond the actual configurations of my earlier work but beyond the whole notion of configuration that has driven my thinking for almost fifteen years. I am personally excited about the result.

The discussion that follows goes beyond configuration in two ways: It goes back to one and goes past seven. It goes back to one by treating the *forms* as *forces,* in other words by viewing the configurations as a single integrative framework of fundamental forces that act on every organization. And it goes past seven by suggesting that truly creative organizations design forms uniquely suited to their own needs.

Were I asked to state the single most important prescription for developing effective theory, I would answer without hesitation "cherish anomalies." Weak theorists, in my view, dismiss anomalies; they ignore what they cannot readily explain. Breakthroughs, in contrast, come from anomalies that have been identified and held onto, sometimes in the conscious mind, probably more often somewhere below it, until they are explained. The same seems to be true of organizations: The real advances in practice seem to come from difficulties that are put aside and periodically mulled over until they are resolved creatively.

Our discussion of the last seven chapters has all been very pat, a game of jigsaw puzzle with seven ways to combine the pieces. Here, to conclude and integrate that discussion, I set out to play "organizational LEGO" with some of the anomalies I have encountered over the years.

I read somewhere of a professor who told his doctoral students: "Keep your theories simple; reality is complex enough." Well, the discussion of our seven configurations has been simple enough; it is time to face some of the complexities of reality.

LUMPING AND SPLITTING

Charles Darwin once made the distinction between "lumpers" and "splitters." Lumpers categorize; they are the synthesizers, prone to consistency. Once they have pigeonholed something into one box or another, they are done with it. To a lumper in management, strategies are generic, structures are types, managers have a style (X, Y, Z, 9–9, etc.). Splitters nuance; they are the analyzers, prone to distinction. Since nothing can ever be categorized, things are never done with. To a splitter in management, strategies, structures, and styles all vary infinitely.

I believe a key to the effective organization lies in this distinction, specifically in its simultaneous acceptance and rejection (which themselves amount to lumping and splitting). Both are right and both are wrong. Without categories, it would be impossible to practice management. With only categories, it could not be practiced effectively.

For several years I worked as a lumper, seeking to identify types of organizations. Much as in the field of biology, I felt we in management needed some categorization of the "species" with which we dealt. We long had too much of "one best way" thinking, that every organization needed every new technique or idea that came along (like MBO or formal planning or participative management). Thus, in my books on structure and power, I developed various "configurations" of organizations. My premise was that an effective organization "got it all together" as the saying goes—achieved consistency in its internal characteristics, harmony in its processes, fit with its context.

JIGSAW PUZZLE AND LEGO

Every once in a while someone asks you a question that stops you dead in your tracks. Some years back, a doctoral student of mine, Alain Noël, after reading this material on structure and power, asked whether I was intending to play "jigsaw puzzle" or LEGO with it. In other words, did I mean all these elements of organizations to fit together in set ways—to create known images—or were they to be used creatively to build new ones? I had to answer that I had been promoting jigsaw puzzle even if I was suggesting that the pieces could be combined into several images instead of the usual one. But I immediately began to think about playing "organizational LEGO." All of the anomalies I had encountered—all those nasty, well-functioning organizations that refused to fit into one or another of my neat categories—suddenly became opportunities to think beyond configuration. I could become a splitter too.

This chapter is presented in the spirit of playing "organizational LEGO." It tries to show how we can use splitting as well as lumping to understand what makes organizations effective as well as what causes many of their fundamental problems.

FORMS AND FORCES

I shall refer to the configurations of organizations as *forms*. The original five of my structure book—here labeled entrepreneurial, machine, diversified, professional, and innovative—are laid out at the nodes of a pentagon, shown in Figure 14–1. (I shall return to the other two configurations of my power book—the missionary and the political—shortly.)

Many organizations seem to fit naturally into one or another of these categories, *more or less*. We all know the small aggressive entrepreneurial firm, the perfectly machinelike Swiss hotel, the diversified conglomerate, the professional collegial university, the free-wheeling intrapreneurial Silicon Valley innovator. But some organizations do not fit, much to the chagrin of the lumpers. And even many that may seem to, on closer examination reveal curious anomalies. It is difficult to imagine a more machinelike organization than McDonald's; why then does it seem to be rather innovative, at least in its own context? And why is it that whenever I mention to an executive group about a 3M or a Hewlett-Packard as innovative in form, someone from the audience leaps up to tell me about their tight control systems. Innovative adhocracies are not supposed to rely on tight controls.

FIGURE 14–1

An Integrating Pentagon of Forces and Forms

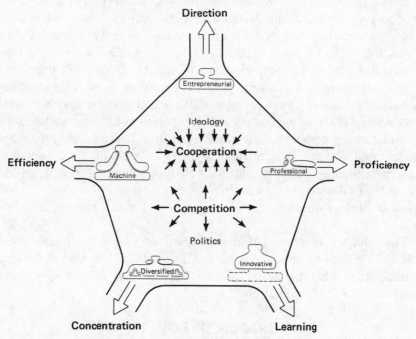

All this of course pleases the splitters. "Come on, Henry," a colleague chided me recently, "in my consulting practice I never see any one of these forms. I can find all of them in all serious organizations." To him, organizations float around the inside of my pentagon; they never make it to any one node. In response, therefore, to the valid claims of the splitters, I recently added *forces* to the pentagon, shown as arrows emanating out from each of the forms. In other words, every form can be thought to represent a force too:

- The entrepreneurial form represents the force for *direction,* for people looking up to the apex of authority, or the leader looking down, and saying, "What we need around here is some *direction,* someone to tell everybody where we all should go."
- The machine form represents the force for *efficiency,* for the staff analysts of the technostructure to look across at everyone else and say, "What they all need there is some order, some work rules and standards to make sure everything comes out as planned."*

---

* Recalling that this, and the diversified configuration, can take the form of instrument or closed system, it should be added that this force for efficiency can be thought to

- The professional form represents the force for *proficiency*, for those in the operating core of the organization to look up and say, "Leave us alone, we're professionals; let us hone our skills and apply them autonomously and all will be well."
- The diversified form represents the forces for *concentration*, for managers in the middle line looking up and down, and saying, "No, we're the ones who should be left alone, to receive clear product–market mandates and then be free to manage them as we see fit, subject only to the performance controls."
- And the innovative form represents the force for *learning*, for experts throughout the organization to look around and say, "What this place really needs is change, adaptation; let's all work together to innovate."

I have so far left out the two forms from my book on power. We can certainly find examples of the missionary configuration, as in the traditional Israeli kibbutz or some radical political movements. Likewise, such organizations as regulatory agencies, sometimes even business corporations, can become so captured by conflict for a time that they come to look like political organizations. But these forms are relatively rare, at least compared with the other five, and so I prefer to show them only as forces (placed in the middle of the pentagon for reasons to be discussed later).

- Ideology represents the force for *cooperation*, for "pulling together" (hence the arrows focus in toward the middle).
- And politics represents the force for *competition*, for "pulling apart" (hence the arrows flare out).

To recap to this point, we have two views of organizational effectiveness. One, for the lumpers, concentrates on a *portfolio of forms*, from which organizations are encouraged to choose if they wish to become effective. The other, for the splitters, focuses on a *system of forces*, with which organizations are encouraged to play in order to become effective. If the lumpers are right, form works; if the splitters are right, we must turn to the forces.

The basis of my argument here is that both views are critical to the practice of management. One represents the most fundamental forces that act on organizations: All serious organizations experience all seven of them, at one time or another if not all the time. And the other represents

---

represent service to a dominant external constituency or else to the organization (and its administrators) as a system unto itself.

the most fundamental forms that organizations can take, which some of them do some of the time. Together, as conceived on the pentagon, these forces and forms appear to constitute a powerful diagnostic framework by which to understand what goes on in organizations and to prescribe effective change in them.

Sometimes one force dominates the behavior of an organization; then we get *configuration*—the appearance of a form. The problem with configuration, however, is that the dominant force can get too powerful, and so have a *contaminating* effect on the other forces. Then the organization risks going *out of control*. Thus the other forces, however secondary, are needed to counterbalance, or *contain*, the dominant one. The lumpers need the splitters.

Some other times, no one force logically dominates, but rather two or more have to exist in a rough balance, as a *combination*. But that creates another problem, which can be called *cleavage*—conflict between the opposing forces. And then there are organizations that experience *conversion*, having to make the transition from one form or combination to another. This also produces opposing forces and cleavage. Splitting has its disadvantages too.

Now containment and cleavage give rise to the need to manage *contradiction*, to reconcile opposing forces. And here the forces of the center of the pentagon come into play, those of cooperation and competition. Lumping for splitters, splitting for lumpers.

We now proceed to lump and to split, to begin by playing jigsaw puzzle and then move quickly to play LEGO. We consider first the configuration of forms, then the combination and conversion of forces (also discussed in a postscript), and finally the management of contradiction, before concluding with a discussion of what makes an organization competent.

CONFIGURATION

When one force dominates the others, based on an organization's particular needs or perhaps just the arbitrary exercise of power, then we should look for the organization to fall close to one of the nodes, to take the form of one of our configurations, more or less. In other words, a force becomes a form when the organization yields to it. Much of what takes place within the configuration then reflects that dominant force. The sociologist Max Weber used the label "ideal type" for the caricatures of reality that our configurations represent. He meant the word "ideal" as pure, not perfect, and we shall refer to our configurations as pure forms. While no real organization matches any one of our pure forms perfectly, as in the examples presented earlier some do come remarkably close.

In the earlier summary chapter of my book on structure, I posed a question: "Do any of these configurations really exist?" I believe my answer to that question bears repeating here.

In one sense, these configurations do not exist at all. After all, they are mere words and pictures on pieces of paper, not reality itself. Real organizations are enormously complex, far more so than any of these caricatures. What these constitute is a kind of theory, or at least the components of a theory, and every theory necessarily simplifies and therefore distorts the reality. The problem, of course, is that in some areas at least, we cannot get by without theory (implicit if not explicit), much as a library cannot get by without a cataloging system.

Thus, our choice is often not between theory and reality but between alternate theories. No one carries reality around in his or her head, no head is that big. Instead we carry around impressions of reality, which amount to implicit theories. Sometimes these are supplemented with explicit frameworks for identifying concepts and interrelating them—in other words, with formal theories, built on systematic investigation known as research, or at least on systematic consideration of experience. In fact, some phenomena cannot be comprehended without such formal aid—how is one to develop an implicit theory of nuclear fission, for example?*

Therefore, I prefer to conclude that the configurations do exist. If I have done my job correctly, they exist where all knowledge ultimately has to exist—in people's minds. With *this* in mind, let us consider some evidence on the occurrence of configurations.

For several years, we have sent out our MBA students at McGill to study organizations in the Montreal area, exposing them, among other things, to my book on structure. At year end, I have circulated a questionnaire asking them if they would categorize their organization as one of the forms, a hybrid of two or more, or none of the above. While the results are only the impressions of a group of students after an exercise of a few months, they do give a rough indication of how the world of organizations appears to a group of intelligent observers. In just over

---

* Sometimes, of course, what we think of as personal implicit theories are just formal ones we have internalized long ago. As John Maynard Keynes put it, "Practical men who believe themselves to be quite exempt from any intellectual influences, are usually the slaves of some defunct economist."

half the cases—66 out of 123—the students felt that a single form fitted best. There were 25 entrepreneurial, 13 machine, 11 diversified, 9 innovative, and 8 professional.* All the rest were labeled combinations, in most cases of two of the forms.

Lumping is, of course, convenient; it appeals to our sense of order. Organizations can be quickly and easily understood. Sometimes we find specific forms favored in particular sectors, for example, the machine configuration in such mass industries as automobile production and airline and postal services, the professional configuration in such highly skilled areas as education and health care, the innovative configuration in the dynamic industries of high technology. Of course, there are also sectors where organizations can choose their form according to how they choose their niche. In restauranting, for example, there is the small "greasy spoon" personally controlled by its entrepreneurial owner, the fast-food machine obsessed with standardizing everything, and, of course, that epitome of professional craft, the gourmet French restaurant. Likewise, consulting firms can be divided into the innovators, which look upon every new client as an opportunity to solve a novel problem in a creative way, and the professionals, which seek to slot all new contracts into some existing category or other and so get on with applying to it a well-established program.

For the lumpers who like cultural stereotypes, we can even extend the idea of forms to national preferences. Perhaps that might reveal some comparative advantages. For example, the Swiss, with their love of order, seem eminently well suited to the machine form. Perhaps that is why their hotels, banks, and railroads function so effectively. And studies of the overseas Chinese suggest that they have a strong propensity to favor the entrepreneurial form, sometimes building up huge empires on a base of personal initiative.[1] And to return to our last two configurations momentarily, the Japanese preference for the ideology of the missionary form is well known, as perhaps is the Italian predisposition toward the political organization.

My own suspicion is that the innovative form works best in Sweden, where the work force is highly educated, there is a long history of creative design, and the preferences for collaboration and consensus

---

* The high incidence of entrepreneurial forms may be thought to reflect the students' bias toward studying small organizations, but I think not. There are many more small organizations (in business and otherwise) than large ones, in many cases entrepreneurial in form. Of the larger ones, I would expect the machine form to predominate in any Western society.

are quite strong in contrast to the tendency to denigrate leadership. In casting about for the nation that seems most suitable to the professional form, where the experts work alone and less creatively, I discovered it right around me. Canadians too have a highly educated work force and a tendency to denigrate leadership, but we lack the Swedish inclinations to innovate and to collaborate—we prefer to let people work on their own. That, I believe, makes us quite good at managing professional organizations: We have the most collegial universities I have found any-where in the world and a health care system that seems to strike the right balance between private initiative and public control.

Big American business, and for that matter big organizations in many spheres of American life, tend to favor the diversified form. Ironically, the same can be said for Eastern bloc nations, where communism can be seen to drive all organizations into one giant divisionalized structure. Indeed, there is a second irony here, because one would expect Americans, with their emphasis on individual initiative and their preference for innova-tion, to favor the entrepreneurial or at least the intrapreneurial (innovative) configuration. That they may do in principle; there is certainly no shortage of either in the United States. But American industry and other sectors today seem to me to be inundated with machine organizations, as divisions of large diversified ones. I believe this derives from the enormous growth of American organizations over the past several decades, a reflection of the exercise of power as much as the consequence of economic forces. As American organizations grew, as they embraced the concepts of ''pro-fessional'' management, and as they increasingly diversified and tried to manage their divisions as instruments subjected to bottom-line controls, they greatly bureaucratized their activities. Earlier I argued that the advan-tages of configuration come with internal harmony coupled with external fit. But here external fit seems to be lacking—markets seem increasingly to want more quality and innovation than many American organizations offer—while internal harmony is disrupted by workers (even managers) who don't particularly relish their roles as cogs in the bureaucratic ma-chinery. Remove harmony and fit, and configuration becomes dysfunc-tional.

When it does fit, however, configuration helps not only to understand organizations but also to manage them. It facilitates diagnosis—everything new that comes along can be assessed in terms of a clear model of the organization—and that in turn facilitates prescription. We know a good deal about each of the common forms—their structures and strategies, their managerial work and management styles, many of their expected problems and opportunities, their people and their systems. We also have a sense of the concepts and techniques that seem to work best in each of them: work-study procedures in the machine form, financial control systems in the diversified, leadership vision in the entrepreneurial, collegiality in the professional, project management and matrix structure in the innovative.

Configuration can also help people who try to make sense of an organization from the outside. A few simple questions can sometimes suggest what form might be expected:

- What are the main groups of operators?
- For each, is their work unskilled or does it require considerable training?
- Do they work alone or must they interact in groups?
- Are their outputs standardized or customized?

Unskilled, standardized work carried out alone suggests the machine configuration. Extensively trained and standardized work done alone suggests the professional one. And the presence of extensively trained workers who require group collaboration and produce customized outputs suggests the innovative form.

Other obvious factors that might be considered in categorizing an organization are the size of its support staff compared with its operators (ratios of three or four to one suggest the professional configuration, sometimes the innovative), the clarity of definition between line and staff (which implies machine or diversified, its absence implying the innovative), the lack of staff altogether (implying the entrepreneurial), and so on. One must, of course, also look for evidence of a preferred mechanism of coordination and clear indications of a center of power. As we shall see, the answers to such questions need not always be unambiguous. But it sure makes things simple when they are.

It can also make them fun. For example, each configuration can be associated with a metaphor (the machine itself, the portfolio for the diversified, the halo for the missionary, the crystalline structure for the innovative, etc.), or with a corresponding animal (the circle of musk-oxen, or perhaps lemmings, for the missionary, the bucket of crabs for the political, the team of beavers for the innovative, etc.). Some configurations also seem to fit naturally with certain sports, American football being the perfect machine (formal leadership, sharp division of labor, preprogrammed work, all highly specialized), perhaps Canadian hockey for the innovative (or is it the political?!).

Thus, for classification, for comprehension, for diagnosis, and for prescription, configuration is most convenient. But it is not without its problems.

CONTAMINATION

Configuration, as noted, represents harmony, consistency, fit. The organization knows what it must do and how; the structure, the distribution of power, and even the culture are clear—you can quickly tell the difference, for example, between a machine and an innovative organization (by who greets you at the door, how he or she is dressed, what the offices—or space in the absence of them—look like). Herein lies its great strength. And its debilitating weakness.

The fact is that configuration contaminates. Just try to be the innovative pocket in an otherwise machine organization, say the research lab in a mass production firm of mature products. Your facility was built in the country, in the belief that distance would shield you from the forces of technocracy. Well, lead may block radiation, but there is no known medium to block the influence of an organizational culture. A director drops in to have a look—"What, no shoes?" Or the controller schedules a visit: "It's 9:15. Where is everybody?" (They quit at 2 A.M.) Of course, contamination is not a problem restricted to the machine configuration. Every time I have done a session with an innovative organization, the question "Who's the most miserable person in adhocracy?" evokes the same response: brief silence, then a few smiles, finally growing laughter as everyone turns to some poor person cowering in the corner. Of course, it is the controller, the person who is supposed to keep the lid on all the madness, the victim of adhocracy's contamination.

Contamination is really just another way of saying that the configurations are not just structures, not even just power systems: They are cultures. Being machinelike or innovative is not just a way of organizing; it's a way of life!

CONTAINMENT

Of course, the argument could be made that this is the price an organization must pay for achieving configuration. No organization can be all things to all people. It is better to select and then concentrate than try to be comprehensive and so end up diffusing efforts. Contamination of innovation is the price paid by the machine organization in order to be efficient, just as contamination of efficiency is the price paid by the innovative organization in order to concentrate on learning. Small prices both. Maybe. And for a time. Until things go out of control.

The fact seems to be that truly successful configurations exist not in pure form. The other forces of our pentagon may be secondary, but their presence is necessary to contain the dominant one. Otherwise the organization risks running out of control. Remove all the arrows but one in our pentagon, and the balance is lost. Without the other forces to anchor it, the organization will fly off in the direction of that remaining arrow. For example, people inclined to break rules may feel hard pressed in the machine organization. But without some of them, the organization may be unable to deal with unexpected problems. Similarly, administration may not be the strongest in the professional organization, but when really weak, anarchy arises as the absolute power of the professionals corrupts them absolutely.

Each configuration thus contains the seeds of its own destruction, residing in its own dominant force. Too much technocratic control destroys the machine organization, unimpeded leadership destroys the entrepreneurial one, and so on. But held in check by the other forces, each configuration can be very effective (in its own favored context). Without what we call *containment,* however, each must eventually become dysfunctional.

My colleagues Danny Miller and Manfred Kets de Vries have published a book that considers neuroses in organizations.[2] They present a cheerful set of five—the dramatic organization, the paranoid organization, the schizoid organization, the compulsive organization, and the depressive organization—each a system having run out of control. Very roughly, if I can be pardoned this lumping, I believe these capture the directions in which each of our five forms tend to run out of control.

Entrepreneurial organizations tend to become dramatic as their leaders, unconstrained by, say, the efficiency forces of the analysts or the proficiency forces of the workers, take their systems off on personal ego trips. Machine organizations, for their part, seem predisposed to compulsion once those analysts, with their obsession for efficiency controls through the intricacy of procedures, take over completely. As for the professional organization, anyone who works in a university or the like well understands their paranoid tendencies. Professionals feel set upon at the best of times; a whole organization of them free to pursue their obsessions with proficiency, independent of the forces of administration or innovation, cannot help but become collectively paranoid. I need not dwell on the depressing effects of the obsession with that mercenary bottom line in the diversified organization; the effect of turning the financial screws on morale, on innovation, and on commitment and culture are now widely appreciated. Finally, the problem in innovative organizations is that while they must continually innovate, which requires divergence, they must also exploit the benefits of their innovation, which requires more of a convergent orientation. The presence of forces other than learning can help balance that pressure; without them the organization can easily become schizoid, as it fails to make up its collective mind what to do.

In discussing the containing effects of the other forces, I do not wish to destroy my case for configuration. The point is not that every organization must do everything, rather that the dominant force must somehow be tempered by the secondary ones.

COMBINATION

The world of management would be awfully convenient (for us lumpers at least) if organizations simply pigeonholed themselves neatly into one category or another. Fortunately, many organizations refuse to cooperate, forcing us to play LEGO. IBM makes my life miserable by appearing to be so efficient in its operations ("the big blue machine") and then turning around periodically and innovating in a most adhocratic way. Equally unnerving is the symphony orchestra that blends the personal leadership of its conductor with the trained skills of its musicians. Is it top-down entrepreneurial or bottom-up professional? There are diversified organizations that work wonderfully well with loose formal controls and innovative organizations that thrive with unexpectedly tight ones.

We can understand these organizations as *combinations* of the forces, sometimes as *hybrids* of the forms. They attend to different forces without letting only one dominate, doing so either in a steady-state balance or else at least in a dynamic equilibrium over time.

The symphony orchestra is an example of a stable and uniform combination. The organization cannot exist without great levels of proficiency coupled with strong central direction. (The Russians apparently tried a leaderless symphony orchestra shortly after their revolution but soon gave it up as unworkable.*) Here combination pervades the entire system as a balance among forces rather than forms.

In other cases, however, the organization combines different forms that dominate different parts. For example, newspapers must couple machine structures in their printing function with what are probably best described as professional structures in their editorial function.[†] Banks sometimes combine a machinelike retailing service for the mass market with a more innovative wholesaling service for merchant banking. And mass production firms that experience frequent or at least important changes in market demand must somehow achieve a balance between innovation in their development work and machinelike efficiency in their production—apparently the case of an IBM. In fact, an employee of Apple of Canada, upon hearing these ideas, suggested to me that in his firm I would have to add the entrepreneurial form in sales due to a dynamic chief, the professional form in marketing as well as in the training unit, and the innovative form also in the new venture unit.

As I noted earlier, in the McGill MBA student reports combinations appeared almost as frequently as configurations. They so labeled 57 of the 123 organizations, 51 as hybrids of two forms, 5 of three, and 1 of four. These combinations ranged widely—there were seventeen different types in all, with diversified machines being the most common (9), followed by innovative professionals (8), entrepreneurial professionals (6), and entrepreneurial machines (5).[††]

---

* The state administrative apparatus did not wither away either, as predicted. Machine bureaucracy hardly has less of a need for administration than the symphony orchestra!

[†] Earlier in the book, I described the editorial function as adhocracy. But a study by a group of students at Laval University suggested that reporters work on relatively standardized assignments from rather well-defined pigeonholes ("beats"), as in professional bureaucracy. (Indeed, for one story that fell between the pigeonholes, reporters from three different beats showed up!) Some of my own work with engineering groups likewise suggests that when engineering is oriented toward modifying standard designs rather than creating new ones, the structure of this function is better described as professional than as innovative.

[††] I personally believe that the diversified and innovative forms are the most difficult to sustain in pure configuration (the former a conglomerate with no links between the divisions, the latter a very loose and free-wheeling structure). Thus they should be common in hybrid combinations. Also, some of these hybrids reflect common transitions in organization life cycles (as in the entrepreneurial firm that eventually settles down as a mature mass production machine), which suggests that hybrids occur commonly during transitions between the forms as well (as I shall discuss below).

Of course, since most people see it when they believe it, students exposed to my structure book are apt to see organizations at least as hybrids of the configurations if not as pure types. But real "organizational LEGO" involves playing with the forces and forms in broader ways. I encountered one successful Dutch company in computer software whose founder prided himself on having diversified his firm into regional divisions all over Holland yet not having the machinelike divisions I would have predicted. In front of an audience of six hundred of his compatriots, he said he could not find his organization in my pentagon. He was looking for it at the nodes. I suggested I could find it in the middle. Since he wanted entrepreneurial or intrapreneurial divisions, he relied for control not on the performance systems of the traditional diversified configuration, but on the norms of ideology. Division managers shared ideas and so developed their own approaches, to which they all conformed. That allowed him to eliminate most of the staff groups normally found at corporate headquarters, which tend to impose machinelike structure on the divisions. The regional divisions were thus free to be more innovative. But as a modest Dutchman, he left out one other important element, in my opinion, at the top of the pentagon: Without his central direction, it was doubtful the whole thing would have held together as it did. His organization thus seemed to combine very effectively the force of concentration with those of cooperation and direction, in order to promote that of innovation. Of course, he may not have needed my pentagon to do this, but I could still use it to help explain what was going on in his firm and, more importantly perhaps, to help predict and deal with what might go wrong later.

Even for an organization that has achieved configuration, we must sometimes play LEGO too. The Brookhaven National Laboratory used my book on structure to classify nuclear power plants for purposes of assessing supervisory influences on plant safety. They concluded that with their plethora of controls and standards, these plants looked primarily like machine organizations. I concurred. But on examination of the plants, we found more going on. For one thing, the design of the facility in the first place, and its construction, required another form of organization, professional or innovative, depending on how established was the technology at the time of construction. And the design of the standards—the system "software" in a sense—an ongoing activity that involved great numbers of engineers in the technostructures, looked rather professional in nature. (Indeed, there was so much of this going on that the plants could almost be characterized as professional organizations in the business of writing standards!) It was the execution of the design, the day-to-day operations and maintenance of the facility, that looked machinelike, because compliance to the standards was so critical. But further consideration suggested that these systems had a need for learning too, that the operators occasionally had to cope with unexpected problems in the short term and to ensure their correction in the long term by communicating their occurrence back to the engineers (in their plants and others). This seemed to require an innovative overlay on the machine structure. And finally, the managers of all this had to deal with the contradiction between machinelike compliance on the one hand and innovative learning on the other. To do that effectively, as I shall discuss later, they probably had to turn to the forces in the center of our pentagon.

My point is that there is always the splitting of gray between the black-and-white of lumping. Theories are used in management not to mirror reality but to help explain it. They may do so deductively by helping us to slot the behavior of organizations into categories, but they must also do so inductively by providing the concepts through which we can see new things, and so make better diagnoses. In our pentagon, we identify the nodes so that we can map the space.

CLEAVAGE

Combinations may not experience contamination—since one strong force can hold another in check—but they instead experience *cleavage*. That is, they tend to conflict along their natural fault lines, where their strong forces meet. Thus, the musicians dispute with the conductor, for they are, after all, professionals who do not need anyone to tell them what to do. Of course, that is not true, as Fellini illustrated so graphically in his film *Orchestra Rehearsal*. The revolting musicians, after experiencing complete anarchy, finally defer to the leader they realize is so necessary to their performance. (Fellini was supposed to have meant the film as an allegory on Italian politics, which suggests that our pentagon may have relevance for governments too.)

Likewise the researchers promoting innovation in a manufacturing firm will often conflict with the manufacturing people who want to get the system stabilized for operating efficiency. Newspapers may be fortunate in this regard, since cleavage is alleviated by the formal decoupling of its different functions (referred to as "truncation" in Chapter 11): Editorial produces camera-ready copy, which it hands over to the printing department. The two functions are thus independent in a way that the *inter*dependent industry people in research and manufacturing, who must not only interact closely but often even reach joint decisions, can only envy.

Cleavage is a necessary evil, an expected cost of organizing in combination. My own belief is that, newspapers and the like aside, it must usually be managed by alleviation more than elimination, or, perhaps better, by its redirection to constructive ends. Thus I conclude that configuration is the preferred way of organizing, that combination is effective only so long as the organization has no choice. Configuration promotes definition and discipline rather than conflict and contradiction. The organization knows what its dominant orientation must be and so can get on with pursuing it. For example, it can act like a bureaucratic machine and be proud of its efficiency even if that means a reduced capacity to innovate.

Most of the examples of hybrid combinations given above appeared in organizations that seemed to have no choice. For example, a management in need of significant degrees of productive efficiency as well as research innovation has to combine these different forces. But there is no shortage of examples of hybrid combinations that are dysfunctional because they are arbitrary, or because they reflect a management that cannot make up its mind. In wanting the best of more than one world, it often ends up with the worst of several. There are, for example, firms whose human resource people promote the professionalism of worker participation while their work-study analysts continue to impose stifling efficiency controls on those same workers. And there are those diversified corporations that no sooner give operating autonomy to their division managers to manage as they see fit than they usurp it by centralizing some function critical to that management at headquarters. Sometimes this may be necessary—retail chains with regional divisions, for example, often need to centralize certain merchandising functions. But at other times such behavior is arbitrary, as management wavers between the forces for central efficiency and divisional concentration.

Unfortunately, there are times when the arbitrary forces are imposed on the organizations from without. A common instance is the public school system subject to the controls of government people who believe that all organizations, no matter how professionally trained their people, should be managed like bureaucratic machines. To these technocrats, the machine configuration is not just *a* structure, it *is* structure; it is not *one* way to organize, it is *the only* sensible way to organize. Common too, for the same reason, is the diversified corporation or even government department that tries to force all its units, no matter what their own needs for learning or proficiency, to organize like bureaucratic machines. (In a seminar I gave recently for people in the Australian government, one frustrated manager who had seen enough of such things offered me a label for it to go along with my "bureaucracies" and "adhocracies"—"hypo-cracy," he called it. It amounts to saying one thing while doing another, such as the common practice of centralizing in the name of decentralization. Alongside our configurations, conversions, etc., we might call this just plain "con"!)

Organizations certainly need to give attention to conflicting forces, but not in ways that confuse and frustrate their people. Closely controlled workers may not be happier than more autonomous ones, but they are certainly better off than confused ones. Innovative or professional divisions may not be as *efficient* as machinelike ones, but they can sometimes be more *effective*. Diversified corporations unable to respect the intrinsic needs of certain of their divisions are better off divesting them. And governments have no business trying to force all professional institutions to act like bureaucratic machines.

CONVERSION

Sometimes organizations have to convert from one configuration, or combination, to another, usually because of a change in the forces acting upon them.

That change may be external to the organization or intrinsic. To consider the former, the appearance of a new operating technology may require much higher levels of worker training and so force a machine form to become more professional. Of course, such transitions can also be temporary, the result of forces that arise for a limited time. Thus, for example, when faced with dramatic external change, a machinelike organization may have to turn temporarily to a strong entrepreneurial leader for new direction. Some organizations even oscillate between two forms, making periodic transitions back and forth, for example favoring the efficiency of the machine form during recessions when customers are price conscious and the learning of the innovative form as economic growth favors product differentiation.[3]

But change does not always come arbitrarily from the outside. Sometimes it is intrinsic to the organization's very nature, often a reflection of its own internal development and so necessitating a permanent conversion. In these cases, forces within a configuration sow the seeds of its destruction and drive it to another form. For example, the intrinsic vulnerability of the entrepreneurial form stems from its centralization of power in the hands of a single individual. So long as the organization remains small and simple, this may not pose a problem—assuming containment of the dramatic neurosis. But growth and increasing complexity can undermine such personalized power, and stabilization of markets can require more efficiency than is usually provided by this configuration. A transition to the machine form may then become necessary. In a consulting firm, the tendency to be innovative at the outset may wane over time as the consultants tire of constant change; in their efforts to settle on more standardized applications of their skills, they naturally drive the organization toward the professional form.

While the externally driven conversions may be inflicted on the organization unexpectedly, the internally driven ones are somewhat predictable: They tend to sequence themselves in particular ways over time, known as "life cycles." Common, for example, is the sequence along the left side of our pentagon, from entrepreneurial to machine to diversified forms as a business first establishes itself, settles down eventually to exploit a secure market, and later enters new businesses once its traditional one has been saturated. The postscript to this chapter presents a fairly elaborate model of organization life cycles, based on transitions of power.

Either way, conversion can occur quickly or slowly. When it is intrinsically natural and long overdue, it may take place very rapidly, much as a super-saturated liquid freezes as soon as it is disturbed. But more commonly, it would seem, whether internally or externally driven, transitions tend to be prolonged and agonizing, as the organization sits suspended between its old and new forms, with one group promoting change and another resisting it. The period during the transition amounts, of course, to a hybrid combination, and given the inevitable confrontation between the two forces, generally leads to cleavage. Thus a John Sculley trying to settle Apple down confronts its founder, Steve Jobs, who wishes to sustain its free-wheeling entrepreneurial spirit. Or those consultants who wish to keep innovating challenge their colleagues who wish to converge on more standardized activities. Of course, conversion becomes combination when the organization gets stalled in such a transition and so remains suspended between the opposing forces.

CONTRADICTION

One important conclusion that comes out of our discussion so far is that the achievement of effectiveness in an organization generally requires the management of *contradiction*. This was especially evident in the point about cleavage in the combinations and conversions, but it is also true of contamination and the need for containment in the configurations. Here, I believe, is especially where the two forces in the center of our pentagon came into play. Each has much to do with contradiction, acting to exacerbate it or working to alleviate it. Indeed, I believe that these two forces themselves represent a contradiction that must be managed if an organization is not to run out of control.

I have placed the cooperative pulling together of ideology and the competitive pulling apart of politics in the center of the pentagon for two reasons. First, as noted earlier, while examples of their corresponding forms (the missionary and political organization) can be found, I believe that compared to the others, it is the forces that are common here, not the forms. Certainly one is hard pressed to find any reasonably large organization that is free of politics. And ideologies, while hard pressed themselves in these days of restructuring, etc., are nonetheless somewhat common.

But instead of considering these forces as merely two more alongside the other five, I prefer to see them differently, as *catalytic* forces that *infuse* organizations in which the other five interplay. This is my second reason for placing them in the center of the pentagon.

COOPERATION

Ideology represents the force for cooperation in an organization, for collegiality and consensus. People "pull together" for the common good—"we" are in this together.

I use the word ideology here to describe an organizational culture that is rich and unique and so binds the members tightly to the organization. They commit themselves personally to it and identify with its needs. Such ideologies usually arise with a charismatic leader who has a vision for his or her organization; hence they are commonly associated with the entrepreneurial form, at least initially. But ideologies often outlive their developers and so can infuse other forms of organization as well. Thus we have the ideological machine called McDonald's that Ray Kroc created and the ideological innovator that Messrs. Hewlett and Packard built up. And in Chapter 12 we discussed Clark's "distinctive" colleges, small liberal arts colleges such as Swarthmore and Antioch whose professional forms were infused with powerful ideologies.[4]

Ideology encourages people to look inward—to take their lead from the imperatives of the organization's own vision instead of looking outward to what comparative organizations are doing. (Of course, when ideology is strong, there are no comparable organizations!) Is that not one meaning of Hewlett-Packard's famous "next bench syndrome"—that product designers get their stimulus for innovation not from the aggregations of marketing research reports but from the needs of particular colleagues working alongside them. This notion is indicated by the direction of the arrows in the pentagon—a circle facing inward, as if to shield the organization from outside forces. Such ideology above all draws people to cooperate with each other, to work together to take the organization where they, all of them, duly indoctrinated into its norms, believe it must go. In this sense, ideology should be thought of as the spirit of the organization, the life force that infuses the skeleton of its formal structure.

The important effect of this is to reduce cleavage and contamination, which in turn facilitates the management of contradiction. People in the organization can more easily reconcile opposing forces when it is the organization itself they believe in rather than any one of its particular parts. This is what helps me to understand how big blue machines like IBM are able to innovate—"snappy bureaucracies" is what I like to call such organizations. The presence of strong internal ideologies—related in IBM as well as McDonald's to owner or family control in the recent past—allows them to overlay adhocracy as a kind of shadow structure on their machine form to promote necessary change. If you believe in IBM instead of productive efficiency or marketing finesse per se, then when things really matter you will suspend your departmental rivalries to enable IBM to adapt. Great organizations simply pull together when they have to, because they are rooted in great systems of beliefs.

In his popular book *Competitive Strategy,* Michael Porter warns against getting "stuck in the middle" between a strategy of "cost leadership" (corresponding to the machine force for routine efficiency) and one of "differentiation" (including an emphasis on quality or innovation).[5] How, then, has Toyota been able to produce such high-quality automobiles at such reasonable cost? Why didn't it get stuck in the middle?

I believe Porter's admonition stems from the view, prevalent in American management circles throughout this century, and reflected equally in my own case for configuration, that if an organization favors one particular orientation, others must suffer. If the efficiency experts have the upper hand, quality must get slighted; if it is the elite designers who get their way, productive efficiency lags; and so on. This may be true so long as an organization is treated as just a collection of different activities—a portfolio of products and functions, etc. But when the spirit of ideology is infused into the bones of its structure, the organization takes on an integrated life of its own and this ceases to be true.

Workers on the American automobile assembly lines have long had good reason to consider themselves only cogs in their bureaucratic machines. Indeed, even within the administrative structure of a General Motors, critics continue to bemoan the effects on engineering design of having had all those financial people in the chief executive's chair. But at Toyota, one has the impression that even if you sweep the floor you do not regard yourself as doing a menial job of little consequence; rather you are doing your part to make Toyota great. Is that not why the assembly workers are allowed to shut down the line? Each and every one can be treated as an individual capable of making decisions for the good of Toyota. The only thing that gets stuck in the middle at Toyota, then, is conventional Western management theory!

The infusion of ideology into a configuration can alleviate the effects of contamination; in a combination it can alleviate the effects of cleavage. Contradictory forces are not just tolerated but respected, however, grudgingly: "Old Joe, over there, that nut in the engineering office—we accountants sometimes wonder about him. But we know this place could never function without him." Or in the symphony orchestra, the musicians respect their conductor because together they produce great music.

Even better than reconciling the contradictory forces expressed by different parts of the organization, ideology can cause these forces to be expressed within individuals themselves. Instead of building a laboratory out in the country and hoping it will be able to impose innovation on the rest of the system, everyone in the organization is charged with innovation alongside his or her regular job, as in those quality circles in Japan. Or, to take the opposite case, control in the ideological innovative organization is not reserved for that poor controller cowering in the corner; even the most creative scientist is expected to worry about costs and efficiency too. That presumably explains the tolerance for rather tight control systems in companies like 3M or H-P. In metaphorical terms, it is not so difficult to change hats in an organization when they are all emblazoned with the same insignia!

All in all it sounds like a great thing, this ideology. Unfortunately, consulting promises notwithstanding, it is not there for the taking, to be plucked off the tree of management systems like just another piece of technological fruit. As Karl Weick has argued, "A corporation doesn't *have* a culture. A corporation *is* a culture. That's why they're so horribly difficult to change."[6] The fact is that there are no techniques for building ideologies, no five easy steps to a better culture. These are built slowly and patiently by committed leaders who have found interesting missions for their organizations and care deeply about the people who perform them. To my mind, the critical ingredient is authenticity. In fact, I believe in a kind of psychic law of management here: that workers, customers, every one involved with a management, no matter how physically distant, can tell when it is genuine in its beliefs and when it is just mouthing the right words.

At best, those five easy steps overlay a thin veneer of culture that washes off in the first political storm. Usually, however, these steps don't even do that; instead they often destroy whatever is left of the ideology that existed before. Indeed, any one of a number of the easy steps of "modern" management can do that with great effectiveness: "Focus on the bottom line, as if you make money by managing money." Or "move managers around so they can never get to know anything but 'management' well." Or "hire and fire workers the way you buy and sell machines (for everything is, after all, just a portfolio)."

But is ideology always such a great thing? An answer to this question lies in the arrows of the pentagon. While those of ideology form what looks like a protective halo around the organization, the fact that they all face inward means that in the absence of other forces to anchor them, they too can go out to control: Their inward thrust leads eventually to *implosion*. Earlier I claimed that ideologies cause people to look within the organization for direction. Too much of this and the organization loses touch with its context, closes in on itself. Even its capacity to innovate can become a liability as it continues to improve outmoded strategies, themselves rooted in ideology and so immutable. We have no need for the extreme example of a Jonestown to appreciate the negative consequences of ideology; we all know firms with strong cultures that, like the proverbial bird, flew in ever diminishing circles until they disappeared up their own rear ends!*

COMPETITION

Politics represents the force for competition in an organization, for conflict and confrontation. People pull apart for their own benefit. "They" get in our way.

Politics can infuse any of the configurations or combinations, exacerbating contamination or cleavage. Indeed, both problems were characterized as intrinsically conflictive in the first place; politics only worsens them. The people behind the dominant force in a configuration—the technocrats in the machine organization, the creative types in the innovative one—lord their power over everyone else, while those behind each of the main forces in a combination relish any opportunity to do battle with the other to gain advantage. Thus, in contrast to a machinelike Toyota pulling together is the Chrysler Iaccoca found when he arrived pulling apart; the culture of an innovative Hewlett-Packard stands in contrast to the politics of a NASA during the Challenger tragedy; for every "distinctive" college there are other "destructive" ones.

Of course, it is clear from the outward facing arrows of the pentagon what politics can do to an organization when unconstrained by other forces: cause *explosion,* as everything pulls apart.

Politics seems to be a more natural force in organizations than ideology. That is to say, organizations left alone seem to pull apart rather more easily. Getting systems of human beings to pull together, in contrast, appears to require continual deliberate effort on the part of dedicated managers. In fact, those easy steps listed above that inadvertently kill ideology generally do so by encouraging politics in its place. The quick fix in place of careful consideration, superficial pronouncements instead of genuine commitments, worrying about the numbers while people are treated as objects—all these are breeding grounds for political conflict.

---

* This may seem to contradict the point just made about how an infusion of ideology can make a machine organization capable of change. But it must be borne in mind what kind of change that is: *within* the perspective of the ideology. To reiterate an earlier example, McDonald's introduction of Egg McMuffin constituted the addition of a position within its existing perspective—in other words, the product brought the firm into the breakfast market, but it remained purely McDonald's. In fact, the company would probably have great difficulty changing perspective. (How about McDuckling à l'Orange served at your candle-lit table?)

Thus in contrast to ideology as ostensibly all things good, we have politics as the force for evil. Or do we? The fact is that politics can also act as a catalytic force for the benefit of an organization.

In my own work with organizations, the single most commonly asked question—the virtual obsession of today's managers—is how can we get bureaucracies to change. I have already tried to show how ideology, alongside entrepreneurial direction and intrapreneurial innovation, can be a force for revitalization, and also a force for the opposite, for resistance to fundamental change. Likewise some of the other forces in organizations—especially those for efficiency, for proficiency, and for concentration—often act to resist fundamental change. When these all team up and overwhelm an organization's entrepreneurial and intrapreneurial capabilities, then, ironically, politics may be the only force available to stimulate the necessary change. The organization must, in other words, pull apart before it can adapt: "Young Turks" must confront the "old guard." Even when the protagonists act out of pure self-interest, the effect of their actions can be to shock the organization into adapting despite itself. It appears to be an inevitable fact of organizational life today that a great deal of the most significant change is driven, not by managerial insight or specialized expertise or ideological commitment, let alone the technology of planning, but by political challenge.

To recap, both ideology and politics can promote organizational effectiveness or undermine it. Ideology infused into another configuration can be a force for revitalization, energizing the organization and making its people more responsive. But that same ideology can also hinder fundamental change, since everything must be interpreted in terms of "the word." Likewise, politics can impede change and waste resources. But it can also promote change that may be available in no other way, by allowing those who recognize the need for the change to challenge those who do not. Thus ideology, that harmonizing force for cooperation, can make an organization insular; politics, that mercenary force for competition, can enable an organization to adapt.

COOPERATION COMBINED WITH COMPETITION

How do organizations counter the imploding effects of ideology and the exploding effects of politics? My belief is that these two catalytic forces in the center of the pentagon must naturally counter each other. In fact, I suspect that another clue to the effective organization lies in

FIGURE 14–2
Combining the Catalytic Forces

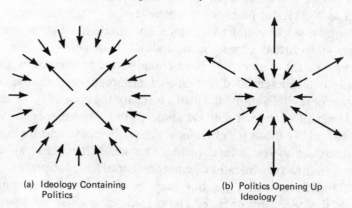

(a) Ideology Containing
    Politics

(b) Politics Opening Up
    Ideology

maintaining a balance between these forces of cooperation and competition: They must form their own combination, must exist in a kind of dynamic tension. Politics challenges the insularity of ideology, ideology constrains the destructiveness of politics.

Again the arrows can tell the story. As shown in Figure 14–2, enveloping the exploding circle of politics within the imploding circle of ideology creates one kind of balance. Consider, for example, those Talmudic scholars who fight furiously with each other over the interpretation of every word in their ancient books yet close ranks to present a united front to the outside world. Is this not exactly the behavior we find in some of the most effective business corporations, IBM among others? Likewise, is not surrounding the converging force of ideology by the diverging force of politics, in order to challenge the organization's most basic assumptions, not the most effective way to counter its inclination to implode?*

Of course, these two catalytic forces need not interact continuously. My own belief is that the pulling together of ideology is probably the preferred state most of the time, so that the organization can pursue its given mission with full vigor. But periodically it must pull apart through

* A doctoral student at McGill, Joe Lampel, came up with the ingenious idea, in the spirit of LEGO, that we think of the children's game of paper, scissors, and stone, extending the rules a bit to consider the interplay of these forces—for example, paper (ideology) covers scissors (politics), but scissors cut paper; stone (machine form) crumples paper (ideology), but paper also covers stone, and so on.

the force of politics to ensure necessary change that has been discouraged by the prevailing ideology.

COMPETENCE

One final issue in this summary chapter on organizations: competence. What makes an organization effective? The question has been an elusive one in organizational theory, and I have no intention of dwelling on it here. In fact, I believe this whole section, indeed this whole book, addresses that question, in a variety of ways. What I do wish to do in closing is summarize briefly the various views of organizational effectiveness that have infiltrated our discussion, presented below as a series of hypotheses. Some have been mentioned previously, but this discussion draws them all together.

CONVERGENCE. First is the *convergence* hypothesis. "One best way" is its motto, the single lens its image. There is a proper way to view, and so to design, an organization. As we saw, this is usually associated with the machine form. A good structure is one with a rigid hierarchy of authority, with spans of control no greater than six, with heavy use of strategic planning, MIS, and whatever else happens to be in the current fashion of the rationalizers.

Of course, "one best way" thinking need not always promote the machine configuration. In *In Search of Excellence*, Peters and Waterman argued that ideology was the key to an organization's success.[7] We concurred for a time here too, but later pointed out the negative effect ideology can have on organizations. (In fact, Peters and Waterman give little attention to the need for strategic renewal in their book, concentrating instead on how ideology can promote operating excellence.)

Thus, while we cannot dismiss this hypothesis—sometimes there *are* proper things to do in most if not all organizations—we must take issue with its general thrust. Society has paid an enormous price for "one best way" thinking over the course of this century, on the part of all its organizations that have been drawn into using what is fashionable rather than functional. We need to look beyond the obvious, beyond the convergence hypothesis.

CONGRUENCE. Beyond convergence is the *congruence* hypothesis, "it all depends" being its motto, the buffet table its image. Introduced in organization theory in the 1960s, it suggests that running an organization is like choosing dinner from such a table—a little bit of this, a little bit of that, all selected according to specific needs. Organizational effectiveness thus becomes a question of matching a given set of internal attributes, treated as a kind of portfolio, with various situational factors. The hypotheses presented in Chapter 6—what attributes of structure best suit large size, a stable environment, an automated technical system, etc.—were presented in the spirit of this view of organizational effectiveness. The congruence hypothesis has certainly been an improvement, but like a dinner plate stacked with an odd assortment of foods, it has not been good enough.

CONFIGURATION. And so the *configuration* hypothesis was introduced and became the basis for the seven previous chapters of this section. "Getting it all together" is its motto, the jigsaw puzzle its image, the lumpers its champions. Design your organization as you would do a jigsaw puzzle, fitting all the pieces together to create a coherent, harmonious picture. There is certainly reason to believe that organizations succeed in good part because they are consistent in what they do; they are certainly easier to manage that way. Configuration entered our discussion as structure, then became also situation and later power, and finally emerged as all of them woven together into culture. But, as we have seen, configuration has its limitations too.

CONTRADICTION. While the lumpers may like the configuration hypothesis, the splitters prefer the *contradiction* hypothesis. Manage the dialectic, the dynamic tension, is their call, perhaps "to each his own" their motto, the tug of war their image. They point to the common occurrence of combinations and conversions, where organizations are forced to manage contradictory forces. And while those in favor of the convergence approach might applaud the role of ideology, even that of politics (cooperation, or competition, as the one best way), the splitters would respond with justification that these two are themselves contradictory, and so must be managed as a dialectic. This is an important hypothesis, together with that of configuration (in their own dynamic tension) certainly an important clue to organizational effectiveness. But still it is not sufficient.

CREATION. The truly great organization transcends convergence, congruence, configuration, and contradiction, while building on them to achieve something more. It respects the *creation* hypothesis. Creativity is its forte, "understand your inner nature" is its motto, LEGO its image. The most interesting organizations live at the edges, far from the logic of conventional organizations, where as Raphael has pointed out in biology (for example, between the sea and the land, or at the forest's edge),[8] the richest, most varied, and most interesting forms of life can be found. These organizations invent novel approaches that solve festering problems and so provide all of us with new ways to deal with our world of organizations. Their effectiveness depends on the two things we have sought to promote throughout this book: a rich understanding of the world of organizations and a propensity to play with that knowledge in creative ways.*

POSTSCRIPT: A LIFE CYCLE MODEL OF ORGANIZATIONS

Earlier, the notion of life cycles of organizations was mentioned. Here we return to it, presenting an elaborate model of how organizations undergo sequences of conversions as they develop over time. In presenting this, I put my natural colors back on: This is lumping with a vengeance (even the sixth and seventh forms return to our discussion). I believe this model has important consequences for a society of organizations; this point will be discussed briefly in conclusion here but pursued vigorously in the final chapter of this book.

Given our seven configurations, it is not difficult to think of examples of all the possible transitions between pairs of them, forty-two in all counting both directions, or really forty-nine adding in the transition that each configuration can make to another form of itself (for example, replacing the leader in the entrepreneurial form). But certain transitions do seem to be far more common, for example from the entrepreneurial configuration to the machine configuration as an organization grows and matures.

It is the transitions that reflect the *intrinsic* forces on organizations that appear to be most common—the naturally occurring forces that sow the seeds of the destruction of one configuration and drive it toward another (or drive the organization itself to demise). The less common

---

* In this spirit, I would like to invite anyone who has been able to play organizational LEGO constructively with these forces and forms to write to me at McGill University (Montreal H3A 1G5, Canada) about their experiences. I hope to collect this for a subsequent book.

transitions, in contrast, appear to reflect the external changes that occur independently of the organization—for example, a shift in technology, new government legislation, the arrival of a new competitor. The variety of these is far wider, as are their causes, and so they cannot be predicted (at least not by studying the organization itself). Moreover, there are configurations that appear most often in young organizations, notably the entrepreneurial, or in more established organizations, notably the machine, or during decline, notably the politicized. This suggests a life cycle model of organizations.

Two key assumptions underlie life cycle models of organizations. The first is that organizations spend most of their lives in steady states, in other words as forms that are stable and enduring, but that these states change periodically as an organization undergoes brief periods of transition. Earlier we referred to this as a "quantum theory" of organizational change. The ecologists call it "punctuated equilibrium," while in organization theory, William Starbuck has referred to "metamorphosis models," in which organizations grow not in "a smooth continuous process" so much as in one "marked by abrupt and discrete changes" in conditions and structures.[9] The second assumption is that the actual steady-state forms organizations adopt over time tend to arrange themselves in sequences according to their stage of life. In other words, there are forms associated with birth, growth, maturity, and decline, perhaps even with the death of organizations.

Life cycle models have long been popular in the literature of organization theory. They have also long been criticized, since particular organizations exhibit all kinds of idiosyncratic changes over time, caused by the changes I called external. Moreover, some organizations settle into particular forms for long periods of time, while others break common sequences by reverting back to what seem to be earlier stages. Nonetheless, life cycle models do capture something important about organizations, namely *leading tendencies* in many of them if not compulsory changes in all of them—in other words, sequences that are common rather than imperative.

Most of the well-known life cycle models track changes in structure. The model I shall present here is oriented more to changes in power (though particular structures do, of course, correspond to particular systems of power). Thus, it reintroduces to our discussion forms that I earlier associated with power, namely the missionary and political configurations, as well as the instrument and closed system forms of the machine configuration.

Figure 14–3 presents our life cycle model in four stages, labeled

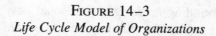

FIGURE 14–3
Life Cycle Model of Organizations

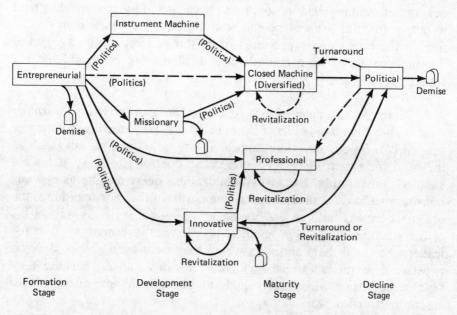

formation (as an entrepreneurial configuration), *development* (as a missionary, instrument-machine, or perhaps innovative configuration), *maturity* (as a closed-machine, professional, or perhaps innovative configuration), and *decline* (as a political configuration, which is also shown accompanying some of the earlier transitions). The demise of the organization is shown (by a tombstone) as common at certain points of the formation and development stages as well as after decline. The model is described below as a series of propositions, each with a label. Note that these propositions are presented in declarative form to highlight them as hypotheses to be considered, not as definitive conclusions. They appear to me to represent leading tendencies in many organizations, but while there is evidence for some, others are in the realm of speculation. All remain to be verified by systematic research.

FORMATION

1. Organizations are typically established in the entrepreneurial form ("personal creation"). A new organization generally finds itself with a mission, some resources, and a leader. The rest must be created. That usually gives the founding leader great personal power: Others defer to him or her to get on with the building of the organization. Moreover, new organizations (even in nonprofit areas, including government) tend to attract forceful leaders, people who prefer to "do their own thing" free of the bureaucratic pressures of established organizations. Hence the entrepreneurial form tends to appear at the outset in all kinds of situations.

2. *Many young organizations remain in the entrepreneurial form as long as their founding leaders remain in office* ("perpetuation of entrepreneurship"). Forces may soon appear in the new organization (such as the need for expertise or for technocratic controls) to drive it toward another configuration. But many organizations delay making an obvious transition so long as their founders remain in office. For one thing, the organization was built around its leader's personal style, as well as his or her strategic vision. For another, people tend to remain loyal to the leader who hired them and with whom they have been able to develop a personal relationship. Furthermore, founding leaders, because they tend to be strong-willed individuals to begin with, are often able to sustain personal power.

DEVELOPMENT

3. *Entrepreneurial organizations tend to be vulnerable; many die, while others tend sooner or later to make a transition to another configuration* ("precariousness"). There are some entrepreneurial organizations that remain under the personal control of their founders for long periods. But the entrepreneurial configuration is fundamentally precarious, relying as it does on a single individual. As mentioned earlier, one heart attack can literally wipe out its prime mechanism of coordination. Moreover, entrepreneurial leaders, because they have so much personal power, can easily lose touch. Some get so involved with the operating detail that they loose touch with the need to change strategy. Others become so opportunistic, constantly flitting from one strategic change to another, that they lose touch with the operations.

No matter what its manifestation, the fundamental problem for the entrepreneurial configuration is that there is usually no rational mechanism for self-correction. So much power focuses on the leader that there is often no one able or willing to make things right, at least not in the context of the entrepreneurial configuration. Hence, the demise of the organization or, failing that, of the configuration would seem likely to follow leadership problems in the entrepreneurial organization.

4. The most natural, if not common, transition for the entrepreneurial organization is to the missionary configuration, at least after the departure of a charismatic, visionary leader ("institutionalization of charisma"). Left on their own, with a strong sense of mission after the departure of a revered leader, the followers who remain have a tendency (in the vocabulary of sociology) to *institutionalize* his or her charisma, in other words to form a missionary configuration in which selection, socialization, and indoctrination are used to reinforce the established system of beliefs. But relatively few such organizations seem to be left on their own.

5. New organizations dependent on expertise tend to make a relatively quick transition to the innovative or the professional configuration ("meritocratization"). A new organization that is highly dependent on expert skills and knowledge will be likely to make a relatively rapid transition to one of the expert configurations, the innovative form if its mission focuses on creative design, or the professional form if it applies standardized skills. This transition tends to happen quickly, because experts are generally hired with their skills already in place; hence they generally insist on power early, rather than defer to the personalized power of a leader. For example, a new hospital can adopt the professional configuration in a surprisingly short period of time simply because its staff, imported from other hospitals, brings long-established medical procedures along with them.

6. Given a choice between the professional and the innovative configuration, many young organizations will opt for the innovative one, although some will later be inclined to make a transition to the professional one ("early experimentation"; *later* "institutionalization of innovation"). New expert organizations, given the choice (as in theater companies or consulting firms, less so in hospitals!), are often experimental. The system is new, the people are enthusiastic, there are unexploited opportunities to be pursued and the organization itself may have to be differentiated from its competitors to survive. The innovative configuration may be preferred to the professional in the developmental stage. But later, as things settle down—procedures get established, the experts develop preferences, client needs recur, and so on—there may be a tendency, again given the choice, to make a transition to the professional configuration. In other words, the ad hoc development of novel solutions is replaced by the routine delivery of standardized ones.

7. *Entrepreneurial organizations not susceptible to ideological pressures and not dependent on expertise tend to be driven eventually to the machine configuration, usually first in its instrument form* ("takeover"). Being vulnerable after the departure of their founding leaders, or even during the leaders' reign, developing organizations largely free of expertise and ideology become prime candidates for takeover and so tend to fall prey to external influencers (or sometimes yield to them voluntarily, for protection). And as noted in Chapter 8, the way in which an external influencer consolidates power over an organization is by encouraging the establishment of technocratic controls through a subservient management. In other words, the natural tendency for the organization taken over in this way is to convert to the machine configuration, in its instrument form.

The classic example of this is, of course, the entrepreneurial firm that comes under the control of a large diversified corporation, whether it sells out or gets seized by it. But a similar process occurs when a government finally consolidates its control over a new agency hitherto personally controlled by its strong-willed founder.

It will be recalled that the difference between the instrument and closed system forms of the machine configuration is that in one power resides with an external influencer (or a group of them acting in concert), while in the other power rests with the internal administrators. The former tends to appear first simply because there is usually no firmly established administrative apparatus to seize the power when the founder departs. A small organization may simply not have had a chance to develop; moreover, entrepreneurial leaders often expressly discourage formalized administration because they consider it a threat to their personalized control. The instrument form of the machine configuration that follows therefore becomes the means to establish the administrative apparatus.

But some organizations do manage to grow quite large under entrepreneurial leadership, including the development of an extensive administrative apparatus to cope with their size. In effect, they develop a hybrid of the entrepreneurial and machine configurations. And these can, of course, make a transition directly to the closed system form of machine, as the administrators take over directly from the founder after he or she departs. Government dictatorships, for example, are sometimes succeeded by closed system bureaucratic regimes, as in the Soviet Union after Stalin. The same thing tends to happen in a large labor union after the departure of the leader who built it (unless that leader has established a strong ideology, in which case we might look for a transition to the missionary configuration instead). Despite these examples, however, I show this transition as a dotted line in Figure 14–3 because I believe it to be less natural—personalized leadership and formalized administration being somewhat incompatible—and therefore less likely to occur.

MATURITY

8. *Missionary configurations, barring the commonly occurring demise of the organization, as well as instrument machine configurations, tend eventually to make a transition to the closed system machine configuration* (the "imperatives of administration"). This is an important proposition, suggesting (as can be seen in Figure 14–3) that organizations not dependent on expertise tend to end up as machine bureaucracies largely impervious to the exercise of external influence. In effect, the administrators come to think of the organization as serving not some external constituency or noble mission, but rather themselves. Yet at the same time, ironically, it may be only through this transition that organizations in certain sectors are able to achieve a scale large enough for the full and efficient exploitation of their products or services.

Many organizations with missionary configurations simply die. As discussed in Chapter 12, those organizations exist on a knife edge between isolation and assimilation. Isolation may protect the ideology, but it can kill the organization. Thus, many religious communities, political movements, even missionary-type business firms die for want of members or resources, or else simply burn themselves out in their ideological fervor.

Those that do survive are instead subjected to the pressures of assimilation. And in a society of large bureaucratic organizations, it is clear what those pressures are. Over time, the organization may have to build an administrative apparatus, especially if it is intent on carrying its mission far and wide; that acts to bureaucratize the structure. Eventually, then, the organization may yield to what I prefer to call the "imperatives of administration," what sociologists might label (paraphrasing Max Weber) the routinization of ideology. Indeed, the Italian political scientist Robert Michels, writing early in this century, was so convinced of the inevitability of this transition (in our terms, from missionary to closed machine) that he labeled it the "iron law of oligarchy."[10] In effect, time blunts the ideology, converting enthusiasm into obligation, traditions into dogmas, norms into rules. Administration thereby replaces ideology at the center of power.

Organizations as instrument machines tend not to die because they are protected by external influencers. But these commonly undergo a similar kind of conversion, to the closed system machine, which seems an almost imperatively iron law in its occurrence. The instrument machine serves an external constituency directly; that is its purpose and its major strength. But this arrangement contains the seeds of its own destruction, namely the difficulty of maintaining external surveillance of internal behavior. The external influencers may have the formal power, but they can exercise it only through the internal administrators, and it is they who develop the information base necessary to manage the organization. And in information, of course, lies power. Furthermore, it is the administrators who have the time and energy to devote full time to the organization. Thus, as an instrument machine organization grows larger and more complex, its internal administrators are able to enhance their power at the expense of the external influencers. A transition to the closed form of machine may become inevitable.

This process is evident in many business corporations, whose growth to large size has been shown to be accompanied by a dispersal of their shareholding until the internal managers rather than the external "owners" exercise effective control.[11] The same result has been shown for large government corporations, in which the internal managers tend gradually to wrest effective control from the government officials until they are able to run the organizations as systems unto themselves.[12]

9. *The closed system nature of the machine configuration encourages, and is in turn encouraged by, a transition to the diversified configuration* ("diversification"). Closed system organizations prefer to retain their earnings (in whatever form), and use them to enhance their own size and influence. A prime way to do this is through diversification, in other words, extending the mission across different sectors of activity, which also helps to spread their risk and to reduce external influence. (As was noted in Chapter 9, for example, diversification may help to diffuse shareholding in a business corporation.) Thus, the closed machine configuration has an incentive to diversify, in order to strengthen its closed system nature.

But conversion to the diversified form does not really induce a major transition, because the diversified configuration is really just an elaborated form of the machine one (typically comprising a set of machine configurations as divisions grouped together under a headquarters umbrella). Thus, this transition tends to amount to an enhancement of the status of the organization as a bureaucratic structure controlled by its administrators and closed to external influencers.

Let me review our discussion to this point, particularly with respect to the identification of different configurations with the various stages of an organization's development. The entrepreneurial configuration has been clearly and solely associated with the formation stage. The missionary and instrument machine configurations, because they are susceptible to transition to the closed machine configuration, have been discussed, and are shown in Figure 14–3, in the development stage. In other words, they are considered to be means by which an organization develops beyond formation toward maturity. The closed machine form, however, is shown in the maturity stage, because the organization by this time tends to be large and firmly established in one or several sectors, to have a well-developed administrative apparatus with highly standardized procedures, and to be relatively free of external influence.

So too is the professional configuration shown at the stage of maturity, for similar reasons. It also tends to be firmly established, with well-defined (if highly skilled) standardized procedures. It is likewise able to seal itself from much external influence and concentrate its power in the hands of insiders (in its case, operating professionals), who are similarly able to use much of it to serve themselves.

Both of these configurations, for all of these reasons, are considered to be highly stable and therefore enduring, it being difficult to displace entrenched administrators or experts. Hence, both are associated with maturity. We can therefore conclude that, barring unpredictable external changes, organizations that survive and grow tend to end up as closed machine configurations (whether or not diversified) when they are fully developed, unless their need for expertise drives them toward the professional configuration in their maturity instead.

The innovative configuration is shown between development and maturity, because on one hand that form of organization is sometimes inclined to make a transition to the more stable professional form (as described earlier), and on the other hand the innovative form can also constitute a basic state (if never fully stable) in its own right. (Recall our discussion in Chapter 11 of the two types of innovative organizations, the operating adhocracy, as found in consulting firms, which tends to be drawn to the professional form as it ages, and the administrative adhocracy, as found in automated or high-technology sectors, which must often remain in the innovative form.)

10. Most of the transitions so far discussed tend to be driven and impeded by forms of the political configuration, typically brief confrontations, although sometimes prolonged by shaky alliances ("transitional politicization"). The transition from the entrepreneurial to the missionary configuration, as the beliefs of a charismatic leader get institutionalized, tends to be smooth, without conflict. All the other transitions so far discussed can be divisive, as an old guard representing the established system of power resists those promoting the change. Outright confrontation may occur and recur, or else, to avoid damaging an organization that is slow to make the transition, the two sides may form a shaky alliance for a time, a transitional hybrid, with considerable cleavage.

Considering the various transitions that have been introduced above, the founder of an entrepreneurial organization, or his or her successors, may resist takeover by a group of external influencers intent on rendering the organization their instrument. Confrontations will thus result unless the transition either is realized through a sudden seizure of power or takes place gradually and the two sides settle down to forming a shaky alliance. Much of the same should happen in the transition from the entrepreneurial directly to the closed machine configuration, except that the conflict here will be between the leader who favors personalized control and the administrators inclined toward the formalized systems that enhance their own influence.

As for organizations dependent on expertise, the transition from the entrepreneurial founding configuration to one of the expert configurations should be similar. The experts would normally be expected to try to gain considerable influence quickly while the leader might try to hang on to his or her personal control, in which case the two will do battle, or else form a shaky alliance until the transition is completed. In the case of the transition between the two expert configurations, from an innovative to a professional one, the experts will be likely to do battle with each other or to settle into a temporary shaky alliance, one side representing creative adhocracy, the other stable professionalism.

Considering the transition from instrument to closed machine, the external influencers probably will not cherish relinquishing power to the administrators they hired to run the organization as their instrument. But the odds are not in their favor, simply because it is the internal administrators who control decision-making directly. At best, the external influencers can form an implicit shaky alliance with the administrators in the hope of stemming their gradual loss of power. Of course, they can also confront the administrators on visible issues, though not too often. (In the case of the publicly owned Air Canada, for example, over the years the government has challenged it on the selection of new aircraft, the location of a new maintenance base, even on a change in the airline's name.) The external influencers may even win these occasional confrontations—social legitimacy is, after all, on the side of the external constituency the organization is supposed to serve. But the external influencers are likely to lose out eventually, at least if the organization grows rather large, simply because they cannot control the great many internal decisions made on a daily basis. In effect, though they may win the wars, they are likely to lose the peace.

Our remaining transition is from the missionary configuration to the closed system machine. Here we should expect both forms of political configuration, as a combination of what was described above. Members of an organization who remain true to the norms of its traditional ideology will not take kindly to administrative types trying to routinize it, to enhance their own formalized power at the expense of the established system of beliefs. Furious confrontations are to be expected. But like the transition previously described, the power of the administrators can be more subtle and pervasive, allowing them to gain influence gradually through the many small decisions they make regularly. Those people true to the ideology may be drawn into a shaky alliance to try to hold their ground, but like the external influencers of the instrument configuration, this may just prolong the inevitable transition to administrative control.

DECLINE

11. The absence of external control tends to have a corrupting influence on the mature configurations, closed machine and professional, driving them eventually toward the political configuration ("eventual politicization"). The seeds of the destruction of the two mature configurations are sown by the very power of their own dominant insiders. To quote Lord Acton, while "power tends to corrupt, absolute power corrupts absolutely." The power of the administrators of the closed system machine or of the experts of the professional configuration can sometimes get so close to absolute that corruption becomes inevitable, first of all in the form of arrogant exercise of that power.

In universities, for example, students can become incidental pawns, there to support what the professors really want to do, namely research.

But that research itself may get done for no constituency other than the professors themselves. To serve is considered crass; the real object of the research becomes methodological elegance, as small communities of "scholars" publish for each other in progressively narrower and more irrelevant journals. In business, it is the customers who get that treatment from the closed system bureaucracies (the students, of course, never being acknowledged as customers in the university). Thus, there was that General Motors chief executive who claimed there was "something wrong" with people who bought small cars, while another commented that "what's good for General Motors is good for the country." And so-called social responsibility can become the closed system executives' smokescreen for ensuring that external influencers cannot penetrate their power base—if they are "responsible," their behavior need not be monitored.

If power produces corruption, then corruption produces conflict. Without the constraint of service beyond themselves, these insiders must be drawn into conflicts with one another. The professionals strut around trying to be superior to each other, while the administrators battle over the building of private empires. The internal coalition then becomes increasingly politicized.

Meanwhile, external influencers, long pacified by the myth of expertise or by the power of the administrative system, begin to take notice of these conflicts. What these indicate is the fundamental illegitimacy of the organization's power system. The organization may have to rely on professionalism or on the formal authority of its administrators to function, but the arrogance and conflicts make it increasingly evident to outsiders that these legitimate means are being used to further illegitimate ends. And so they begin to challenge the insiders, as well as the legitimacy of their power, and thereby politicize the external coalition as well. Students and government administrators question the goals of the university and the actions of its professors. Ralph Nader, listening to the utterances of General Motors executives, begins a series of attacks on the corporation—the safety of its products, its record on pollution, the criteria by which people are named to its board of directors.

With conflict infusing the organization from both inside and outside, the organization begins to take on the form earlier labeled the politicized organization, in which conflict is pervasive but, because it is moderate, also tends to be enduring.

Of course, this need not happen quickly. Organizations can remain in the stage of maturity for long periods, held in check perhaps by a certain degree of market competition or by professional standards. (Or the advent of new competition or renewed professional standards may drive ones on the way to conflictive decline back to more viable maturity.) The vestiges of an earlier ideology can have the same effect. Indeed, the longevity of a healthy state of maturity in certain closed machine or professional organizations is probably best explained by strong ideology in their earlier lives. (It is my suspicion that this last factor is what explains the "excellence" of the companies Peters and Waterman wrote about. In effect, *In Search of Excellence* seems largely to be about the exceptions, those few companies that managed to remain responsive despite growing to a very large size. Thus it should have come as no surprise that many soon slipped out of the ranks of excellence.[13])

Figure 14–3 also shows a line from the innovative to the political configuration, but this conclusion must be qualified. This configuration is certainly predisposed to internal conflict, indeed, far more than the closed machine if not the professional configuration. But this is conflict of a different kind. The structure is so organic, the work so variable, that friction inevitably arises in the normal functioning of the organization. It is true that the experts of the innovative organization tend to have a good deal of power. But external legitimacy is less of a question here because these organizations are characterized by responsiveness to their markets. If anything, adhocracies are too quick to react to external changes. Thus, transition to a political status here may reflect more a temporary difficulty than a permanent shift to a state of decline. (That probably happens to the innovative organization via transition first to a more bureaucratic configuration.)

12. Barring renewal or some form of artificial support, an enduring political configuration eventually leads to the demise of the organization ("artificial support," "political demise"). The politicized organization is hardly effective in the long run. As noted in the last chapter, organizations are in the business of producing products and services, not providing an arena for people to fight with one another. So sustained pervasive politicization should lead to the demise of the organization. That is, of course, a common enough occurrence (or, perhaps more accurately, as demise becomes imminent, conflict increases as those who remain fight over the leftovers, giving rise to a complete political arena that finally destroy the organization). But two things can impede it.

One is organizational renewal, to be described below. The other is the presence of artificial support. An organization that can find an artificial means to sustain itself may be able to maintain a state of pervasive politics for a long time. In the last chapter, examples given of this included the controversial regulatory agency whose funding keeps coming from the government and the politicized business corporation that sustains itself by means of a privileged position already established in a market place. But even artificial support cannot last forever, especially since politics feeds on itself and when left unchecked tears an organization apart. Thus, demise must come eventually unless there is renewal.

RENEWAL

13. Organizational renewal may take place in the form of gradual revitalization or, in the absence of that, dramatic turnaround, the former likely during maturity, the latter during demise ("revitalization," "turnaround"). Every organization must adapt eventually if it is to survive. Some do seem capable of renewing themselves; others do not and simply die. Ironically, the latter occurrence seems to be more common in the earlier stages of the life cycle, as shown by the tombstones in Figure 14–3. As already noted, the missionary configuration often kills organizations that use it simply because it isolates them from the rest of the world. Likewise, entrepreneurial configurations tend to kill organizations when their leaders lose their ability to adapt (or adapt too freely, the main reason why innovative configurations are also often implicated in the death of organizations).

Faced with crisis, therefore, an organization in an early stage of its life seems more likely to survive by moving on to a subsequent stage, making the transition to another configuration, than by renewing itself with the configuration it has. Threatened entrepreneurial configurations tend to become instrument machines or expert organizations, as the leaders are replaced not by other entrepreneurs but by different centers of power; threatened missionary organizations tend to become closed system machines, since their ideologies must be destroyed if the organizations are to adapt beyond them; and so on.

Thus, renewal seems to be a phenomenon of the later stages of the organizational life cycle. This would seem to make sense, because by then the organization may have no choice. The mature configuration can only move on to decline, the declining one to demise. Moreover, while the demise of an entrepreneurial or missionary organization may not concern many people, because it tends to be small and insular and often to operate in an inconsequential market niche, the threatened organization that has reached maturity usually attracts a great deal of attention: It is typically large and entrenched in a central market with all kinds of trading relationships established around it, not to mention the institutional status that comes from a long history. Thus, there tends to be a great incentive to save the organization, often even when the organization is not worth saving.

Renewal can take two forms, as was suggested in Chapter 8. Some organizations are capable of revitalizing themselves periodically. Others, which are not, must be subjected to turnaround under crisis if they are to survive.

Revitalization is a gradual process that operates within, reflecting the capacity of an organization to renew itself, in other words to change while maintaining its basic configuration. As implied by points made earlier in this chapter, revitalization would seem to be encouraged by a healthy mixture of politics and ideology in an organization, the former stimulating all kinds of people to promote changes that challenge the status quo, the latter creating the culture that facilitates their acceptance. Thus, we should not expect to find revitalization so much in the decline stage, where politicization has already undermined the healthy functioning of an organization, as in the mature stage, where remaining vestiges of ideology can function alongside the inevitable political games. Of course, we should expect the capacity for revitalization to be greatest in organizations whose ideologies are sufficiently strong to allow them to sustain the various forces of our pentagon concurrently.

The configurations of maturity are the closed system machine, the professional, and, in part, the innovative. Each is shown in Figure 14–3 with a loop underneath to represent this capacity for revitalization. In other words, these alone are considered able to make a natural transition to a renewed form of themselves. (Of course, it is this capacity for self-renewal that helps to define maturity, since this allows an organization to sustain itself in its state for a long time.)

The innovative configuration is the one most naturally amenable to revitalization. After all, it exists to change, to revitalize itself continually in direct response to changes in its environment through its grassroots process of strategy-making. Indeed, its main problem is not to change but to direct that change, find convergence periodically in its many strategic initiatives. Ideology can help in this regard, by focusing perspective.

As its strategy-making process was presented in Chapter 10, the professional organization tends to be in a state of incessant revitalization. But that is at its narrowest level, in the creation of particular pigeonholes and in activities inside of each. It is at the broadest level that the professional organization has difficulty revitalizing itself because its power tends to be so diffuse. Professional organizations are spinning all the time, even when they are headed in the wrong direction. The problem is to get them to change overall direction periodically. Again ideology may help: Politics can promote individual changes, but ideology may be necessary to weave them together into systematic revitalization. Thus, it is the professional organization devoid of ideology that seems most susceptible to decline through transition to the political configuration.

In both of these expert configurations, revitalization, of one kind or another, is driven by forces intrinsic to the configuration itself. In our third mature configuration, the closed system machine, such natural forces for change do not exist. So to revitalize itself, the configuration needs a push from something beyond itself (hence, the loop underneath is shown as dotted). That push appears to come from the two forces in the center of a pentagon, working in concert. Politics helps to generate and to promote strategic initiatives, for example, through games such as strategic candidates and young Turks, while ideology helps to engender a climate of receptivity to such initiatives, at least for the ones that fit the strategic perspective. Thus, the revitalizing machine configuration, what we earlier labeled the ''snappy bureaucracy,'' really has need for both ideology and politics to adapt.

Mature organizations unable to revitalize themselves may coast until their advantages run out, and then become politicized and decline. In decline, they may try to protect themselves politically by exploiting some artificial means of support. But when that fails, and their survival becomes threatened, efforts may be made to renew them economically, through *turnaround*.

Operating turnaround is the popular label for acting on the cost side of an organization's benefit-cost ratio, by economizing; *strategic turnaround*, for acting on the benefit side, by changing direction. (*Political turnaround* should be added as the label for acting externally, through artificial means to protect themselves.) One involves surgery, the removal or reduction of diseased parts; the other involves reconstruction through the improvement or addition of parts. (And the third involves projecting the problem, and the cost of solving it, onto others.) Generally, as noted in Chapter 8, turnaround appears to involve reversion to the entrepreneurial configuration temporarily, as the exercise of established power is suspended to allow a forceful leader with vision (or determination to cut costs) to resolve the crisis in a personal way.

Of the mature configurations, the closed machine seems most amenable to turnaround. For one thing, its centralization of authority facilitates takeover by a single leader. (Zald and Berger write of the "organizational coup d'etat" in such organizations, where the leader is replaced while the structure remains intact.[14]) For another, these organizations tend to be so large and influential that there is bound to be tremendous pressure for renewal when they decline. (Illustrative of both these points is the Chrysler turnaround effected by Lee Iacocca.) For a third, lacking ideology, as many machine configurations do, revitalization does not occur, and so when the crisis eventually arises, turnaround is the only hope.

On the other hand, true turnaround is not easy to effect here. These are machines; they do not take kindly to dramatic change. That is why political and operating turnarounds, which keep the strategies and systems intact, tend to be favored over strategic turnarounds. (Again, consider the Chrysler turnaround, with its heavy dose of the political, in the form of loan guarantees from the government, and the operating, including cost cuts and layoffs of all kinds.) But these forms of turnaround are often just palliatives, cosmetic or temporary relief that only delays recurrence of the real problem.

Thus the line on Figure 14–3 labeled "turnaround," from the political configuration of decline back to the closed machine configuration of maturity, is dotted, to suggest that true turnaround, permanent resolution of the fundamental problem, may not be all that natural here, or all that common. Indeed, it may not be all that necessary: The costs of such turnarounds can be large yet the effort fruitless. Sometimes it simply does not pay to try to save a sick institution, no matter how important it once was and how strong are the social pressures for doing so. (Witness the steady decline of British Leyland.)

In the professional configuration, power is so diffused that it is almost impossible for an entrepreneurial leader to effect a serious turnaround. Even in the best of times, with the aid of a strong ideology, it is no simple matter to change these organizations in an integrated way. Politics having taken over hardly makes this easier. Sometimes it seems that an organization of professionals is more inclined to destroy itself through conflict than to cede its power to a single leader for turnaround. (Of course, why not? Most of the professionals can simply join another professional organization and pick up right where they left off. If the organization is for them just a shell that provides support, then why should they care if it dies?)

On the other hand, the professionals themselves will sometimes reduce their own political activities to allow the organization to survive, if for nothing more than the convenience of being able to get back to what they most want to do, namely practice their professions. Thus, a dotted line is shown from the political organization back to the professional, though it is not labeled turnaround.

The line from the political organization back to the innovative one is solid, because that transition is considered to be more natural, and common. As noted earlier, innovative organizations slip easily into a political state, not because of decline but simply because their fluid structures easily go out of control. Likewise they are easily brought back, as indicated by the use of one solid line in Figure 14–3, with arrows going both ways. This may be done by an entrepreneurial leader who effects a turnaround, probably strategic through the imposition of a new strategic umbrella, but possibly also operating, simply by bringing order to all the chaos. Or it may take place through the organization's own internal processes of revitalization that, ironically, can use politics to focus direction and so to convert a politicized structure back into an innovative one.

One final issue concerning renewal: Can the mature or declining organization begin the overall life cycle anew, emerging as a fresh entrepreneurial configuration, much as the mythical phoenix arises from its own ashes every five hundred years? Despite intimations of this in the popular management press, I think not. Some organizations captured by politics in an enduring way may be turned around, to revert to a machine or expert configuration, though our conclusions were not very optimistic even on this. But to be turned around by entrepreneurship does not mean to become entrepreneurial, in the sense of becoming a simple, supple, and flexible structure ready to go on adapting.

Turnaround tends to be a one-time event, a temporary, sometimes even superficial change during which normal practices are suspended to allow for change. In the machine organization, the procedures do not go away, nor do the analysts who design them or the managers who supervise them. They merely wait for the organization to be secured so that they can continue to get on with their own tasks. Likewise, turnaround of the innovative or professional configuration does not dispense with the power of its experts. The mythical phoenix may arise in the freshness of youth; the real organization does not. Legacies remain, which influence behavior. The organization may be the wiser for its experiences, but it must also be the wearier.

If reversion to the entrepreneurial form on a sustained basis is unlikely, what about reversion to some earlier configuration of the development stage? Again, I find this equally unlikely. There are certainly examples of old, lethargic organizations having developed bright new systems of beliefs. But for every one that truly internalizes a rich new ideology, let alone becomes a missionary configuration, there appear to be a great many others whose beliefs amount to a thin veneer that washes off in the first storm. At best, with a dedicated, patient, and charismatic leadership, the mature organization gets an infusion of ideology, which may be able to exist alongside its conventional structure for a time.

Likewise, reversion to the instrument form does happen, but it is also difficult to sustain in a machine organization that has already become large and established. Corporate raiders may be able to capture large, sick organizations, turning closed systems into their instruments for a time to restructure them. But restructuring these monoliths is different from controlling them externally on a regular basis, much as turning them around is different from sustaining entrepreneurial management of them.

The one reversion that seems possible in our model is from the political back to innovative configuration, as noted above, because the former state tends to be a frequent, natural, and, most important, temporary one for these organizations. But another reversion is less likely: While I have come across many examples of the less stable innovative form (sitting between the stages of development and maturity) making a transition to the more stable professional one (in maturity), I cannot recall a single example of the opposite transition.

Once having commenced this life cycle, therefore, many organizations seem more or less destined to complete it, unless, of course, they stall or die along the way, or get diverted by external changes that have nothing to do with the forces within themselves. Our model suggests that as organizations survive and develop, they become more diffuse in their power relationships, more complex in their functioning, more ambiguous in their intentions, and eventually less functional in their performance, though, ironically, more stable in their makeup. The forces of direction, belief, and service to an external constituency give way to protection of themselves as systems and of their influential members, and later to pervasive conflict.

At some point, as a result, organizations tend to peak in their service to society and then they decline. But there seems to be no going back, at least not in any sustained way. Applying the model to our world of organizations, we would therefore expect a healthy society to maintain a steady level of the replacement of old, spent organizations by fresh new ones. In other words, *it is not the renewal of single organizations that should concern us so much as the renewal of our system of organizations*. But the two would seem to call for very different approaches.

Organizations cannot be renewed very easily, at least not in terms of invigorating long-established ones with the energy of youth. What we have called a life *cycle* model then, is really a life *sequence;* it is the society of organizations that experiences the cycle.

Or at least it should. The problem is that in contemporary society we seem to discourage this cycle of organizational life by allowing spent organizations to survive, indeed even by protecting them artificially. This is done at the expense of new organizations that ought to be able to grow up in their place, using their freed-up resources more judiciously and more productively. That doing this has grave consequences for our society of organizations will be the subject of the closing chapter of this book.

Part III
ON OUR SOCIETY OF ORGANIZATIONS

As I noted in the first sentence of this book, ours is a society of organizations for better *and* for worse. We create organizations to serve us, but somehow they also force us to serve them. Sometimes it feels as if our institutions have run out of control, like the machinery of Charlie Chaplin's film *Modern Times.* Why we should become slaves to our servants is the theme taken up in this section of the book. With an understanding of management developed in the first section and an understanding of organizations developed in the second, we can begin to suggest some answers.

A society of organizations is one in which organizations enter our lives as influential forces in a great many ways—in how we work, what we eat, how we get educated and cured of our illnesses, how we get entertained, and how our ideas get shaped. The ways in which we try to control our organizations and our organizations in turn try to control us become major issues in the lives of all of us.

Foremost among the organizations that influence us may be the large business corporation. Yet the debate over the control of it has advanced hardly at all over the course of more than half a century. This section therefore opens with the question, "Who should control the corporation?," suggesting a series of answers around a "conceptual horseshoe," which represents the political spectrum.

Then we consider "A note on that dirty word efficiency," because an important message lies in the fact that efficiency, that paragon of all good things organizational, should have developed such a reputation. While that message is considered in the second chapter, its full implication is really addressed in the third one of this section, and the final essay of this book. Based on an unpublished speech I gave a few years ago, it seems to bring together virtually every major point made in this book. Its conclusion is not an encouraging one, but is presented in the belief that we must understand our problems before we can deal with them. This closing essay is entitled "Society Has Become Unmanageable as a Result of Management."

15
WHO SHOULD CONTROL THE CORPORATION?

The life cycle model has suggested that as organizations grow large, they tend to seal themselves off from external influence and instead exert their own influence as powerful closed systems, under the control of their own insiders. But clearly, society cannot sit by and be dictated to by systems that were created to serve it. And so a debate arose and has raged for more than half a century,* particularly over the large, widely held business corporation: Who should control it, how, and for whose benefit? As the shareholding of these powerful institutions spread, so that none of their official owners held enough stock to exercise direct control, effective power over many of them passed to their full-time managers. But this was unacceptable to many people, and a host of proposals arose to temper that control, even, in some cases, to eliminate it altogether.

These proposals have run the whole gamut of political persuasions. Yet the issue remains as muddied and unresolved today as it ever was. Indeed, the issue is as important for the "communist" East, which is right now struggling over how to control its large enterprises, as for the "capitalist" West and, in that West, as important for other large public and parapublic institutions as it is for business. How is society to bring its large organizations under adequate social control without endangering their capacity to produce goods and services efficiently?

In discussing the various answers that have been proposed and suggesting a way to reconcile them, I here take less a political stand than an organizational one, arguing in essence that the resolution of the issue may have less to do with debates over "radical left" or "reactionary right" than with the teachings of organization theory:

---

* The publication in 1932 of the Berle and Means book *The Modern Corporation and Private Property* (Macmillan Publishing Company), while not the start of this debate, certainly brought it into sharp focus by presenting evidence that the large business corporation was more likely to be controlled by its managers than its shareholders.

what works in an administrative or organizational sense. "A plague on both your houses" is my response to extremist positions on both sides, simply because they seldom work, not even from the perspective of the proponents themselves. As we shall see, nationalization of industry does not engender social responsibility, often not even service to the state, while absolute shareholder control can lead to concentrations of power that threaten the free market itself. Again, we must understand how organizations work and how and why they get broken before we run off half-cocked trying to fix them.

In a sense, I guess that does position me politically: as a pragmatist. I believe capitalism is no less a failure than communism when pushed to the extreme end of the political spectrum. Extremism is the problem, and ironically, from the perspective of organization theory, the two extremes look remarkably alike. Both, I argue, assume the organization to be the instrument of some dominant group of external influencers, and so a machine configuration. The influencers may differ, even in the goals they ostensibly pursue, but the nature of the resultant organizations does not, nor do the consequences on how they function. My own inclination, therefore, is to favor the combination of proposals that range from the moderate left to the moderate right.

This paper was first published, in a somewhat longer version, in the *California Management Review,* Fall 1984, that version itself based on a fairly long final section of my book *Power In and Around Organizations.* In addressing the issue in question, the paper also shows how organization theory can be used to consider such issues. "Who should control the corporation?" has been considered from the perspective of economics, political science, law, industrial relations, sociology, and a range of other disciplines. I believe organization theory is able to bring special insight to it. In my opinion, nowhere in this book are the benefits of using organization theory better demonstrated than right here.

Who should control the corporation? How? And for the pursuit of what goals?

Historically, the corporation was controlled by its owners—through direct control of its managers if not through direct management—for the pursuit of economic goals. But as shareholding became dispersed, owner control weakened; and as the corporation grew to very large size, its economic actions came to have increasing social consequences. The giant, widely held corporation came increasingly under the implicit control of its managers, and the concept of social responsibility—the voluntary consideration of public social goals alongside the private economic ones—arose to provide them with a basis legitimacy for their actions.

To some, including those closest to the managers themselves, this was accepted as a satisfactory arrangement for the large corporation. "Trust it" to the goodwill of the managers was their credo; these people will be able to achieve an appropriate balance between social and economic goals.

But others viewed this basis of control as unacceptable. The corporation was too large, too influential, its actions too pervasive to be left free of the direct and concerted influence of outsiders. At the extreme were those who believed that managerial control alone was fundamentally illegitimate and had to be subjected to formal and direct external control. "Nationalize it," said those at one end of the political spectrum, to put ultimate control in the hands of the government so that the corporation would pursue public social goals. No, said those at the other end, "restore it" to direct shareholder control, so that it will not waver from the pursuit of private economic goals.

Other people took less extreme positions. "Democratize it" became the rallying cry for some, to open up the governance of the large, widely held corporation to a variety of affected groups—if not the workers, then the customers, or conservation interests, or minorities. "Regulate it" was also a popular position, with its implicit premise that only by being subjected to certain government controls would the corporation's managers attend to particular social goals. Then there were those who accepted direct management control so long as it was tempered by other, less formal types of influence. "Pressure it," said a generation of social activists, to ensure that social goals are taken into consideration. But others argued that because the corporation is an economic instrument, you must "induce it" by providing economic incentives to encourage the resolution of social problems.

Finally, there were those who argued that this whole debate was unnecessary, that a kind of invisible hand ensures that the economic corporation acts in a socially responsible manner. "Ignore it" was their implicit conclusion.

What this implies is that the various positions concerning who should control the corporation, and how, can be laid out along a political continuum, from nationalization at one end to the restoration of shareholder power at the other. From the organization theory perspective, however, those two extremes are not so far apart. Both call for direct control of the corporation's managers by specific outsiders, in one case the govern-

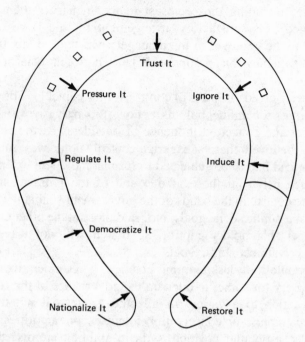

FIGURE 15–1
The Conceptual Horseshoe

ment to ensure the pursuit of social goals, in the other case the shareholders to ensure the pursuit of economic ones. It is the moderate positions—notably, trusting the corporation to the social responsibility of its managers—that are farthest from the extremes. Hence, we can fold our spectrum around so that it takes the shape of a horseshoe.

Figure 15–1 shows our "conceptual horseshoe," with "nationalize it" and "restore it" at the two ends. "Trust it" is at the center, because this position postulates a natural balance of social and economic goals. "Democratize it," "regulate it," and "pressure it" are shown on the left side of the horseshoe, because all seek to temper economic goals with social ones. "Induce it" and "ignore it," both of which favor the pursuit of economic goals, are shown on the right side.

This conceptual horseshoe provides a basic framework to help clarify the issues in this important debate. We begin by discussing each of these positions in turn, circling the horseshoe from left to right. Finding that each (with one exception) has a logical context, we conclude—in keeping with our organization theory perspective—that they should be thought of as forming a portfolio from which society can draw to deal with the issue of who should control the corporation and how.

Nationalization of the business corporation is a taboo subject in the United States . . . in general, but not in particular. Whenever a major corporation runs into serious difficulty (i.e., faces bankruptcy with possible loss of many jobs), massive government intervention, often including direct nationalization, inevitably comes up as an option. And this option has been exercised: U.S. travelers now ride on Amtrak; Tennessee residents have for years been getting their power from a government utility; indeed, the Post Office was once a private enterprise. Other nations have, of course, been much more ambitious in this regard.

From an organizational theory perspective, the question is not whether nationalization is legitimate, but whether it works—at least in particular, limited circumstances. As a response to concerns about the social responsibility of large corporations, the answer seems to be no. The evidence suggests that social difficulties arise more from the size of an organization and its degree of bureaucratization than from its form of ownership. On the other hand, contrary to popular belief in the United States, nationalization does not necessarily harm economic efficiency. Renault was long one of the most successful automobile companies outside Japan; it was nationalized by the French government shortly after World War II. Likewise, the state-owned Canadian National has long been an innovative and effective railroad. The prophecy may be a self-fulfilling one: When people believe that government ownership leads to interference, politicization, and inefficiency, that may be exactly what happens. However, when they believe that nationalization *has* to work, then state-owned enterprises may be able to attract the very best talent in the country and thereby work well.

But economic efficiency provides no more reason to favor nationalization than does concern about social responsibility. Nationalization does, however, seem to make sense in at least two particular circumstances. The first is when a mission deemed necessary in a society will not be provided adequately by the private sector. That is presumably why America has its Amtrak and why third world nations often create state enterprises. The second is when the activities of an organization must be so intimately tied to government policy that it is best managed as a direct arm of the state. The Canadian government created Petrocan to act as a "window," a source of knowledge, on the sensitive oil industry.

Thus, it is not rhetoric but requirement that should determine the use of this position as a solution to who should control the corporation. "Nationalize it" should certainly not be embraced as a panacea. But neither should it be rejected as always irrelevant.

"DEMOCRATIZE IT"

A less extreme position—at least in the context of the American debate—is one that calls for formal devices to broaden the governance of the corporation. The proponents of this position either accept the legal fiction of shareholder control and argue that the corporation's power base is too narrow, or else respond to the reality that has evolved and question the legitimacy of managerial control. Why, they ask, do stockholders or self-selected managers have any greater right to control the profound decisions of these major institutions than do workers or customers or the neighbors downstream?

This stand is not to be confused with what is known as "participative management." The call to "democratize it" is a legal rather than an ethical one and is based on power, not generosity. Management is not asked to share its power voluntarily; rather, that power is to be reallocated constitutionally. That makes this position a fundamental and important one, *especially* in the United States, with its strong tradition of pluralist control of its institutions.

The debate over democratization of the corporation has been confusing in part because many of the proposals have been so vague. We can bring some order to it by considering, in organization theory terms, two basic means of democratization and two basic constituencies that can be involved. As shown in Figure 15–2, they suggest four possible forms of corporate democracy. One means is through the election of representatives to the board of directors, which we call *representative democracy*. The other is through formal but direct involvement in internal decision-making processes, which we call *participatory democracy*. Either can focus on the *workers* or else on a host of outside interest groups, the latter giving rise to a *pluralistic* form of democracy. These are basic forms of corporate democracy in theory. With one exception, however, they have hardly been approached—let alone achieved—in practice. But they suggest where the "democratize it" debate may be headed.

FIGURE 15–2

Four Basic Forms of Corporate Democracy

GROUPS INVOLVED

		Internal Employees	External Interest Groups
FOCUS OF ATTENTION	Board of Directors	Worker Representative Democracy (European style, e.g., "co-determination" or worker ownership)	Pluralistic Representative Democracy (American style, e.g., "public interest" directors)
	Internal Decision-Making Process	Worker Participatory Democracy (e.g., works councils)	Pluralistic Participatory Democracy (e.g., outsiders on new product committees)

WORKER REPRESENTATIVE DEMOCRACY. The European debate has focused on worker representative democracy. This has, in some sense, been achieved in Yugoslavia, where the workers of all but the smallest firms elect the members of what is the equivalent of the American board of directors. In Germany, under the so-called *Mitbestimmung* (''co-determination''), the workers and the shareholders each elect half of the directors.

The evidence on this form of corporate democracy has been consistent, and it supports neither its proponents nor its detractors. Workers' representation on the board seems to make relatively little difference one way or the other. The worker representatives concern themselves with wage and welfare issues but leave most other questions to management. Worker-controlled firms (not unlike the state-owned ones) appear to be no more socially responsible than private ones.

On the other hand, worker representative democracy may have certain positive benefits. Helmut Schmidt, when Chancellor of West Germany, is reported to have said that ''the key to [this] country's postwar economic miracle was its sophisticated system of workers' participation.''[1] While no one can prove this statement, co-determination certainly does not seem to have done the German economy much harm. By providing an aura of legitimacy to the German corporation and by involving the workers (at least officially) in its governance and opening up some lines of communication, co-determination may perhaps have enhanced the spirit of enterprise in Germany (while having little real effect on how decisions are actually made). More significantly, co-determination may have fostered greater understanding and cooperation between the managers and the union members who fill most of the worker seats on the boards.

PLURALISTIC REPRESENTATIVE DEMOCRACY. The embryonic debate over representative democracy in the United States has shown signs of moving in a different direction. Consistent with the tradition of pluralism in America's democratic institutions—the town council and the school board, if not the corporation itself—there has been increasing pressure to elect outside directors who represent a wide variety of special interest groups, consumers, minorities, environmentalists, and so on.

Critics have pointed out the problems of defining constituencies and finding the means to hold elections. "One-person, one-vote" may be easily applied to electing representatives of the workers, but no such simple rule can be found in the case of the consumer or environmental representatives, let alone ones of the "public interest." Yet it is amazing how quickly things become workable in the United States when Americans decide to put their collective mind to it. Indeed, the one case of public directors that I came across is telling in this regard. According to a Conference Board report, the selection by the Chief Justice of the Supreme Court of New Jersey of six of the twenty-four members of the board of Prudential Insurance as public directors has been found by the company to be "quite workable."[2]

THE POWER OF THE BOARD. Proposals for representative democracy, indeed those for nationalization and the restoration of shareholder control as well, rest on assumptions about the power of the board of directors. It may, therefore, be worth considering at this point the roles that boards of directors play in organizations and the board's resulting powers.

In law, traditionally, the business of a corporation was to be "managed" by its board. But of course, the board does no such thing. Managers manage, although some may happen to sit on the board. What then are the roles of the board, particularly of its "outside" directors?

The most tangible role of the board, and clearly provided for in law, is to name, and of course to dismiss as well, the chief executive officer, that person who in turn names the rest of the management. A second role may be to exercise direct control during periods of crisis, for example when the management has failed to provide leadership. And a third is to review the major decisions of the management as well as its overall performance.

These three constitute the board's roles of control, in principal at least because there is no shortage of evidence that boards have difficulty doing even these effectively, especially outside directors. Their job is, after all, part-time, and in a brief meeting once in a while they face a complex organization led by a highly organized management that deals with it every day. The result is that board control tends to reduce to naming and replacing the chief executive, and that person's knowledge of that fact, nothing more. Indeed, even that power is circumscribed, because a management cannot be replaced very often. In a sense, the board is like a bee hovering near a person picking flowers. The person must proceed carefully, so as not to provoke the bee, but can proceed with the task. But if the bee does happen to be provoked, it only gets to sting once. Thus many boards try to know only enough to know when the management is not doing its job properly, so that they can replace it.

But if boards tend to be weak in exercising *control over* the organization, they also tend to be strong in providing *service to* the organization. Here board membership plays at least four other roles. First, it "co-opts" influential outsiders: The organization uses the status of a seat on its board to gain the support of people important to it (as in the case of the big donors who sit on university boards). Second, board membership may be used to establish contacts for the organization (as when retired military officers sit on the boards of weapons manufacturing firms). This may be done to help in such things as the securing of contracts and the raising of funds. Third, seats on the board can be used to enhance an organization's reputation (as when an astronaut or some other type of celebrity is given a seat). And fourth, the board can be used to provide advice for the organization (as in the case of many of the bankers and lawyers who sit on the boards of corporations).

How much do boards serve organizations, and how much do they control them? Some boards do, of course, exercise control, particularly when their members represent a well-defined constituency, such as the substantial owner of a corporation. But, as noted, this tends to be a loose control at best. And other boards hardly do even that, especially when their constituencies are widely dispersed.

To represent everyone is ultimately to represent no one, especially when faced with a highly organized management that knows exactly what it wants. (Or from the elector's point of view, having some distant representative sitting on a board somewhere hardly brings him or her closer to control over the things that impinge on daily life—the work performed, the products consumed, the rivers polluted.) In corporations, this has been shown to be true of the directors who represent many small shareholders no less than those who represent many workers or many customers, perhaps even those who represent government, since that can be just a confusing array of pressure groups. These boards become, at best, tools of the organization, providing it with the variety of the services discussed above, at worst mere façades of formal authority. That is why we cannot expect a great deal from the representative forms of corporate democracy.

WORKER PARTICIPATORY DEMOCRACY. Despite its problems, representative democracy is crystal clear compared with participatory democracy. This describes a kind of bottom-up, grassroots democracy in which the workers participate directly in decision-making (instead of overseeing management's decisions from the board of directors) and also elect their own managers (who then become more administrators than bosses). Yet proposals to this effect are inevitably vague, and I have heard of no large mass production or mass service firm—not even one owned by workers themselves or by a union—that comes close to this.

What has impeded worker participatory democracy? In my opinion, something rather obvious has stood in its way, namely the structure required by the very organizations in which the attempts have been made to apply it. Worker participatory democracy—and worker representative democracy too, for that matter—have been attempted primarily in organizations containing large numbers of workers who do highly routine, rather unskilled jobs that are typical of most mass production and service, in other words, ones structured as machine bureaucracies. The overriding requirement in machine bureaucracy is for tight coordination, the kind that can be achieved only by central administrators. For example, the myriad of decisions associated with producing an automobile at Volvo's Kalmar works in Sweden cannot be made by autonomous groups, each doing as it pleases. The whole car must fit together in a particular way at the end of the assembly process. These decisions require a highly sophisticated system of bureaucratic coordination. That is why automobile companies are structured into rigid hierarchies of authority.

Participatory democracy *is* approached in other kinds of organizations, for example in autonomous professional ones such as universities and hospitals or the innovative ones in such fields as high technology, which have very different needs for central coordination. But the proponents of organizational democracy are not lobbying for changes in hospitals or high technology. It is the giant mass producers they are after, and unless the operating work in those corporations becomes largely skilled and professional in nature, nothing approaching participative democracy can be expected.

PLURALISTIC PARTICIPATORY DEMOCRACY. In principle, the pluralistic form of participatory democracy means that a variety of groups external to the corporation can somehow control its decision-making processes directly. In practice, of course, this concept is even more elusive than the worker form of participatory democracy. To fully open up the internal decision-making processes of the corporation to outsiders would mean chaos. Yet certain very limited forms of outside participation would seem to be not only feasible but perhaps even desirable. Imagine telephone company executives resolving rate conflicts with consumer groups in quiet offices instead of having to face them in noisy public hearings.

To conclude, corporate democracy—whether representative or participatory in form—may be an elusive and difficult concept, but it cannot be dismissed. It is not just another social issue, like river pollution or forced retirement, but one that strikes at the most fundamental of values. In a more detailed article on this subject, I argued "why America needs but cannot have corporate democracy." It cannot have it, at least not in organizations that depend on the efforts of many relatively unskilled workers, because effective coordination precludes it. The important decisions must be made at one center, and no part-time representatives of the many workers who produce the outputs or the many customers who buy them, etc., can change that fact. (One Yugoslav has written, regarding industrial democracy in his country, that "decisions are no longer made at the top; they are only integrated and coordinated there."[3] Only!)

But America, alongside other developed nations, must pursue corporate democracy, because in a society of organizations democracy can have meaning only if it applies to the organizational activities that most impinge upon citizens in their daily lives—as workers, consumers, and neighbors. Organizations that prove unresponsive to other forces will have to be opened up to external control, one way or another. Indeed, as the legitimacy of large closed system organizations becomes increasingly questioned by workers inside as well as pressure groups outside, generating greater levels of politicization, the issue will become no less one of economic efficiency than of social democracy.

"REGULATE IT"

In theory, regulating the corporation is about as simple as democratizing it is complex. Practice is, of course, another matter. To the proponents of "regulate it," the corporation can be made responsive to social needs by having its actions subjected to the controls of a higher authority, typically government, in the form of a regulatory agency or legislation backed up by the courts. Under regulation, constraints are imposed externally on the corporation while its internal governance is left to its managers.

Regulation of business is at least as old as the Code of Hammurabi, and has increased steadily through this century, although in recent years it has experienced waves of reduction. To some, regulation is a clumsy instrument that should never be relied upon; to others, it is the only means of ensuring social responsibility. The truth lies in between. At best, regulation sets minimum and usually crude standards of acceptable behavior; when it works, it does not make any organization socially responsible so much as stop some from being grossly irresponsible. Because it is inflexible, regulation tends to be applied slowly and conservatively, usually lagging behind public sentiment. Also, regulation often does not work because of difficulties in enforcement. The problems of the regulatory agencies are legendary—limited resources and information compared with the industries they are supposed to regulate, the co-optation of the regulators by those industries, and so on. When applied indiscriminately, regulation either fails dramatically or else succeeds and creates havoc.

Yet there are obvious places for regulation. A prime one is to control tangible "externalities"—costs incurred by corporations that are passed on to the public at large. When, for example, costly pollution or worker health problems can be attributed directly to a corporation, then there seems to be every reason to force it (or its customers) to bear those costs directly, or else to terminate the actions that generate them. Likewise, regulation may have a place where severe competition pulls all firms down to some base level of behavior, forcing even the well-intentioned manager to ignore the social consequences of his or her actions. Indeed, in such cases, the socially responsible behavior is to encourage sensible regulation. "Help us to help ourselves," businesspeople who want to be socially responsible should be telling the government.

Most discouraging, however, is Theodore Levitt's revelation some years ago that business has fought every piece of proposed regulatory or social legislation throughout this century, from the Child Labor Laws on up. In Levitt's opinion, much of that legislation has been good for business—dissolving the giant trusts, creating a more honest and effective stock market, and so on. Yet, "the computer is programmed to cry wolf."[4]

In summary, regulation is a clumsy instrument but not a useless one. Were the business community to take a more enlightened view of it, regulation could be applied more appropriately, and we would not need those periodic waves of deregulation to eliminate the excesses.

"PRESSURE IT"

"Pressure it" is designed to provoke corporations to act beyond some base level of behavior, usually in areas that regulation misses entirely. Here, activists bring ad hoc campaigns of pressure to bear on one or a group of corporations to keep them responsive to the activists' interpretation of social needs.

"Pressure it" is a distinctively American position. While Europeans debate the theories of nationalization and corporate democracy in their cafés, Americans read about the exploits of Ralph Nader et al. in their morning newspapers. Note that "pressure it," unlike "regulate it," implicitly accepts management's right to make the final decisions. Perhaps that is one reason why it is favored in America.

While less radical than the other positions so far discussed, "pressure it" has nevertheless proved far more effective in eliciting behavior sensitive to social needs. Activist groups have pressured for everything from the dismemberment of diversified corporations to the development of day care centers. Of special note is the class action suit, which has opened up a whole new realm of corporate social issues. But the effective use of the pressure campaign has not been restricted to the traditional activist. President Kennedy used it to roll back U.S. Steel price increases in the early 1960s, and business leaders in Pittsburgh used it in the late 1940s by threatening to take their freight-haulage business elsewhere if the Pennsylvania Railroad did not replace its coal burning locomotives to help clean up their city's air.

"Pressure it" has been highly successful because it is an informal, flexible, and focused way to change corporate behavior. Yet it is irregular and ad hoc, with different pressure campaigns sometimes making contradictory demands on management. Compared to the positions to its right on the horseshoe, "pressure it," like the other positions to its left, is based on confrontation rather than cooperation.

"TRUST IT"

To a large and vocal contingent which parades under the banner of corporate "social responsibility," the corporation has no need to act irresponsibly, and there is thus no reason for it to be nationalized by the state, democratized by its different constituencies, regulated by the government, or pressured by activists. This contingent believes that the corporation's leaders can be trusted to attend to social goals for their own sake, simply because it is the noble thing to do. This is the twentieth-century version of *noblesse oblige,* literally "nobility obliges."

We call this position "trust it," or, more exactly, "trust the corporation to the goodwill of its managers," although looking at it from outside the corporation, it might just as well be called "socialize it." We place it in the center of our conceptual horseshoe because it alone postulates a natural balance between social and economic goals—a balance that is to be attained in the heads (or perhaps the hearts) of responsible business-people. And, as a not necessarily incidental consequence, power can be left in the hands of the managers: The corporation can be trusted to those who reconcile social and economic goals.

ATTACKS ON SOCIAL RESPONSIBILITY. The attacks on social responsibility have been many and varied, from the right as well as the left. They boil down to whether corporate managers should be trusted when they claim to pursue social goals; if so, whether they are capable of pursuing such goals; and finally, whether they have any right to pursue such goals.

The simplest attack is that managerial discussion of social responsibility is all rhetoric, no action. E. F. Cheit refers to the "Gospel of Social Responsibility" as "designed to justify the power of managers over an ownerless system."[5]

Others argue that businessmen lack the personal capabilities required to pursue social goals. Levitt claims that professional managers reach the top of the hierarchy by dedication to their firms and their industries; as a result, their knowledge of social issues is highly restricted.[6] Others argue that an orientation to efficiency renders business leaders inept at handling complex social problems (which require flexibility and political finesse, often involving solutions that are uneconomic).

The most far-reaching criticism, however, is that businesspeople have no right to pursue social goals. "Who authorized them to do that?" asks Braybrooke,[7] attacking from the left. What business have they—self-selected or at best appointed by shareholders—to impose *their* interpretation of the public good on society? Let the elected politicians, directly responsible to the population, look after the social goals.

But that attack comes from the right, too. Milton Friedman writes that social responsibility amounts to spending other people's money—if not that of shareholders, then of customers or employees. Drawing on the pejorative vocabulary of right-wing ideology, Friedman concludes that social responsibility is a "fundamentally subversive doctrine," representing "pure and unadulterated socialism," supported by businessmen who are "unwitting puppets of the intellectual forces that have been undermining the basis of a free society these past decades." To Friedman, "there is one and only one social responsibility of business—to use its resources and engage in activities designed to increase its profits so long as it stays within the rules of the game."[8] Let businessmen, in other words, stick to their own business, which is business itself.

EVIDENCE ON SOCIAL RESPONSIBILITY. The empirical evidence on social responsibility is hardly more encouraging. Brenner and Molander, comparing their 1977 survey of *Harvard Business Review* readers with one conducted fifteen years earlier, concluded that the "respondents are somewhat more cynical about the ethical conduct of their peers" than they were previously. Close to half the respondents agreed with the statement that "the American business executive tends not to apply the great ethical laws immediately to work. He is preoccupied chiefly with gain."[9] Only 5 percent listed social responsibility as a factor "influencing ethical standards" whereas 31 and 20 percent listed different factors related to pressure campaigns and 10 percent listed regulation.

The modern corporation has been described as a rational, amoral institution—its "professional" managers "hired guns" who pursue any goals asked of them in an "efficient" manner. The problem (for reasons that will be discussed in the next chapter) is that efficiency really means measurable efficiency, so that the guns load only with goals that can be quantified. Social goals, unlike economic ones, just don't lend themselves to quantification. As a result, the performance control systems—on which modern corporations so heavily depend—tend to drive out social goals in favor of economic ones.[10]

In the contemporary large corporation, then, professional amorality turns into economic morality. And when the screws of these performance control systems are turned really tight, economic morality can turn into social immorality. And it happens often: A *Fortune* writer found that "a surprising number of [big companies] have been involved in blatant illegalities" in the 1970s, at least 117 of 1,043 firms studied.[11]

How, then, is anyone to "trust it"?

THE NEED FOR SOCIAL RESPONSIBILITY. The fact is that we have to trust it. Social responsibility may be a naive concept, but it is also a necessary one, for two reasons. First, the strategic decisions of large organizations inevitably involve social as well as economic consequences that are inextricably intertwined. The neat distinction between economic goals in the private sector and social goals in the public sector just doesn't hold up in practice. Every important decision of the large corporation—to introduce a new product line, to close an old plant, whatever—generates all kinds of social consequences. There is no such thing as a purely economic decision in big business. Only a conceptual ostrich, with his head deeply buried in the abstractions of economic theory, could possibly use the distinction between economic and social goals to dismiss social responsibility.

The second reason we have to "trust it" is that there is always some degree of discretion involved in corporate decision-making, discretion to thwart social needs or to attend to them. Things could be a lot better in today's corporation, but they could also be worse. It is primarily our ethics that keep us responsible. If the performance control systems favored by large, diversified corporations cut too deeply into our ethical standards, then we shall have to rethink how these corporations are organized—rethink their size, their bureaucratization, their diversification.

To dismiss corporate social responsibility is to allow corporate behavior to drop to the lowest level, propped up only by external controls such as regulation and pressure campaigns. Solzhenitsyn, who has experienced "a society without any objective legal scale," warns us (in sharp contrast to Friedman) that "a society with no other scale but the legal one is not quite worthy of man either. A society which is based on the letter of the law and never reaches any higher is scarcely taking advantage of the high level of human possibilities."[12]

This is not to suggest that we must "trust it" categorically. We certainly cannot trust it unconditionally by accepting the claim popular in some quarters that only business can solve the social ills of society. Business has no business using its resources without constraint in the social sphere—whether to support political candidates or to dictate through its donations how nonprofit institutions should allocate their efforts.

But in situations where business is necessarily involved, where its decisions have inherent social consequences of importance, that is where social responsibility has a role to play: where business creates externalities that cannot be measured and attributed to it (in other words, where regulation is ineffective); where regulation would work if only business would cooperate with it; where the corporation can fool its customers or suppliers or government through superior knowledge; where useful products can be marketed instead of wasteful or destructive ones. In other words, we have to realize that in many spheres we must "trust it," or at least we must socialize it (and perhaps change it) so that we can trust it. None of us will want to live in a society without responsible, ethical, and committed people in important posts.

"IGNORE IT"

"Ignore it" differs from the other positions on the horseshoe in that explicitly or implicitly it calls for no change in corporate behavior. It assumes that social needs are met in the course of pursuing economic goals. We include this position in our horseshoe because it is held by many influential people and also because its validity would make the other positions irrelevant. We must therefore investigate it alongside the others.

It should be noted at the outset that "ignore it" is not the same position as "trust it." In the latter, to be good is the right thing to do; in the present position, "it pays to be good." The distinction is subtle but important, for now it is economics, not ethics, that elicits the desired behavior. One need not strive to be ethical; economic forces will ensure that social needs fall conveniently into place. Thus by moving one notch to the right on our horseshoe, we enter the realm where the economic goals dominate.

"Ignore it" is sometimes referred to as "enlightened self-interest," although some of its proponents are more enlightened than others. Many a true believer in social responsibility has used the "it pays to be good" argument to ward off attacks from the right that corporations have no business pursuing social goals. After all, even Milton Friedman must admit that they have every right to do so if it pays them economically.

The danger of such arguments, however—and a prime reason "ignore it" differs from "trust it"—is that they tend to support the status quo: Corporations need not change their behavior because it already pays to be good.

Sometimes the case for "ignore it" is made in terms of corporations at large, that the whole business community will benefit from socially responsible behavior. Other times the case is made in terms of the individual corporation, that it will benefit directly from its own socially responsible actions. Others make the case for "ignore it" in "social investment" terms, claiming that socially responsible behavior pays off in a better image for the firm, a more positive relationship with customers, and ultimately a healthier and more stable society in which to do business.

Then, there is what can be called the "them" argument: "If we're not good, *they* will move in"—"they" being Ralph Nader, the government, whoever. In other words, "Be good or else." The trouble with this argument is that reducing social responsibility to simply a political tool for sustaining managerial control of the corporation in the face of outside threats tends to encourage general pronouncements instead of concrete actions, unless, of course, "they" actually deliver with pressure campaigns.

I conclude that the "ignore it" position rests on some shaky ground. It promotes average behavior at best—the status quo of corporate social responsiveness—and we have already seen that for many people that average is not good enough. In fact, the "ignore it" position cannot stand alone; its argument collapses without the "pressure it" position. For without the pressure campaign of the activist, corporations need not worry about their behavior. And if this position cannot stand alone, then by its very nature it cannot stand at all.

"INDUCE IT"

Continuing around to the right, our next position drops all concern with social responsibility per se and argues simply: "Pay it to be good," or, from the corporation's point of view, "be good only where it pays." Here, the corporation does not actively pursue social goals at all, whether as ends in themselves or as means to economic ends. Rather, it undertakes socially desirable *programs* when it is induced economically to do so— usually through government incentives. If society wishes to clean up urban blight, then let its government provide subsidies for corporations that renovate buildings. If pollution is the problem, then let corporations be rewarded for reducing it.

"Induce it" faces "regulate it" on the opposite side of the horseshoe for good reason. While one can penalize the corporation for what it does do, the other rewards it for doing what it would not otherwise do. Hence the two positions can be direct substitutes: Pollution can be alleviated by introducing penalties for the damage done or by offering incentives for the improvements rendered.

Logic does, however, dictate an appropriate role for each of these positions. Where a corporation is doing society a specific, attributable harm—as in the case of pollution—then paying it to stop hardly seems to make sense. If society does not wish to outlaw the harmful behavior altogether, then surely it must charge those responsible for it. Offering financial incentives to stop causing harm would be to invite a kind of blackmail—for example, encouraging corporations to pollute so as to get paid to stop. And every citizen would be charged for the harm done by only a few.

On the other hand, where social problems exist that cannot be attributed to specific corporations yet require the skills of business for solution, then financial incentives clearly make sense (so long, of course, as solutions can be clearly defined and tied to tangible economic rewards). Here, then, and not under "trust it," is where the "only business can do it" argument belongs. When it is true that only business can do it (and business has not done it to us in the first place), then business should be encouraged to do it.

"RESTORE IT"

Our last position on the horseshoe tends to be highly ideological, the first since "democratize it" to seek a fundamental change in the governance and the goals of the corporation. Like the proponents of "nationalize it," those of this position believe that managerial control is illegitimate and must be replaced by a more acceptable form of external control. The corporation should be restored to its former status as a "closely held" instrument, in other words, returned to the direct control of its "rightful" owners, the shareholders. The only way to ensure the relentless pursuit of economic goals—and that means the maximization of profit, free of the "subversive doctrine" of social responsibility—is to put control directly into the hands of those to whom profit means the most.

THE FRIEDMAN DOCTRINE. Some years ago this may have seemed to be an obsolete position. But thanks to its patron saint Milton Friedman, it has come back into prominence. Friedman has written:

> In a free-enterprise, private-property system, a corporate executive is an employee of the owners of the business. He has direct responsibility to his employers. That responsibility is to conduct the business in accordance with their desires, which generally will be to make as much money as possible while conforming to the basic rules of the society, both those embodied in law and those embodied in ethical custom.[13]

Interestingly, what seems to drive Friedman is a belief that the shift over the course of this century from owner to manager control, with its concerns about social responsibility, represents an unstoppable skid around our horseshoe. In the opening chapter of his book *Capitalism and Freedom,* Friedman seems to accept only two possibilities—traditional capitalism and state socialism as practiced in Eastern Europe. The absence of the former must inevitably lead to the latter, with social responsibility acting as the catalyst.

> The preservation and expansion of freedom are today threatened from two directions. The one threat is obvious and clear. It is the external threat coming from the evil men in the Kremlin who promise to bury us. The other threat is far more subtle. It is the internal threat coming from men of good intentions and good will who wish to reform us.[14]

The problem of who should control the corporation thus reduces to a war between two ideologies—in Friedman's terms, "subversive" socialism and "free" enterprise. In this world of black and white, there can be no middle ground, no moderate position between the black of "nationalize it" and the white of "restore it," none of the gray of "trust it." Either the owners will control the corporation or else the government will. Hence, " 'restore it' or else." Anchor the corporation on the right side of the horseshoe, Friedman seems to be telling us, the only place where "free" enterprise and "freedom" are safe.

All of this rests on a series of assumptions—some technical, some economic, some political—that I believe are faulty. The issues are important enough in my opinion to merit their consideration at some length.

ASSUMPTION OF SHAREHOLDER CONTROL. First is the technical assumption of shareholder control. Most large corporations are simply beyond the reach of individual shareholders. Those people's vehicle of control, formally at least, is the board of directors. But the boards of widely held corporations are typically controlled by the managers, not the shareholders. Traditions have grown up whereby it is the full-time chairmen who propose new board members, and there is a good deal of evidence that the selection is based not on shareholding per se, certainly not on any inclination by the managers to chose people who will control their behavior, but at best on the ability of the directors to serve the organization, at worst on their propensity to sit quietly and leave the management alone.

It is true that occasionally someone amasses enough stock to wrest control of a board from the management. But more often the volume of the publicly traded stock is so huge that even the largest private shareholders cannot hope to own more than an insignificant portion of it, far too little to challenge the management. (Of course, one corporation, or financial institution, can amass considerable stock ownership of another, but that just bumps our argument up one level, to the question of who can control the controller.)

Every trend in stock ownership throughout this century refutes the assumption that small shareholders are either able or willing to exercise control over the large corporation. As was pointed out in our earlier discussion of the board of directors, wherever power is widely dispersed among a constituency—shareholders no less than workers or customers—those who share it tend to remain passive. It simply does not pay any one of them to invest the effort to exercise it. If shareholders are unhappy with the behavior of a corporation, it is so much easier for them simply to sell their stock.

Interestingly, then, the one place where the free market still clearly exists is in stock ownership, and that has served to detach property from control. Shareholding has become more and more dispersed, and the ease of the market transaction discourages the exercise of control. To use the terms of a fascinating little book by Albert Hirschman, "exit" is preferred to "voice," let alone "loyalty."[15] Thus, while there may occasionally be shareholder *autocracy*—control of the corporation by a single important shareholder—there is never likely to be shareholder *democracy*—true control of the management by many small shareholders.

ASSUMPTION OF COMPETITIVE MARKETS. The economic assumptions of free markets have been discussed at length in the literature. Whether there exists vibrant competition, unlimited entry, open information, consumer sovereignty, and labor mobility is certainly subject to debate. Less subject to debate, though, is the assertion that the larger the corporation, the greater is its ability to interfere with those things. The issues we are discussing center on the giant corporation. It is not Joe's Body Shop that Ralph Nader is after, but General Motors, a corporation that employs more than half a million people and earns greater revenues than many national governments.

Those who laid the foundation for conventional economic theory—such as Adam Smith and Alfred Marshall—never dreamed of chemical complexes that cost more than a billion dollars; of the massive amounts now spent for advertising campaigns, designed for affect more than for effect; of the waves of conglomeration that have combined all kinds of diverse businesses into single corporate entities; and of the intimate relationships that now exist among giant corporations and between them and governments, as customers and partners as well as supporters. The concept of the arms-length relationship in such conditions is, at best, nostalgic.

How does government contract objectively for a major weapons system when only a few firms are capable of supplying it, ones that are likely to have been involved in the previous development of the technologies to be used, not to mention staffed with ex-military personnel with ties deep in its defense department? And the coffers of the politicians who must make the decision have been filled with funds from the corporate managers, if not the corporations themselves (however indirectly)? What happens to consumer sovereignty when Ford knows more about its gas tanks than do its customers? And what does labor mobility mean in the presence of an inflexible pension plan, or commitment to a special skill, or to a one-factory town? Indeed, it is an ironic twist of conventional economic theory that the worker is the one who typically stays put, rendering false the assumption of labor mobility, while the shareholder is the mobile one, thus spoiling the case for owner control.

ASSUMPTION OF FREEDOM THROUGH "FREE" ENTERPRISE. The political assumptions are more ideological in nature, although usually implicit, namely that the corporation is essentially amoral, society's instrument for producing goods and services, and, more broadly, that a society is "free" and "democratic" so long as its governmental leaders are elected by universal suffrage and do not interfere with the legal activities of its businesspeople. Freedom becomes associated with "free" enterprise. But many people—a large majority of the general public, if the polls are to be believed—seem to subscribe to one or more contrary assumptions.

One is that the large corporation is a social and political institution as much as an economic instrument. Economic activities, as noted previously, produce all kinds of social consequences. Jobs get created and rivers get polluted, cities get built and workers get injured. These social consequences cannot be factored out of corporate strategic decisions and assigned to government.

Another contrary assumption is that society cannot achieve the necessary balance between social and economic needs so long as the private sector attends only to economic goals. Given the influence of business in society, it is argued that the acceptance of Friedman's prescriptions would lead to a one-dimensional society—excessively materialistic and mercenary. Economic morality, as noted earlier, can amount to a social immorality.

Finally, the question is asked: Why the owners? In a democratic society, what justifies owner control of the corporation any more than worker control, or consumer control, or pluralistic control? This is not Adam Smith's society of small proprietors and shopkeepers. His butcher, brewer, and baker have become Swift, Anheuser-Busch, and Ralston Purina. What was once a case for individual democracy now becomes a case for oligarchy.

Free enterprise comes to mean, not the freedom of individual entrepreneurs to maneuver in a market place, but the autonomy of large established organizations to sustain their power in good part free of external influence. And there is, as already noted, no democracy within those organizations. They are technically oligarchies, structures of hierarchical authority in which the few at the top direct the activities of the many down below. There is nothing wrong with this, at least not so long as it is viewed for what it is: not freedom itself but rather the suspension of freedom for the sake of productive efficiency. Indeed, it must be considered a curious fact that, as argued back in Chapters 8 and 9, "free" enterprise is structured on the business level in America in much the same way that "subversive" socialism is structured on the state level in the Soviet Union.

Thus, I personally see Friedman's form of "restore it" as a rather quaint position in a society of giant corporations, managed economies, and dispersed shareholders—a society in which the collective power of corporations is coming under increasing scrutiny and in which the tradeoff between economic and social goals is being reconsidered.

OTHER WAYS TO RESTORE IT. Of course, there are ways other than those of Milton Friedman to "restore it." In some cases, divestment can return the corporation to the business or central theme it knows best, restoring the role of allocating funds between different businesses to capital markets. Likewise, it may sometimes be advantageous to do away with certain forms of vertical integration, so that the large corporation trades with its suppliers and customers instead of ingesting them indiscriminately. Boards could be restored to positions of influence by increasing the directors' legal responsibility for their actions and by making them more independent of the management (for example, by giving them the right to personal staffs and by excluding full-time managers from their ranks, especially the position of chairman). And the size of large enterprises can be reduced where that reflects not current economic competitiveness but rather the legacies of historical successes or other political powers.*

Some of these proposals may not be much more easily attainable in today's society than those of Friedman, even though they may be desirable to large segments of the population. "Restore it" is the nostalgic position on our horseshoe, a return to our fantasies of a glorious past. In this society of giant organizations, it flies in the face of powerful economic and political forces. But efforts must be made to correct at least the obvious deficiencies.

CONCLUSION: IF THE SHOE FITS . . .

I believe that today's corporation is no more capable of riding on one position of this horseshoe than is a horse of stepping on any one part of its shoe. In other words, we need to treat the conceptual horseshoe as a portfolio of positions from which we can draw, depending on circumstances. Exclusive reliance on any one position will lead to a narrow

---

* Of course, a number of these proposals might be worthwhile to pursue in parts of the public and parapublic sectors as well, for example to divide up overgrown hospitals, school systems, social service agencies, and all kinds of government departments.

and dogmatic society, with an excess of concentration of power. The use of a variety of positions, can encourage the pluralism I believe most of us feel is necessary to sustain democracy. If the shoe fits, then let the corporation wear it.

I do not mean to imply that some of the positions do not represent fundamentally different ideologies. Clearly they do. But I also believe that anyone who makes an honest assessment of the realities of power in and around today's large corporation, no matter to which side he or she tilts, must conclude that a variety of positions have to be relied upon.

I tilt to the left of center, as has no doubt been obvious in my comments to this point. Let me summarize my own prescriptions as follows, and in the process provide some basis for considering when it is appropriate to use each of the eight positions.

First "trust it," or at least "socialize it." Despite my suspicions about much of the rhetoric that passes for social responsibility and the discouraging evidence about the behavior of many large contemporary organizations (not only corporations), I remain firmly convinced that without honest and responsible people in important places, we are in deep trouble. We need to trust it because, no matter how much we rely on the other positions on the horseshoe, managers will always retain a great deal of discretionary power. And that power necessarily has social no less than economic consequences.

The positions on the right side of our horseshoe ignore these social consequences, while some of those on the left fail to recognize the difficulties of influencing these consequences in large, hierarchical organizations. Sitting between these two sets of positions at "trust it," managers can use their discretion to satisfy or to subvert the wishes of the public. Ultimately, what managers do is determined by their sense of responsibility as individual members of society.

Although we must "trust it," we cannot *but* "trust it." As I have argued, there is an appropriate and limited role for social responsibility—essentially to get the corporation's own house in order and to encourage it to act responsibly in its own sphere of operations. Beyond that, social responsibility needs to be influenced by other positions around our horseshoe.

Then "pressure it," ceaselessly. As we have seen, too many forces interfere with social responsibility. The best antidote to these forces is the ad hoc pressure campaign, designed to pinpoint unethical behaviors and to raise social consciousness about issues. The existence of the "pressure it" position is what most clearly distinguishes the Western from the Eastern "democracies." Give me one Ralph Nader to all those banks of government functionaries.

In fact, "pressure it" underlies the viability of most of the other positions. Pressure campaigns have, for example, brought about necessary new regulations and have highlighted the case for corporate democracy. And, as we have seen, the "ignore it" position collapses without "pressure it."

After that, try to "democratize it." A somewhat distant third in my portfolio is "democratize it," a position I view as radical only in terms of the current U.S. debate, not in terms of fundamental American values. Pluralistic control of institutions is very much in the tradition of American democracy. And democracy matters most where it affects us directly— in the water we drink, the jobs we perform, the products we consume. How can we call our society democratic when many of its most powerful institutions are closed to governance from the outside and are run as oligarchies from within?

As noted earlier, we have yet to find the means to achieve corporate democracy. But we also know how resourceful people can be when they decide to resolve a problem—and this is a problem that badly needs resolving. Somehow, ways must be found to open the corporation up to the formal influence of the constituencies most affected by it— employees, customers, neighbors, even owners of small numbers of shares—without weakening it as an economic institution. At issue is nothing less than the maintenance of basic freedoms in our society.

Then, only where specifically appropriate, "regulate it" and "induce it." Facing each other on the horseshoe are two positions that have useful if limited roles to play. Regulation is neither a panacea nor a menace. It should be used where the corporation can abuse the power it has and can be penalized for that abuse—especially where externalities can be identified with specific corporations. Financial inducements belong not where a corporation has created a problem but where it has the capability to solve a problem created by someone else.

Occasionally, selectively, "nationalize it" and "restore it," but not in Friedman's way. The extreme positions should be reserved for extreme problems. If "pressure it" is a scalpel and "regulate it" a cleaver, then "nationalize it" and "restore it" are guillotines.

Both these positions are implicitly proposed as alternatives to "democratize it." One offers public control, the other "shareholder democracy." The trouble is that control by everyone often turns out to be control by no one, while exclusive control by the owners—even if attainable— would remove the corporation even further from the influence of those most influenced by it.

Yet, as noted earlier, nationalization sometimes makes sense, namely, where private enterprise cannot provide a necessary mission, at least in a sufficient or appropriate way, and sometimes where the activities of a corporation must be intimately tied to government policy.

As for "restore it," I believe Friedman's particular proposals will aggravate the problems of political control and social responsibility, strengthening oligarchical tendencies in society and further tilting what I see as the current imbalance between social and economic goals. In response to Friedman's choice between "subversive" socialism and "free" enterprise, I say "a plague on both your houses." Let us concentrate our efforts on the intermediate positions around the horseshoe.

However, other forms of "restore it" are worth considering: to "divest it" where diversification has interfered with capital markets, competition, and economic efficiency; to "*dis*integrate it" vertically where a trading network is preferable to a managerial hierarchy; to "strengthen its board" so that directors can assess managers objectively; and to "reduce it" where size represents a power game rather than a means to provide better and more efficient service to the public. I stand with Friedman in wishing to see competitive markets strengthened; it is just that I believe his proposals lead in exactly the opposite direction.

Finally, above all, don't "ignore it." I leave one position out of my portfolio altogether, because it contradicts the others. The one thing we must not do is ignore the large, widely held corporation. It is too influential a force in our lives. Our challenge is to find ways to distribute the power in and around our large organizations so that they will remain responsive, vital, *and* effective.

16

A NOTE ON THAT DIRTY WORD "EFFICIENCY"

The title of this piece may seem cute, its tone whimsical. Don't be fooled. It deals with a critical issue in our society of organizations. The problem is not that people sneer at "efficiency experts"; it's that trying to be efficient can sometimes make us ineffective. Recalling our earlier discussion of analysis and intuition in Chapter 4, what we find here is that an obsession with being "objective" can prove subjective, that professional managers who claim to be "amoral" may find themselves drawn into decidedly immoral behaviors.

The suggestion is that management as conventionally practiced may prove to be the problem, not the solution. It may have worked against our best interests, not only as consumers of the products of organizations who seek quality and economy, but also as citizens who expect organizations to treat us as human beings. This theme underlies our discussion here; it becomes the focus of attention in the next chapter, our last. Thus, "A Note on That Dirty Word Efficiency" helps to set up our closing essay.

Why should "efficiency" be considered a dirty word in so many quarters? It is one thing when assembly line workers or student radicals rail against it, but quite another when a Harvard Business School publication refers to the label "efficiency expert" applied to a manager in one of its cases as "most uncomplimentary in connotation."[1]

Efficiency, Herbert Simon argued in *Administrative Behavior,* is a value-free concept, in his words, "completely neutral." He defined the "criterion of efficiency" as dictating "that choice of alternative which produces the largest result for the given application of resources."[2] In other words, to be efficient means to get the most of whatever goal an organization wishes to pursue—for example the most growth, the happiest employees, or the highest-quality products. Efficiency means the greatest *benefit* for the *cost,* in the words of McNamara's whiz kids at the Pentagon back in the 1960s, "the biggest bang for the buck." And since resources are always constrained in a competitive world, efficiency is a logical goal of every organization, indeed every human endeavor. It too is like "motherhood." How could anyone possibly be against efficiency?

I believe the root of the problem lies not in the definition of the term but in how that definition is inevitably put into operation. In practice, efficiency does not mean the greatest benefit for the cost; it means the greatest *measurable* benefit for the *measurable* cost. In other words, efficiency means *demonstrated* efficiency, *proven* efficiency, above all, *calculated* efficiency. A management obsessed with efficiency is a management obsessed with measurement. The cult of efficiency is the cult of calculation. And therein lies the problem.

A simple experiment demonstrates the point. I asked fifty-nine MBA students, cold, at the start of a class on another subject, to write down the first thing that came into their heads when I said that a restaurant was efficient. (Readers are invited to stop here and record their own answers.) According to Simon's definition, the answers should have varied widely. According to my contention, however, easily quantified goals should have predominated.

In fact, forty-three of the students named that most operational of goals, speed of service, in one form or another (for instance, "fast service," "no delays"). The quality of the food—surely at least as important a goal for restaurants, although less easily measured—did evoke thirteen positive comments (such as "serves good meals," "tasty food"), but also five specifically negative ones (for example, "terrible food," "serves what should be thrown out," "bland, boring, and dehumanizing"; my father, to whom I put the same question, remarked, "I don't see what efficiency has to do with food," but then, on further reflection, added, "If I heard that a restaurant was efficient, I would wonder about the food.")* I polled twenty-two more students a year later, and this time all but two mentioned speed of service (fourteen exclusively).

I also polled both groups of students on the statement that my house was efficient. Forty of the fifty-nine as well as ten of the twenty-two referred to something related to getting around in it or cleaning it up quickly. Seven of the first group and ten of the second commented on its fuel consumption. Issues of comfort, beauty, and warmth (in the psychological sense) were hardly mentioned.

---

* It should be added that a few students made comments on price, cleanliness, and profitability; note also that some made more than one comment.

Thus, in practice, efficiency is associated with criteria that are measurable. An efficient restaurant is one that gets its food on the table in thirteen minutes, independent of, or perhaps in spite of, the quality of that food. An efficient home is one that warms the bodies of its occupants with only 3,000 liters of oil during a frigid Canadian winter, not one that warms their hearts with its charm.

This orientation has three major consequences.

1. Because costs are typically more easily measured than benefits, efficiency all too often reduces to economy. Compared with benefits, costs more easily lend themselves to expression in quantitative terms—in dollars, person-hours, materials, or whatever. For example, university administrators know with some precision how much it costs to train an MBA student. But no one really has a clue how much is learned in such programs, or what effect that learning has on the practice of management.

The all-too-frequent result of an obsession with efficiency, therefore, is the cutting of tangible costs at the expense of intangible benefits. What university administrator cannot cut 10 percent from the cost of training an MBA with no *measurable* effect on the benefits? Even in a business firm, it is a simple matter for a chief executive to cut certain costs without impacting on benefits—that almighty bottom line—not in the short run, at least. One simply reduces spending on research or advertising. The effect on profits may not show up for years, long after the executive has left. All too often, therefore, efficiency just means economy, with benefits suffering at the expense of costs, so to speak. And efficiency gets a bad name.

2. Because economic costs can usually be more easily measured than social costs, efficiency often produces an escalation in social costs, which are treated as "externalities." Business firms in particular like to measure things. Peter Drucker makes this clear: The "task can be identified. It can be defined. Goals can be set. And performance can be measured. And then business can perform."[3] The problem is that some things are more easily measured than others. The dollars spent, the hours worked, the materials consumed are easily quantified. The air polluted, the minds dulled, the scenery destroyed are costs, too, but they are not so easily measured.

In all kinds of organizations, the economic costs—the tangible resources deployed—are generally easier to measure than the social costs—the consequences on people's lives. An emphasis on efficiency thus encourages the attribution of only the tangible costs to the organization; the intangible costs, usually social, get dismissed as "externalities," for which society is considered responsible. The implicit assumption is that if a cost cannot be measured, it has not been incurred. And so it is not the concern of a management responsible for "efficiency." As a result, the economic costs tend to be closely controlled by "efficient" managers, while the social costs escalate. And efficiency gets a bad name.

3. Because economic benefits are typically more easily measured than social benefits, efficiency often drives the organization toward an economic morality which can amount to a social immorality. Human activities create many benefits, ranging from the tangible to the highly ambiguous. A manager concerned with efficiency naturally favors the former; he or she can measure them and attribute them to his or her efforts. The dean who must base his promotion decisions on "hard facts" will be encouraged to count the publications of professors rather than make subjective assessments of their quality.

An obsession with efficiency therefore means that tangible, demonstrable, measurable benefits (such as speed of service) are allowed to obscure intangible, less easily specified and quantified benefits (such as the quality of food). Indeed, the more serious problem is that the former are often allowed to drive out the latter, even when the latter are generally recognized as more important. If one marches to the tune of efficiency, if one is "measured" on one's performance, then there may be no choice. Again, it is those things economic—associated with tangible resources—that best lend themselves to measurement. The social values get left behind.

Pirsig, in his popular book, *Zen and the Art of Motorcycle Maintenance,* helps us to take this point one step further, by suggesting that such social values may be beyond our skills of logic and analysis (and, therefore, measurement): "I think there is such a thing as Quality, but as soon as you try to define it, something goes haywire. You can't do it. . . . Because definitions are a product of rigid, formal thinking, Quality cannot be defined." And yet, "even though Quality cannot be defined, you know what Quality is."[4] But do the efficiency experts? Or at least, do they allow themselves to "know" that which is beyond the power of their tools?

Thus efficiency emerges in practice not as a neutral concept but as one associated with a particular system of values—economic values. In fact, an obsession with efficiency can force the trading off of social benefits for economic ones that can drive an organization beyond an economic morality to a social immorality. In Chapter 9, I cited Ackerman on how the systems of objectives used in large corporations "may actually inhibit social responsiveness" by driving out the less operational social goals.[5] And it is worth repeating here Bower's illustration of this, the turning of the financial screws in one such system, at General Electric, that contributed to the famous price-fixing scandal of 1961. As he noted, in the giant corporation, people

> . . . are rewarded for performance, but performance is almost always
> defined as short-run economic or technical results. The more objective
> the system, the more an attempt is made to quantify results, the harder
> it is to broaden the rules of the game to take into account the social role
> of the executive.[6]

Thus proeconomic behavior becomes antisocial behavior. And efficiency gets a bad name.

Thus, in practice if not in theory, efficiency is associated with a particular system of values. The call to "be efficient" is the call to calculate, where calculation means economizing, means treating social costs as externalities, and means allowing economic benefits to push out social ones. At the limit, efficiency emerges as one pillar of an ideology that worships economic goals, sometimes with immoral consequences. Thus efficiency, that "completely neutral" concept, as well as the managers and management schools obsessed with it, get a bad name.

17

SOCIETY HAS BECOME UNMANAGEABLE AS A RESULT OF MANAGEMENT

The title is a sentence from a talk I gave in 1982 at a symposium held in St. Gallen, Switzerland. The talk was my diatribe against all the things that bothered me about management and organizations. The audience of businessmen and students received it rather well, I thought. But I never published it, waiting, I guess, for the right moment. This seems to be it. The issue, the integration, the tone all seem appropriate right here, to close and cap this book.

It is interesting that a talk on the problems of management and organizations should bring together so much of my work. But that it does: Virtually every major theme I developed over these last twenty years somehow gets integrated here. I did not set out to do this; it just occurred naturally as I wove together a series of ideas. One consequence is that you will find some repetition here. In my revision and editing of the speech, I chose to leave some of that repetition in, even the occasional quotation that I felt merited being reread, because this last chapter is meant not only to highlight what I believe are critical issues in society but also to summarize the themes of this book.

I have purposely left in the speechlike tone of the discussion as well. It may seem casual in places, but I feel it helps to retain the pace of the presentation and the forcefulness with which the points are made. You might wish to consider this the literary license of an author in the concluding chapter of his book.

What I have to say here may also strike you as pessimistic. I think it is necessarily so. In my opinion, management as contemporarily practiced and organizations as contemporarily run, the two together in a society of large institutions, pose grave dangers for us all. I prefer to overstate my case to bring more attention to it. Clearly the issues are not as one-sided as presented here. But what I have written elsewhere in this book, on planning and the role of analysis in general and on the functional aspects of bureaucracy, among other things, outline my views with more balance. This final presentation is meant to be a polemic.

A business school dean once commented that while the consultants get paid for the answers, the academics get paid for the questions. This sounds like a sensible division of labor to me! It is true, though, that this paper is longer on the problems than it is on the solutions. But I do make a number of suggestions at the end (one colleague managed to identify thirteen proposals buried there). I present them, however, to stimulate thinking about these issues. This is not a finished paper but an intermediate step on the way to understanding and dealing with what I consider to be some serious problems. I suspect I shall never finish writing this article, no matter how often I try.

In the final analysis, I would like to think that the tone of this paper is really optimistic. If we can only understand how our organizations work, how and why they go out of control, and why our conventional managerial interventions have often aggravated this, then we might be able to work toward resolution of these problems. Our organizations must serve us, as workers, consumers, and citizens, by using and reflecting the best of our human qualities—our capabilities, intuitive and emotional as well as analytical, and our fundamental spirit. We need to manage organizations in ways that will make our society manageable.

In time gone by, Inuit* hunters could find their way across dozens of miles of flat white tundra to visit the camp of a friend, guided only by their intuition. A few years ago, the snowmobile of three young Inuit broke down only a few miles from their home and they froze to death because they could not make their way back.

This story disturbed me, and has since come to symbolize for me the problems of our society. I believe we are in danger of freezing to death for the same reason: Our machinery, in the broadest sense, not just our technologies, but our social systems and especially our organizations, has likewise dulled our senses, driving out our intuition and making it increasingly difficult to find our way out of our problems. My theme,

---

* "Eskimo" is actually an Indian word, a pejorative term for their neighbors to the north, meaning "eaters of raw flesh." "Inuit" is the term "the people" use for themselves.

specifically, is that society has become unmanageable as a result of management.

I am an organization theorist, interested in how organizations and the management processes that underlie them really work. I began my research career by studying the work of the managers who run organizations. I found that there were tremendous pressures on them to be superficial and concluded that managers had to learn to be effective in their superficiality. I have since begun to question that conclusion, to wonder how effectively anyone can manage a large, complex organization.

After that, I began research on the processes by which organizations make their strategies—how they establish basic directions for themselves. In my work and that of others, this turned out to be far more complicated than had been generally thought. In fact, the long favored approach, called "strategic planning," proved to be a myth: There turned out to be no systematic way to create strategy. And so I came to describe two less systematic approaches, a centralized one based on entrepreneurial vision and a decentralized one based on "grassroots" learning. But recently I have begun to wonder if either process can really work all that well in a large organization with its pressures of superficiality. Can any leader know enough to conceive a vision in an entrepreneurial way or even to deal with all those initiatives coming up from below?

In parallel work, seeking to make sense of the research on structure and power, I found it necessary to describe organizations as configurations, concluding that they succeed because they put things together in some integrated way—around central leadership or machinelike procedures or professional skills, among other things. In other words, the effectiveness of an organization lay more in integration itself than in the form that a particular integration happened to take. Later I came to realize that each integrated configuration naturally sows the seeds of its own destruction. And so I began to consider life cycle models of organizations, to show how various forms rise and fall over time. In particular, there appeared to be an entrepreneurial form for initial development, a machine or professional form for maturity, and a political form for decline, the latter eventually killing the moribund organization to allow its replacement by new entrepreneurial ones. But increasingly, I see interference with that cycle in our society, as old, spent organizations, incapable of finding new direction or inspiring their people, are sustained through political means, at the expense of the creation of fresh new ones.

Thus I now suspect that superficiality may be the problem, that as a result management may not be capable of providing new direction to our large organizations, and instead of replacing them in natural cycles, we sustain them at the expense of renewal in society.

What I wish to do here is pull together my various concerns, to assail in one place all the things I see as wrong in our highly organized societies. Please bear with me as I do this, because in some sense every sentence that follows is an overstatement (including this one!). My reason is to draw attention to a set of trends in society that I find both consequential and disturbing. I shall proceed through a series of highlighted points.

My first point is that ours is a society of organizations. What happens in our society happens in the context of organizations, from our birth in hospitals to our burial by funeral homes, including most of our work and our recreation in between.

I once looked at something called the *Encyclopedia of Associations*. In fact, it is an encyclopedia of American associations, because Americans are undoubtedly the greatest organizers of them all. (Witness the popularity of that most structured of sports, American football, with its formal field leadership, sharp division of labor, carefully planned procedures, etc.) In that encyclopedia I found, for example, The Flying Funeral Directors of America, an organization that brings together funeral directors "to create and further a common interest in flying and funeral service; to join together in case of mass disaster, and to improve flying safety"! Skipping past the National Horseshoe Pitchers' Association (15,000 member!) and the Pen Fanciers' Club (only 1000), I came to Pickle Packers International, an organization that every two years gives a "Hall of Fame" award to the person who has done the most for the pickle industry. It publishes *Picklepak* bimonthly. Nearby was the Popcorn Institute, which exists to promote the consumption of popcorn. Significant about the Popcorn Institute, according to the Encyclopedia, is that in 1960 it absorbed the Popcorn Processors Association, a harbinger, no doubt, of the wave of mergers that was to sweep across America in that decade.

If you wish to do something in this kind of society, no matter how private or recreational, do it in an organization. Otherwise you will have to explain yourself. If it's work, even the private work of, say, pulling teeth, join an organization of dentists; if it's bicycling, don't just hop on your bike and go, find a touring club that will plan it all out for you. And even if you insist on actually doing it yourself, you probably need to rely on an organization to get you there or at least to provide you with the means of doing it, if not to have informed you about being able to do it in the first place.

My second point is that our society of organizations is in good part a society of large organizations. We swim in a sea of big business, big government, big labor, big education. This has an important consequence for my own field, because it is organization theory that focuses its attention on the organization itself. Indeed, in this kind of society, organization theory may be better disposed to explain social behavior than the more established social sciences to which we have traditionally turned, notably economics and political science.

Every field of research has its central concept: In economics, it is the market, in political science, it is politics. But conventional markets and politics do not tell us a great deal about systems that operate as collections of large organizations. Large business organizations can interact in part free of purely competitive economic markets, taking on more of a political orientation, while, ironically, governments have come to look more and more like conglomerate clusters of organizations somewhat free of the formalities of legislative politics. Thus, considering "rational" entrepreneurs who maximize profit under conditions of competition, as economists traditionally do, reveals little about the behavior of big business, just as studying legislative bargaining among politicians, as in traditional political science, reveals little about the network of interlocking organizations of big government.

Of interest in this society of organizations is what most influences our thinking about how to construct organizations. Picking up on the idea of configuration, a number of different forms of organization seem to be possible, including an entrepreneurial configuration based on personal intuition, a missionary configuration based on ideology, a machine-like configuration (sometimes diversified) based on formal standardization, a professional configuration based on trained expertise, and an innovative configuration based on flexible teamwork.

My third point is that a form of structure called machine bureaucracy dominates our thinking about how organizations should be constructed. This form is familiar to us all, although not necessarily by that name (since we tend to associate bureaucracy with red tape and other dysfunctions, without stopping to realize that "getting organized," "being rational," and "achieving efficiency" are part and parcel of the same package). Machine bureaucracy is characterized by specialized and standardized work, formalized procedure, close control through rules and regulations, clear hierarchy of authority, formalized planning to formulate strategies before implementation, and so on.

I believe that to most people in our society of large organizations, what I am calling machine bureaucracy is not just *a* way to organize, it is *the* way to organize; it's not *one* form of structure, it *is* structure. This thinking dominates not only big government and big business, not just big management consulting, but also big labor, big social service, big fundraising, as well as big pickles and big popcorn.

The question thus arises, why machine bureaucracy? And the explanations are several.

The most obvious explanation—and the most "functional"—is that when operating tasks are simple and repetitive, as in the mass production of automobiles or the delivery of mail, then machine bureaucracy becomes the most natural way to organize. In other words, these conditions make it necessary to formalize, standardize, and rationalize behavior. But if these were the only reasons, then our automobile companies and post offices would be organized as machine bureaucracies but many of our other businesses and government departments might not, our schools would not, our welfare agencies would not. There must, therefore, be other forces that drive organizations to this structure.

One is the notion of countervailing power that John Kenneth Galbraith wrote about some years ago.[1] Since some organizations are big, other organizations must become big in response. And big generally means impersonal, and therefore machine bureaucratic. Big business generates big labor, big business and big labor generate big government, big government generates bigger business and bigger labor and also encourages big school systems, big social welfare organizations, perhaps big popcorn institutes as well. It all becomes one big power game.

The Cree Indians of northern Quebec have not had a tradition of centralized structure; each community, given its historical physical isolation, organized independently. But when the government bureaucrats of the "south" went in to build their dams to suck out the electricity, and, incidentally, flood the Cree lands, the Indians, in order to protest, had to "get organized." The government, being "Liberal," was, of course, willing to negotiate. But in *its* courts, by *its* system of justice. "Take us to your leader," said the government. And so the Cree had to centralize, to strengthen the leadership over its loose network of villages. And to that leadership, the system said, "Make your case. Show us the 'facts.' Collect the data, rationalize them, and present them to impress the judges, our judges." So the Cree had to formalize too—develop procedures and harden their data (count the dead animals, for example).* And centralization coupled with formalization is exactly what machine bureaucracy is. Thus, to save their traditional way of life, the Cree had to forfeit it: They had to organize like us. We didn't set out to bureaucratize the Cree culture. But moving it in that direction was an inevitable consequence of our actions.

Countervailing power is probably behind another factor that drives organizations toward machine bureaucracy: obsession with control. Control is the central driving force in these structures—control of workers, control of markets, control of the future, control of whatever might control them, including, if necessary, owners and elected governments. Bringing things under control is exactly what their planning systems are designed to do. They specify what is wanted and then program whatever is necessary to get it. (In fact, it is the obsession with planning, as a form of control, that explains all the fuss made in our society about "turbulent" conditions, about this so-called "age of discontinuity," and the like. It is not that our world has become any more unstable— quite the contrary, in fact, when anyone considers the 1930s and the 1940s. It is just that any perturbation at all, anything unexpected, such as a new competitor or a changed technology, upsets the carefully honed procedures of the planning systems and so sets the machine bureaucracies into a quivering panic. When the planners run around like Chicken Little crying, "The environment is turbulent! The environment is turbulent!," what they really mean is that something happened which was not anticipated by their inflexible systems.)

Now, in theory, an organization can control its future by being independent of outside forces. But in a society of machine bureaucracies, all obsessed with control, there is hardly anywhere to hide. So to be in control generally means doing the controlling yourself. The organization must grow bigger and try to dominate other organizations to avoid being dominated by them instead.

Consider the waves of mergers that have swept across the United States during the past century, first to consolidate firms of single industries

---

* A friend and former doctoral student, Fritz Rieger, who worked with the Cree, wrote to me in response to my request to review these comments: "The need for harder data reached extremes. I understood that in order to establish that natural foods were an essential part of the Cree diet, not only dietary inputs (quantity of natural foods consumed) but also human waste products (in significant quantities) were collected by native research assistants under direction of some McGill anthropologists and geographers for analysis!"

into giant trusts, then to extend the operating chains of these firms forward and backward in so-called vertical integration, and in more recent times to agglomerate all kinds of diversified businesses into single corporations. Some of the forces that drove these were no doubt economic. But many have also been political, when not representing a sheer lust for power then at least reflecting the reality that to avoid being taken over by another organization, you had better take it over first. How many small, healthy organizations have been destroyed over the years by having been gobbled up by the big bureaucracies (which immediately bureaucratized them—"What, no organization chart?" say the technocrats)? Unless, of course, they voluntarily forfeited that small size to become those voracious bureaucracies themselves.

But there is still another set of forces that gives rise to machine bureaucracy, in my opinion the most fundamental.

My fourth point is that an irrational form of "rationality" underlies our attraction to machine bureaucracy. Certain fields try to control words. The statisticians, for example, have tried to take over the word "significant," and in so doing may have reversed its meaning (since so much that proved "statistically significant" turned out to be trivial). So too, the economists have tried to take over the word "rational," with much the same effect. As human beings, we must above all be "rational," meaning to emphasize a strictly logical, explicit, and analytical—basically linear—form of reasoning. Everything must be worked out in advance, ideally based on numerical calculation.

This notion of rationality really amounts to mental control—mind over matter—and to the "rational" mind, mental control is the most important kind of control. And so organizations obsessed with control become organizations obsessed with this form of rationality.

To be in control in the machine bureaucracy means, above all, to have it down on paper. A market is controlled if a high number appears next to the label "market share"; quality is controlled if a low number appears next to "defects"; work is controlled if its accomplishment has been duly ticked off on a sheet of paper; people are controlled if each is connected to a boss on an organigram; the whole system is controlled if everything that must happen is recorded in a document called a "plan." It matters not that the real world goes its own merry way, so long as the mind controls the records of that world on paper. We deal with the discrepancies that arise through a process known as "creative accounting"!

How rational is this form of "rationality"? If no other form of thinking existed short of the haphazard, or if any other form that did exist was demonstrably inferior, then it would appear to be rational.

In fact, however, there is another form of thinking. We have long sensed it, have even had labels for it, although it has only been in recent years, through the hard science of physiology, that we discovered it. It appears to have been hiding all along in the mute right hemisphere of the human brain. We still do not know much about it—our words for it, "intuition" and "judgment," just label our ignorance—except that it seems to be inaccessible to our conscious ("rational") minds and appears to be neither linear nor analytical in its workings. Processing seems to take place in parallel, in a more holistic manner, oriented to synthesis.

If to be rational really means to use the process that most effectively achieves your goals, then intuition, no matter how mysterious, has never been demonstrated to be any less rational than conventional, formal "rationality"—no one has ever proved it to be an inferior process. Of course, how could they? The concept of proof itself resides in conventional rationality. How can we allow "rational" argument to prove or disprove the inferiority of a thought process that itself is beyond such rationality? That would be like using black-and-white photography to study the colors of the rainbow.

If this is true, then machine bureaucracies, because they accept only the narrow form of rationality, must be considered irrational organizations. Such rationality has been their obsession since Frederick Taylor began his time and motion studies of factory workers a century ago. Taylor's purpose was to root out instinct, intuition, and judgment in favor of this narrow form of rationality. From the factory, this same orientation moved into the office, as "rational" operations research techniques and formal information systems become popular after World War II. It then moved up the hierarchy, to culminate in the use of "strategic planning" in the executive suite. Such "rational" thinking has likewise dominated our business schools, which ostensibly train managers as if their brains had only one hemisphere. That old joke about MBA meaning "management by analysis" is no joke at all.

Bear in mind what "rationality" means in management, whether business, government, or the parapublic sector—it makes no difference. To rationalize almost inevitably means to cut, to reduce, to eliminate, not to integrate or grow or create. In effect, rationalizing is to the contemporary manager what bloodletting was to the medieval physician. No matter what form it takes—firing workers, cutting budgets, restructuring, etc.—rationalizing becomes the machine bureaucracy's solution to all of its problems. Integrating, growing, and creating depend in good part on the other mode of thinking—on viewing things holistically, from the perspective of synthesis, processes that seem to be beyond the machine bureaucracy.

Such rationalizing tends to be promoted by numerically literate people—the technocrats—for whom control means rules not skills, behavior means standards not norms, decision-making means analysis not intuition. When the other form of thinking is called for, the machine bureaucracy usually cannot respond. Thus small firms taken over by large ones are not allowed to be loose and informal; inspired organizations captured by conglomerates are not allowed to believe in anything beyond measurable ("bottom line") efficiency; creative and professional organizations that come under the control of big governments are not allowed to be innovative or to be proficient. All behavior must come under the technocratic control of the rules, the standards, the analyses.

We see this most clearly—most irrationally—in our school systems, which in my opinion have become areas of unmitigated disaster. In the name of rationality, education has been inundated with curricula carefully planned in offices distant from the classroom and has been forced into facilities cleverly rationalized to be efficient. Both look wonderful on paper. Yet both, by imposing forms of control incompatible with the activities in question (for reasons to be discussed later), have produced unprecedented alienation. We end up, here and in many other spheres of human activity, with "rationally" designed organizational machines that affront us—machines for which people hate to work and from which people hate to take service.

If formal proof is rooted in the conventional view of rationality, then "prove it" is the motto of a society of organizations. This means that you win points by proving it explicitly, quantitatively—by "rational" argument, analytical and logical, based on "hard," replicable data. "Sense" doesn't count, not intuitive sense. As an Inuit, you would be expected to make your way across the tundra with a map and a compass tucked under the seat of your snowmobile. Even if no one had charted the territory before and there existed no magnetic field for guidance. That way at least you could show how you did it, prove it to people who have never seen snow. If you got out alive. As a Cree, you have to dress up as a lawyer (or better, hire one of ours) and present logical arguments, eloquently, supported by facts and figures. And you must do this in a perfectly orderly courtroom, a thousand miles from the chaos of your swamped land and its dead animals.

"Prove it" manifests itself most pointedly in the question period of parliamentary democracy, where each day opposition members bombard government ministers with embarrassing questions. Under the glare of the television lights (in Canada at least), ministers have to justify to the nation what they have done (or, more often, what some civil servant they never met did in Moose Jaw, Saskatchewan). Imagine the Prime Minister arising in response to a question about why he funded some project or other with the comment, "because it felt good, because deep in my gut I knew it was right." No, he must have facts, formal justifications, logical arguments. The same, of course, holds true for presidential press conferences in the United States.

But how else can you run a modern state, you might wonder? We can't have politicians running around doing whatever they please. True enough. But neither can we have them denying their innate feel for things. Or more to the point, neither can we afford to have people in positions of influence who lack such feelings. Maybe they never had a chance to develop them in the first place; most were, after all, lawyers who spent their careers in those orderly courtrooms, far from the snow and the dead animals. But people with richer experiences do sometimes make it to government too. But how can innate sense work in that environment? What happens to feel and intuition when all these people see around them are facts and figures, files and filibusters, slick technocrats professing analytical arguments and superficial politicians mouthing easy opinions?

Certainly, when there are reliable facts our leaders had better get them right. But how often are the facts reliable? How often do different "facts" contradict each other? And how often do superficial facts suppress deeper wisdom? Where does intuition come in? The parliamentary question period and the U.S. presidential press conference have certainly proved a boon to problem recognition. But they turn out to be a menace to problem solution. They expose problems in a marvelously public way, and then impose superficial solutions on them, solutions that violate our real needs.

If you are in business, you may be inclined to dismiss some of this, attributing it to the pressures of the political process. But that would miss a major point: The problem is fundamentally organizational. It is rooted in a major premise of machine bureaucracy, private no less than public, that it is those people who sit on the top of an organizational hierarchy—whether called manager or minister—who must decide. It is they who are responsible. And the reason is that they know better. All the information comes together right there, at their level. Anyone can see this on the organigram, right there on paper, where all the lines join.

Of course, you might wonder how this can be. How can people who sit in offices wearing shirts and ties all day long know so much about the services rendered in Moose Jaw, the lands flooded in James Bay, the products produced in Saskatoon and sold in Trois Pistoles? Simple, they have a system to inform them. It is called an MIS—management information system. Everything they need to know gets recorded— black figures on white paper. All they have to do to get informed is to read. And if there is too much to read, the system takes care of that too: It aggregates. It combines data, packages them neatly and dispenses them to the leaders in neat periodic reports. In government, it's the opinion poll. So much more convenient than having to talk to real citizens. In business, it's the accounting statement and the marketing research report. A lot quicker and more ''rational'' than having to visit factories and meet customers. Or it's capital budgeting, a procedure whereby senior managers are expected to approve major proposals on the basis of reviewing aggregated figures of costs and benefits, neatly combined into projections of return on investment. Another form of ''prove it.''

The problem with all this aggregated rationality is that it drives out judgment and intuition. How can you feel if you cannot see for yourself? How can you sense if you cannot experience firsthand?

Nowhere is this better reflected than in the world of the contemporary MBA. How do we train managers, the leaders of our organizations, where products are hammered out in messy factories and then sold in busy market places? We lock bright and inexperienced people up in austere buildings and inundate them with paper. They never set foot in a factory, never meet a customer. Cases do it for them instead, much like those MIS reports in practice. The cases describe the real world, right there on paper—the products, the personalities, the politics, they're all there, in black on white. The MBAs ''know'' because they've read it all in a pithy twenty-page report the night before. On a given day it might be General Motors: what that hundred billion dollar corporation should do to secure its future. They all decide together, all those eager young MBAs, all challenging each other to ''prove it.''

Recently I got into a discussion with a group of MBA students about the excessive reliance on numerical scores to assess applicants to the program. I wondered what that had to do with native managerial ability, including intuition. One student asked: How can you select for intuition if you can't even measure it?! But another raised a more reasonable point: Would not the use of judgment introduce bias into the selection process? Absolutely, I replied, because bias is the other side of judgment. The best way to get rid of bias is to get rid of judgment. But at what price?

Is it not the elimination of judgment that so characterizes the bureaucratic institutions of our age? Is that not in good part why government is so bureaucratic—to ensure that citizens are not discriminated against or that the minister does not sneak his mistress onto the payroll? It's all very efficient at rooting out bias. Too bad it destroys organizational effectiveness.

Let us return to that court of law, where "proving it" is the means to eliminate bias. In the case of a challenge by an employee who has been fired, the courts say to the employer: "Don't tell us that person was incompetent, disagreeable, an impediment to the work of everyone else. No opinions please, just the facts and figures. Prove it. How many days off? How do you know she wasn't sick? Maybe the lighting at work made her sick. He insulted the customers? Well, customers can be disagreeable too. Prove they weren't." Better to keep the employee than face all that. (And bear in mind which organizations can afford to keep that employee.) Thus, in seeking to protect the individual from false (biased) dismissal, certainly a proper thing to do, we build bureaucratic systems free of the exercise of judgment that tie everyone else in knots.* Surely we must face the dilemma of having to balance the exercise of judgment with the avoidance of bias. As Solzhenitsyn has commented:

> I have spent all my life under a communist regime and I will tell you that a society without any objective legal scale is a terrible one indeed.

---

* I must add a note on academic tenure here. It, too, was introduced to eliminate bias, in this case the arbitrary dismissal of faculty members with unpopular views by governments or university trustees. Tenure was designed to protect freedom of expression. But today it's effect is exactly the opposite: It suppresses freedom of expression. That is because the threat to the maverick academic now comes not from the outside but from his or her own colleagues. Whereas once *having* tenure may have protected those who spoke out, today *getting* tenure menaces them. Their offended colleagues will seek to deny it to them. Thus tenure works to weed out those who do not toe the accepted line, whether that be conservative economics at one university or radical sociology at another.

But a society with no other scale but the legal one is not quite worthy of man either. A society which is based on the letter of the law and never reaches any higher is taking very scarce advantage of the high level of human possibilities. The letter of the law is too cold and formal to have a beneficial influence on society. Whenever the tissue of life is woven of legalistic relations, there is an atmosphere of moral mediocrity, paralyzing man's noblest impulses.[2]

Thus no matter who wins, it is inevitably *judgment* that the courts strike down, *gut feel* that the government procedures preclude, *intuition* that the corporate systems eliminate. Judgment, gut feel, and intuition can't be justified, not the way "rational" argument can. No matter where you function in a bureaucratic society, then, you have to "prove" your case, even if there are no maps, no compasses, no magnetic fields. And if you have to prove it, you can't feel it, you can't sense it. You forget how to use your intuition. So when the machinery breaks down, you're stranded.

My fifth point is that a society of large, "rational," machine bureaucratic organizations dictates an age of capital letter MANAGEMENT, so-called professional, that often proves thin, superficial, and sometimes immoral. What characterizes this dominant configuration of machine bureaucracy above all is the power of its administrators. The rules, the standards, the data, the rationales, these come from the administrators—line managers as well as staff analysts, the planners, systems people, accountants, and many others of the technostructure. When Robert Michels set out his "iron law of oligarchy" early in this century ("who says organization, says oligarchy") he was talking about the inevitable power of the administrators in machine bureaucracy.[3]

It is not just management that matters in our society of large organizations, but "rational" management, analytical management, management defined as "professional." But what does the word "professional" mean in the context of managing? It surely does not mean the same as in medicine or engineering, for these fields have certified methods for diagnosing and for solving practical problems in particular contexts. We certainly have techniques in management, no shortage of those, but none certified in that way. Indeed, we know a lot more about the failure of our techniques—whether PPBS, "total" information systems, giant models of the firm, or strategic planning—than we do about their successful applications. In other words, we have almost no systematic evidence on the successful practice of management, at least as compared with the complexity of the everyday job of managing. Against the occasional study of what managers actually do, and the no less rare study of how a particular technique actually functioned in practice, are the reams of publications imploring managers to use the latest techniques because they are so elegantly rational. And our universities do no better. A good part of MBA training is devoted to drill in techniques, free of context, most of whose abilities have never been demonstrated in practice. The occasional student who asks the nasty question is likely to be told that the reason the technique is not used is because it is so far ahead of those neanderthal managers practicing out there.

Thus, formal education can hardly be considered a prerequisite to practicing this so-called profession. No one identifies successful managers on the basis of holding an MBA (apart from the fact that it starts them off on that fast track). Indeed, if the success of the Japanese in practicing management compared with their reluctance to teach it is any indication, then conventional MBA training should be considered part of the problem, not part of the solution.

What "professional" means, then, is really "generic," that is, people armed with this arbitrary set of techniques can manage anything. They are specialists in nothing more than the management process itself. The context in which it is to be applied is not relevant. In medicine, this would be equivalent to physicians who, because they know how to cut, assume they can replace hearts as well as remove gallbladders; in engineering, to engineers who, because they know how to design (or more to the point, have a computer-aided program to do so on their desks), assume they can construct nuclear reactors as well as build bridges.

"Professional management" is the great invention of this century, an invention that produced gains in organizational *efficiency* so great that it eventually destroyed organizational *effectiveness*. The idea grew out of Taylor's early time and motion study work. Taylor's idea was that you programmed a task by studying it meticulously so that you could decompose it into clear steps, and then set up a specific procedure for carrying out each one. His work rendered enormous improvements in the efficiency of the highly routine physical work of the factory and equivalent clerical work of the office. This hardly endeared Taylor and the many time study analysts who followed him to the workers in question, but it worked. In other words, it proved *efficient* to treat workers as machines, with arms and legs but no brains. Personal involvement with the task may have been sacrificed, even quality and capacity for innovation, but the effects on the costs of production were dramatic.

Through professional management, Taylor's approach was brought to all areas of organizational activity, from scheduling production and selecting employees to formulating strategy. But not his basic message, because that was in fact misunderstood.

Taylor did not try to program work that he did not fully comprehend. His studies and experiments were meticulous. He described before he prescribed. Many of his imitators never learned that lesson. Strategic planners, for example, leapt into prescription in the face of almost total ignorance about how strategies really do form. We had barely any empirical evidence on strategy-making throughout the 1960s and 1970s, when strategic planning was promoted so aggressively. It was simply assumed that the "rational" approach was better. Now we do have some evidence, and it shows how naïve the assumptions that underlie strategic planning really were. For one thing, strategy-making depends importantly on synthesis, while formal planning offers only analysis. Disaggregating a process into steps and checklists does not reintegrate it. For another, strategy-making is a highly dynamic process, one of slow learning over time in response to unpredictable events. For this, formal planning offered a static sequence of steps, converting a future considered predictable into a set of prescheduled strategies.

In 1979, in order to explain the success of Texas Instruments, Marianne Jelinek published *Institutionalizing Innovation*. Her argument, in essence, was that Taylor's successes in the factory could be replicated in the executive offices by processes that were fundamentally the same, though on a different level of abstraction. "It is through administrative systems that planning and policy are made possible because the *systems* capture knowledge about the task."[4] But those systems captured nothing; they failed soon after the book was published: Texas Instruments' own fancy planning system was subsequently believed to *dis*courage innovation.[5] In fact, there never was any evidence that the company's success stemmed from anything more than a capable leader who knew how to learn and whose own energy and enthusiasm enabled him to attract good people and to invigorate them. Good people, of course, make for good organizations. They also design good systems, at least systems that are good for them. But remove the good people and the systems collapse. Innovation, it turned out, could not be institutionalized.

But strategic planning and other techniques failed not only because of ignorance of the processes they tried to replace. They also failed because Taylor's approach was not suited to other contexts, to situations where the mind and the motivation of the worker mattered more than his or her ability to do simple, routine tasks.

Taylor said, many years ago, "In the past the man has been first; in the future the system must be first."[6] Prophetic words indeed. It is the procedure that counted, not the person who happened to execute it. Now, if you are dealing with the carrying of pig iron—to cite one of Taylor's famous studies—then such an attitude may not matter all that much, at least not to those concerned strictly with an organization's efficiency. The work gets done, quickly, so long as people remain willing to do it, even if it makes them miserable. But when the work requires the thinking of the worker, then it also requires that person's motivation—his or her involvement and commitment. Formal systems do not put the brain into gear; rather they disengage it. Removing control over the work from the worker—as, for example, strategic planning did to the managers expected to carry out the plans—had the eventual effect of destroying that motivation.

Thus professional management, by putting the systems ahead of the people, has had the effect of bleeding out of organizations, slowly and gradually, their capacity to do mental work as it must be done—with energy, vigor, and imagination. Taylor's "scientific management" has exacted its toll not only on the workers who don't care about the products of their labor, but also on the managers and analysts who have been equally dehumanized by the whole effort.

Thus has the cult of rationality, as manifested in so-called professional management, served to destroy the deep-rooted effectiveness of many of our large organizations, by squeezing out their very humanness. In its own form of *reductio ad absurdum,* professional management made organizations so rational, so efficient, that they ceased to function effectively. Alfred Chandler and Oliver Williamson have published highly acclaimed books about the advantages of administrative systems over market relationships.[7] Managers were described as being able to manage certain transactions within their administrative hierarchies (for example, through vertical integration) more efficiently than could trading relationships deal with them in the marketplace. But at what cost in human terms? And in organizational effectiveness? Chandler titled his Pulitzer Prize-winning book *The Visible Hand,* to contrast the power of administration with Adam Smith's "invisible hand" of market forces. "The Visible Claw" might have been a more appropriate title.

Why do we persist in imputing such powers to management systems?

How can we so condemn the centralized management of governments in Eastern Europe while remaining so enamored of the same form of management in our Western corporations? Why do we insist on attributing every human success in organizations to systems, pretending that we can sustain idiosyncratic human initiative by perpetuating the formal procedures that merely aid it? What is wrong with recognizing success as residing in the energy, the intelligence, and the commitment of individual flesh-and-blood human beings?

Two personal stories illustrate well, I believe, the widespread feelings about the effects of impersonalized management. Shortly after I published my article "The Manager's Job: Folklore and Fact," the *New York Times* ran a story on it in which they characterized my description as "calculated chaos" and "controlled disorder."[8] A few days later I received calls from a radio station in Winnipeg and a television network in Toronto, in both cases from production assistants working on morning programs who requested interviews on the air. Both added a curious comment in those calls, to the effect that "Are we glad someone finally let managers have it!"

Now one thing my article certainly did *not* do was let managers have it; both women who called had read only the *Times* account, but that did not give such an impression either. Indeed, managers themselves have been the most enthusiastic recipients of my article. Why then the comments? I believe they were a reaction to what those people experienced management to be—the impersonal directives coming down from above. It was not flesh-and-blood managers they saw up there, not people struggling like them to deal with complex problems, but cold, impersonal systems. I was certainly letting *that* have it, if not them. But to the people who called, the two seemed synonymous. And so words like "chaos" and "disorder" appeared to them to debunk managers rather than to humanize them.

The second story reinforces the first. Some time ago, I was asked to join a group that was screening a series of National Film Board of Canada films called "Corporation," about the Steinberg supermarket chain and especially about its colorful leader, Sam Steinberg. I am hardly a right-wing reactionary, but this was a particularly radical group. (It was shortly after 1968, and this was a retreat on Vancouver Island.) One member of the group referred to the films as "subversive" because they made Sam Steinberg seem so affectionately human: Everyone *knew* that managers were really sons of bitches!

Some years ago, a professor named Albert Shapero expressed the point well with an article entitled "What MANAGEMENT Says and What Managers Do." Like him, I believe it is capital-letter MANAGE-MENT that is the son of a bitch, not small-letter managers. "Twenty-five years of MANAGEMENT have resulted in an Analysis in Wonderland outlook where abstractions are reality and where people and things are ciphers or difficulties to be dealt with."[9] It is the impersonal systems that people rail against, the dehumanizing nature of a professional manage-ment that believes it can function free of context, free of human initiative. The systems will do it. Of course, there is no shortage of capital-letter MANAGERS who believe they can capital-letter MANAGE by staying in their offices and using their authority to dictate bottom-line performance by playing with numbers on financial statements and boxes on portfolio grids. But we should not forget that there does still exist another form of management, in which very human people work hard to understand their world and those who populate it, people who feel the need to be more rational than the rationality that surrounds them and so find the need to work in calculated chaos. Of course, the reason we sometimes forget this, as did those two production assistants, is that we are so inundated with the systems of MANAGEMENT.

Earlier, I mentioned that I had changed my views on the issue of superficiality in managerial work. In my own study, I found that the pressures of their job drove managers to be superficial; I concluded that the effective managers were the ones who had learned to be proficient at their superficiality. For example, they knew they had to make decisions with inadequate information, that deciding, even superficially, was prefer-able to not deciding at all because that at least enabled their organization to do *something*. Or else, lacking knowledge of the details of specific proposals, they could choose the sponsors of those proposals instead, allowing their intuition to function where they did have knowledge, namely about the character of their people.

Increasingly, however, I have begun to believe that superficiality *is* the problem. To continue with overstatement, but as always in the hope of conveying an important grain of truth, inherent in the job of being a manager is the need to make decisions on things one knows nothing about. Now, of course, the job of the manager is to know things, to get informed. And in small organizations, as well as in larger ones concentrated on a particular business, managers can do that, at least if they have some deep-rooted knowledge of the issues in question (which means that there had to have been life before management, in the factories and with the customers, which probably also means there was no MBA early in the career to project the inexperienced directly into the abstractions of administration). But I would maintain that to be so informed in other organizations has become enormously difficult due to distance and detachment. In other words, to manage at the senior levels of today's large, complex, and especially diversified organization is to have only the most superficial knowledge of the things that must be decided about.

The purpose of the management information system is, of course, to inform the manager. As noted earlier, the professional manager is supposed to sit back in his or her office and read MIS reports. Because there is too much to absorb, the data are aggregated, periodicized, and packaged neatly (thereby magically making the unknowable knowable). That is how professional managers in machine bureaucracies are supposed to "know."

But how much does anyone who reads words and numbers on pieces of paper really know? Not much, I suspect, because there is another kind of "knowing," one more relevant for the management of organizations. Borrowing a word from the anthropologist Clifford Geertz, I shall call it "thick knowing," resulting in "thick management."[10] "Thin management" remains distant from the subject of its efforts, acting as if it moved pieces on a chessboard (the "portfolio" of businesses is one popular conception), making little effort to influence what those pieces really do, even how they relate to each other in any but the most superficial ways. Faced with an organization's lack of innovation, thin management throws cash at a research and development facility; faced with declining profits in a division, thin management sells it or fires its manager; faced with the need to bring the wonders of electronics to its products, thin management acquires an electronics firm and slaps it together with its own activities; faced with public accusations of the organization's social irresponsibility, thin management appoints a vice president in charge of social responsibility to be responsible for everyone else.

A management informed by the MIS, a management whose knowledge consists of black symbols on white paper, is afraid to intervene in any but these most superficial of ways. Epitomizing the "thin" form of information—aggregated, analytical, detached—were the body counts of Vietnam. That is how Secretary of Defense McNamara "knew" what was going on in that unfortunate war. Robert McNamara was, of course, the archetypal professional manager, the hero of a generation of MBAs, just as the U.S. Army was the archetypal machine bureaucracy.

"Thick" information, in contrast, is information rich in detail and color, far beyond what can be quantified and aggregated. It must be dug out, on site, by people intimately involved with the phenomenon they wish to influence. In Vietnam, it was the look on a peasant's face; in business, the will of a customer, the mood of the factory, the intricacies of a technological change; in government, it is the service that actually gets delivered and the citizen's response to that service at the moment of delivery. This is the kind of information, it seems to me, that informs intuition and that allows for "thick management," a management that intervenes deeply to influence and to integrate activities. Those who practice this kind of management bypass the MIS to ensure that they get informed. They drop in on their facilities unexpectedly or, better, work in them periodically; they meet their customers or, better, *are* their customers, consuming their own products and services whenever they can.

Unfortunately, when organizations become large, complex, and diversified, managers can't do these things very easily; they are precluded from managing in thick ways. There is simply too much to do, too much to know. That is why our political leaders live on aggregated opinion polls instead of speaking with ordinary citizens (a recent Canadian news story accused the Conservative government of averaging four polls a *week* for its several years in office!), and why business leaders do the same with market research reports instead of meeting ordinary customers. What they get are abstractions often as deadly as those body counts. The statistic replaces the flesh-and-blood human being, and the managers think they are informed, while the citizens and the customers burn.

Of course, the machine bureaucracy, at least the one with diversified markets, has an answer for this problem too, one rooted in its belief in the division of labor. The managers at headquarters, who cannot be well informed about many diverse businesses, manage the strategic portfolio—they buy and sell businesses. It is the managers of the divisions who manage the individual businesses, where the necessary knowledge can be obtained. Unfortunately, it does not work out quite as planned. The division managers, who are supposed to be looking down to manage their own businesses, feel the gaze from above; they thus get distracted by having to glance up from time to time. There is just something about being controlled superficially, by having to satisfy someone who cannot see beyond that bottom line. To manage is to control, in one way or another. Too many levels of management has to mean too much control. Thus, the administrative arrangements promoted by Chandler and Williamson are not better at all, not after they have squeezed the human energy and involvement out of the people through their continual pressures and rationalizations, through their obsession with controlling performance directly.

This brings us back to the subject of strategy formation, setting the direction for an organization. Now strategy can be viewed as simply *position,* or else as more complex *perspective.* One focuses on the products and markets selected, the other on the business idea conceived, the organization's way of doing things. Portfolio management treats strategy as position, or at least a set of positions loosely coupled. That is compatible with thin management. But it is insufficient, because positions must have substance too; there must be some rich perspective behind each one. And such perspective cannot be developed without thick knowing, without deep-rooted involvement. Put another way, rich, creative strategy formation requires rich knowledge and mental synthesis. But synthesis, as noted, is quite different from rational analysis; it seems to be the province of the brain's mysterious right hemisphere and appears to be fed primarily by soft data. Thus, because our machine bureaucracies, whether or not diversified, are oriented to hard data and analytical thinking, they tend to treat strategy as no more than position. And so they tend to end up with thin strategies, bland and lifeless, at best imitations of the strategies already invented by other organizations—the "Whoppers" of this world in response to the "Big Macs."

For some time, in fact, machine bureaucracies have recognized the problem—that their managers are often incapable of generating rich new strategies. So they have relied on a system to do it for them instead, namely strategic planning. But as suggested earlier, that system has no real substance: It is just another set of black words on sheets of white paper. Each is placed in its appropriate box, labeled, for example, "assess your competitive advantage" or "generate strategies to match strengths with opportunities." But inside, the boxes are empty—no one ever explained how these things are to be done.

Behind the boxes are, of course, the planners. So it is really they who take charge of the process, using the cover of technique to promote their own influence. The "whiz kids"—the "best and the brightest," to use Halberstam's label for those responsible for the Vietnam debacle[11]—claim to do what thin management cannot do. They will pull the strategic rabbit out of an overgrown left hemisphere, so to speak. Of course, they never could. They could read all the documents, all the hard data; they could analyze furiously; they could write eloquently.

But it all lacked substance. Their strategies, like their knowledge, were thin; ultimately there was no wisdom.

Wisdom is a word that seems to have been lost in the English language. It suggests deep knowledge, based on substantial experience—intimate experience. The whiz kids lack wisdom, indeed, in their bias toward systematic analysis, they tend to denigrate it.

I collect definitions of the expert. Best known, perhaps, is: "An expert is a guy from out of town." The whiz kids tend to be from out of the industry. They are professionals; they don't let an ignorance of specifics interfere with their application of analysis. Another favorite definition is: "An expert is someone with no elementary knowledge." This captures the idea that the whiz kids have the facts and figures, all the sophistication that comes out of the computer, but they lack "street sense," wisdom. My own favorite definition is: "An expert is a person who avoids all the many pitfalls on his or her way to the grand fallacy." Pitfalls are sins to be avoided in order to serve the almighty, in this case rational analysis. But the pitfalls claimed by the experts in the "science" of management are superficial, only skin deep, and in any event are blamed on others, never on analysis. For example, planning fails because managers are not committed to it; analytical studies are ignored because organizations are too political. What trips up the whiz kids, however, are not these pitfalls at all (managers have given far more commitment to planning than it ever deserved; and analysis has done its share to politicize organizations), but some more fundamental fallacies, for example that discontinuities can be forecast in systematic ways, that hard data can substitute for soft, that decomposition and rationalization are what matter. The grand fallacy is that analysis magically provides synthesis.

In all these ways, the age of management has become the age of the "quick fix." Call in your technocrats, throw a lot of technique at a problem, drown it in hard data, the data you can get without ever having to leave your comfortable office, and all will be well. Resolve it quickly so that you can get on with the next problem. Better still, call in the consultants to resolve it; they know even less about your industry; you get a slick report from the experts; the board will be impressed (what do they know anyway?). If it's a strategy you need, they have a nice list of generic ones to choose from. If your culture is no longer any good, they have four easy steps to a new one. Quality, you say? Well, they can measure that.

Then, once you have the final answer, let others lower down in the hierarchy work it all out. It is called "implementation." Implementation means dropping a solution into the laps of people informed enough to know it won't work but restricted from telling anyone with power what can. So while administrators in the executive suites are smiling about how "Quality is Job 1" or whatever, the implementers are running around the factories trying to plug the holes. (I was on a panel recently with a top Ford executive who talked about their quality program; I mentioned a report I had seen just before about an awful work situation in a Ford assembly plant. The executive dismissed it as an isolated problem in one factory. After the session, two people came up to tell me of similar situations they had encountered in two other Ford plants. Sometimes I wonder how much such programs—whether or not conceived in good faith—amount to substance and how much to administrative wheel-spinning, and whether a distant management can even tell the difference.)

Occasionally someone does write about the reality of management, and the effect can be stunning. Let me recount two examples. Some years ago, the British Government hired the Boston Consulting Group (BCG) to help explain how it was that the Japanese firms, especially Honda, took over the U.K. firms' markets for motorcycles in the United States. (In 1959, they had a 49 percent market share; by 1966 Honda alone had 63%!) They issued their report in 1975 and it was vintage BCG, and classic rational MANAGEMENT (so much so that the report became the basis for well-known cases used at American business schools to teach the students exemplary strategic behavior). The report was all about experience curves and high market shares and carefully thought-out deliberate strategies and the like, especially how a firm dedicated to low cost, using the scale of its domestic production base, attacked the American market by forcing entry through a new segment—the sale of small motorcycles to middle-class consumers. Very clever, those Japanese. To quote from the BCG report:

> The Japanese motorcycle industry, and in particular Honda, the market leader, present a [consistent] picture. The basic philosophy of the Japanese manufacturers is that high volumes per model provide the potential for high productivity as a result of using capital intensive and highly automated techniques. Their marketing strategies are, therefore, directed towards developing these high model volumes, hence the careful attention that we have observed them giving to growth and market share.[12]

Wondering about all this, Richard Pascale, co-author of *The Art of*

Japanese Management, [13] flew to Japan and interviewed the Japanese managers who had done all this in America. They told a different story.

"In truth, we had *no* strategy other than the idea of seeing if we could sell *something* in the United States." Honda had to obtain a currency allocation from the Japanese Ministry of Finance, part of a government so famous for supporting the competitiveness of its industry abroad. "They were extraordinarily skeptical," said the managers, finally granting Honda the right to invest $250,000 in the U.S., but only $110,000 in cash!

"Mr. Honda was especially confident of the 250cc and 305cc machines," the managers continued about their leader. "The shape of the handlebars on these larger machines looked like the eyebrow of Buddha, which he felt was a strong selling point."

The managers rented a cheap apartment in Los Angeles; two of them slept on the floor. In their warehouse in a rundown section of town, they swept the floors themselves and stacked the motorcycles by hand, to save money. Their arrival in America coincided with the *closing* of the 1959 motorcycle season.

The next year, a few of the larger bikes began to sell. Then, as they put it, "disaster struck." Because motorcycles are driven longer and faster in the U.S., the Hondas begun to break down. "But in the meantime," to use their words, *"events had taken a surprising turn"*:

> Throughout our first eight months, following Mr. Honda's and our own instincts, we had not attempted to move the 50cc Supercubs. While they were a smash success in Japan (and manufacturing couldn't keep up with demand there), they seemed wholly unsuitable for the U.S. market where everything was bigger and more luxurious. As a clincher, we had our sights on the import market—and the Europeans, like the American manufacturers, emphasized the larger machines.
>
> We used the Honda 50cc ourselves to ride around Los Angeles on errands. They attracted a lot of attention. One day we had a call from a Sears buyer. While persisting in our refusal to sell through an intermediary, we took note of Sears' interest. But we still hesitated to push the 50cc bikes out of fear they might harm our image in a heavily macho market. But when the larger bikes started breaking, *we had no choice.* We let the 50cc bikes move. [14]

The rest is history. Sales rose dramatically. Middle-class Americans began to ride on Hondas, first the Supercubs, later the larger bikes. Even the famous ad campaign—"You meet the nicest people on a Honda"—was serendipitous: It was conceived by a UCLA undergraduate

for a class project. Shown the idea, the Honda managers—still tryin,
to straddle the market and not antagonize the black leather jacket types—
were split. Eventually the sales director talked his more senior colleague
into accepting it!

Well, then, what in the world makes the Japanese so smart? This i
a story of success, not failure, yet they seemed to do everything wrong
Indeed, the story violates everything we believe about effective manage
ment (and much that BCG imputed to those clever Japanese). Just conside
the passive tone of the Japanese managers' comments ("events took
surprising turn," "we had no choice," etc.) compared with the willfu
vocabulary of the BCG report.

If this story is any indication, then the Japanese advantage lies nc
in their cleverness at all, but in our own stupidity. While we run aroun
being "rational," they use their common sense. Their secret seems t
be as much in what they *avoid* as in what they *have*. Honda avoide
being too rational. Rather than believing they could work it all out i
Tokyo, they came to America prepared to *learn*. As Pascale put it
"success was achieved by senior managers humble enough not to tak
their initial strategic positions too seriously." We build organization
so they cannot learn. The formulators lack the information, the implemen
ters lack the power. The Honda managers let the market hit them ove
the head with its needs until they got the message.

And what the Japanese *have* is a different form of organization. Th
managers of the Honda story had commitment—they were in Americ
to work it out, without having to report to some silly controller in Toky
every week or two. (Jay Galbraith, a consultant and researcher in manage
ment, tells the story of the headquarters managers who pull up the youn
shoots that the divisions have planted to have a look with the commer
"no roots yet"!) And they had involvement, on site—they met the dealer
and customers, drove the motorcycles on the streets of America.

Now imagine two British motorcycle manufacturers wanting to ge
back into the American market. You give one the BCG report, th
other the Honda managers' account. What would each do? In the obviou
answers—one going back upstairs to do even more clever strategy analy
sis, the other buying a pair of jeans and moving to Driggs, Idaho, t
ride motorcycles—you get the perfect juxtaposition of thin and thic
management.

In fact, the most revealing aspect of this story for me came in a boo
I recently discovered called *Whatever Happened to the British Motorcyc
Industry?* Here, Bert Hopwood recalls as an executive of BSA, one o

the principal British motorcycle producers, that "not a soul on the Parent Board [meaning full-time senior executives] knew the first thing about single track vehicles." More significantly, "in the early 1960s," at precisely the moment when the Japanese managers were in America learning,

> . . . the Chief Executive of a world famous group of management consultants tried hard to convince me that it is ideal that top level management executives should have as little knowledge as possible relative to the product. This great man really believed that this qualification enabled them to deal efficiently with all business matters in a detached and uninhibited way.[15]

That is where we were not so many years ago!!

The second story reflects exactly the same philosophy, except that its consequences were far more serious than losing a market for motorcycles. This philosophy was implicated in the most devastating chapter in British military history, the World War I battle of Passchendaele. The chiefs had their plan at headquarters. It was a clever plan. Unfortunately it did not account for the possibility of rain while the battle was fought; 250,000 British troops fell as a result:

> The critics argued that the planning of Passchendaele was carried out in almost total ignorance of the conditions under which the battle had to be fought. No senior officer from the Operations Branch of the General Headquarters, it was claimed, ever set foot (or eyes) on the Passchendaele battlefield during the four months that battle was in progress. Daily reports on the condition of the battlefield were first ignored, then ordered discontinued. Only after that battle did the Army chief of staff learn that he had been directing men to advance through a sea of mud.[16]

To quote Stokesbury's account in his history of World War I, the "great plan" was implemented despite the effect the steady, drenching rain had on the battlefield—despite the fact that guns clogged, that soldiers carrying heavy ammunition slipped off their paths into muddy shell holes and drowned, that the guns could not be moved forward and the wounded could not be brought backward. "Still the attack went on; they slept between sheets at corps headquarters and lamented that the infantry did not show more offensive spirit."

> [A] staff officer . . . came up to see the battlefield after it was all quiet again. He gazed out over the sea of mud, then said half to himself, "My God, did we send men to advance in that?" after which he broke down weeping and his escort led him away. Staff officers . . . complained that infantrymen failed to salute them.[17]

The formulators finished formulating and then the implementers had to implement. One decided, the other saluted. Thus does the age of management become an age of superficiality; thus does efficiency produce ineffectiveness.

Perhaps these officers were well-intentioned, even if misguided. But professional management can sometimes produce not just superficial behavior but immoral behavior as well. The systems simply deflect good intentions, or else encourage bad ones. To quote Singer and Wooton with reference to Albert Speer's seemingly enlightened management of the Nazi wartime production machine, "It's not that managers are authoritarian themselves; rather . . . it may be that the process of management is authoritarian."[18]

The professional manager claims to be a "hired gun," so to speak, there with the technique to apply to any set of needs. "Tell us what you want," such managers claim, "and we can get you the most of it." Professional managers are ostensibly "amoral," their techniques supposedly neutral. But it doesn't always work out that way. The "hired gun" analogy holds up in more ways than one.

Technique is not amoral when its very nature drives organizations to a certain type of morality. Calculation is not neutral when some things are more easily calculated than others—costs more than benefits, tangible costs more than intangible costs, economic benefits more than social benefits. All of this can lead strictly professional managers into all kinds of questionable behaviors. Economizing cuts the needs of the workers and the customers alongside the costs of production (for example, by speeding up assembly lines beyond human capacity, or by eliminating experimentation on new products, which can also reduce the long-term economic viability of an organization by eliminating investments such as research treated as costs). "Rational" accounting slips social costs off the ledgers by treating them as "externalities," which means that society has to foot the organization's bills (for example, by calculating that unsafe gas tanks are cheaper than safe ones, or by letting the health care system pay for the mental breakdowns of the workers on those speeded-up assembly lines). Amorality thus becomes economic morality and when pushed to the limit becomes social immorality. We end up with a one-dimensional society in which innocent people get run over by professional managers racing down the fast track, trampling whoever gets in the way of serving that almighty bottom line.

In his study at the Harvard Business School, Robert Ackerman[19] noted that the control systems intrinsic to the very functioning of the diversified corporation—bottom-line systems based on quantifiable, specifically financial goals—discouraged consideration of the social goals simply because the latter could not easily be measured. He found this to be the case even when the chief executive sincerely believed in the social goals and wished to promote them. The very control system the leader had to use to run the organization precluded attention to those goals. ''Listen, boss, do you want me to treat people nice or meet the targets?''

My sixth point is that machine bureaucratic organizations run by professional management, by emphasizing calculation, drive out commitment, and so reduce human systems to impersonal shells. Earlier, in our discussion of Taylor's procedures, I mentioned the effect that rationalization has on motivation—how it discourages involvement and commitment. Here I wish to pursue at greater length what I believe may be the worst consequence of this syndrome of machine bureaucracy run by professional management: its stifling effect on commitment. James Worthy, once an executive at Sears, Roebuck, attributes this directly to the machine notion of the organization and its emphasis on planning for control:

> The obsession for control springs from the failure to recognize or appreciate the value of spontaneity, either in everyday work or in economic processes. Hence the need for planning. Hence the machine as the idea for human organization. For the machine has no will of its own. Its parts have no urge to independent action. Thinking, direction—even purpose—must be provided from outside or above.[20]

The problem of commitment can be partly attributed to professionalism in management too. A professional is someone who ''knows better,'' who takes care of your needs for you. When I am lying on an operating table with my appendix about to burst, I am hardly inclined to second-guess the surgeon. That person really does know better. But when I am sitting in a classroom or doing difficult work in an organization, having someone above who thinks he or she knows better only impedes my efforts, because I need a good deal of personal control over such work.

That is why I am opposed to the strict notion of professionalism in education. True, it may have helped reduce the influence of educational administrators, whose excessive controls have, in my opinion, had a devastating effect on the process. But professionalism fares no better if it is used to concentrate power over the learning process in the hands

of the teacher instead of the student. That is why children who go craz
being forced to learn a language in school turn around and pick it u
on the street with no effort at all. (If we could measure it, what woul
we find to be the efficiency of the average classroom, in terms of th
capacity of the students' potential used? Would it get as high as 1
percent? Why do we continue to tolerate this?) To draw on an old expres
sion, a teacher cannot teach children anything, only help them to fin
it within themselves. And the same holds true for the relationship betwee
managers and people doing difficult work. Managers who claim that a
professionals they must take control of that work through planning an
other technocratic procedures, like professional teachers who claim the
must control the learning process through detailed specification of th
curriculum, destroy the need for commitment and spontaneous learnin
in these activities.

Is that not what we have seen so much of in our organizations–
administrative systems that have squeezed the commitment out of thos
subjected to them? Formal structure, together with these systems, const
tutes the bones of an organization. Every system needs its skeleton
But an organization in which these dominate remains no more than a
empty shell. Only when it is infused with human spirit—with energy
ideology, culture, call it what you like—does the organization com
alive. And that energy cannot reside exclusively at the top of a forma
hierarchy, any more than our human energy can flow exclusively from
our brains.

Someone once claimed that to be objective is to treat people as object
"Nothing but the facts, ma'am," Sergeant Friday used to say on telev
sion. But that just doesn't work in management, because facts themselve
are infused with value, in their content and in their origin as well as i
their selection. In an important way, calculation and commitment ar
mutually exclusive. You can sit back and calculate or you can dive i
and commit. The Honda story contrasted these. In the early 1960
IBM committed to remaking its entire line of computers as an act c
faith. It decided to eliminate its traditional lines without being sure wha
the new ones would look like. "We'll work it out" was the attitude
(Imagine the looks on the faces of MBA students specializing in financ
when asked what bottom-line calculations could have informed that dec
sion.) In contrast, an airline we studied introduced a shuttle servic
without reserved seating. When passengers kept trying to book seat
the airline scuttled the shuttle a few days later. Far from working
out, their attitude was, "We tried, didn't we?"

It is amazing how such attitudes get communicated throughout an organization, how what is inside the heads—really the hearts—of the senior management, the intentions that really drive them, somehow gets conveyed to everyone else. It's almost psychic. Maybe that is why the managers of one organization, who get personally involved, can so fire everyone up, while those of another, sitting back and pontificating through systems, can have such a deadening effect. Consider the toll that has been exacted from so many people in organizations by the obsession with the bottom line. How in the world did the idea spread in management that you make money by managing money, instead of dealing with people and products? It is as if everybody pretends to be managing a bank (although it probably doesn't work even there!). With these kinds of ideas so current in the executive suites—now it is the absurd notion of managing "shareholder value," the assumption of direct links between all the fuzzy decision-making that goes on and the price of the stock in some distant capital market—is it any wonder that so few workers care what is being produced, let alone how or for whose benefit?

Thus, with understanding, intuition, belief, and commitment driven out, along with social concerns, it should come as no surprise that the population at large has become so alienated from its large organizations, private as well as public. As workers, customers, citizens, often even as managers themselves, people have come increasingly to question whether organizations are there to serve them or to enslave them. And that is a formula for failure, economic no less than social.

My seventh point is that every form of organization sows the seeds of its own destruction; in machine bureaucracy devoid of human commitment, that manifests itself as enveloping politicization. Success breeds failure; in strength lie the roots of weakness. Organizations succeed by balancing the competing forces of conflict with the committing forces of ideology. But when the latter get squeezed out, the former take over.

The strength of machine bureaucracy lies in its ability to "buffer" itself from environmental forces, to seal itself off from external perturbations in order to rationalize its operations and so attain a high level of efficiency. But no one need be reminded that "power tends to corrupt, and absolute power corrupts absolutely." In sealing itself off, the machine bureaucracy concentrates its power in its administrators, those people who run its systems of authority and control. Commitment, in the form of culture or ideology, can temper that power. Everyone works for the common good. But when that force is removed, power becomes corrupting. The large bureaucratic organization becomes a closed system in the service of its administrators (despite their self-serving claims of "social responsibility").

When this happens, the whole system begins to deteriorate. Administrators become increasingly greedy, seeking satisfaction through the building of larger personal empires rather than the serving of customers or even owners. That puts pressure on the organization to grow, no matter what the consequences, so that all the demands can be met without excessive conflict. Other insiders get the message too, for example the workers who insist on their share of the spoils. And since the one thing a closed system management cannot tolerate is public challenge, which might expose the fundamental illegitimacy of its power base, it is inclined to give in. More growth can always pay for the excessive wage settlements, or, failing that, greater exploitation of the organization's market power.

But as excess piles upon excess—stories of executive jets and golden parachutes and bonuses growing faster than performance (consider the rise in Fortune 500 executive salaries over the last decade or so compared with industrial profits or workers' salaries)—outsiders take notice too. Some may try to get a piece of the action, while others, further removed, may instead challenge the legitimacy of the whole system of power. "Why is what's good for General Motors good for the country?" they ask, especially when they see the management, not the board, controlling the corporation. And so pressure campaigns arise, and government intervention follows.

All of this ends up, however, less correcting the excesses than further politicizing the organization. Whereas before the large corporation may have looked like an economic entity with political power, now it appears to be a political entity that happens to operate in the economic sphere. It takes on the form of a political arena for some, who use it to fight out their ideological battles, and a fountain of benefits for others, who compete with each other for personal gain. And once the large organization has been so captured by conflict, it is unlikely ever to free itself of it. Which of our giant, highly politicized organizations—in business, government, or any other sphere—is ever likely to be left alone by any of the demanding influencers who surround it?

All this would be fine if politicization served the role that equivalent processes serve in nature. When an animal can no longer function effectively, it becomes prey to attackers and is eventually cut down. The system is brutal but functional—resources get redistributed, and nature wins. Were the dysfunctional animals to survive, then nature would lose, because its resources would be misallocated. That, I maintain, is exactly what is happening in our society of organizations.

My eighth and final point is that large politicized organizations are increasingly allowed to sustain themselves by political means, threatening the destruction, not of the single spent organization, but of the whole society of organizations instead. How can an organization that has lost sight of its central mission possibly survive? The answer is suggested in its own politicization. It acts as a political entity, seeking to sustain itself through the sheer exploitation of its political power.

In a world of large organizations, the competition of Adam Smith's brewer, baker, and butcher becomes the oligarchy of giant corporations, massive governments, and huge trade unions making deals with one another for their mutual convenience. Organizations, especially business organizations, may have grown large because they were sharper, smarter, more competitive—that was "getting there." It was essentially economic. But "staying there" is another matter. Large organizations are often able to sustain themselves in other ways. One is through past successes— not what they do now so much as today's consequences of what they did earlier. For example, a corporation may have locked up the best retailing sites or the cheapest sources of supply, or established the reputation to which purchasing agents must defer. Another way is through sheer exploitation of the power they have, in ways more political than economic. Large organizations can, for example, make reciprocal trading arrangements with each other to preempt competitive markets; they can mount huge advertising campaigns of image to manipulate public opinion; in the airline business, they can use a modern form of "payola" that offers points to private individuals whose companies paid for their tickets, thereby discouraging travel on the smaller carriers with less extensive networks; they can bring the influences of the many people and organizations that depend on them to lobby for favorable government legislation. Even government regulation can be favorable to the large organization, by keeping out smaller would-be competitors discouraged by the paperwork alone.

In Canada, large corporations secure government grants by threatening to close down existing plants. Like their response to the occasional dramatic plane crash as compared with the steady stream of carnage on the highways, governments have become obsessed with job losses and gains large enough to be reported by the press. In America, essentially bankrupt corporations lobby for trade barriers or government loan guarantees, pointing to the consequence on the economy if they fail (short-term, anyway). Lee Iacocca may have turned Chrysler around, but the hidden cost of that may prove to be enormous. That is because every argument that Iacocca used, and every political stop he pulled out—drawing on Chrysler's suppliers and workers to pressure their politicians about the consequences of the jobs and business that would be lost—can be used by any failing large corporation. If it becomes considered proper to have saved Chrysler—and its very survival seems to make that case—then never again can the American government let any large corporation go bankrupt.

The Chrysler episode signifies the growing trend toward mutual relationships among large organizations, public and private, outside the forces of open competition. It is not new, however; President Eisenhower warned when he left office in 1959 of the dangers of the "military–industrial complex." But today such arrangements cut increasingly across, not just large corporations, not just those corporations and their governments, but private and public organizations of all kinds around the world. Many people applaud the cooperation of the huge consortiums of businesses and governments—joint ventures of all kinds—without stopping to think what effect these can have on bureaucratization, on politicization, and on competition. (Consider all the vigorous young organizations that are simply too small to join.)

Of course, all these problems are not those of business alone. They can be found in large organizations in every sector of human activity. The politicization of government departments is widely acknowledged; and here there is often not even a semblance of competition to provide some countervailing force. And so we get festering public bureaucracies that continue to squander public resources. Likewise in other sectors: Powerful unions entrench themselves in political ways, sometime even through the use of physical violence, and large politicized welfare agencies and universities work themselves into positions of invulnerability and then sit back and waste society's resources.

Thus we end up with a vicious circle in our society. An irrational obsession with "rationality" produces a society of large, bureaucratic organizations run by a "professional" management that proves thin, superficial, and sometimes immoral. That drives out human commitment, which in turn leads to the politicization of organizations. This should destroy them, but it does not, for they turn around and use their political power to sustain themselves artificially. Organizations thereby get larger, more bureaucratic, and more politicized, and their managements as a consequence get thinner, more superficial, and less moral. It is an irony of contemporary society that the large organizations designed to serve themselves as closed systems are so stable and those dominated by politics so protected, while younger organizations that respond to creative leadership or that exhibit a strong sense of mission are inherently so vulnerable. Today it almost seems wrong to believe in what is produced, as opposed to how, or, more to the point, for whose personal benefit. Should we not be encouraging the demise of our large, spent organizations, so that they can be replaced in a natural cycle of renewal by younger, smaller, less constrained and more vigorous ones? Does the society that discourages the demise of its spent organizations not risk its own demise instead?

To conclude, we are a world of large organizations in an age of capital-letter MANAGEMENT, and as a result society has become unmanageable. Like those Inuit boys, our machinery has broken down and we cannot find our way home.

Well, this is an awfully bleak picture. We might be consoled by the fact that I have overstated my points. But not for long, I fear. The situation today may not be as bad as I have described, but I believe the trends are evident. Overall, the prognosis is not encouraging.

We do need machine bureaucracies to bring us mass-produced goods and services efficiently. But we do not need them to dehumanize us and to dominate our lives, public and private. Likewise we do need analysis and we do need planning. I am not arguing for a return to the cults of personality of times gone by. Unchecked intuition is as dangerous as unchecked analysis. It is just that I see the latter as the problem today. I am arguing for a return to balance, to allow intuition to function alongside analysis, recognized as a valid and necessary process in organizations. Shapero puts it perfectly in his article cited earlier: "We need to return to a rationality tuned to the natural messiness of life, and not one dedicated to abstractions."[21]

Of course, there are great organizations out there, even great large ones. Rich culture and dedicated management hold many a large organization together and render it effective and humane. But this is accomplished against the natural pressures created by bigness and rationalization. In my opinion, Peters and Waterman's book *In Search of Excellence* attained its enormous success precisely because it was about the exceptions, about organizations that didn't give in to those pressures. It was exciting to read of organizations that managed to maintain their vigor and effectiveness, their very human qualities, despite their growth to large size—typically, it appeared, because of the strong ideologies infused in them by founding leaders still present or recently departed. These organizations seemed so different from the ones we all knew. But that vigor and that humanness are not easy to maintain, not even in the Peters and Waterman organizations, as the subsequent *Business Week* story on the faltering "excellent" companies, with a cover labeled "Oops," pointed out.[22] I see pockets of excellence out there too, but bobbing up and down in a stormy sea of increasing bureaucratization, increasing politicization, increasing alienation. Unless we break that vicious circle, I am not terribly optimistic about our future.

Where to intervene, how to break the vicious circle? Ideally, of course, it would break itself. Small organizations would nip at the heels of the ineffective large ones until the latter collapsed. While we can, of course, see this on many fronts, we also see too much of the opposite—of governments and other organizations coming to the rescue of spent big ones by kicking away the small ones or by building protective shelters around the big ones. Thus, I believe there will have to be concerted intervention, based on a change of attitude. And sooner rather than later. The longer this goes on, the more established our politicized organizations become, and the more we adapt ourselves to them (the final stage of slavery being when you no longer realize that you are a slave).

Milton Friedman's solution, to wind down the role of government and, in his words, allow "free" enterprise to displace "subversive" socialism, is no solution at all, but simply a formula for a particular kind of oligarchy. Today the problem is not private versus public but bureaucracy in all its forms. Who cares if the system that regulates us is owned by thousands of shareholders as opposed to millions of citizens, since neither exercises control over the management. At the limit, the difference between America and the Soviet Union from an organization theory perspective is that one is controlled by a single giant closed system machine bureaucracy while the other is dominated by several hundred. "A plague on both your houses" is my answer to Friedman. Don't compound the problem by compounding the bureaucracies. Give me a system in which all organizations have to be responsive to me, as a worker, a client, a citizen, an owner.

Thus, neither nationalization nor privatization is a fundamental solution, nor is regulation or deregulation, for that matter. We can keep bouncing back and forth between these, perhaps correcting some deficiencies at the margin, but never solving any fundamental problem. Nor is the "democratization" of our large organizations a basic solution, because that won't make them much more responsive, not even the proposals for "self-management," a wonderful idea as soon as someone figures out what it means in places that need a great deal of systematic coordination. (There are not many ways to bolt a bumper onto a Volvo.) Certainly we must work to democratize our large organizations, to open them up to broader forms of social control. That will temper their power and provide them with a certain legitimacy. But let's not pretend that will resolve any basic issue.

As for social responsibility, that is a fine and noble concept. We critically need responsible people in important places. But how can even decent, well-meaning people be responsible in places that are impersonal and that breed alienation by their very nature? If power really does corrupt, then we will have to make some fundamental changes in the nature of our organizations before we can expect them to exhibit greater social responsibility.

Our best hope may lie in subtle and clever interventions where things can be changed in basic ways. We can certainly afford to promote small organizations, ones of a human scale, wherever feasible. We may not be able to afford small petrochemical refineries or small automobile firms, but we can certainly afford human-sized businesses in many other spheres, manufacturing and especially service. And it is not at all clear why we need all those huge hospitals, schools, libraries, social services, and so on. The tradeoff between the commitment and personalized services offered by "human scale" and the cost savings offered by "economies of scale" has never been firmly established. Yet how often do we opt for the latter, in response to the hard data accumulated by the large organization, or else simply as a result of the power game played by its administrators? Who, after all, is in the best position to "prove it"?

To illustrate with an exception, some years ago, a vice principal at McGill University proposed to close our small management library and incorporate its collection into the large general library. Concerned by the thought of having to deal with that big impersonal system, we marshaled our resources to study the issue. On every quantifiable criterion, our little library was two to three times more efficient than the big one. (And imagine what might have been suggested by the nonquantifiable ones!) And why not? It did naturally all those things that big organizations tie themselves in knots trying to accomplish through formal programs: "job enrichment" (everyone naturally pitched in to help do everything), "managerial involvement" (if someone had to step out, the boss became a worker), "motivation" (the librarians knew the people they were serving), and so on. We saved our library and learned a lesson in the bargain (and, incidentally, found that we had been "had" by a clever administrator—all he wanted was a free study of library efficiency, and so he got a group of worried academics to "prove it"!)

If we are to promote small organizations, then we shall have to demote many large ones. We must not attack them arbitrarily, but we should challenge their effectiveness. Put the onus on them: "Give us good reasons why you should be sustained." And when those reasons are lacking—when they cannot "prove it" beyond questionable numbers in slick reports, cannot show significant benefits in operating efficiency and strategic responsiveness to the people they were designed to serve—then we should pull out every plug that favors them. Especially when they show signs of pervasive politicization—a form of rot no less evident than the black spots that appear on a piece of fruit. Size alone gives large organizations a huge advantage; offering them other advantages, or even allowing more subtle intrinsic advantages to dominate, simply throws the whole society of organizations out of balance.

Likewise we should question conglomeration wherever it appears. The popular arguments about the benefits of hierarchies over markets notwithstanding, there is no evidence that anyone knows how to manage effectively a diversity of businesses under one corporate umbrella, except by the sheer power of personality. (But think how much more productive such personality could be if dedicated to the development of new focused businesses. Indeed, think of the consequences of marshaling all that creative energy now devoted to restructuring and other financial games toward the production of better products and services!) A great deal of diversification and conglomeration has been nothing more than a giant power game played for the benefit of administrators and financial types who keep score by the number of digits on the bottom line. ("Diversific-tion," the [Freudian?] slip of a former secretary of mine, better describes this phenomenon.) Above all, let us get rid of the multiple layers of management—authority piled upon authority, increasingly detached and superficial—that serves only to sap the energy of involved, committed people.

Likewise, let us question vertical integration where a network of trading relationships involving negotiations among smaller, autonomous units is superior to a monolithic hierarchy of captive divisions. By the same token, let us question the trend toward the contractual associations of organizations, public and private, on an international basis. Some of this will no doubt serve us well, but much will not: We must scrutinize these relationships carefully. And let us question agglomeration in other sectors too, of "multiversities," huge school systems, large chains of newspapers, huge unions, and on and on. Many of these giant organizations have exacted a cost in human commitment and economic effectiveness far in excess of the benefits to any but the few who rule them.

We should be encouraging young organizations to establish themselves and attain adulthood; we should be encouraging small organizations that involve their people and provide eclecticism in the marketplace; we should be encouraging autonomous, focused organizations that understand their missions, "know" the people they serve, and excite the ones they employ; we should be encouraging "thick" management, deep knowledge, healthy competition, and authentic social responsibility. We need to get back to our basic senses, to feel genuine commitment, to use informal intuition, by promoting forms of organization that encourage these things. Only in these ways, it seems to me, shall we find our way back from the frozen wastes of our strange world of organizations.

Notes

Part I Introduction

1. J.-J. Servan-Schreiber, *The American Challenge* (New York: Atheneum, 1968).

Chapter 1 The Manager's Job

1. F. Andrews, "Management: How a Boss Works in Calculated Chaos," *New York Times,* October 29, 1976.

2. The data from my study can be found in Henry Mintzberg, *The Nature of Managerial Work* (New York: Harper & Row, 1973).

3. Robert H. Guest, "Of Time and the Foreman," *Personnel,* May 1956, p. 478.

4. Rosemary Stewart, *Managers and Their Jobs* (New York: Macmillan, 1967); see also Sune Carlson, *Executive Behaviour* (Stockholm: Strömbergs, 1951), the first of the diary studies.

5. Irving Choran, unpublished McGill MBA thesis, reported in Mintzberg, *Nature of Managerial Work.*

6. Robert T. Davis, *Performance and Development of Field Sales Managers* (Cambridge: Division of Research, Harvard Business School, 1957), and George H. Copeman, *The Role of the Managing Director* (London: Business Publications, 1963).

7. Stewart, *Managers and Their Jobs,* and Tom Burns, "The Directions of Activity and Communication in a Departmental Executive Group," *Human Relations,* February, 1954, p. 73.

8. Richard E. Neustadt, *Presidential Power* (New York: Wiley, 1960), pp. 153–54; italics added.

9. George C. Homans, *The Human Group* (New York: Harcourt Brace & World, 1950), based on the study by W. F. Whyte, *Street Corner Society,* revised edition (Chicago: University of Chicago Press, 1955).

10. Neustadt, *Presidential Power,* p. 157.

11. Peter F. Drucker, *The Practice of Management* (New York: Harper & Row, 1954), pp. 341–42.

12. Leonard R. Sayles, *Managerial Behavior* (New York: McGraw-Hill, 1964), p. 162.

13. James S. Hekimian and Henry Mintzberg, "The Planning Dilemma," *Management Review,* May 1968, p. 4.

Chapter 2 Crafting Strategy

1. Richard T. Pascale, "Perspective on Strategy: The Real Story Behind Honda's Success" *California Management Review,* Spring 1984, pp. 47–72.

2. James B. Quinn, "IBM(A): The System/360 Decision," in J. B. Quinn, H. Mintzberg, and R. M. James, *The Strategy Process: Concepts, Context, and Cases* (Englewood Cliffs, N.J.: Prentice-Hall, 1988), pp. 189–203.

3. See Danny Miller and Peter H. Friesen, *Organizations: A Quantum View* (Englewood Cliffs, N.J.: Prentice-Hall, 1984).

4. See Chapter 11. The term *adhocracy* was coined by Warren G. Bennis and Philip L. Slater in *The Temporary Society* (New York: Harper & Row, 1964).

5. See Danny Miller and Peter H. Friesen, "Archetypes of Strategy Formulation," *Management Science,* May 1978, pp. 921–23.

Chapter 3 Planning on the Left Side, Managing on the Right

1. Richard Restak, "The Hemispheres of the Brain Have Minds of Their Own," *New York Times,* January 25, 1976.

2. Robert Ornstein, *The Psychology of Consciousness* (San Francisco: Freeman, 1975), p. 60.

3. Henry Mintzberg, Duru Raisinghani, and André Théorêt, "The Structure of 'Unstructured' Decision Processes," *Administrative Science Quarterly,* 1976, pp. 246–75.

4. Clyde T. Hardwick and Bernard F. Landuyt, *Administrative Strategy and Decision Making,* 2d edition (Cincinnati: South Western, 1966).

5. This point is elaborated upon in Henry Mintzberg, a forthcoming book on *Strategic Planning.*

6. Ornstein, *Psychology of Consciousness,* p. 10.

Chapter 4 Coupling Analysis and Intuition in Management

1. P. M. S. Blackett, *Studies of War: Nuclear and Conventional* (Edinburgh: Olivier and Boyd, 1962), p. 199.

2. David B. Hertz, "Has Management Science Reached a Dead End?," *McKinsey Quarterly,* Winter 1972, p. 44.

3. Herbert A. Simon, *Administrative Behavior* (New York: Macmillan, first published in 1947); *Organizations* (with James G. March) (New York: Wiley, 1957); *The Sciences of the Artificial* (Cambridge: MIT Press, 1964);

and *The New Science of Management Decision* (New York: Harper & Row, first published in 1960); among others.

4. Herbert A. Simon, *The New Science of Management Decision,* revised edition (Englewood Cliffs, N.J.: Prentice-Hall, 1977), p. 69.

5. Henry Mintzberg, *The Nature of Managerial Work* (New York: Harper & Row, 1973), pp. 132–33.

6. Simon, *New Science,* p. 69.

7. David Halberstam, *The Best and the Brightest* (New York: Random House, 1972).

8. Charles J. Hitch and Roland N. McKean, *The Economics of Defense in the Nuclear Age* (Cambridge: Harvard University Press, 1960).

9. Halberstam, *Best and Brightest,* p. 256.

10. See Robert W. Ackerman, *The Social Challenge to Business* (Cambridge: Harvard University Press, 1975).

11. In Halberstam, *Best and Brightest,* p. 81.

12. Simon, *New Science,* p. 68; italics added.

13. Simon, *New Science,* p. 81; and Roger Sperry, "Messages from the Laboratory," *Engineering and Science,* January 1974, p. 30; italics added.

14. Simon, *New Science,* p. 71; italics added.

15. Herbert A. Simon, "Making Management Decisions: The Role of Intuition and Emotion," *Academy of Management Executive,* February 1987, pp. 58–59, citing with regard to the evidence of the last paragraph, R. H. Doktor, "Problem Solving Styles of Executives and Management Scientists," in A. Charnes, W. W. Cooper, and R. J. Niehaus, eds., *Management Science Approaches to Manpower Planning and Organization Design* (New York: Elsevier North-Holland, 1978), and R. H. Docktor and W. F. Hamilton, "Cognitive Styles and the Acceptance of Management Science Recommendations," *Management Science,* 1973, pp. 884–94.

16. Simon, "Making Management Decisions," pp. 60, 61.

17. *Ibid.,* pp. 61, 63.

18. George A. Miller, "The Magic Number Seven, Plus or Minus Two: Some Limits on Our Capacity for Processing Information," *Psychology Review,* March 1956, pp. 81–97.

19. F. Bello, "The Magic That Made Polaroid," *Fortune,* April 1959, p. 158; italics added.

20. J. T. Peters, K. R. Hammond, and D. A. Summers, "A Note on Intuitive vs. Analytical Thinking," *Organizational Behavior and Human Performance,* August 1974, p. 126, quoting Brunswik.

21. *Ibid.,* p. 129; see also K. R. Hammond, R. M. Hamm, J. Arassca, and

T. Pearson, "Direct Comparison of Efficiency of Intuitive and Analytical Cognition in Expert Judgement," in *IEEE Transactions on Systems, Man, and Cybernetics,* September–October, 1987, pp. 753–768.

22. Polanyi, paraphrased in D. Braybrooke and C. E. Lindblom, *A Strategy of Decision* (New York: Free Press, 1963), pp. 44–45.

23. C. P. Curtis and F. Greenslet, *The Practical Cogitator* (Boston: Houghton Mifflin, 1945), p. 18.

24. F. E. Kast and J. E. Rosenzweig, *Organization and Management: A Systems Approach* (New York: McGraw-Hill, 1970).

25. Jay W. Forrester, "The Counter-Intuitive Behavior of Social Systems," in *Collected Papers of J. W. Forrester* (Cambridge: Wright-Allen Press, 1975).

26. J. McKenney and P. G. W. Keen, "How Managers' Minds Work," *Harvard Business Review,* May–June 1974, p. 84.

27. P. M. Morse, "The History of the Development of Operations Research," in G. J. Kelleher, ed. *The Challenge to Systems Analysis: Public Policy and Social Change* (New York: Wiley, 1970), p. 28.

28. In J. de Montigny, review of speech by Harold Lardner, *Bulletin of the Canadian Operational Research Society,* 1972, p. 5.

29. Aaron Wildavsky, "The Political Essay of Efficiency: Cost-Benefit Analysis, Systems Analysis, and Program Budgeting," *Public Administration Review,* 1968, p. 298.

30. Halberstam, *Best and Brightest,* p. 610.

31. Herbert A. Simon, "The Future of Information Processing Technology," *Management Science,* 1968, p. 622.

32. Aaron Wildavsky, "If Planning Is Everything, Maybe It's Nothing," *Policy Sciences,* June 1973, pp. 127–53.

Chapter 5 Training Managers, Not MBAs

1. R. H. Hayes and W. J. Abernathy, "Managing Our Way to Economic Decline," *Harvard Business Review,* July–August 1980, pp. 67–77.

2. Herbert A. Simon, *The Sciences of the Artificial* (Cambridge: MIT Press, 1969).

3. S. Zalaznick, "The MBA—the Man, the Myth, and the Method," *Fortune,* May 1, 1969, p. 168 ff.

4. J. A. Barks, "Here They Come: Master's Admissions at Sloan," *Sloan Magazine,* Winter 1987.

5. J. Stirling Livingston, "The Myth of the Well-Educated Manager," *Harvard Business Review,* January–February 1971, pp. 79–89.

6. Herbert A. Simon, *The New Science of Management Decision,* revised edition (Englewood Cliffs, N.J.: Prentice-Hall, 1977), p. 44.

7. Abraham Kaplan, *The Conduct of Inquiry: Methodology for Behavioral Science* (San Francisco: Chandler, 1964).

8. C. R. Christensen, K. R. Andrews, J. L. Bower, R. G. Hammermesh, and M. E. Porter, *Business Policy: Text and Cases*, 5th edition (Homewood, Ill.: Irwin, 1982).

Part II Introduction

1. George A. Miller, "The Magic Number Seven, Plus or Minus Two: Some Limits on Our Capacity for Processing Information," *Psychological Review*, March 1956, pp. 81–97.

Chapter 6 Deriving Configurations

1. Pradip Khandwalla, *The Effects of Environment on the Organizational Structure of Firms*, doctoral dissertation, Graduate School of Industrial Administration, Carnegie–Mellon University, 1970.

Chapter 7 The Entrepreneurial Organization

1. Peter Brook, *The Empty Space* (Harmondsworth, Middlesex: Penguin Books, 1968).

2. *Ibid.*, p. 154.

3. Lee Iacocca with William Novak, *Iacocca: An Autobiography* (New York: Bantam Books, 1984), p. 141.

4. Edwin Land, "People Should Want More From Life . . . ," *Forbes*, June 1, 1975, p. 50.

5. "The Most Basic Form of Creativity," *Time*, June 26, 1972, p. 84.

6. D. Wise, "Apple's New Crusade," *Business Week*, November 26, 1984, p. 146.

7. Albert Speer, *Inside the Third Reich* (New York: Macmillan, 1970), p. 16.

8. Brook, *Empty Space*, p. 157.

9. A. H. Cole, *Business Enterprise in Its Social Setting* (Cambridge: Harvard University Press, 1959).

10. Kurt Lewin, *Field Theory in Social Science* (New York: Harper & Row, 1951).

11. Thomas J. Peters, "A Style for All Seasons," *Executive*, Summer 1980, Graduate School of Business and Public Administration, Cornell University, pp. 12–16.

Chapter 8 The Machine Organization

1. Thomas A. Murphy, interviewed in *Executive* magazine, Summer 1980, Graduate School of Business and Public Administration, Cornell University, p. 4.

1a. A. L. Stinchcombe, "Social Structure and Organizations," in J. G. March, ed., *Handbook of Organizations* (Chicago: Rand McNally, 1965), Ch. 4.

2. Studs Terkel, *Working* (New York: Pantheon Books, 1972), pp. 186, 406.

3. Charles Perrow, *Complex Organizations: A Critical Essay* (New York: Scott, Foresman, 1972), p. 199.

4. John Kenneth Galbraith, *The New Industrial State* (Boston: Houghton Mifflin, 1967).

5. James C. Worthy, *Big Business and Free Men* (New York: Harper & Row, 1959), p. 77.

6. H. Constas, "The USSR—From Charismatic Sect to Bureaucratic Society," *Administrative Science Quarterly,* 1961–62, p. 294.

7. Michel Crozier, *The Bureaucratic Phenomenon* (Chicago: University of Chicago Press, 1964), p. 176.

8. H. H. Gerth and C. Wright Mills, eds., *From Max Weber: Essays in Sociology* (New York: Oxford University Press, 1958).

9. Worthy, *Big Business and Free Men,* pp. 67, 79, 70.

10. Quoted in *ibid.,* p. 73.

11. Victor A. Thompson, *Modern Organizations* (New York: Knopf, 1961).

12. James C. Worthy, "Organizational Structure and Employee Morale," *American Sociological Review,* April 1950, p. 176.

13. R. G. Hunt, "Technology and Organization," *Academy of Management Journal,* 1970, pp. 235–52.

14. Danny Miller and Peter H. Friesen, *Organizations: A Quantum View* (Englewood Cliffs, N.J.: Prentice-Hall, 1984).

15. Mihaela Firsirotu, "Strategic Turnaround as Cultural Revolution: The Case of Canadian National Express," doctoral dissertation, Faculty of Management, McGill University, 1985.

Chapter 9 The Diversified Organization

1. D. F. Channon, "The Strategy, Structure and Financial Performance of the Services Industries," working paper, Manchester Business School, 1975.

2. From Richard P. Rumelt, *Strategy, Structure, and Economic Performance.* Boston: Division of Research, Harvard Business School, 1974. Republished as a Harvard Business School Classic (Boston: Harvard Business School Press, 1986). Copyright © 1974, 1986 by the President and Fellows of Harvard College. Used with permission of the publisher and author. (Figure 1.4, p. 21, in source.)

3. L. C. Martin, "How Beatrice Foods Sneaked Up on $5 Billion," *Fortune,* April 1976.

4. Oliver E. Williamson, *Markets and Hierarchies* (New York: Free Press, 1975), and *The Economic Institutions of Captitalism* (New York: Free Press, 1985).

5. R. C. Moyer, "Berle and Means Revisted: The Conglomerate Merger," *Business and Society,* Spring 1970, pp. 20–29.

6. J. L. Bower, "Planning Within the Firm," *The American Economic Review: Papers and Proceedings of the 82nd Annual Meeting,* May 1970, p. 194.

7. L. Smith, "The Boardroom's Becoming a Different Scene," *Fortune,* May 8, 1978.

8. J. Bacon, *Corporate Dictatorship Practices: Memberships and Committees of the Board* (Conference Board and American Society of Corporate Secretaries, Inc., 1973), p. 40.

9. L. Wrigley, "Diversification and Divisional Autonomy," DBA dissertation, Graduate School of Business Administration, Harvard University, 1970, p. V78.

10. Rumelt, *Strategy, Structure, and Economic Performance.*

11. Wrigley, "Diversification and Divisional Autonomy," p. V86.

12. Bower, "Planning Within Firm," p. 193.

13. Robert W. Ackerman, *The Social Challenge to Business* (Cambridge: Harvard University Press, 1975), pp. 55, 56.

14. Bower, "Planning Within Firm," p. 193.

15. John Kenneth Galbraith, *American Capitalism: The Concept of Countervailing Power* (Boston: Houghton Mifflin, 1952).

Chapter 10 The Professional Organization

1. R. Gosselin, "A Study of the Interdependence of Medical Specialists in Quebec Teaching Hospitals," doctoral dissertation, Faculty of Management, McGill University, 1978.

2. F. C. Spencer, "Deductive Reasoning in the Lifelong Continuing Education of a Cardiovascular Surgeon," *Archives of Surgery,* 1976, pp. 1179, 1182.

3. K. E. Weick, "Educational Organizations as Loosely Coupled Systems," *Administrative Science Quarterly,* 1976, p. 8.

4. J. G. March and J. P. Olsen, *Ambiguity and Choice in Organizations* (Bergen, Norway: Universitetforlaget, 1976).

5. W. H. Taylor, "The Nature of Policy Making in Universities," *The Canadian Journal of Higher Education,* 1, 1983, p. 18.

6. M. D. Cohen, J. G. March, and J. P. Olsen, "A Garbage Can Model of Organizational Choice," *Administrative Science Quarterly,* 1972, p. 1; also March and Olsen, *Ambiguity and Choice.*

7. Spencer, "Deductive Reasoning," p. 1181.

8. J. W. Garbarino, "Faculty Unionization: The Pre-Yeshiva Years, 1966–1979," *Industrial Relations,* 1980, p. 229.

9. *Ibid.,* p. 228.

Chapter 11 The Innovative Organization

1. Warren G. Bennis and Philip L. Slater, *The Temporary Society* (New York: Harper & Row, 1964), and Alvin Toffler, *Future Shock* (New York: Bantam Books, 1970).

2. C. Reeser, "Some Potential Human Problems of the Project Form of Organization," *Academy of Management Journal,* 1969, p. 463.

3. Alvin Toffler, *Future Shock,* p. 133.

4. Charles E. Lindblom, *The Policy-Making Process* (Englewood Cliffs, N.J.: Prentice-Hall, 1968), p. 25.

5. Tom Burns and G. M. Stalker, *The Management of Innovation,* 2d edition, (London: Tavistock, 1966), pp. 122–23.

6. C. Reeser, "Some Potential Human Problems," pp. 459–67.

Chapter 12 Ideology and the Missionary Organization

1. Max Weber, "The Three Types of Legitimate Rule," trans. by H. Gerth, in Amitai Etzioni, ed., *A Sociological Reader on Complex Organizations,* 2d edition (New York: Holt, Rinehart and Winston, 1969), p. 12.

2. Philip Selznick, *Leadership in Administration: A Sociological Interpretation* (New York: Harper & Row, 1957).

3. B. R. Clark, "The Organizational Saga in Higher Education," *Administrative Science Quarterly,* 1972, p. 178.

4. B. R. Clark, *The Distinctive College* (Chicago: Aldine, 1970), p. 235.

5. R. A. Scott, "The Selection of Clients by Social Welfare Agencies: The Case of the Blind," *Social Problems,* Winter 1967, pp. 248–57.

6. A. Jay, *Management and Machiavelli* (Harmondsworth, Middlesex: Penguin, 1970), p. 70.

7. D. L. Sills, *The Volunteers* (Glencoe, Ill.: Free Press, 1957).

8. From M. Rosner, "Principal Types and Problems of Direct Democracy in the Kibbutz," working paper, Social Research Center on the Kibbutz, Givat Havina, Israel, 1969.

9. E. Goffman, "The Characteristics of Total Institutions," in Amitai Etzioni, ed., *Complex Organizations: A Sociological Reader* (New York: Holt, Rinehart and Winston, 1961).

10. W. G. Ouchi and A. M. Jaeger, "Type Z Organizations: Stability in the Midst of Mobility," *Academy of Management Review,* 1978, p. 308.

11. *Ibid.,* p. 309.

12. W. G. Ouchi, *Theory Z: How American Business Can Meet the Japanese Challenge* (Reading, Mass.: Addison-Wesley, 1981).

13. W. G. Ouchi and B. Johnson, "Types of Organizational Control and Their Relationship to Emotional Well Being," *Administrative Science Quarterly*, 1978, p. 302.

Chapter 13 Politics and the Political Organization

1. Graham T. Allison, *Essence of Decision: Explaining the Cuban Missile Crisis* (Boston: Little, Brown, 1971), p. 170.

2. M. N. Zald and M. A. Berger, "Social Movements in Organizations: Coup d'Etat, Insurgency, and Mass Movements," *American Journal of Sociology*, 1978, p. 841.

3. David Mechanic, "Sources of Power of Lower Participants in Complex Organizations," *Administrative Science Quarterly*, 1962, pp. 349–64.

4. Aaron B. Wildavsky, "Budgeting as a Political Process," in D. L. Sills, ed., *International Encyclopedia of the Social Sciences* (New York: Crowell, Collier, Macmillan, 1968), vol. 2, and *The Politics of the Budgeting Process*, 2d ed. (Boston: Little, Brown, 1974).

5. D. J. Hickson, C. A. Lee, R. E. Schneck, and J. M. Pennings, "A Strategic Contingencies' Theory of Intraorganizational Power," *Administrative Science Quarterly*, 1971, pp. 216–29.

6. Zald and Berger, "Social Movements," p. 833.

7. David C. McClelland, "The Two Faces of Power," *Journal of International Affairs*, 1970, pp. 29–47.

8. Allison, *Essence of Decision*, p. 145.

9. T. Burns, "Micropolitics: Mechanisms of Institutional Change," *Administrative Science Quarterly*, 1961–62, p. 260.

Chapter 14 Beyond Configuration

1. S. Gordon Redding, *The Spirit of Chinese Capitalism* (Cambridge: Cambridge University Press, forthcoming in 1989).

2. Manfred F. R. Kets de Vries and Danny Miller, *The Neurotic Organization* (San Francisco: Jossey-Bass, 1984).

3. See "Sequential attention to goals" in Richard M. Cyert and James G. March, *A Behavioral Theory of the Firm* (Englewood Cliffs, N.J.: Prentice-Hall, 1963), p. 118.

4. B. R. Clark, *The Distinctive College* (Chicago: Aldine, 1970).

5. Michael E. Porter, *Competitive Strategy: Techniques for Analyzing Industries and Competition* (New York: Free Press, 1980).

6. Quoted in Walter Kiechel III, "Sniping at Strategic Planning (Interview with himself)," *Planning Review*, May 1984, p. 11.

7. Thomas J. Peters and Robert H. Waterman, Jr., *In Search of Excellence* (New York: Harper & Row, 1982).

8. R. Raphael, *Edges* (New York: Knopf, 1976), pp. 5–6.

9. William Starbuck, "Organizational Growth and Development," in J. G. March, ed., *Handbook of Organizations* (Chicago: Rand McNally, 1965), p. 486.

10. Robert Michels, *Political Parties: A Sociological Study of the Oligarchical Tendencies of Modern Democracy* (New York: Free Press, 1958).

11. See, for example, Adolph A. Berle and G. C. Means, *The Modern Corporation and Private Property,* revised edition (New York: Harcourt, Brace & World, 1968).

12. See, for example, T. Hafsi, "The Dynamics of Government in Business," *Interfaces,* July–August 1985, pp. 62–69.

13. "Who's Excellent Now?" *Business Week,* November 5, 1984, pp. 76–78.

14. M. N. Zald and M. A. Berger, "Social Movements in Organizations: Coup d'Etat, Insurgency, and Mass Movements," *American Journal of Sociology,* 1978, pp. 823–61.

Chapter 15 Who Should Control the Corporation?

1. G. D. Garson, "The Codetermination Model of Workers' Participation: Where Is It Leading?" *Sloan Management Review,* Spring 1977, p. 63.

2. J. Bacon and J. K. Brown, *Corporate Directorship Practices: Role, Selection and Legal Status of the Board* (Conference Board and American Society of Corporate Secretaries, Inc., 1975), p. 48.

3. J. Kralj, "Is There a Role for Managers?" *Journal of General Management,* Winter 1977, p. 13.

4. Theodore Levitt, "Why Business Always Loses," *Harvard Business Review,* March–April 1968, p. 83.

5. E. F. Cheit, "The New Place of Business: Why Managers Cultivate Social Responsibility," in E. F. Cheit, ed., *The Business Establishment* (New York: Wiley, 1964), p. 172.

6. Levitt, "Why Business Always Loses," p. 83.

7. D. Braybrooke, "Skepticism of Wants, and Certain Subversive Effects of Corporations on American Values," in Sydney Hook, ed., *Human Values and Economic Policy* (New York: NYU Press, 1967), p. 224.

8. Milton Friedman, "A Friedman Doctrine: The Social Responsibility of Business Is to Increase Its Profits," *New York Times Magazine,* September 13, 1970, pp. 32 ff.

9. S. N. Brenner and E. A. Molander, "Is the Ethics of Business Changing?" *Harvard Business Review,* January–February 1977, pp. 59, 62.

10. Robert W. Ackerman, *The Social Challenge to Business* (Cambridge: Harvard University Press, 1975).

11. I. Ross, "How Lawless Are the Big Companies?" *Fortune,* December 1, 1980, p. 57.

12. Aleksandr Solzhenitsyn, "Why the West Has Succumbed to Cowardice," *Montreal Star, News and Review,* June 10, 1978, p. B1.

13. Friedman, "A Friedman Doctrine," p. 33.

14. Milton Friedman, *Capitalism and Freedom* (Chicago: University of Chicago Press, 1962), p. 20.

15. Albert O. Hirschman, *Exit, Voice and Loyalty: Responses to Decline in Firms, Organizations, and States* (Cambridge: Harvard University Press, 1970).

Chapter 16 A Note on That Dirty Word "Efficiency"

1. Teaching note for "The Rose Company," Case 9–453–002, Intercollegiate Case Clearing House, Graduate School of Business Administration, Harvard University.

2. Herbert A. Simon, *Administrative Behavior,* 2d edition (New York: Macmillan, 1957), pp. 14, 179.

3. Peter F. Drucker, *Management: Tasks, Responsibilities, and Practices* (New York: Harper & Row, 1973), p. 347.

4. Robert M. Pirsig, *Zen and the Art of Motorcycle Maintenance: An Inquiry into Values* (New York: Bantam, 1974), pp. 200, 201.

5. Robert W. Ackerman, *The Social Challenge to Business* (Cambridge: Harvard University Press, 1975), p. 56.

6. J. L. Bower, "Planning and Control: Bottom Up or Top Down?" *Journal of General Management,* 3, 1974, pp. 22–23.

Chapter 17 Society Has Become Unmanageable as a Result of Management

1. John Kenneth Galbraith, *American Capitalism: The Concept of Countervailing Power* (Boston: Houghton Mifflin, 1952).

2. Aleksandr Solzhenitsyn, "Why the West Has Succumbed to Cowardice," *Montreal Star, News and Review,* June 10, 1978, p. B1.

3. Robert Michels, *Political Parties: A Sociological Study of the Oligarchical Tendencies of Modern Democracy* (New York: Free Press, 1958). Originally published in 1915.

4. Marianne Jelinek, *Institutionalizing Innovation* (New York: Praeger, 1979), p. 139. italics added.

5. *Business Week,* September 19, 1983, pp. 56–64, and November 5, 1984, pp. 82–87.

6. Quoted in James C. Worthy, *Big Business and Free Men* (New York: Harper & Row, 1959), p. 73.

7. Alfred D. Chandler, *Strategy and Structure* (Cambridge: MIT Press, 1962) and *The Visible Hand: The Managerial Revolution in American Business* (Cambridge: Harvard University Press, 1977), and Oliver E. Williamson, *Markets and Hierarchies* (New York: Free Press, 1975) and *The Economic Institutions of Capitalism* (New York: Free Press, 1985).

8. F. Andrews, "Management: How a Boss Works in Calculated Chaos," *New York Times,* October 29, 1978.

9. Albert Shapero, "What MANAGEMENT Says and What Managers Do," *Interfaces,* February 1977, p. 107.

10. Clifford Geertz, *The Interpretation of Cultures* (New York: Basic Books, 1973).

11. David Halberstam, *The Best and the Brightest* (New York: Random House, 1972).

12. Boston Consulting Group, *Strategy Alternatives for the British Motorcycle Industry* (London: Her Majesty's Stationery Office, 1975), p. 59.

13. Richard T. Pascale and A. G. Athos, *The Art of Japanese Management* (New York: Simon & Schuster, 1981).

14. All quotations above are from Richard T. Pascale, "Perspectives on Strategy: The Real Story Behind Honda's Success," *California Management Review,* Spring 1984, pp. 47–72; italics added.

15. Bert Hopwood, *What Ever Happened to the British Motorcycle Industry?* (San Leandro, Calif.: Haynes Publishing, 1981), p. 173.

16. M. D. Feld, "Information and Authority: The Structure of Military Organization," *American Sociological Review,* February 1959, p. 21.

17. J. L. Stokesbury, *A Short History of World War I* (New York: Morrow, 1981), pp. 241, 242.

18. E. A. Singer and L. M. Wooton, "The Triumph and Failure of Albert Speer's Administrative Genius: Implications for Current Management Theory and Practice," *Journal of Applied Behavioral Science,* 1976, p. 100.

19. Robert W. Ackerman, *The Social Challenge to Business* (Cambridge: Harvard University Press, 1975).

20. James C. Worthy, *Big Business and Free Men* (New York: Harper & Row, 1959), p. 29.

21. Shapero, "What MANAGEMENT Says," p. 108.

22. "Who's Excellent Now?" *Business Week,* November 5, 1984, pp. 76–78.

FOR FURTHER DETAIL

Chapter 1 The Manager's Job

My book *The Nature of Managerial Work* (Harper & Row, 1973; Prentice-Hall, 1980), contains detailed discussion of all the characteristics and roles described in this chapter, as well as the implications of that discussion for managers and management scientists. One chapter also considers variations in managerial work by level, function, and other factors. An appendix to the Harper & Row edition also presents detail on the research method used.

Chapter 2 Crafting Strategy

This material was drawn from various published articles; perhaps most relevant are "Patterns in Strategy Formation," *Management Science,* May 1979, on Volkswagenwerk (as well as on our study of U.S. strategy in Vietnam), "Tracking Strategy in an Entrepreneurial Firm" (with Jim Waters), *Academy of Management Journal,* September 1982, on Steinberg, Inc., and "Strategy Formation in an Adhocracy" (with Alexandra McHugh), *Administrative Science Quarterly,* June 1985, on the National Film Board of Canada. Some of this and related other material will be considered in Part II of this book. In addition, I have discussed different definitions of strategy in "Five P's for Strategy," *California Management Review,* Fall 1987, and different types of strategies (umbrella, process, etc.) in "Of Strategies, Deliberate and Emergent" (with Jim Waters), *Strategic Management Journal,* July–September 1985. An application of these ideas to the public sector is contained in "Emergent Strategy for Public Policy" (with Jan Jorgensen), *Canadian Public Administration,* Summer 1987. My earlier reference to my first article on the subject is "The Science of Strategy Making," published in what is now called the *Sloan Management Review,* Spring 1967. In addition, I am currently completing a rather long paper on "ten schools of thought" on strategy formation, to be published in J. W. Fredrickson (ed.), *Perspectives on Strategic Management* (New York: Ballinger, 1989).

Chapter 3 Planning on the Left Side, Managing on the Right

Aside from references to my other work (cited, or contained elsewhere in this book), further detail can be found in the next chapter.

Chapter 4 Coupling Analysis and Intuition in Management

My review of Simon's book can be found in the *Administrative Science Quarterly,* June 1977; his revised book *The New Science of Management Decision* was published by Prentice-Hall in 1977, while the article from which his passages are quoted, "Making Management Decisions: The Role of Intuition and Emotion," appeared in the *Academy of Management Executive* in February 1987. My ideas on the strengths and weaknesses of analysis and intuition, as well as the role of analysis in strategic decision-making, appeared in "Beyond Implementation: An Analysis of Resistance to Policy Analysis," published in K. B. Haley, ed., *Operations Research '78* (Elsevier North-Holland, 1979), pp. 106–62. *Impediments to the Use of Management Information*, which takes up the role of MIS in management and also provides more detail on the limitations of brains, organizations, and systems in information processing, appeared as a monograph published in 1975 jointly by the National Association of Accountants of the U.S. and the Society of Management Accountants of Canada. My forthcoming book on planning, tentatively entitled *Strategic Planning: An Irreverent Review* and to be published in 1990, goes into considerable detail on the meaning and models of strategic planning, the evidence on its performance over the years, its pitfalls and fallacies, and what seem to me to be the appropriate roles for planning, plans, and planners in various organizational contexts. I am also working with a number of colleagues and doctoral students on a paper entitled "Opening Up Decision Processes: The View from the Black Stool," which, among other issues, probes into the roles of insight and inspiration in decision-making and why these have tended to be slighted in the formal research and literature.

Chapter 5 Training Managers, Not MBAs

The implications of these ideas for management practice will be discussed in the final chapter of this book. A similar paper on research methods in management can be found in my "An Emerging Strategy of Direct Research" (*Administrative Science Quarterly*, December 1979) or, more of a diatribe; "If You're Not Serving Bill and Barbara, then You're

Not Serving Leadership'' (in Hunt et al., eds., *Leadership: Beyond Establishment Views* (Southern Illinois University Press, 1982).

Chapter 6 Deriving Configurations

Every concept, every attribute, every hypothesis presented here has been elaborated in one or the other of two books (which together comprise 1,200 pages), sometimes in a paragraph, sometimes in a section, not infrequently in an entire chapter (as is true for each of the design parameters and sets of conditions as well as the configurations themselves). The material on structure can be found in *The Structuring of Organizations* (Prentice-Hall, 1979), or the shorter version by that publisher, *Structure in Fives: Designing Effective Organizations* (1983), while the material on power can be found in *Power In and Around Organizations* by the same publisher (1983). The full ''Case for Configuration'' of the introduction to Part II, by Danny Miller and myself, can be found in Miller and Friesen's *Organizations: A Quantum View* (Prentice-Hall, 1984), Chapter 1.

Chapter 7 The Entrepreneurial Organization

Most of this chapter has been drawn from *The Structuring of Organizations* (Prentice-Hall, 1979), which devotes one chapter to ''simple structure.'' Some also comes from a chapter in *Power In and Around Organizations* on the ''autocracy.'' The material on strategy formation comes from three papers which present these conclusions in greater depth: ''Visionary Leadership and Strategic Management,'' *Strategic Management Journal*, forthcoming in 1989, co-authored with Frances Westley; ''Tracking Strategy in an Entrepreneurial Firm,'' about Steinberg's, published in the *Academy of Management Journal* in 1982, pp. 465–99; and ''Researching the Formation of Strategies: The History of Canadian Lady, 1939–1976,'' in R. B. Lamb, ed., *Competitive Strategic Management* (Prentice-Hall, 1984) about Canadelle, the last two articles co-authored with Jim Waters.

Chapter 8 The Machine Organization

The structure and conditions as well as the social issues associated with the machine organization are discussed at length in the chapter ''Machine Bureaucracy'' in my book *The Structuring of Organizations* (Prentice-Hall, 1979). A full chapter on both the ''Instrument'' and the ''Closed System'' can be found in my book *Power In and Around Organizations* (Prentice-Hall, 1983). And the material on strategy formation in this type of organization is discussed at greater length in three articles: ''Patterns in Strategy Formation,'' on Volkswagenwerk and U.S. Strategy in Vietnam, *Management Science,* 1978; "Does Planning Impede Strategic Thinking? The Strategy of Air Canada, 1937–1976" (with Pierre Brunet and Jim Waters), in R. B. Lamb and P. Shrivastava, eds., *Advances in Strategic Management, Volume IV* (JAI Press, 1987); and "The Mind of the Strategist(s)" (with Jim Waters), in S. Srivastva, ed., *The Executive Mind* (Jossey-Bass, 1983). Of further interest may be my book *Strategic Planning: An Irreverent Review*, forthcoming in 1990, on the nature and difficulties of formal planning.

Chapter 9 The Diversified Organization

All the points discussed here, especially those of the diversified configuration's social consequences, are developed at greater length in Chapter 20 of *The Structuring of Organizations* (Prentice-Hall, 1979). An article entitled "Diversi*fiction* (what a difference an "a" makes)," on "thick" and "thin" management, is in progress (also further developed in Chapter 17 of this book).

Chapter 10 The Professional Organization

The structure, context, and social issues of the "professional bureaucracy," including considerable detail on the pigeonholing process and other aspects, is discussed at length in Chapter 19 of *The Structuring of Organizations* (Prentice-Hall, 1979). Strategy-making in these organizations—specifically in academia—is discussed at greater length in the paper by Cynthia Hardy, Ann Langley, Janet Rose, and myself entitled "Strategy Formation in the University Setting," published in J. L. Bess, ed., *College and University Organization* (New York University Press, 1984). Finally, the full text of "A Note on the Unionization of Professionals from the Perspective of Organization Theory," including discussion of the U.S. Supreme Court decision concerning the unionization of faculty at Yeshiva University (and why I believe it was the right one for the wrong reason), can be found in the *Industrial Relations Law Journal* of 1983, pp. 623–34.

Chapter 11 The Innovative Organization

The adhocracy structure, including its operating and administrative forms and its contexts and issues, are discussed at length in Chapter 21 of *The Structuring of Organizations* (Prentice-Hall, 1979). Strategy-making in this configuration, especially aspects of the "grassroots" model, can be found in "Strategy Formation in an Adhocracy," co-authored with Alexandra McHugh and published in the *Administrative Science Quarterly* (1985), pp. 160–97, and "Strategy of Design: A Study of 'Architects in Co-Partnership,' '' co-authored with Suzane Otis, Jamal Shamsie, and Jim Waters and published in J. Grant, ed., *Strategic Management Frontiers* (J.A.I. Press, 1988).

Chapter 12 Ideology and the Missionary Organization

Chapter 11 of *Power In and Around Organizations* (Prentice-Hall, 1983) discusses "the system of ideology," including its three stages of development, at greater length, while Chapter 21 goes into considerable detail on the goals and power relationships of the missionary configuration as well as the various forms it can take—pure (reformer, converter, cloister), quasi (overlays), and pseudo (only seemingly ideological).

Chapter 13 Politics and the Political Organization

Two chapters in *Power In and Around Organizations* (Prentice-Hall, 1983) elaborate at some length on all the points raised here. Chapter 13, "The System of Politics," discusses each of the political games at length as well as why politics is played in organizations and with what equipment (will, skill, privileged information, privileged access, and so on). Chapter 23, "The Political Arena," then discusses each of the four forms of political organization at length, with a number of illustrations, and also describes in detail the life cycle model of the political organization.

Chapter 14 Beyond Configuration

Much of this discussion is new to this book, although some of the basic ideas (pulls, hybrids, transitions, a simple pentagon) were introduced briefly in the concluding chapter of *The Structuring of Organizations* (Prentice-Hall, 1979). The life cycle model was developed in more detail and in a more academic way in Chapter 24 of *Power In and Around Organizations* (Prentice-Hall, 1983). Examples of all the possible transitions between the configurations and the reasons I consider some intrinsically more natural than others can also be found in that chapter.

Chapter 15 Who Should Control the Corporation?

As noted, this article was drawn from my book *Power In and Around Organizations* (Prentice-Hall, 1983), which devotes one section to this issue, including a full chapter on each of the eight positions. Readers interested in more detail, as well as the support (and published references) behind the arguments presented here, are referred to these chapters. Two of these positions have also been presented in articles in their own right, one called "Why America Needs, but Cannot Have Corporate

Democracy'' (*Organizational Dynamics,* Spring 1983), the other ''The Case for Corporate Social Responsibility'' (*The Journal of Business Strategy,* Fall 1983, although I preferred the paper's original title, ''That Naïve and Necessary Concept Called Social Responsibility''). I feel the critique of Milton Friedman's views, discussed under ''restore it,'' really requires the longer, original version for a full understanding; this can be found on pages 632–44 of my ''Power'' book. Finally, the brief comments on the board of directors, inserted here into the discussion of ''democratize it,'' are drawn from Chapter 6 of my ''Power'' book, which reviews the directors' roles and powers at some length. A late decision eliminated a full discussion of that subject in its own chapter in this book, but interested readers can turn to the original source. Otherwise, the summary of all this material presented here is similar to an article that appeared by the same title in the *California Management Review* (Fall 1984) or the *McKinsey Quarterly* in 1986.

Chapter 16 A Note on That Dirty Word ''Efficiency''

This paper was published in *Interfaces,* October (1982), more or less as presented here. A slightly longer version, under the title ''Efficiency as a Systems Goal,'' can be found in *Power In and Around Organizations* (Prentice-Hall, 1983), on pages 268–73. The same chapter, ''Specific Goals in Organizations,'' also discusses survival, control, and growth as systems goals of organizations, and how these can displace mission as a goal. ''The Determination of Organizational Goals,'' including the argument that organizations do have intrinsic goals, which must be inferred from their actions, and discussion of how conflicting goals are reconciled in organizations, is taken up in the preceding chapter of that book.

Chapter 17 Society Has Become Unmanageable as a Result of Management

No further detail. Go back to Chapter 1!

Credits and Acknowledgments

Figure 4–1: From "A Note on Intuitive vs. Analytic Thinking," by J. T. Peters, K. R. Hammond, and D. A. Summers, in *Organizational Behavior and Human Performance* (August 1974), p. 128. Used by permission of Academic Press, Orlando, Fla., and author.

Figure 7–1: Used by permission of Steinberg, Inc., Montreal.

Figure 9–3: From Richard P. Rumelt, *Strategy, Structure and Economic Performance.* Boston: Division of Research, Harvard Business School, 1974. Republished as a Harvard Business School Classic. Boston: Harvard Business School Press, 1986. Copyright © 1974, 1986 by the President and Fellows of Harvard College. Used with permission of the publisher and author. (Figure 1.4, p. 21, in source.)

Figure 11–1: Used by permission of the National Film Board of Canada, Montreal.

INDEX